A history
of the mental
health services

International Library of Social Policy

General Editor   Kathleen Jones
Professor of Social Administration
University of York

Arbor Scientiæ
Arbor Vitæ

A catalogue of the books available in the **International Library of Social Policy** and other series of Social Science books published by Routledge will be found at the end of this volume.

A history
of the mental
health services

Kathleen Jones

Routledge & Kegan Paul
London and Boston

First published 1972
by Routledge & Kegan Paul Ltd
Broadway House, 68-74 Carter Lane,
London EC4V 5EL and
9 Park Street,
Boston, Mass. 02108, U.S.A.
Printed in Great Britain by
C. Tinling & Co. Ltd London and Prescot
© Kathleen Jones 1972
No part of this book may be reproduced in
any form without permission from the
publisher, except for the quotation of brief
passages in criticism

ISBN 0 7100 7452 2

To Gwyn
— as in 1955

Per que tuit le fin aman
Sapchan qu'amors es fina bevolenza

Contents

Preface

Part One of this book, originally published as *Lunacy, Law and Conscience, 1744–1845*, was begun in 1950. It was written from a house in the grounds of one of the large Lancashire mental hospitals— within sight of the chimneys and the water-towers, the wired-in airing courts for 'refractory' patients and the locked doors. The National Health Service was something of an innovation then, and not everyone thought that it would last. Some of the committee members used to speak with nostalgia of the old Lancashire Asylums Board. The hospital had a flourishing institutional life—so flourishing indeed, that patients' relatives were advised not to visit them for the first month after admission, 'to give them time to settle down'. The Lunacy Act of 1890 was still in force. Mr Enoch Powell, who was later to attack the chimneys and the water-towers as Minister of Health, was a new back-bencher in the House of Commons. Mr Erving Goffman was writing his Ph.D., and had not yet coined the phrase 'total institution'.

Part Two, originally published as *Mental Health and Social Policy, 1845–1959* was written in the late fifties, when the impact of the psychotropic drugs, the open-door system and the debate which led up to the Mental Health Act had produced a swirl of new ideas and experimentation, and it was difficult to estimate either the force of change or its direction. Though the locked doors and the airing courts were going, and the average length of stay per patient was dropping, our thinking was still very hospital centred. We talked of 'pre-care' and 'after-care', not 'community care'.

Because they were grounded in what is now part of history, Part One and Part Two have required considerable revision for this new edition. Both have been abridged, and I hope that this makes the central line of argument run more clearly. Part Three, which starts at the point where documentary evidence on the mental health services is supplemented by my own experience, is new, apart from a section on the provision of the 1959 Act. The appendices are also new, and Appendix I gives a detailed analysis of the statistics of mental illness and mental handicap.

The first person to offer help with the text was Dr Barbara Hammond. Her book (with J. L. Hammond) on Lord Shaftesbury set me thinking about the plight of the lunatics; and she was kind enough, in her distinguished old age, to go and look up references in the British Museum library for a very undistinguished and junior research student. The most recent help has come from Dr Alexander Walk, formerly Librarian of the Royal Medico-Psychological Association, who has offered many corrections and suggestions on Part One and Part Two from his own considerable knowledge of the history; and from Dr Arthur Bowen of York, who has read and commented on Part Three. To these three, and to many others who have helped in between (particularly my former colleagues at the University of Manchester) I am deeply grateful.

K.J.

Introduction

Some time in the first half of the eighteenth century, in a quieter but harsher England, the idea began to develop that there was a group of people who needed special protection because of their mental condition. The idea grew under its own momentum. Influential men in the larger cities compared notes, discovered a state of quite appalling misery, and began to plan reforms. In time, these local experiments began to attract the attention of members of Parliament, and there were further revelations which brought home to the general public (or at least that small proportion who could read and vote) the plight of a group of helpless people. Chained, beaten and half-starved, they lived in cellars and garrets, in prisons and workhouses; but William Tuke had proved at the Retreat that 'lunatics' could respond to kindness and trust, and Godfrey Higgins defied an Archbishop of York in making the story public. In London, a group of members of Parliament investigated Bethlem, the oldest Lunatic Hospital in England, and others forced their way into the filth and the squalor of the private madhouses. In Gloucester, Sir George Onesiphorus Paul set in train a service of events which led to the passing of the County Asylums Act of 1808, and the first local authority institutions designed for 'criminal and pauper lunatics'.

The tide of industrial change brought an intensification of social distress of many kinds. The social problems with which small rural communities had dealt casually, but often effectively, became acute in the dirt-ridden and disease-ridden life of the towns; but industrialization, if it increased social distress, also provided the means of dealing with it. The very force of misery produced a new social conscience, a desire to tackle the problems of poverty and sickness and ignorance which had been taken for granted by the 'reasonable man' of the eighteenth century. A booming economy provided the money; the growth of the middle and artisan classes provided the staff; the new ease of communication by road and rail made it possible to establish national standards where previously only local standards had been possible. It is no accident that the establishment of national inspectorates in factories and asylums and public health followed so closely on the work of Telford and Macadam and Stephenson.

If any one man can be said to have embodied the social conscience of the mid-Victorian era, it is unquestionably Lord Ashley, later the seventh Earl of Shaftesbury. His work for the climbing boys, the children of the Ragged Schools, the labouring women in mines and factories, is well-known. A sickly child who became a fastidious and gentle adult, he faced more squalor and corruption than most of his stronger-stomached contemporaries. No issue occupied so much of his time and energy as the care of the 'lunatics'. His appointment as a Metropolitan Commissioner in Lunacy was his first public appointment at the age of twenty-seven; he was still chairman of the national Lunacy Commission when he died at the age of eighty-four.

The Act of 1845—known as Shaftesbury's Act—was the crown of his early work in this field. As Chairman of the Lunacy Commission, he was in a position to see that the Act was operated as he wished, and all the good will of a successful reform movement was focused on him and his work. There was a new spirit of humanity in treatment, a rising class of competent 'asylum doctors', and the beginnings of a training for nurses; and Shaftesbury had over forty years of active public life ahead of him.

Yet, somehow, things went wrong. Even as the new county asylums were built—and it is not easy for a generation which is intent on knocking them down to remember what a social advance they represented—the system was becoming the System. Perhaps it was too complete, too highly organized, for human beings to live comfortably within it. Perhaps the causes lay elsewhere—in the pressure of a relentlessly growing population which kept the asylums constantly overcrowded; in the local parsimony and unimaginativeness which dragged down standards and turned good new ideas into bad old ones; in the sublime sufficiency of a generation to whom radical self-criticism was unthinkable; in a bitterly inegalitarian class structure; in a volatile and unthinking public which would cry 'scandal' one minute and withhold help the next. For some or all of these reasons, the clear vision of the early reformers faded in a welter of local politics and medical inertia. Large, impersonal buildings were put up for the reception of patients in their thousands—buildings which from their very size and structure spoke of authority and repression, and made it almost impossible to create a sense of community.

When the first part of this study was begun, twenty years ago, we knew the problems, and we were beginning to have an inkling of some of the answers; but much has happened since then—the open-door movement, the Mental Health Act, the development of community care, the movement to abolish the mental hospital (surely one of the very few topics on which the Monday Club and the Fabians have spoken in chorus?) and the rise of two groups of anti-psychiatrists—those who want treatment for mental illness absorbed into general medicine, and those who deny that mental illness and mental handicap have any objective reality.

It might be thought that the study of some 230 years of English history, even in so limited a specialism, over twenty years of the writer's own existence would yield some general results: for instance, that it would be possible to develop views on the historian's conundrum of whether history has a shape and a purpose, or whether shape and purpose are merely imposed upon it by historians; or some modest ability to predict what is likely to happen next. Disappointingly, it has shed no light in either direction. If history has a shape and a purpose, they are so unimaginable in scope that the small fragment recorded here is no more than a dot in the corner of a vast Persian carpet; as to the future, if there is any lesson to be learned from the past, it must be a sense of the surprisingness of change—the way in which apparently major trends in one decade die out in the next, and minor ones come to unforeseen prominence; the almost inevitable inaccuracy of forecasts; the multiplication of quite unpredictable variables.

So there are no simple answers. It is important to recognize that the way in which the mentally ill and the mentally handicapped are defined and cared for is primarily a social response to a very basic set of human problems. The purpose of this survey is simply to show how succeeding generations have answered the fundamental questions: What are mental illness and mental handicap? How and why do we define them? What forms of care should the community provide? Who should be responsible for administering them? What is liberty, and how can it best be safeguarded?

All societies have these problems. How they answer them depends on what they are, and the values they hold.

Part One

1744–1845

1　Eighteenth-century custom

England in the early eighteenth century was a country of some five and a half million people who lived for the most part in small towns and villages. There were few towns of appreciable size— London had a population of little over half a million and Bristol had about fifty thousand inhabitants. In most parts of England, people lived in semi-isolated communities, remote from each other and from any central stream of influence. Travel was slow and hazardous. There were few books, and no national newspapers. Many of the rich were cultured and sceptical; most of the poor were illiterate and superstitious; and some of the poor starved.

From an economic point of view, it was a society undergoing a slow process of disintegration, in the final stages of the decay of feudalism; from a social point of view, it was scarcely a society at all, for it lacked the homogeneity necessary to social action. The medieval conception of charity as a duty which each man owed to his neighbour was dying, and there was as yet nothing to take its place. The community recognized little corporate responsibility for the well-being of its citizens, and inevitably its weakest members—the very poor, the very old, the sick, and the insane—suffered.

There was no clear definition of what mental disorder was, and certainly no recognition of the mentally ill or handicapped as a category requiring a distinct form of treatment. The problem was a submerged one. Only a small proportion of the total number were recognized as being insane, and the majority were treated as though they were fully responsible for their actions. If their mental condition reduced them to penury, they came within the purview of the Poor Law. If it led them to break the criminal code, they were judged by the penal law. If they wandered abroad from their legal place of settlement without means of support, they were involved in the rigours of the vagrancy laws.

The person who was recognized as insane—that is, the person whose actions were obviously a danger to himself or to others—had no protection in law. If he lived in or near London, he might be sent to Bethlem or 'Bedlam', the only institution of any public standing which dealt with the mentally abnormal. If he were wealthy, he might be sent by his relatives to one of the small private madhouses which combined high fees with a pledge of absolute secrecy, or confined alone with an attendant. If he were poor, he might be kept by his family in whatever conditions they chose, or sent to the workhouse or prison for greater security; but whether he lived in London, or in a small and remote village, whether he was rich or poor, he was almost certain to be confined, neglected, and intimidated, if not treated with open cruelty.

Since the lunatic or idiot was so dependent on those around him, our first task is to inquire what the eighteenth century thought about insanity, and what fundamental beliefs lay behind this treatment. The attitude of the labouring classes will be considered first, and then that of the medical practitioners, who were responsible for what little treatment of insanity there was; the clergy, who considered mind as a function of spirit, and all human misfortunes as falling within their province; and philosophers, who were at this time obsessed with that study of the rational faculties of man which later laid the foundations of the science of psychology.

The labouring classes

Society in its more primitive forms sees the manifestations of mental disorder as proof of divine powers, or evidence of divine disfavour. The Bible abounds in cases of reputed demoniac possession, and Renaissance Christendom, in its orgy of witch-hunting, persecuted thousands whose only crime was that they suffered from mental aberration. The so-called 'Devil's Claw'—a patch of insensitive skin on the body of the supposed witch into which pins and knives might be inserted without causing pain—is to-day widely recognized as a form of localized anaesthesia found in some cases of hysteria;[1] yet it was believed to be an infallible proof of witchcraft, for which the penalty was trial by ordeal, or death at the stake. The harmless lunatic was generally treated with respect in the Middle Ages, as being different from other people, and thus standing in a special relation to the Deity. *Piers Plowman* refers to the 'lunatik lollers'[2]:

> Moneyles thei walke
> With a good wil, witlees, meny wyde contreys
> Ryghte as Peter dude, and Paul, save that thei preche nat.

and the author continues:

Mattheu ous techeth
We sholde have hem to hous, and help hem when thei come.

The penal laws against witchcraft were removed in 1736, and beliefs
in witchcraft had certainly been superseded by rationalism in the
minds of the educated classes; but among the uneducated, this belief
lingered on, and local trials for witchcraft were not uncommon in the
mid-eighteenth century. A case is noted in the *Percy Anecdotes*—'so
recently as the year 1759'—in which an elderly woman named
Susannah Hannokes was accused at Wingrove in Hertfordshire of
bewitching her neighbour's spindle, and was tried by the time-
honoured method of weighing against the Church Bible. The Bible
appears to have been a comparatively small one, for 'to the no small
astonishment and mortification of her accuser, she actually outweighed it, and was honourably acquitted of the charge'. Sir Frederick
Eden, writing in 1797, found it 'mortifying to a philosophic mind'
that a British jury could be persuaded that the crime of witchcraft
existed, and that a woman could converse with the devil in the shape
of a cat.[3] It is interesting to note in this connection that Mr Montague
Summers, that modern believer in witchcraft, relating the case of a
female witch convicted and hanged in 1670, referred to her as 'this
miserable lunatic',[4] apparently regarding mental abnormality as
proof that the sufferer was allied to the powers of darkness.

When burning witches became prohibited by law, and witchcraft
became a doubtful hypothesis which only the totally uneducated took
seriously, the poorer classes turned to other methods of driving the
devil out of the lunatic. D. H. Tuke, in his *Chapters in the History of
the Insane in the British Isles*, mentions the existence of several wells in
the remoter parts of the British Isles where superstitious rites connected with insanity were practised even in the nineteenth century.
The usual procedure was a combination of repeated duckings and
religious rites—a system which differed little in practice from the
'ordeal by water' formerly used in witchcraft trials, and which had
more than a little in common with the 'cold bath' and the 'bath of
surprise' which were favourite remedies for insanity among the
medical profession. At St Nun's Pool in Cornwall, the sufferer was
made to stand with his back to the pool, and was then thrown
suddenly into it. After being repeatedly ducked until half-drowned
and thoroughly exhausted, he was taken to the church, and certain
masses were sung over him. If there was no marked improvement in
his condition, the process was repeated as long as life remained. At a

well in Scotland, the lunatic was stripped of his clothes, bound hand and foot, immersed in the sacred pool, and then left all night in the chapel. If he manged to free himself of his bonds during the night there was a good hope of recovery. 'It sometimes happens,' added Tuke's informant, 'that death relieves him during his confinement of the troubles of life.'[5]

If the insane were no longer judicially executed, they were certainly regarded with superstitious fear by the lower classes, who clung to the belief that harsh treatment would drive out the devil. Thus there was no hope of pressure for the amelioration of conditions from this quarter.

The medical profession

Medical qualifications were at this time unstandardized, and the title of 'doctor' bore no settled meaning. A Master of Arts of the Universities of Oxford or Cambridge could still acquire an MD degree by expounding a book of Galen in three written or six spoken lectures,[6] the Royal College of Physicians and the Company of Barber-Surgeons held their own examinations, but the examining boards were completely irresponsible, and the standard required was low.[7] The Society of Apothecaries licensed its own men, but anyone who had served a nominal apprenticeship as a druggist might set up in his own right and call himself an apothecary. No legal action against the unqualified practitioner was possible, and none of the licensing bodies had any real authority outside the metropolitan area. One witness before a Select Committee which examined this problem in 1834 spoke of a man who had set up as a 'chemist, druggist, surgeon, apothecary and man-midwife' without qualifications of any description.[8]

Since professional standards were so low, the average medical practitioner contented himself with a rough-and-ready knowledge of the ailments of the body, and had little or no apprehension of the complexities of the mind-body relationship. There were no facilities for research, and few ways of disseminating information. Medical knowledge was still dominated by the belief in the four 'humours' of blood, choler, phlegm and bile, and the theory that all human ailments were due to an excess of one or more of these substances. The means employed in driving out the excess humours were in some ways akin to those used in driving out the devil, since they consisted in systematically weakening the patient, and sometimes in a calculated terrorism.

The Anatomy of Melancholy, first published in 1621, gives a detailed analysis of the beliefs which were commonly held by medical men up to the end of the eighteenth century and beyond. Burton's treatise derived partly from Hippocrates, with a superstructure of religious and superstitious ideology. The original cause of madness was the Fall of Man. 'We are ... bad by nature, bad by kind, but far worse by art, every man the greatest enemy unto himself.' Mental and moral defect were synonymous.

Although he attributed the basic causes of insanity to sin and the activities of the devil, Burton also believed that the 'six non-natural things' were contributory causes. These were bad air. the retention of bodily excretions, bad diet, lack of sleep—'which causeth dizziness of the brain, frenzie, dotage, and makes the body lean, dry, hard and ugly to behold', too much or too little exercise, and emotional disturbances.

Burton's outline of physiology was almost entirely derived from Hippocrates. The body consisted of parts contained and containing, the most important of the former being the four humours. The treatment of mental disturbance was a matter of removing the excess of these substances by means of evacuation.

The most readily accessible means of evacuation were 'simples', or purges and vomits. Burton recommended laurel, white hellebore, antimony and tobacco—'divine, rare, super-excellent tobacco . . . a sovereign remedy to all diseases. A good vomit, I confess, if it be well qualified, opportunely taken, and medicinally used; but as it is commonly abused by most men . . . hellish, divelish and damned tobacco.' Senna, aloes, herb mercury and half-boiled cabbage were also useful. Many of these substances had been used in the treatment of insanity in antiquity, and were probably still being used by country doctors in 1845.

Bodily evacuation could also be achieved by blood-letting, and other 'chirurgical' methods, such as the use of horse-leeches, and the practice of raising blisters through the application of plasters and hot irons. 'Cauteries and hot irons are to be used in the suture of the crown, and the seared or ulcerated place suffered to run a good while.' Burton also cited a number of authorities for the efficacy of the ancient practice of trephining, which involved boring holes in the skull of the sufferer in order to allow the humours affecting the brain to escape.[9]

The Anatomy of Melancholy was widely current in the eighteenth century, and received the public commendation of an archbishop in 1777.[10] The foreword to the 1821 edition shows that, even at that date, Burton's diagnoses and treatment were acceptable.

The Church

The Church of England was the only considerable religious force in England in the first half of the eighteenth century; nonconformity suffered an eclipse from the Restoration to the advent of the Wesleys, and Roman Catholics were still unpopular, possessing no assessable national influence; but the Church of England was a decaying institution in which the parson was often a gentleman, sometimes a scholar, seldom a pastor, and never a priest. In the country parishes, no doubt, existed men of the calibre of George Herbert, but they did not usually obtain preferment, and their influence was restricted to their own charges. The fox-hunting parson perhaps did little or no harm to the human race, but he was not the man to lead a crusade; the socially eligible parson—like Mr Tilney in *Northanger Abbey*—found ample leisure from his pastoral duties to take part in the social round; and the obsequious parson, of whom Jane Austen's Mr Collins is the epitome,[11] had no time or thought to spare for the unfortunate.

It is doubtful whether the majority of the clergy at this time possessed a coherent social philosophy other than that implied in the defence of privilege; but if they turned for assistance to contemporary theology, it merely reinforced their own inclinations. At different periods in history the Church tends to stress varying aspects of the Christian Gospel, and until the eighteenth century the laity had lived under the perpetual shadow of Death, Judgment and Hell. Now the emphasis changed. The new philosophical fashion of 'natural law' produced a new theology—a rationalized theology which proclaimed that the world was as God made it, and that doubtless His reasons for doing so were good. The old ideas and the new came together in a synthesized theory of judgment—that human misery was a result of personal sin. What Man, with his limited vision, called evil, was divinely ordained. It followed from this premise that the poor, the sick, and the insane deserved their fate, and that it was not for Man to interfere with the plans of an inscrutable Deity. 'God moves in a mysterious way' wrote Cowper, and it was not the task of the clergy to plumb the mystery.

This thesis, outlined by Bishop Butler,[12] was taken a step forward by the poet and theological expositor Soame Jenyns, in his *Free Enquiry into the Nature of Good and Evil* (1757). 'The beauty and happiness of the whole,' he wrote, 'depend on the just inferiority of the parts,' and 'the sufferings of individuals are absolutely necessary to human happiness.' Jenyns seems to have envisaged a kind of cosmic hierarchy dependent on moral worth, where in a scale ranging from archangels to the lower animals, men appeared high or lowly placed according to their deserts. Each had his use, and each his appointed place.

Such a view of theology made possible a complete acceptance of poverty and disease. The wealthy and powerful owed no duty to the less fortunate members of society. The emphasis had shifted from an immanent God who redeemed Mankind and healed the sick in mind and body to a transcendent God who created and judged in supreme and uncaring isolation.

'Observe him', said Burton of the lunatic:

... for as in a glass
Thine angry portraiture it was.
His picture keep still in thy presence,
'Twixt him and thee, there's no difference.[13]

In this respect, the Anglican clergy probably differed from Burton. Many saw every possible difference between themselves and the lunatic. Moral condemnation of the mentally abnormal was as strong a component of eighteenth-century rationalist theology as it was of medical thought, or the inarticulate beliefs of the labouring classes.

Philosophy

Philosophers did not condemn the mentally disordered, but this was largely because they ignored them and their problems completely. Many philosophers of the period occupied themselves with the workings of the human mind, but the question of the existence of the whole field of abnormal psychology was never raised. David Hume, in his *Inquiry Concerning the Principles of Morals*, postulated that there were no absolute standards, personal merit being merely the possession of qualities 'useful or agreeable to the person himself or to others'.[14] Professor Willey, commenting on Lord Chesterfield's letters to his son, remarks that Chesterfield betrayed a similar belief.[15] The highest good was to be well thought of, and the virtuous man was he who won universal approbation. There was no place in this philosophy of life for those who wished to fight social injustice.

Hartley, in his *Observations on Man*, recognized the existence of certain types of mental aberration. He described hallucinations—'a vivid train of images which forces itself on the patient's eye'—and obsessions—'the frequent recurrency of the same ideas'. He noted in passing the existence of 'violent passions' and 'vapours, hypochondriacal and hysterical disorders'; but his own preoccupation with the 'natural' phenomena—the working of the sane and normal mind—precluded more than a passing interest in these things. His section on 'Imperfections in the Rational Faculty' occupies only nine pages in a work of over six hundred. As a doctor, we are told by his translator,[16] David Hartley 'visited with affectionate sympathy the humblest recesses of poverty and sickness as well as the stately beds of pampered distemper'.[17] Yet neither his medical training, his knowledge of the mind, nor his human instincts induced him to consider in detail the problems of insanity.

That cultured philosopher and man of letters, the third Earl of Shaftesbury, showed an unusual compassion when he wrote in his curiously elliptical style: 'Poor mad people and naturals, how treated? The diversion of seeing Bedlam—what a better laugh? See the malignity of this . . . vulgar, sordid and profane laughter.'[18] Yet he subscribed to the prevalent philosophy of *laisser-faire*: 'What wouldst thou? That which is good for the world.—Who knows what is good for the world? Who should know but the Providence that looks after it?'[19]

Superstition, moral condemnation, ignorance, and apathy: these were the mental attitudes which dominated the treatment of mental disorder in the eighteenth century; and they were inevitably reflected in the pattern of administration. The main ways in which the insane were confined in the first half of the eighteenth century may be distinguished as follows:

(*a*) *Those confined under the Poor Laws.* The 'pauper lunatic' was the responsibility of the parish overseer, and was subject to the rigours and inconsistencies which characterized the old Poor Law.

(*b*) *Those confined under the criminal law.* Insanity was until 1800 technically ineffective as a defence against a criminal charge. In certain cases, an individual jury might refuse to convict where the prisoner was obviously insane, but as a general rule, the criminally insane went to gaols and Bridewells in exactly the same way as other prisoners.

(*c*) *Those confined under the vagrancy laws.* The common vagrant was at this time heavily penalized. Poor Law legislation drew a sharp distinction between the respectable pauper who applied for relief in his own parish, and the pauper who wandered abroad begging. Since each parish had to provide for the relief of its own paupers by means of a rate, it followed that each was concerned to prevent casual

vagrants from becoming a charge on its funds, and any beggar who was found in a place other than his legal place of settlement was treated with the utmost severity. Administering the vagrancy laws was one of the functions of the local justice of the peace. Vagrants were usually sent to the county Bridewell.

(*d*) *Those confined in private madhouses.* These institutions were run for private profit, and among their inmates were not only people in need of care and treatment but also people detained at the instance of their relatives. Private madhouses varied in size from those taking only two or three patients to those which accommodated three or four hundred. A few of the larger ones took military or naval cases, or received pauper lunatics sent in by the parish overseer because their presence in the workhouse was disturbing to the other inmates. In these cases, the establishments were subject to the inspection of the authorities concerned, but the average private madhouse was such an unpleasant place that the inspection was likely to be a nominal one. Other patients—and these were the vast majority—were without any form of legal protection. The only possible defence which could be raised against the illegal detention of a sane person was by means of a writ of Habeas Corpus,[20] but this means was not often employed, and such was the secrecy with which the proprietors of private madhouses surrounded their activities, that it was seldom successful.

(*e*) *Patients in Bethlem.* Bethlem Hospital in London had been in use since the year 1377 as an institution for the reception of those suffering from acute forms of mental disorder. It was financed by public subscriptions and legacies.

(*f*) *Single lunatics.* This term is used, as it was used in the nineteenth century, to indicate all who were confined alone. The state of single lunatics varied enormously, since it depended entirely on the arrangements made by relatives and friends for their confinement. They can be divided into three main classes—patients of some social standing who remained in their own homes and received medical attention; patients who were 'put away' by their families, usually in some deserted place where their existence might be forgotten, and the family scandal allowed to die down; and those in poorer families who were simply tied or chained in a corner of the house to prevent them from becoming a nuisance to other people. A writer in the *Westminster Review* as late as March 1845, considered that this class was in the worse case of all.

The portion of the domestic accommodation usually assigned to these unfortunates is that commonly devoted to the reception of coals . . . namely, that triangular space formed between the stairs and the ground-floor. In this confined, dark and damp corner may be found at this very time no small number of our fellow-beings, huddled, crouching and gibbering, with less apparent intelligence and under worse treatment than the lower domestic animals.

Nothing further can be said at this juncture concerning single lunatics and those in private madhouses,[21] as no public records were kept at this period, and the whole object of such confinement was secrecy; but it is possible to form a picture of the conditions under which the insane lived in Bethlem, and in workhouses and prisons throughout the country.

Bethlem

Early history

This hospital, which gave the English language a new and descriptive word, was in 1744 the largest public hospital in England devoted to the care of the insane.[22] It originally derived its name from a priory of the Order of St Mary of Bethlehem founded in London in 1247. It was seized by the Crown in 1375 on the grounds that it was in the possession of an alien Order, and was used from 1377 as an institution for the reception of those suffering from acute forms of mental disorder. It was apparently controlled by the Crown until 1546, when the Lord Mayor of London, Sir John Gresham, petitioned Henry VIII to grant the hospital to the City. The Charter was granted on 13 January 1547 —only a few days before the King's death. Eight years later, control passed for a short time into the hands of the Governors of Christ's Hospital, but this experiment in government was apparently a failure. In 1557, the management was transferred to the Governors of the original Bridewell at Blackfriars; this arrangement was later confirmed by Act of Parliament,[23] and endured throughout the joint life of the two institutions until Bethlem became part of the National Health Service in 1948. Governors were elected by the freemen of the City, the Court of Aldermen and the Common Council of the City serving *ex-officio*.

The institution was financed by public subscriptions and legacies; money received in donations and bequests was invested in house property in London, and by the early eighteenth century, when the value of such property was rising, Bethlem was a comparatively wealthy institution, being spared the financial anxieties which beset other ventures in philanthropy.

Patients were liable for their own maintenance unless they were paupers, in which case the responsibility for maintenance fell upon the parish of settlement. Up to the middle of the seventeenth century, 'Toms o' Bedlam'—discharged patients with a recognizable badge[24] which gave them licence to beg in order to pay their arrears—were a familiar sight in towns and villages throughout England. John Aubrey's description is a well-known one:

> Till the breaking out of the Civill Warres, Tom o' Bedlams did travell about the countrey. They had been poore distracted men that had been put into Bedlam, where, recovering to some sobernesse, they were licentiated to goe a-begging . . . they wore about their necks a great horn of an oxe in a string or bawdric, which, when they came to an house for almes, they did wind.[25]

The profession, if it can be called such, suffered greatly from the intrusion of other beggars who counterfeited the distinguishing marks of the Bedlam beggar in order to escape the penalties of the vagrancy laws. A poem composed by a pretended Bedlamite in the seventeenth century sings of:

> The lordly lofts of Bedlam
> With stubble soft and dainty,
> Brave bracelets strong,
> Sweet whips, ding-dong,
> And wholesome hunger plenty.[26]

'Old Bedlam' was rebuilt after a fire in 1678. The new building was a reproduction of the Tuileries, a fact which is said to have given considerable offence to Louis XIV. Prints[27] show an imposing frontage surrounded by pleasant greenery. On either side of the main gate stood the two famous figures of Raving and Melancholy Madness, designed by Caius Gabriel Cibber, and commemorated by Alexander Pope in *The Dunciad*:

> Close to those walls where Folly holds her throne,
> And laughs to think Monroe would take her down,
> Where, o'er the gates, by his famed father's hand,
> Great Cibber's brazen brainless brothers stand.[28]

'Monroe' refers to James Monro, son of a Principal of Edinburgh University, who became resident physician of Bethlem in 1728, the year in which *The Dunciad* was written. He held office until 1752, when he was succeeded by his son John; the management of Bethlem remained largely in the hands of an unbroken line of Monros, the office of physician passing from father to son, until 1852.

Conditions in the eighteenth century

Bethlem has always had its defenders and attackers. Since some of the early records of the hospital have now been destroyed, we are largely dependent on partisan accounts of the treatment at this time. The official *Story of Bethlehem Hospital*, published as recently as 1913, and written by the chaplain of the hospital, continues this partisanship to some extent, and displays a distressing geniality: 'I have a whole budget of literary associations to gossip over as we saunter through the wards,' writes the author. 'Will you allow me to open the pack and spread out some of my attractive wares?' Until 1770, idle and curious visitors were allowed to enter Bethlem at a fee of a penny or twopence a time, in order to watch the antics of the inmates.[29] The official historian's attitude seems to have more in common with them than with the sober and responsible philanthropists who made it their business to investigate conditions in the nineteenth century.

As an instance of the two attitudes, two poems quoted by historians of Bethlem are here reproduced. The first, which appears in the official history, was written by one J. Clark in 1744, and was sold to visitors:

> . . . to our Governors, due praise be giv'n
> Who, by just care, have changed our Hell to Heav'n.
> A Hell on earth no truer can we find
> Than a disturbed and distracted mind.
> . . . our learned Doctor gives his aid,
> And for his Care with Blessings ever paid,
> This all those happy Objects will not spare
> Who are discharged by his Skill and Care.
> Our Meat is good, the Bread and Cheese the same,
> Our Butter, Beer and Spoon Meat none can blame.
> The Physic's mild, the Vomits are not such,
> But, thanks be prais'd, of these we have not much.
> Bleeding is wholesome, and as for the Cold Bath,

All are agreed it many Virtues hath.
The Beds and Bedding are both warm and clean,
Which to each comer may be plainly seen,
Except those rooms where the most Wild do lie. . . .[30]

This skilful if naïve propaganda was dedicated to the Governor,[31] Admiral Vernon, and may have served to quiet the consciences of the fashionable visitors.

An anonymous poem written in 1776 is quoted by Daniel Hack Tuke, sometime President of the Royal Medico-Psychological Association, and member of a family famous in the history of lunacy reform:

Far other views than these within appear
And Woe and Horror dwell forever here;
Forever from the echoing roofs rebound
A dreadful Din of heterogeneous sounds.
From this, from that, from every quarter rise
Loud shouts and sullen groans and doleful cries. . . .
Within the Chambers which this Dome contains
In all her 'frantic' forms, Distraction reigns . . .
Rattling his chains, the wretch all raving lies
And roars and foams, and Earth and Heaven defies.[32]

Perhaps the most famous representation of these conditions occurs in the eighth scene of *The Rake's Progress*, which Hogarth painted in the incurable ward in 1733. It shows two fashionable ladies watching the inmates without a visible sign of compassion. The Rake lies on the floor, practically naked, and with his head shaven, while a keeper manacles his feet and another, or an apothecary, examines his head. His expression shows an extreme of cynicism, bitterness, and despair. Another print, dated about 1745 and in the Gardner Collection, shows a similar scene. The patient is again shorn; his hands are chained, and he struggles violently while three keepers hold him down in order to affix a leg-lock to his ankles. A bowl for bleeding or vomit lies in front of the group, and one of the onlookers is a woman— presumably, from her clothes, a female attendant.

An interesting and probably authentic account of the conditions of those whom Tuke's anonymous rhymer called the 'most Wild' occurs in Harrison Ainsworth's *Jack Sheppard*. It refers to the year 1720. Jack Sheppard, who is wanted for murder, risks arrest in order to visit Bethlem to see his mother, who has been driven insane by his crimes:

Jack recoiled before the appalling object that met his gaze. Cowering in a corner upon a heap of straw sat his unfortunate mother, the complete wreck of what she had been. Her eyes glistened in the darkness—for light was only admitted through a small grated window—like flames, and as she fixed them on him, their glances seemed to penetrate to his very soul. A piece of old blanket was fastened across her shoulders, and she wore no other clothing except a petticoat. Her arms and feet were uncovered, and of almost skeleton thinness. Her features were meagre and ghastly white, and had the fixed and horrible stamp of insanity. Her head had been shaved, and around it was swathed a piece of rag, in which a few straws were stuck. Her thin fingers were armed with nails as long as the talons of a bird. A chain, riveted to an iron belt encircling her waist, bound her to the wall. The cell in which she was confined was about six feet long and four feet wide.

This description might be dismissed as over-painted were it not for the fact that reliable investigators in 1815 discovered patients in almost identical conditions.[33]

The management of Bethlem was marred during the period by a series of financial scandals concerning the misappropriation of money and goods by the staff. In 1752, a pamphlet entitled *Low Life: or, One Half of the World does not know how the Other Half Lives*, accused the keepers of stealing food and personal possessions from the patients.[34] In 1772, the House Governor himself was dismissed for obtaining large quantities of provisions from the buttery for his personal use.[35]

'Patients are ordered to be bled about the latter end of May, or the beginning of June, according to the weather,' stated Dr Thomas Monro in evidence before the Select Committee of 1815, 'and after they have been bled, they take vomits once a week for a certain number of weeks; after that, we purge the patients. That has been the practice invariably for years, long before my time; it was handed down to me by my father, and I do not know any better practice.' The control of the Monro family over the medical treatment of the patients was complete and unchallenged, and consisted in an unvarying and indiscriminate use of weakening agents to reduce violence, coupled with the frequent use of mechanical forms of restraint.

Most patients, male and female, appear to have been kept in a state of near or complete nakedness,[37] either because the authorities would not provide clothes or because the patients might destroy them. Bedding usually consisted of straw for the paupers and unclean patients, since this was cheap and easily cleared away when fouled.[38]

While casual visitors who paid for admission and came only for entertainment were welcome, serious and responsible visitors who wished to observe and ameliorate conditions were not. Medical practitioners were forbidden to see the patients, and an entry in John Wesley's diary shows that the same prohibition extended to evangelical preachers: 'I went to see a young woman in Bedlam; but I had not talked to her long before one gave me to know that none of the preachers were to come here. So we are forbidden to go to Newgate for fear of making them wicked, and to Bedlam for fear of making them mad!'

It is easy to overstate the case against the authorities of Bethlem. They provided care and treatment of a kind when this was otherwise unknown and had no precedents against which to test their methods. An institution for the reception of violent patients can never be wholly a pleasant place, and, however enlightened the policy of the authorities, there will always be patients who suffer extremely through delusions of persecution, depression, or squalid habits that defy the most patient and sustained attempts at cleanliness; but the available evidence shows that the policy of the authorities, even by eighteenth-century standards, was very far from enlightened.

Workhouses and poorhouses

By 1774, pauperism—genuine poverty, as opposed to habitual vagrancy—had assumed alarming proportions. There is probably no other period in English history in which the social classes were so clearly divided. A small book entitled *An Account of the Workhouses in Great Britain in the Year* 1732, compiled apparently from official returns, gives a vivid picture of the treatment of the poor at this time. The rich, who had to pay the rates, were obsessed with the idea that institutions for the poor must be run as cheaply as possible. The Guardians of the workhouse in the parish of St George's, Hanover Square, recorded with some pride that as a result of the 'frugality of management under Honourable Persons' they had succeeded in reducing the cost of maintenance per head to the sum of one and ninepence halfpenny per week. At Maidstone, the Poor Law authorities were satisfied that 'very great numbers of lazy People, rather than submit to the Confinement and Labour of the Workhouse, are content to throw off the Mask and maintain themselves by their own Industry'. 'A Workhouse', they added, 'is a Name that carries with it an idea of Correction and Punishment'. A prayer 'proper to be used in Workhouses', and couched in the language of the 1662 Prayer Book, includes the plea that the poor may not 'cherish Sin with the Bread of Idleness'.

It is impossible to assess the number of mentally disordered people who were housed in institutions of this stringent and corrective nature. The parliamentary committee of 1807 came to the conclusion that the previous year's estimate of 1765 was a gross under-estimate[39] and in 1828, the figure was put at 9000.[40] Even allowing for the increase of population in the late eighteenth and early nineteenth centuries, it would be safe to say that there must have been four or five thousand people suffering from psychotic disorders or mental deficiency in workhouses before 1789. The significant fact is that their existence was hardly recognized. The *Account of Workhouses in* 1732, which included returns from all the principal Poor Law institutions in the country, mentions them in only two instances, and then in passing. There was no special administrative practice for dealing with pauper lunatics as a class, so that their treatment depended on the policy—or lack of policy—of the local authorities.

Treatment under the Poor Law

The basis of Poor Law legislation was the Act of 1601 (43 Eliz. c. 2), which stated that unpaid overseers of the poor were to raise money 'weekly or otherwise by taxation' in each parish for the relief of its own paupers. Outdoor relief was common in most parishes before 1723, the year of the Workhouse Test. It was widely used again towards the end of the century,[41] when the volume of distress became so great that it was impossible for the workhouses to deal with the problem; but in the period under review, outdoor relief was not in general use, and many parishes used the workhouse as a weapon to deter the poor from seeking relief.

The great failure of the Poor Law lay in the apparent inability of its administrators to distinguish between the 'impotent poor' who could not work, and the able-bodied poor who would not. Conditions varied greatly from parish to parish, but the number of authorities was so great, and the administrative area of each so small, that it was impossible for most of them to devise a system of classification which would allow for differentiation in treatment.

A scheme for making more sympathetic provision for the 'impotent poor' was put forward by the Earl of Hillsborough in 1753; he proposed that county hospitals should be set up, and that 'none be admitted into the hospital except the children of parents not able to maintain themselves; all exposed and deserted children, diseased persons who cannot work, and are too poor to purchase medicines; idiots, climatics, lame, old, blind, and others having no means to maintain themselves.'[42] Such a scheme would have been impossible to put into practice without great financial outlay and extensive reorganization of the whole framework of poor relief.

It has been estimated[43] that under the old Poor Law there were between twelve and fifteen thousand separate parishes and townships, each controlling its own institution for the relief of pauperism. The principles on which relief was organized differed widely. In some of the smaller parishes, the poorhouse was primarily an almshouse for the infirm and aged of respectable character; but in the larger cities, the organized workhouse had superseded the poorhouse, and the succour of the impotent was at best only a secondary aim.

The common justification for the existence of the man on parish relief was his ability to work, and provide at least in part for his own maintenance. Institutions like that at Strood, Kent, where the infirm and aged were said to be 'wholly removed from the Cares of this Life' and had 'nothing to do but to prepare themselves for the next', were rare and merciful in comparison with the majority. At St Andrew's, Holborn, seven old men and women 'of which two are upwards of fourscore and one an Ideot' picked oakum and were said to be 'continually refreshed by the Balsamick Odour of it'. Oakum-picking and the spinning of mop yarn, both lowly-paid and tedious occupations, were the methods of employment almost universally used.

The punishments for not working or for 'mischievous conduct' were frequently severe. They included solitary confinement in a dark room, deprivation of food, and being made to stand on a stool 'with the Crime pinned to their Breast'. A pauper whose mental condition precluded the possibility of normal employment, or led him into erratic conduct would thus be penalized in a way which was likely to aggravate the condition.

Violence and excitability were sternly discouraged in institutions which placed great emphasis on orderliness and quietude. At St Giles-

B

in-the-Fields, paupers who were 'very clamorous' or who made 'great Disturbances' were debarred from meals until they became amenable. At St Andrew's, Holborn, those who were guilty of 'prophane Cursing or Swearing' were sent to the stocks. The workhouse at Norwich was accustomed to use leg-locks and manacles on troublesome inmates.[44]

Medical attention

At St Albans, the Guardians recorded with some pride that the sick were nursed by the women paupers, thus saving fifteen to twenty pounds a year in apothecaries' bills. 'There are many workhouses,' wrote an official at Winchester, 'where medicines are dispensed; but they are generally given without the advice of a doctor.'[45] Where medical attention was provided, the general practice was for the contract to be farmed out to the local doctors, and the lowest tender automatically accepted. The doctor or apothecary gave nominal attention to all paupers, providing his own drugs and medicines, for a sum of perhaps twenty pounds a year.[46] Since a degree of physical debility would render the more troublesome lunatics weaker and thus more amenable, it is unlikely that any sustained attempt would be made to restore them to robust and violent health.

St Peter's, Bristol

In most workhouses, no attempt was made to separate even the small proportion of the mentally disordered who were recognized as such from the other paupers, for the benefit of either class. Some few of the larger workhouses possessed infirmaries, but these appear to have been mainly used for those suffering from infectious and contagious diseases, such as smallpox and syphilis.

The outstanding exception to the rigours of the Workhouse Test as it affected the mentally disordered was the workhouse where that test was initiated. The records of St Peter's Workhouse, Bristol,[47] show that it was one of the very few where pauper lunatics were treated as a separate class, and almost certainly the only one where they received treatment as distinct from confinement. Almost from its inception in 1696, the first building, known as the Mint, was used for the 'impotent poor' of the city, and other premises were acquired as a 'manufactory' for the able-bodied. By degrees, the aged and those suffering from ailments of a mainly physical nature were housed elsewhere, until the

Mint became the general asylum for what was then one of the largest cities in England.

The lunatic patients seem to have been placed in separate wards almost from the first, an early regulation recommending that 'the lunatic wards be floored with planks'—presumably because stone floors were injurious to the patients' health. Medical attention was provided by surgeons and physicians of local standing, who gave their services voluntarily. A regulation of April, 1768, laid down that they were to visit the 'Frenzy Objects' once a week, and also 'such Objects as shall from time to time be brought in by Warrants of Lunacy.'*

The policy of the authorities at Bristol stands out in complete contrast to that of almost every other Poor Law authority. They established three principles which laid the foundation for the later development of county asylums: the care of the insane should be the responsibility of the parish or township in which they lived; they should be treated as a separate class, their living conditions being adapted to their special needs; and they should receive treatment, not punishment.

Prisons

Bridewells, or houses of correction, were built on the pattern of the original Bridewell raised at Blackfriars in London in 1555. They generally received vagrants and beggars who could not be convicted of any crime save that of wandering abroad or refusing to work. They also housed a number of petty offenders of the kind who under the modern penal system would probably be placed on probation. The chief distinction between a gaol and a Bridewell was that in the former the inmates were responsible for their own maintenance and for the payment of gaolers' fees, since the gaolers were generally not in receipt of a salary. Many prisoners were forced to remain in gaol as debtors long after the original sentence was served. In a Bridewell, the officials received a salary, and the Poor Law authority was responsible for the maintenance of pauper inmates, who were released at the end of their term of imprisonment. At the same time, conditions were such as to deter the sturdiest of beggars. The Master of the Bridewell at Tothill Fields received the sum of £200 a year, out of which he paid the expenses of the entire house, and made his own salary. He was

* The patients are commonly referred to as 'objects of charity'—cp. 'those happy objects' at Bethlem, p. 14.

directed to pay a matron, a chaplain, a porter, and sufficient servants, and to provide the inmates with 'fresh straw every month, and warm pottage thrice a week.'[48]

It would appear from John Howard's *Report on the State of the Prisons* (1777) that the inmates of this Bridewell were comparatively fortunate. 'In many Gaols and most Bridewells,' he wrote, 'there is no allowance of straw for the prisoners to sleep on; and if by any means they get a little, it is not changed for months together, so that it is almost worn to dust.' In writing of the Blackfriars Bridewell, he added, 'The night-rooms are supplied with straw. No other Prison in London has any straw or other bedding.'

> There are several Bridewells . . . in which the prisoners have no allowance of food at all. In some, the keeper farms out what little is allowed them: and where he engages to supply each prisoner with one or two pennyworth of bread a day, I have known this shrunk to half, sometimes less than half, the quantity, cut or broken from his own loaf.

In many cases, there were no tools or materials with which the prisoners might work and earn their keep:

> Some keepers of these houses, who have represented to the magistrates the wants of their prisoners, and desired for them necessary food, have been silenced with these inconsiderate words, 'Let them work or starve.' When these gentlemen know the former is impossible, do they not by that sentence inevitably doom poor creatures to the latter?

When Howard undertook his lengthy and self-imposed travels on behalf of the prisoners, he found hardened criminals, shiftless vagrants and petty offenders confined together with the insane. 'Idiots and lunatics . . . serve for sport to idle visitants . . . where they are not kept separate (they) disturb and terrify other prisoners. No care is taken of them, though it is probable that by medicines and proper regimen, some of them might be restored to their senses, and to usefulness in life.'

At Kingston-upon-Hull Bridewell, Howard found 'two rooms below and two upstairs, about twelve feet square, very offensive; no fireplace. Courtyard only twenty-two feet by ten; not secure, and prisoners not permitted to go to the pump: no sewer: no allowance: no straw. . . .' He visited this Bridewell on three occasions between 1774 and 1779, and found the same 'poor, raving lunatic' there each time. At Swaffham County Bridewell, the lunatic whose existence was noted in 1774 was still there in 1779. At the county gaol, Lancaster, he 'saw only one poor lunatic; who had been there many years, and is since dead.' These instances may be multiplied from his report.

Howard notes in the Appendix to his report, added in 1779, that an Act of 1763 provided for the separation of insane prisoners from others, stating that 'persons of insane mind and outrageous behaviour' were not to 'go in common with the other prisoners' (3 Geo. III c. 27). This is another example of segregation of the insane for the benefit of the sane, since vagrants and petty thieves were to receive what amounted to preferential treatment. This Act appears to have been generally ignored, since most county Bridewells were too small and too badly run to admit of diversity in accommodation; but the reformer's recommendation, that all Bridewells should have 'two wards for the sick, with medical relief' was very far from realization. In many cases, the sick prisoners lacked not only medical relief and separate quarters, but even fresh air: 'One reason why the rooms in some prisons are so close is perhaps the window-tax, which gaolers have to pay; this tempts them to stop up the windows and stifle the prisoners.'[49]

Criminal lunatics

Criminally insane persons were confined to gaol, apparently for life. The only prominent judicial opinion of the period drew such a stringent definition of what constituted criminal insanity that only those beyond the hope of cure could possibly be included in it. At the trial of a man named Arnold in 1723 for the attempted murder of Lord Onslow, Mr Justice Tracey made the following pronouncement:

> It is not every kind of frantic humour, or something unaccount-
> able in a man's behaviour, that points him out to be such
> a man as is exempted from punishment; it must be a man that is
> totally deprived of his understanding and memory, and doth not
> know what he is doing, no more than an infant, than a brute or
> wild beast, such a one is never the object of punishment.[50]

This definition necessarily excluded all cases which were not characterized by chronic and continued incoherence, or the lower grades of mental subnormality, so that the vast majority of those who would now be considered criminally insane and sent to institutions of the Broadmoor type were punished as ordinary criminals. Those who came within the definition of what became known as 'the Wild Beast

Test' were in scarcely better case. They were confined to gaols where the conditions were, if possible, even worse than the Bridewells. At Ely, Howard noted, the gaol was until 1763 in ruins; to prevent them from escaping, the gaoler secured the felons by 'chaining them down on their backs on a floor, across which were several iron bars; with an iron collar with spikes about their necks, and a heavy iron bar over their legs'. An 'excellent Magistrate' named James Colyer brought the plight of the prisoners to the notice of the King, 'upon which His Majesty was much affected, and gave immediate orders for a proper inquiry and redress', but in 1774 the new gaol had an offensive sewer, no water, no infirmary, and no straw for the inmates to sleep on, so that the extent of the redress was apparently not very great. At Bury St Edmunds, the felons lived by night and day in 'a large dungeon down three steps' and were chained by staples fixed to their bedsteads. In places such as these, the criminally insane—who were completely lacking in any power to look after themselves—were confined without attention and without food except what they might obtain through charity. Such was the nature of their 'exemption from punishment'.

2   The growth of public concern

The reform movement began imperceptibly, through a series of apparently disconnected events, each of which aroused the public interest in some aspect of the treatment of the insane. In 1744, dangerous lunatics were specially considered in a revision of the vagrancy laws; in 1763, the general public was alarmed by revelations concerning the conditions in private madhouses, and a movement to obtain statutory control was initiated; in 1789, the nature of the King's illness became generally known, and the topic of madness was widely discussed in a context which excluded the attitude of moral condemnation. It was scarcely possible—at least in Tory circles—to assume that the head of state was being punished for his sins.

It is doubtful whether many people in the eighteenth century sensed the connection between these events; for, as we have seen, the idea of insanity as a single social factor had not yet been evolved. It is only in the light of later developments that these happenings assumed a relevance to each other.

Lunatics under the Vagrancy Laws, 1744

A parliamentary committee was set up in 1742 to consider the treatment of 'rogues and vagabonds' and the revision of the vagrancy laws. The perennial problems of vagrancy tended to be reviewed every thirty or forty years through the sixteenth, seventeenth and eighteenth centuries. By 1744, the population movement to the industrial north and midlands, and the cumulative effect of enclosures, was exacerbating the problems. Today, the interest of the vagrancy laws enacted lies less in the penal solutions found to predominantly economic problems than in the definition of society's rejects. The 1744 Act, which resulted from the committee's recommendations, began: 'Whereas the number of Rogues, Vagabonds and other Idle or Disorderly Persons daily increases, to the great Scandal, Loss and Annoyance of the Kingdom . . . ' It no longer included wandering scholars (a Tudor Act[1] refers to 'all psons [sic] calling themselves Schollers going about the country begging') but it included 'Persons

25

who threaten to run away and leave their Wives and Children to the Parish . . . Persons found in Forests with Guns. . . . All Minstrels, Jugglers . . . All Persons pretending to be Gypsies, or wandering about in the Habit or Form of Egyptians'.[2]

Lunatics had first joined this band of marital defaulters, poachers, travelling showmen and other nomads in 1714.[3] That Act provided for their detention, restraint and maintenance, but not for treatment. The importance of the 1744 Act rests in the fact that it added the words 'and curing'—even though it in fact specified no method by which cure could be carried out.

Under the 1744 Act, anyone could apprehend a vagrant, and the local justice of the peace was directed to order the payment of a reward of five shillings to the informant. Normally, vagrants were sent on a single magistrate's warrant to a Bridewell 'there to be kept to Hard Labour for any Time not exceeding One Month'. The point of incorporating a special section concerning lunatics was probably less to secure treatment for them than to exempt them from the penal clauses applicable to other vagrants.

Section 20 of the Act reads as follows:

It shall and may be lawful for any two or more Justices of the Peace where such Lunatick or mad Person shall be found, by Warrant under their Hands and Seals, directed to the Constables, Churchwardens and Overseers of the Poor of such Parish, Town or Place, to cause such Persons to be apprehended and kept safely locked up in some secure Place . . . as such Justices shall appoint; and (if such Justices find it necessary) to be there chained. . . . The Charges of removing, and of keeping, maintaining and curing such Persons during such Restraint (which shall be for and during such time only as such Lunacy or Madness shall continue) shall be satisfied and paid . . . by Order of two or more Justices of the Peace, directing the Churchwardens or Overseers where any Goods, Chattels, Lands or Tenements of such Persons shall be, to seize and sell so much of the Goods and Chattels, or to receive so much of the annual Rents of the Lands and Tenements, as is necessary to pay the same; and to account for what is so sold, seized or received at the next Quarter Sessions; or, if such Person hath not an Estate to pay and satisfy the same, over and above what shall be sufficient to maintain his or her Family, then such Charges shall be satisfied and paid by the Parish, Town or Place to which such Person belongs, by Order of two Justices directed to the Churchwardens or Overseers for that Purpose.

This section has several significant points, and its omissions convey a certain amount of information about the treatment which the mentally disordered received.

'. . . *to cause such Person to be apprehended* . . .'

The local magistrates, who possessed neither legal nor medical training, were held to be sufficient judges of the existence of a state of insanity. No medical certification was necessary. It should perhaps be pointed out here that responsible medical certification was hardly possible until after 1858—the date of the Medical Registration Act.

'. . . *two or more Justices of the Peace* . . .'

The warrant for the detention of a vagrant under the other sections of the Act required the assent of only one magistrate. The provision of a joint authority in the case of the insane may have been designed to prevent individual magistrates from indulging in a purely personal grudge against an inconvenient neighbour by using their powers under this section.

'. . . *safely locked up in some secure Place* . . .'

The 'secure place' was often a gaol or house of correction, since these were the only places which possessed the means of preventing the inmates from escaping.

'. . . *removing* . . .'

If he was not a resident of the parish in which he was apprehended, the insane person would be removed to his legal place of settlement, if this could be established, so that the responsibility for his maintenance might devolve on the latter parish.

'. . . *keeping, maintaining and curing* . . .'

No machinery was set up for curative treatment or medical attention of any kind. The only form of treatment apparently envisaged was that of mechanical restraint in the form of chains. However, the Act did make it possible to send patients to special accommodation as and where this was provided.

'. . . *during such Time* . . . *as such Lunacy or Madness shall continue*. . .'

Since no medical evidence was necessary to establish that the state of insanity had ceased to exist, the onus of judgment rested presumably on the justices or the gaolers. Two social dangers were implicit in the unsatisfactory clause: a person who regained his sanity might be confined indefinitely if he offered resistance when chained, or fell foul of his gaoler; alternatively, a person suffering from a cyclical condition, the course of which is separable into distinct and recurrent phases, might be released during a lucid spell, to become again a public danger soon after his release.

Behind the framing of this section, and of much subsequent legislation, lay the belief that insanity was one distinct mental state differing so widely from 'normal' mental health that it was easily discernible to the lay eye. It was also believed to be a continuous state. In fact, no state of mental illness or handicap involves unabated violence. Many such states are intermittent in their manifestations, while in others exhaustion would end the intolerable strain placed on the physical system in the absence of drugs.

'. . . *The Charges . . . shall be satisfied and paid . . .*'

The first charge on the estate of the insane person was to pay 'what shall be necessary to maintain his . . . family'. Only when this charge had been adequately met could the local authority distrain his goods and property to pay for his maintenance.

'. . . *to account for what is so seized . . . at the next Quarter Sessions . . .*'

A legal check was to be kept on the administration of property appropriated by the overseers or churchwardens to satisfy maintenance charges, but no provision was made for safeguarding any other property of the insane person during his confinement under the provision of this Act.[4] Such property might be seized by an unscrupulous relative without fear of legal action.

The 1744 Act could hardly be called a positive advance on previous law or practice. It excited no public interest, and gave rise to no controversies. The sole achievement lay in the fact that some of those suffering from mental disorder were for the first time recognized as requiring treatment.

Private madhouses, 1763–74

It was nineteen years before the question of the insane was again raised in parliament, and then in connection with the private madhouses. On this occasion, we have the first hint of outside pressure being brought to bear on the House of Commons. The public interest was aroused by two cases in which a writ of Habeas Corpus had been issued as a means of liberating the inmate of a private madhouse suspected of being wrongfully detained. This procedure was seldom successful, since many devices—such as changing the patient's name, using secret cells which could not be detected by an investigator, or declaring that the patient had escaped—could be used to defeat it.

Judging from reported cases, the usual practice was to require that the relatives and a physician appointed by the Court should be given access to the patient in the madhouse, in order to ascertain whether a state of insanity really existed. If they reported that the patient was sane, the proprietor of the madhouse was then required to produce the patient in court.

In the case of Rex *v*. Turlington (1761)[5] a motion was made on behalf of the relatives of Mrs Deborah D'Vebre for a Habeas Corpus to be directed to Turlington, the keeper of a private madhouse in Chelsea. Mrs D'Vebre had been sent there at the instance of her husband. A rule was made that a physician, together with the patient's nearest blood relation (a gentleman named Peter Bodkin) and her attorney should 'at all proper times and reasonable hours respectively be admitted, and have free access to Mrs Deborah D'Vebre . . . at the madhouse kept by Robert Turlington in Chelsea.'

Two days later, an affidavit from the physician was read in Court. It stated that he 'saw no reason to suspect that she was or had been disordered in her mind: on the contrary, he found her to be very sensible, and very cool and dispassionate'. Mrs D'Vebre was thereupon produced in Court, and allowed to leave with her attorney.

In another case (Rex *v*. Clarke, 1762)[6] the attempt to serve a writ of Habeas Corpus was defeated by an affidavit from the appointed physician that the patient, Mrs Anne Hunt, was in an acute state of mental disorder, and had in fact been sent to the madhouse on his own advice.

The interest aroused by the Turlington case and the Clarke case caused a growing degree of public concern which was fanned by the publication of a now famous article in the *Gentleman's Magazine* of January, 1763.

'When a person is forcibly taken or artfully decoyed into a private madhouse,' stated the anonymous writer:

he is, without any authority or any further charge than that of an impatient heir, a mercenary relation, or a pretended friend, instantly seized upon by a set of inhuman ruffians trained up to this barbarous profession, stripped naked, and conveyed to a dark-room. If the patient complains, the attendant brutishly orders him not to rave, calls for assistance, and ties him down to a bed, from which he is not released until he submits to their pleasure. Next morning, a doctor is gravely introduced who, taking the report of the keeper, pronounces the unfortunate person a lunatic, and declares that he must be reduced by physic. If the revolted victim offers to argue against it by alleging any proofs of sanity, a motion is made by the waiter for the doctor to withdraw, and if the patient, or rather the prisoner, persists in vindicating his reason, or refuses to take the dose, he is then deemed raving mad; the banditti of the whole house are called in, the forcing instruments brought, upon which the sensible patient must submit to take whatever is administered. When the poor patient thus finds himself deprived of all communication with the world, and denied the use of pen and paper, all he can do is to compose himself under the unhappy situation in the hope of a more favourable report. But any composure under such affliction is immediately deemed a melancholy or sulky fit, by the waiter, who reports it as such to the doctor in the hearing of the despairing prisoner, whose misery is thus redoubled in finding that the doctor prescribes a repetition of the dose, and that from day to day, until the patient is so debilitated in body that in time it impairs his mind . . . What must a rational mind suffer that is treated in this irrational manner? Weakened by physic, emaciated by torture, diseased by confinement, and terrified by the sight of every instrument of cruelty and the dreadful menaces of an attending ruffian, hardened against all the tendernesses of human nature. . . .

The writer contrasted this situation with conditions in the public hospitals and concluded with an appeal to parliament to frame regulations designed to prevent the imprisonment of sane people, and parliament responded on the 27th of January by the appointment of a Select Committee of the House of Commons.

The report of this Committee makes curious reading. The members apparently found it necessary to proceed with extreme discretion, since London madhouses confined the relatives of many prominent people, and also because a number of well-known members of the medical profession had financial interests in private madhouses. Accordingly, they confined their investigations to two houses— Miles', at Hoxton, and Turlington's, in Chelsea—and to the detailed study of only one case in each house. They stressed in their short report that these were not selected cases, and that hundreds of similar examples existed, but stated that they refrained from publishing further cases out of consideration for the families of sufferers. One of the witnesses before the Committee was Dr Battie of St Luke's, who was asked if he had ever met with cases in which persons of undoubted sanity were confined as lunatics.

He said, 'It frequently happened.'

Dr Monro of Bethlem, who bore a strong antipathy to Battie, (see p. 41) then gave evidence. He flatly contradicted Battie's statement, and stated that no such cases existed.

The allegations concerning the two madhouses investigated were that persons had been confined there on the representation of relatives without adequate medical examination, and that they were prevented from communicating with the outside world, being denied visits from friends and the use of writing materials. However, the only evidence brought forward related to two relatively mild cases—a Mrs Gold, confined at Hoxton for three weeks eight years previously, and a Mrs Hawley, thought to be an habitual drunkard. Many questions were left unanswered and the impression left on the reader is that, although the Committee was bound to investigate, it did not want to investigate too deeply.

The Act for Regulating Private Madhouses, 1774 (14 Geo. III c. 9)

It was eleven years from the time when the Committee made its report to the time when provisions limiting the power of madhouse proprietors became law. Even then, the opposition of the legal profession was such that the provisions for enforcing the regulations contained in this Act were so ineffectual that it remained almost a dead letter. It did not apply to pauper lunatics in madhouses, to single lunatics, or to public subscription hospitals. The preamble ran:

> Whereas many great and dangerous Abuses frequently arise from the present State of Houses kept for the Reception of Lunaticks, for Want of Regulations with Respect to the Person keeping such Houses, the admission of Patients into them, and the Visitation by proper Persons of the said Houses and Patients: and whereas the Law, as it now stands, is insufficient for preventing or discovering such Abuses. . . .

No person was to take charge of more than one lunatic for profit without a licence. In the metropolitan area ('within the cities of London and Westminster and within seven miles of the same, and within the County of Middlesex') licensing was to be carried out by five Commissioners elected from their number by the President and Fellows of the Royal College of Physicians; the Commissioners were to meet annually in the Hall of the College for this purpose. No Commissioner was to be directly or indirectly concerned in the keeping of a licensed house, on pain of a penalty of fifty pounds. They were to visit all such houses 'between the Hours of Eight and Five in the Day-time', and were to make notes in writing of the condition of the patients. 'In case the Commissioners upon their Visitation shall discover any Thing that, in their Opinion, shall deserve Censure or Animadversion, they shall, in that case, report the same; and such Part of their Report and no more shall be hung up in the Censor's Room of the College, to be perused and inspected by any Person who shall apply for that Purpose.'

A keeper who refused to admit the Commissioners forfeited his licence. Notice was to be sent to the Secretary of the Commissioners by the keeper within three days of the reception of a patient.

Outside the metropolitan area, licensing was to be carried out by the justices at the Quarter Sessions. Two justices and a physician were to be nominated at the Quarter Sessions to visit and make reports on the same terms as the Commissioners in the metropolitan area.

The Act applied only to a limited section of patients, but even so, had many weaknesses. The most glaring of these was the omission of any power by which the Commissioners might refuse to grant licences on the grounds of ill-treatment or neglect of patients. A keeper would forfeit his licence if he refused to admit the official visitors; but as long as he admitted them, whatever the conditions, they could take no action except that of displaying their reports in a place where few could see it and none would have their attention drawn to it.

Visits were to be made 'between the Hours of Eight and Five in the Day-time', and no provision was made to ensure that the proprietors —who might also be members of the Royal College of Physicians— were not warned beforehand. The visit might be a purely cursory one, since the Commissioners were untrained, unpaid (save for nominal expenses) and not instructed what to look for. Since they could not visit at night, they would have no adequate opportunity of inspecting the sleeping conditions.

The proprietors were obliged to send notice of reception within three days, but no medical certificate was needed, and there was no penalty for failure to comply.

Significance of the 1774 Act

Even if the visitation envisaged by the Act had been carried out systematically and conscientiously, the proprietors of private mad-houses would have remained almost as free from the fear of legal penalties as before. The Act said nothing on the subject of the medical supervision of patients, diet, overcrowding, mechanical restraint, or deliberate brutality of treatment. Its primary purpose was to provide safeguards against illegal detention, but it failed even in this simple object, since there was no means of forcing the proprietor to comply with the orders of the Commissioners.

Although its provisions were administratively weak, the Act of 1774 served a purpose. It established five important principles in lunacy legislation:

1. Licensing by a public authority of private institutions run for profit.
2. Notification of the reception into such institutions of a person alleged to be insane.
3. Visitation by Commissioners, whose method of appointment was prescribed by parliament.
4. Inspection to ensure that those wrongfully detained were released, and that those rightfully detained were treated with humanity.
5. Supervision by the medical profession.

It was many years before these points were covered by effective legislation. As in most branches of social reform, the reformers themselves were not entirely aware in these early days of what they wished to achieve. Only as one set of laws was found inadequate, and a new law designed to cover the deficiencies of the old, did a coherent policy emerge.

The King's illness and the Regency question

The nature of the King's illness* did not become public knowledge until 1788, when the attack was so severe that he became incapable of

---

* We are concerned here with the King's symptoms and with public reactions to them. I. Macalpine and R. Hunter (*George III and the Mad-Business*, 1969, pp. 172–5) have recently argued that George III was in fact suffering from a rare metabolic disorder known as variegated porphyria. However, George III's contemporaries believed his condition to be a mental illness—and assumed that it was likely to be hereditary.

carrying out affairs of state for several months. The Prince of Wales later described the onset of the attack to his friends: 'He told us that he was present when the King was first seized with his mental disorder: that His Majesty caught him with both his hands by the collar, pushing him against the wall with some violence, and asked him who would dare to say to a King of England that he should not speak out, or who should prevent his whispering. His Majesty then whispered.'[7]

The King's doctors, who included Dr Warren and Sir Lucas Pepys, were not optimistic about a swift recovery; but the fate of the administration hung precisely on this point. If the King's illness lasted more than a few months, a Regent would have to be appointed. The obvious candidate for the Regency was the Prince of Wales, and he left little doubt in the mind of his adherents that, once he was established, his first action would be to dismiss the younger Pitt and his colleagues, and to install the 'Carlton House set', headed by Charles James Fox, in their place.

The appointment of Dr Willis

The Opposition backed Dr Warren and Sir Lucas Pepys; Pitt and his associates needed another and more optimistic opinion of the King's state of mind to preserve themselves in office. Accordingly Dr Francis Willis was called in. Willis was a former vicar of Wapping who had left his calling in order to practise as a physician, and who was at that time the proprietor of a private madhouse in Lincolnshire.

The King appears to have taken an instant dislike to him. 'Aware of Dr Willis being a clergyman, he taxed him at his first interview with having abandoned his sacred calling for profit—a rebuke to which the latter rejoined that the Saviour had cured demoniacs. "Yes," said the King, "but He did not get £700 a year for it".'[8] Fulke Greville recounts that the King offered Willis any preferment he wished if he would return to his former calling.[9]

Opinions on the competence of the new doctor varied. Lord Sheffield dismissed him with 'Dr Willis . . . is considered by some as not much better than a mountebank, and not far different from some of those that are confined in his house'[10]—while Hannah More described him on the other hand as 'The very image of simplicity, quite a good, plain, old-fashioned country clergyman.'[11]

Mountebank or not, Willis had one great virtue in the eyes of Pitt and his colleagues; he was certain that he could restore the King to sanity within a few months. His first step was to acquire ascendancy

over the mind of his patient by intimidatory means. Fulke Greville
tells how the King was immediately separated from his wife and
family, and kept in constant fear of the strait jacket. Countess
Harcourt goes further:

> The unhappy patient . . . was no longer treated as a human being.
> His body was immediately encased in a machine which left it no
> liberty of motion. He was sometimes chained to a staple. He was
> frequently beaten and starved, and at best he was kept in
> subjection by menacing and violent language. The history of the
> King's illness showed that the most exalted station did not wholly
> exempt the sufferer from this stupid and inhuman usage. . . .[12]

The treatment of the King speaks volumes for the contemporary
view of insanity; one party wanted him cured as soon as possible, and
the other would have been glad to see that cure delayed; but neither
protested that the person of the monarch should not be subjected to
indignities of this description.

By the end of 1788, the King's condition was being openly discussed
in clubs and coffee-houses. There was despondency at White's, the
Tory stronghold, and exultation at Brooke's, where the Prince of
Wales and the Duke of York freely discussed their father's illness,
and made it a subject for merriment. The only person for whom one
can have sympathy is the King himself, the unwitting pawn in party
manoeuvres; but the matter had one good and lasting effect: for the
first time, mental illness and its treatment formed a burning topic of
public discussion. The subject had been brought out of concealment
in a way which defeated the conspiracy of silence.

Willis was still optimistic, though the King's malady continued unabated. At length Pitt's hand was forced, and he rose in the Commons
at the beginning of the new session on 4 December 1788 to inform
members that they were:

> again assembled in the same unhappy circumstances which he
> had been under the melancholy necessity of communicating at
> their last meeting, the continuance of His Majesty's illness still
> preventing any measures either for opening the sessions or
> proroguing the parliament, and rendering it for the present
> impossible for His Majesty personally to attend to any public
> business; . . . and in this situation, the Privy Council had thought
> it their duty to call before them His Majesty's physicians, and
> to examine them on oath concerning the state of His Majesty's
> health.[13]

The Select Committee of 1789

A Select Committee was appointed four days later. It consisted of twenty-one members, of whom five had strongly conflicting interests in the matter. Lord North represented the interest of the King; William Wilberforce was a close personal friend of Pitt. He had not yet embarked on his career as 'the authorized interpreter of the national conscience',[14] though it was three years since his conversion to the religious life put an end to his practice of gambling with the Carlton House set; Lord Grenville, son of George Grenville, who had sat on the two former Committees on lunacy questions, was a cousin of the younger Pitt, and although only thirty, had held office continuously for the past six years. He was a man respected by both parties, and was appointed Speaker of the House of Commons in the following year. Fox and Sheridan were the leaders of the Prince of Wales' party—his personal friends and gambling associates. Sheridan had followed his literary and dramatic triumphs by becoming member of parliament for Stafford in 1780, and had held office in the Rockingham government of 1782 and the coalition of 1783.

It is interesting to note that both Sheridan and Grenville had legal training. Sheridan had been entered at the Middle Temple, and Grenville at Lincoln's Inn, though neither was actually called to the Bar.

The issue before the Committee was a vital one. Sir John Scott (then Solicitor-General, and later better-known as Lord Eldon, the rigid and unyielding Lord Chancellor of Wellington's Government) told Fulke Greville that the Government would back Willis because he stated that recovery was possible within a short time, and that it was essential to stave off the Regency question.[15]

Dr Warren fanned the flames of medical rivalry and party strife by stating that he had no reason to believe that the King's condition was improving. He alleged that Dr Willis had written reports, 'expressing His Majesty to be much better than I apprehended His Majesty to be at that time, declaring progress in cure that I could not discover,' and that he had tried to coerce him (Warren) into doing likewise by making 'a very unwarrantable use of the name of a Great Person'.[16] The Committee inquired, 'Whether Dr Warren knows or has any reason to believe that Dr Willis has signed more favourable accounts of the King's health than Dr Willis believed to be true?'—and Warren answered briefly, 'I cannot possibly tell what Dr Willis believes.' He added that the application of blisters by Dr Willis had 'made His Majesty much more unquiet and increased the necessity for coercion.'

Willis was called, and the Whig members of the Committee posed a most searching series of questions. Fulke Greville reports: 'By my conversation with Dr Willis, I found that he had been very closely pressed and questioned by Mr Burke and Mr Sheridan—that he was angry with them, and with Mr Sheridan particularly.'[17]

The Whigs won their point; a Regency Bill was framed, and passed the Commons on 12 February 1789. Whig ladies wore 'Regency caps' and Regency favours;[18] and it was said in Brooke's that the Whigs had completed their ministerial arrangements in readiness for the moment when the Prince of Wales should have power to eject the Tories. The Duke of York was to be Commander-in-Chief, Sheridan the Treasurer of the Navy, and Fox Secretary of State, while Mrs FitzHerbert was to be created a Duchess.

The Regency Bill was about to be read for the third time in the Lords when the King frustrated these plans, whether because of or in spite of the treatment of Dr Willis, by making a recovery. In March 1789 he was much better; in April the doctors were dismissed; and on 23 April he attended a public service of thanksgiving in St Paul's Cathedral. Dr Willis returned to Lincolnshire, the Whigs shelved their plans of political triumph, and the Prince of Wales made his peace with his father. A play at Drury Lane in which Mrs Siddons and John Kemble were appearing was withdrawn after only one performance solely on account of the title—*The Regent*.

The King's recovery seems to have been greeted with relief and satisfaction by the general public. As the first Hanoverian monarch to identify himself with England rather than Hanover, he was fairly popular, and the Prince of Wales, by reason of his extravagances and his connection with the Roman Catholic Mrs FitzHerbert, was exceedingly unpopular. The King's journey to Weymouth, where he went to convalesce, became a triumphal procession; and although much of the rejoicing may have been officially inspired, and some of it due to the general public's love of a show, there was undoubtedly a spontaneous element also.

The effects on lunacy reform of this first attack suffered by the King are intangible, but nevertheless real. The sympathies of the nation were with the sufferer, and the note of moral condemnation which had previously characterized all approaches to the subject was entirely lacking. Nobody suggested that the King was being punished by heaven for his sins; nobody regarded him as being possessed by the

Devil. Madness had become a respectable malady—one which might happen to anybody; and, which is even more important, one which was susceptible to treatment and capable of cure.

The course of the King's illness

The King became ill again twelve years later—in February 1801. The attack was said at the time to have been caused by Pitt's determination to carry Catholic Emancipation against the King's wishes. Dr Willis and his sons were sent for; again the strait jacket, the cauterizing irons and the herbal remedies were produced. There was despondency among the Tories, and jubilation at Carlton House. Lord Eldon found the King 'In a house at Kew, separated from his family, and with the Willises living with him.'

Pitt, wisely in the circumstances, gave a guarantee that he would not attempt Catholic Emancipation while the King was alive, and the King, freed from the fear that he would be forced into a course of action which he regarded as a betrayal of his coronation oath, promptly recovered.

In May, his balance of mind was again disturbed for a short period, during which he was alleged to be desirous of retiring to Hanover and abdicating in favour of the Prince of Wales. In January 1804 there was another attack; and in May of that year the King appeared at the installation of the Knights of the Order of the Garter wearing a judge's wig with his Garter robes, to the general consternation. In 1805—he was then sixty-seven years of age—his sight began to fail; as a result he became increasingly incapable of living a normal life. The final descent into illness, from which he did not recover, came in 1810, brought about by the death of his favourite child, the Princess Amelia. Francis Willis had died in 1807, but his sons, Dr Robert and Dr John Willis, returned to take charge of the King. He was confined to a suite of rooms at Windsor, where he found solace in Handel's music and the comforts of religion. Madame D'Arblay reported that he imagined himself to be conversing with angels, and the slow drift into religious delusion may have been a merciful end to a troubled reign.

The Regency Bill became law in 1811, and the King lived on until January 1820, through more than thirty years of intermittent illness. His death was little more than a reminder of his long-drawn-out life, the *Gentleman's Magazine* providing a fitting commentary: 'That this brave and honest man should have passed the last years of his long reign in darkness, mental and bodily, and should have died unconscious of his country's glory, is enough to tame all human pride. How little sensation his death occasions! It is indeed but the passing of a shadow.'

Two things are notable about the phrasing of this obituary notice; first, the avoidance of the words 'mad' and 'madness', and the substitution of 'mental darkness' in a context which linked it with the King's physical blindness; and second, the description of an insane person as 'this brave and honest man'. This marked a considerable shift of opinion since the days of the witchcraft trials.

3   Subscription hospitals and county asylums

The improvement in the public attitude to mental disorder was shown in three cities—London, Manchester and York—by the setting up of institutions where treatment of a relatively humane nature could be provided. This action arose in each case primarily from the consciousness felt by a small group of citizens of an overwhelming social evil in their midst. St Luke's Hospital, London, was founded in 1751, the Manchester Lunatic Hospital in 1763, and the York Retreat in 1792. Each formed not only a local but also a national precedent for improvements in treatment and accommodation which were later to find legislative expression.

This was the pioneer stage—the stage of voluntary social action. In these three cities was laid the foundation of nineteenth-century lunacy legislation.

St Luke's Hospital

This hospital, which was to become in many respects a rival to Bethlem, was founded by public subscription in 1751. A pamphlet entitled *Reasons for Establishing St Luke's*, published in 1817, makes the following points: Bethlem was overcrowded, and had a lengthy waiting list; the resultant delay in the admission of patients meant that many whose reason might have been saved by early diagnosis and treatment were not admitted until the disease had become incurable. People of means were frequently reduced to poverty by insanity, and the workhouse was an unsuitable place for their reception, since they were not 'pauper lunatics' in the usual sense of the term; finally, if medical students were to acquire a competent knowledge of the forms and treatment of insanity, a hospital must be established where they would be able to observe and study cases under suitable guidance. Bethlem at this time, and indeed until 1844, forbade the visitation of patients by medical students, or by practitioners other than those on the staff.

St Luke's may thus claim to have been the first teaching hospital in this field of medicine, and quickly developed into an institution

40

rivalling Bethlem in everything but age. In 1758 the physician, Dr Battie,[1] published an apparently innocuous pamphlet[2] in which he gave an account of his methods of treatment. This was construed by John Monro of Bethlem as an attack on his father, and he published a printed reply in the same year.[3] The paragraph which chiefly gave offence was that in which Battie wrote of insanity: 'This distemper is as little understood as any that ever afflicted mankind, because the care of lunatics is entrusted to empiricks, or at best to a few select Physicians, most of whom think it advisable to keep the cases as well as the patients to themselves.'

'By a few select Physicians,' replied John Monro, 'I presume are intended the Physicians of Bethlem Hospital, whom I consider it as a duty incumbent upon me to defend against any injurious reflections.' He described his father as 'A man of admirable discernment (who) treated this disease with an address that will not soon be equalled.'

Dr Battie spoke also of the 'impertinent curiosity of those who think it pastime to converse with Madmen and to play on their passions.' Such visitors were strictly forbidden at St Luke's, while medical practitioners and students were regularly admitted. Battie advocated generally a quiet and natural form of treatment, without violent vomits and purges, and with a sufficiency of simple food, 'not highly-seasoned and full of poignancy.' The practice of inducing repeated vomiting he described as 'a shocking operation, the consequence of a morbid convulsion', and he urged that purges should be given in small doses, at considerable intervals, and with due care for the patient's physical health. He believed that the mental condition of many patients could be alleviated by diversion, and that an asylum should provide 'amusements . . . rendered more agreeable by a well-timed variety'. Although conditions at St Luke's were far from perfect by later standards, the hospital was at least a centre for the serious study of mental disorder, where attempts were made to restore the irrational to mental health by other means than those of coercion and neglect. Evidence on the conditions at this hospital was given before the Select Committees of 1807 and 1815, and will be referred to at a later point in the narrative.

The Manchester Lunatic Hospital

The Lunatic Hospital at Manchester formed part of that city's comprehensive scheme for the treatment of mental and bodily illness in patients of means. The parent body was the Infirmary, founded in

1752, and attached to it when completed were the Lunatic Hospital, the Lying-In Hospital, the Eye Hospital and the Lock Hospital, occupying contiguous sites.[4] This chain of hospitals was raised by public subscription, and largely administered by the trustees of the Infirmary.[5]

Foundation of the Lunatic Hospital

Persons 'disordered in their senses' were specifically excluded by section 45 of the Infirmary Rules from becoming in-patients, though they were free to attend the clinic for out-patients. This expedient proved unsuitable, since lunatic patients were unable to attend the clinic without supervision, and their condition needed more than the sporadic treatment available.

The desire to make provision for patients of this type may have received an impetus from the article on the abuses in private mad-houses published in the *Gentleman's Magazine* in January, 1763.[6] In August of the same year, the Infirmary trustees appointed a committee to consider what provision might be made for lunatics, and the committee's report recommended the raising of a separate building, for which a subscription list should be opened. Patients should have 'advice gratis, paying for all other necessaries', and paupers should only be accepted if maintained by their parish of settlement. The finances of the new hospital should be kept separately from those of the Infirmary; no contribution made to the work of the Infirmary should be applied to the development of the Lunatic Hospital, 'or any other steps taken that will in any manner prejudice the same.'

Before the committee's report was presented to the Board of Trustees, an unsigned article appeared in the *Manchester Mercury* of 13 September 1763; this advocated public provision for the lunatics of the city. The writer pointed out that, though the cost of maintaining a pauper lunatic in a workhouse was low, the lack of treatment in these institutions meant that the majority of such cases became in-curable, and had to be maintained out of public funds for the rest of their lives. It would thus be to the advantage of the Poor Law authorities to pay a larger weekly sum for treatment in a lunatic hospital, since the chances of the patient's recovery and the restoration of his earning power were much greater. He was also concerned with 'many people in middling Circumstances who labour under the very great Misfortune of having a Parent or a Child thus visited by the Hand of Providence, and who would most thankfully pay any moderate Sum . . . for a Place of Security where their Relations might be properly guarded, receive the best Advice, and meet with the most humane Treatment.'

The phrasing of this article is similar to that of the committee's report, and it is difficult to believe that the writer had no knowledge of the steps which were being taken to meet this need. A likely explanation is that the article was inspired by one or more members of the committee as a means of popularizing the scheme by making it appear to spring from public demand.

This hypothesis is strengthened by the fact that, four years later, on 13 January 1767, the same journal published in its leading column a statement by the trustees, laying before the public their reasons for undertaking the project. They stated that they had 'long been solicited to take the Case of poor Lunatics under Consideration, upon Account chiefly of their being denied Admission into all other Infirmaries, and their being in Common at too great a distance from London to receive any benefit from the two noble Hospitals established there . . .' Their aim was to provide for the cure of patients, not merely for their confinement, and they wished to preserve the moderately well-to-do from the 'Impositions of Private Madhouses.'

Patients were to be admitted on application by two friends or relatives, or by the parish overseer. The charge for pauper lunatics was seven shillings a week, and that for 'Persons of middling Fortune' not less than ten shillings. In 1777, the charge for paupers was reduced to four shillings, and it was hoped that the Hospital would eventually be able to take poor patients free, though this was never achieved.[7]

It was reported at the Quarterly Board meeting on 26 September 1765 that the building was completed, though it had still to be staffed and furnished. The administration was to be organized in common with that of the Infirmary, the same secretary, steward, surgeon and physician serving both. The Infirmary was to provide all medicines— 'for which its account shall have credit.' Jonas Wood and his wife were appointed to the positions of master and matron—at first designated 'governor' and 'governess'—at a joint salary of thirty guineas a year. It was also moved at this meeting that 'the printed rules concerning the Hospital for Lunatics for the County of Northumberland'[8] be adopted.

Physical violence was not to be used on the patients, except where it was 'necessary to restrain the Furious from hurting themselves or others'. Mechanical restraint was used, as it was also provided that 'the feet of those in straw or chains be carefully examined, gently rubbed night and morning, and covered with flannel during the winter.' This was designed to prevent mortification due to restriction of the circulation.

Treatment was otherwise mainly medical, and consisted, according to an account written by the Infirmary Physician in 1795,[9] of the usual methods of blood-letting, blistering, purging and drugs. Dr Ferriar noted that tartar emetic acted 'briskly', and 'had an instantaneous effect in restoring a degree of rationality' in maniacal cases. Blood-letting was practised on the 'young and plethoric maniac whose eyes are turgid and inflamed, who passes the night without sleep, and whose pulse is quick and full', but Ferriar also gave warning that frequent repetition might prove dangerous. Opium was used in 'large doses in maniacal cases.'

Although the medical treatment represented no advance on the usual methods of the day, the physicians of the Lunatic Hospital appear to have realized that other factors in the treatment of the insane also affected their mental condition. The situation of the various wards, the provision of gardens, the small amenities given as a reward for an increased degree of self-control—all these formed an adjunct to treatment which had not previously been recognized as important but which was to play an increasing part in the humane treatment of mental disorder in later years.

Complete separation of the sexes was enforced from the opening of the hospital.[10] Special apartments were put aside for the use of convalescent patients, so that they might not be disturbed by those who were noisy or violent. The trustees reported in 1783 that 'those whose condition will admit it are allowed to walk with their friends in a large adjoining garden.' Dr Ferriar wrote, 'I find it useful to remonstrate, for lunatics frequently have a high sense of honour, and are sooner brought to reflection by the appearance of indignity than by violence, against which they usually harden themselves. . . . Small favours, the shew of confidence and apparent distinction, accelerate recovery.'[11]

Public sight-seeing was specifically forbidden by the rules, as at St Luke's. The physician was to visit his patients twice a week, or more often if necessary; he was to keep a regular record of all his cases. The House Visitors of the Infirmary were to visit the Lunatic Hospital daily to investigate the behaviour of the keepers and the domestic staff to the patients, and were also to examine the sleeping accommodation. Four trustees were required to sign the certificates of admission and discharge.

Some idea of the standard of treatment given at the Lunatic Hospital may be gained from an examination of its accounts. In 1769, it received 361 patients at a cost of £444 in addition to the payments made. This sum was met from public subscriptions, and indicates that on an average each patient cost about twenty-five shillings more to maintain than his sureties paid in fees. Since the fees were already fairly high, and the accounts were publicly audited each year, it seems reasonably certain that this relatively large sum was actually expended on the provision of a high standard of treatment and accommodation for the patients.

Although the Manchester Lunatic Hospital dealt with its patients more humanely than was commonly the case, its work can only be described as pioneer work in the most limited sense. It is significant of the trustees' faith in accepted practice that they described Bethlem as a 'Noble Hospital' and adopted the rules of the asylum at Newcastle-on-Tyne. Treatment proceeded by the usual methods, including restraint by chains and manacles, and violent medicines.

The Lunatic Hospital's claim to a place in the history of lunacy reform depends less on its treatment than on its tentative approach to what later became known as 'the moral management of the insane'. Its insistence on the importance of keeping records and case-histories sprang from the close connection with the Infirmary, and the fact of that connection brought a new factor into the treatment of insanity. For the first time, that treatment was recognized as being allied to the treatment of bodily illness, to be sought without shame or secrecy. The terms 'hospital' and 'patient' were used, and statements were published in the local newspapers. It was the first attempt to treat mental disorder in the way that physical ills were treated—with matter-of-fact compassion untinged by sensation, moral condemnation or concealment.[12]

The York Retreat

The Retreat was founded in 1792 by the Society of Friends.[13] It was unique in two ways: first, because it was neither a subscription hospital nor a private asylum, being financed and organized on a non-profit basis by a body of restricted membership; and second, because it evolved a form of treatment based, not on the scanty medical knowledge of the time, but on Christianity and common-sense.

The city of York already possessed a subscription asylum—the York Asylum, founded in 1777. Consideration of the management of this establishment will be deferred, since it was not until 1815 that the conditions under which it operated came fully to light. For the present it is sufficient to say that the conduct of the Asylum was wrapped in secrecy, the Governors and physician resisting any attempt at visitation and inspection. At least one unsuccessful effort was made to secure a public investigation of conditions,[14] but until 1790 would-be reformers could point to nothing more concrete than the general reluctance of the authorities to open the building to responsible inquirers, and the complaints, easily discredited, of ex-patients.

In the latter year,[15] a patient called Hannah Mills was sent to the Asylum, and her relatives, who lived at some distance from the city, recommended her to the care of the Society of Friends. Members of the Society who attempted to visit her were refused admission on the grounds that she was 'not in a suitable state to be seen by strangers', and she subsequently died under circumstances which aroused strong suspicions of ill-treatment or neglect.

The project for the Retreat was a direct result of this occurrence. It was primarily the brain-child of William Tuke (1732–1822), a tea and coffee merchant, and head of a Quaker family which had been resident in York for several generations. He saw that the time was not yet ripe for a full-scale public inquiry at the Asylum. The Government of that institution—who took no part in its management and made no official visits—were a powerful and influential body in the city.[16] Public opinion was not yet sufficiently roused to overcome their opposition to reform. Moreover, reform was impossible until some system of treatment other than that in operation at the Asylum had been tried and found successful. Experiment must precede reform.

Tuke's project met at first with opposition from within the Society of Friends. Some members thought that the incidence of mental disorder was too low to warrant the construction of a special institution for Quakers. Some were 'averse to the concentration of the instances of this disease amongst us', and others thought that York was not a suitable site for such an institution, being 'not central to the Nation.'

A man of outstanding personality and considerable administrative gifts, Tuke overrode all objections. His project was approved at the Quarterly Meeting[17] of the Society in March 1792, and by the end of August nearly £1200 had been subscribed. The Friends proceeded to buy eleven acres of land at a cost of £1357, and to approve a building estimate of nearly £2000. These sums were raised by private donation and covenant from members of the Society by the end of 1797.

It was significant that the new institution was named neither 'hospital' nor 'asylum'. York already possessed an asylum, operating under conditions which made the use of the term a mockery, and the Retreat was not a hospital. William Tuke had a strong distrust of the medical profession and its methods.[18] Daniel Hack Tuke states that 'The Retreat' was suggested by his grandmother, William's daughter-in-law, 'to convey the idea of what such an institution should be, namely . . . a quiet haven in which the shattered bark might find the means of reparation or of safety.'

The pleasantness of the site was described in the first 'Visiter's Book' of the Retreat by a Swiss doctor named Delarive, who visited the establishment in 1798: 'Cette maison est située à un mille de York, au milieu d'une campagne fertile et riante; ce n'est point l'idée d'une prison qu'elle fait naître, mais plutôt celle d'une grande ferme rustique; elle est entourée d'un jardin fermé.'

Conditions of admission

The Retreat was built to accommodate thirty patients, who were to be either members of the Society of Friends, or recommended by members. There were several grades of accommodation, the cost ranging from eight shillings to fifteen shillings weekly. Patients recommended by private donors of £25, or by Meetings subscribing £100, were admitted at the reduced rate of four shillings. The fact that the institution was not primarily intended to provide for the insane poor was stressed by the rule that patients' servants could be accommodated for a further six shillings a week.

Administration

The first superintendent appointed was Timothy Maude, 'a Friend of great worth as well as medical knowledge, who had retired from practice'. Maude died within three months of taking up his appointment, and for some time William Tuke himself acted as superintendent, while Dr Fowler was appointed visiting physician. Thomas Fowler seems to have been an unusually open-minded physician for his generation. After a period of trial and error, he came to believe that 'moral' methods of treatment were preferable to those involving restraint and the use of harsh drugs. So the new method of treatment for which the Retreat became famous was a product of Tuke's humanitarianism and Fowler's empiricism.

In 1797 William Tuke relinquished the day-to-day control of administration, and a male superintendent was appointed. This was George Jepson, who later married the female superintendent, Katharine Allen; together, they shared the responsibility for the immediate care of the patients until 1823. There was a staff of five in addition to the Jepsons—two men and three women. The ratio of staff to patients (7 : 30) was thus very much higher than at any other existing institution for the care of the insane.

The work of the Tuke family

William Tuke continued to act as secretary and treasurer,* and still found time to know the patients individually, and to supervise the details of their treatment in many cases. His work has been commemorated by a minor poet of his time in lines which compensate for their lack of literary merit by the sincerity of their sentiment:

On a fair hill, where York in prospect lies
Her towers and steeples pointing to the skies,
A goodly structure rears its modest head;
Thither my walk the worthy founder led.
Thither with Tuke my willing footsteps prest,
Who, on the subject pondering in his breast,
Went forth alone, and weigh'd the growing plan,
Big with the lasting help of suffering Man.[19]

The inscription on the foundation stone at the Retreat does not bear his name, stating simply, 'Hoc fecit amicorum caritas in humanitatis argumentum'; but his portrait, painted by a descendant,[20] still has the place of honour in the board room.

The philanthropic work of the Tuke family was not confined to the Retreat. William Tuke and his second wife, Esther, were co-founders of the Friends' Girls' School at York; his son Henry (1755–1814) was associated with the educational work of the British and Foreign Bible Society; Henry's son was Samuel Tuke, the author of the *Description of the Retreat*. When William became totally blind—some years before his death in 1822—it was Samuel who took his place as unofficial supervisor and general counsellor at the Retreat. Both William and Samuel Tuke were among the body of citizens who finally achieved the reform of the old York Asylum in 1814–15 (see

* All the early bills preserved at the Retreat are directed to him—
'Mr Tuke, for the Retreat.'

p. 69) and William, then over eighty, gave evidence before the Select Committee on Madhouses which was appointed in 1815.

Although Samuel Tuke studied medicine, he eventually entered the family business in deference to his grandfather's wishes.[21] The first of the family to qualify as a medical practitioner was Daniel Hack Tuke, who only overcame the family prejudice against the profession in 1852 after refusing to enter Tuke, Son & Co., giving up a legal career in its early stages, and failing lamentably to become a poet.[22]

'*Moral*' *treatment at the Retreat*

'People in general,' noted Samuel Tuke in his *Description of the Retreat*, 'have the most outrageous notions of the constantly outrageous behaviour or malicious dispositions of deranged persons: and it has in too many instances been found convenient to encourage these false sentiments to apologize for the treatment of the unhappy sufferer, or to admit the vicious neglect of their keepers.' The Tukes believed that many patients could be rational and controllable, provided that they were not aggravated by cruelty, hostility, or harsh methods of restraint. 'Vous voyez,' wrote Delarive in the 'Visiter's Book', 'que dans le traitement moral, on ne considère pas les fous comme absolument privés de raison, c'est-à-dire, comme inaccessibles aux motifs de crainte, d'éspérance, de sentiment, et d'honneur. On les considère plutôt, ce semble, comme les enfans qui ont un superflu de force, et qui en faisoient un emploi dangereux.'

The patients were never punished for failure to control their behaviour, but certain amenities were given to them in order to foster self-control by a show of trust. The female superintendent gave teaparties, to which the patients were invited, and for which they were encouraged to wear their best clothes. There was an airing court in the grounds for each class of patients, and each court was supplied with a number of small animals—rabbits, poultry, and others—so that the patients might learn self-control by having dependent upon them creatures weaker than themselves. 'These creatures are generally very familiar with the patients, and it is believed that they are not only the means of innocent pleasure, but that the intercourse with them sometimes tends to awaken the social and benevolent feelings,' commented Samuel Tuke.

Every attempt was made to occupy the patients suitably. Some cared for the animals, some helped in the garden, the women knitted or sewed. Writing materials were provided, and books were carefully chosen to form a patients' library. Samuel Tuke stated that this did not contain 'works of the imagination'—probably a wise choice in view of the popularity at that time of horrific novels such as *The Castle of Otranto, Vathek* and *The Monk.* It may be said that members of the Society of Friends were not at this period given to novel-reading. Books on mathematics and the natural sciences were recommended as 'the most useful class of subjects on which to employ the minds of the insane.'

The Friends believed firmly in the integrating influence of religion in cases of mental disorder; religious meetings were held at the Retreat, and parties of patients were taken from time to time to share in the common worship of the city Quakers. In short, the patient was given no excuse for feeling that his mental condition precluded participation in normal human activity, or cut him off from the outside world.

An account by Samuel Tuke of the reception of a violent patient illustrates the complete antithesis between the old system and the new:

> Some years ago, a man of Herculean size and figure was brought
> to the house . . . so constantly during the present attack had he
> been kept chained, that his clothes were contrived to be taken
> off and put on by means of strings, without removing his
> manacles. They were . . taken off when he entered the Retreat,
> and he was ushered into the apartment where the superintendents
> were supping. He was calm. His attention appeared to be arrested
> by his new situation. He was desired to join in the repast, during
> which he behaved with tolerable propriety . . . the maniac was
> sensible of the kindness of his treatment. He promised to
> restrain himself, and he so completely succeeded that during his
> stay no coercive means were ever employed towards him . . . in
> about four months, he was discharged, perfectly recovered.

Mechanical restraint

'Point de barreau, point de grillages aux fenêtres,' wrote Delarive. The windows of the Retreat were specially designed to look like ordinary windows, the iron sashes being painted to look like wooden ones. Restraint was seldom used, except to prevent a patient from injuring himself or his fellows. Chains were never used as a method of restraint, and the strait waistcoat only as a last resort. Extracts from the case-history (preserved at the Retreat) of a patient named Wilson Sutton give a vivid picture of the degree of forbearance which this system demanded of the keepers:

> 1814. 12th August. To-day, after a walk in the country and eating a good dinner, while the attendants were at theirs he became quarrelsome—struck Josh. Whiting hurt Saml. Lays head and neck. After this he was shut up in a room to get calm.
> 1815. 15th January. When S.L. has come into sight, he has fallen on him furiously with his fists.
> . . . 20th February . . . seized Saml Smith his attendant and threatened to throw him downstairs, breaking his watch and chain and straining his thumb.
> . . . 16th September. Fecht him (Smith) a blow betwixt the eyes.

Sutton was then placed in the strait waistcoat for a few hours, but when freed, seized an iron fender, and felled the unfortunate Smith with it.

> . . . 11th October. He has since conducted himself in a peaceable manner, but has not deigned to speak to S. S.

Mortification of the extremities through prolonged cold and physical restraint was frequently met with in institutions for the insane at this time. Reference has already been made to the practice of wrapping the patients' feet in flannel as a preventive measure. This was done not only at the Manchester Lunatic Hospital, but also, according to Samuel Tuke, at Bethlem. He goes on to say that Dr Pinel, himself a pioneer in the humane treatment of the insane, admitted that 'seldom has a whole year elapsed during which no fatal accident has taken place in the Hôpital de Bicêtre (Paris) from the action of cold on the extremities.' Yet Tuke was able to write of the Retreat:

> Happily, this calamity is hardly known, and no instance of mortification has occurred . . . connected with cold or confinement. Indeed, the patients are never found to require such a degree of restraint as to prevent the use of considerable exercise, or to render it at all necessary to keep their feet wrapped in flannel.

Medical treatment

'The physician', wrote Samuel Tuke, 'plainly perceived how much was

c

to be done by moral, and how little by any known medical, means.'
Accordingly, medical treatment took a subordinate place at the
Retreat. Drugs were seldom used to quiet elated patients. Dr Fowler
stressed the curative and soothing effects of warm baths, especially in
cases of melancholia, and Jepson believed that an abundant diet of
'meat, bread and good porter' was more effective than a policy of
semi-starvation. He thought porter as successful as opium in inducing
sound sleep, and less detrimental to the constitution. Good food, air,
exercise and occupation took the place of drastic medical methods
practised in other institutions for the insane.

Diet

The diet contained a generous amount of milk and meat, regular
supplies of fruit, and an extra small meal in the afternoon, when the
women were supplied with the relatively expensive products of tea and
coffee.[23] The 'patients of the higher class' dined at the superintendents'
table, and shared their meals. The household bills of this period show
frequent expenditure on porter, and on such luxury items as wines,
oranges and figs.

Household items

Samuel Tuke frequently referred to the community of staff and
patients as 'the family', and indeed the accounts preserved at the
Retreat show that the expenditure was far more like that of an
ordinary household than of a charitable institution. William Tuke
bought pots and pans, tin trays, beer jugs, coffee mugs, cream jugs,
cutlery, cruets; great emphasis was placed on the steadying effect of
properly served and attractive meals.

Bills for the year 1796, when the Retreat was originally furnished,
show that beds and bedding were supplied for all the patients, including paupers. These beds were made of wood, and a special design
was devised for those suffering from enuresis—patients who in other
institutions for the insane would have been relegated to bundles of
straw. The beds of 'those who are not of the lowest class' were of
better quality, but all patients were provided with sheets, blankets,
bags of goose feathers, and counterpanes.

Visitation

While the Tuke family exercised a regular supervision over the affairs of the Retreat, representatives of the Quarterly Meeting of the Society of Friends were sent regularly to make independent reports,[24] and from 1796 three women Friends were appointed to carry out additional visits.[25] The 'Visiter's Book' shows that from the earliest days, the Retreat received distinguished visitors—English philanthropists such as Robert Owen and Elizabeth Fry; medical men such as Dr Delarive and a Dr Duncan from Dublin who described the Retreat as 'the best-regulated establishment in Europe'; writers and thinkers such as Sydney Smith, who wrote his famous article 'Mad Quakers' for the *Edinburgh Review* of 1813, immediately after reading Samuel Tuke's *Description of the Retreat*. No less than three parties were sent over by the Russian royal family—the first, early in 1814, including Alexander I's Physician and Chamberlain, the second, later in the same year, consisting of the Grand Duke Nicholas and his entourage, and the third, in 1818, headed by the Grand Duke Michael. It is interesting to speculate whether these visits had any connection with the mental instability of the Romanovs in general, and of Alexander I in particular. Perhaps the most picturesque visitors of all were the seven Red Indian braves who had been brought over to England to appear in a London theatre. After they had seen all that was to be seen, their Chief offered up a short prayer of thanks, and Friends and warriors remained for some few minutes in prayerful silence.[26]

It would be unfair to compare the conditions at the Retreat during this period with those at St Luke's and the Manchester Lunatic Hospital. The Retreat catered only for a restricted section of society. It was small enough for the community to be referred to as 'the family', and sufficiently well-endowed to be run on the lines of a comfortable guest-house. The treasurer was not a salaried official whose duty lay in managing as economically as possible, but a wealthy philanthropist who was one of the chief benefactors. The staff, though it lacked formal qualifications, was drawn from the Society of Friends, and had at least the qualification of unimpeachable moral integrity. The Retreat was thus spared the troubles which were likely to beset other institutions for the insane—problems of financial speculation, of apathetic visitors, and untrustworthy staff.

To say all this is not to minimize the extent of the achievement, but merely to point out that conditions were particularly favourable to success. The influence of the experiment at the Retreat on the subsequent conduct of less-favoured institutions was immense. It removed the final justification for neglect, brutality and crude medical methods. It proved that kindness was more effective than rigorous confinement; and it threw a startling light on the activities of private madhouse keepers, many of whom charged large fees for keeping patients in conditions as miserable as those of the parish workhouse.

The foundation of county asylums

Lunacy reform began on a national scale with the foundation of the county asylums, following the Act of 1808; but no reform takes place in a vacuum, and it is necessary to refer briefly to the movements in thought and philanthropic practice which bridge the gap between the small local reforms of the late eighteenth century, and the parliamentary reform movement of the early nineteenth.

Somervell writes that the nineteenth century started in 1789;[27] and certainly the ideas and ideals of the 1790s form an immense contrast to those of fifty years earlier. Reasoned apathy had been replaced by violent emotion. 'Cosmic Toryism' was challenged on all sides—by Paine, by Godwin, by Paley, by Malthus, by Bentham. Changes in agricultural and industrial methods now affected the lives of the whole population, virtually abolishing the traditional pattern of English living. The working classes began to feel their power, and to be aware of wrongs accentuated by the pressure of industrialization. There was a considerable shift of population, as workers from the south moved to the new industrial towns of the north. It is no mere generalization to say that a curious kind of unrest seized the whole country in these years. The Americans had rejected George III, France rejected the Bourbons; the religious became converted, the literary wrote lyrical poetry, the politically-minded talked of revolution; and gradually the word 'revolution' became applicable to almost every sphere of systematized thought, so that ideas and habits of thought which had gone unchallenged for centuries were examined in a new and searching light. Out of this intellectual and social ferment arose two movements which were to have a decisive effect on lunacy reform: Evangelicalism and Radicalism.

The Evangelical movement in the Church of England was, to quote Halévy, 'a species of Anglican Methodism'[28] which owed much to the example of the Wesleys; and, like Wesley's followers, the Clapham Sect—that group of lay 'Saints' which gathered round Wilberforce in the years 1795–1808—made use of experience gained in the world of politics and business to develop a concrete policy for social

action. The individual activities of the earlier philanthropists—
Howard, John Wesley, Elizabeth Fry and the Tukes—were now
replaced to a large extent by group activities. Societies for the reform
of particular abuses became the fashion, and each cause had its small
group of parliamentary adherents who were ready to press for
legislative action. In the years which preceded the passing of the
County Asylums Act, the influence of the Clapham Sect was at its
peak. Wilberforce and Hannah More were its prophets, and lunacy
reform was only one of the many avenues explored.

Evangelical humanism stemmed from an emotional appreciation
of the plight of the poor and oppressed. It may be said to have started
with the Wesleys, and to have reached fruition in the person of the
seventh Earl of Shaftesbury; but Radicalism came from cold reason,
from a fundamental love of order, a hatred of administrative confusion. Its dominant figure was Jeremy Bentham, whose thought was
to have so great an influence on Chadwick and J. S. Mill. Round
Bentham, as round Wilberforce, gathered a group of disciples. The
Benthamites were both a philosophical school and a political party,
and their thought can in some ways be traced back to Hume's
associationism: the belief that all complex ideas could be reduced to
show their dependence on simple sensations led inevitably to the
'pleasure-pain principle', and thus to the belief in 'the greatest
happiness of the greatest number'; but for the Benthamites, any connection with the past was purely accidental. They were without a
sense of history, being characterized by 'a volcanic desire for utter,
organic, sweeping change.'[29] They were not concerned with the plight
of the insane from any sense of pity. Bentham himself considered it
right and proper that lunatics should be kept under constant surveillance and in perpetual solitude, apparently thinking both medical
and 'moral' treatment useless. It is unlikely that he ever gave the
matter much thought; but because he taught his followers to detest
legal anomalies, because they thought in terms of legal action and
public institutions, his disciples are to be found among those who
worked and planned for the reform of the conditions of the insane.

Sir George Onesiphorus Paul

In 1806, the new train of events was set in motion by a Benthamite,
the High Sheriff of Gloucestershire, who addressed a letter to the
Secretary of State urging him to take action concerning the condition
of criminal and pauper lunatics.[30]

Paul was a prison reformer who had known John Howard,[31] and who had also absorbed something of the Howard tradition. He had personally designed the new county gaol and Bridewells erected at Gloucester, being 'the head and heart of the committee, the draftsman of the Bill, the financier who raised the funds . . . the author of the reformed system of discipline, and the scapegoat on whose head were laid all the stupid anathemas that the scheme provoked.'[32]

This energetic man, then sixty years old,[33] was also the president of the Stroud Society for providing medical attention for the poor, and his practical experience led him to consider criminal lunatics and pauper lunatics as two components of a single problem which might be dealt with in a uniform way.

Of pauper lunatics, he wrote in his letter: 'I believe there is hardly a parish of any considerable size in which there may not be found some unfortunate human creature of this description, who, if his ill-treatment has made him phrenetic, is chained in the cellar or garret of a workhouse, fastened to the leg of a table, tied to a post in an outhouse, or perhaps shut up in an uninhabited ruin.'

He added in a footnote, 'I have witnessed instances of each of these methods of securing under 17 George II.'[34]

The condition of pauper lunatics at this time has been partially misrepresented by the Webbs, who state that 'right down to 1835, the typical method of dealing with pauper lunatics was to place them out under contract',[35] that is, to place them in private madhouses. While this statement was true of the large metropolitan parishes, where the workhouse was a highly-organized institution, it did not apply in the provinces; parishes outside London were generally too small, too poor, and too remote to avail themselves of this method of ridding themselves of their most troublesome inmates.

In the prisons, the position had been complicated by the Criminal Lunatics Act of 1800, which provided for the first time for the detention of criminal lunatics 'during His Majesty's pleasure'. This Act applied not only to persons tried for treason, murder and felony, who were found to have been insane at the time of the commission of the offence, but also to those found insane on arraignment, and to any person 'discovered or apprehended under circumstances that denote a derangement of mind and a purpose of committing some crime.' The Act had not directed where these different classes of the criminally insane were to be housed, nor had it provided any machinery by which they might ultimately be released.

There was clearly a case for the construction of a new type of institution where pauper and criminal lunatics could be treated as insane persons, and not primarily as paupers or criminals.

The Select Committee Report of 1807

A select committee 'to inquire into the State of Criminal and Pauper Lunatics in England, and the Laws relating thereto' was appointed in January, 1807,[36] shortly after the setting-up of the Ministry of All the Talents. The prime mover was Charles Williams-Wynn, then Under-Secretary of State for the Home Department, and a nephew of Lord Grenville.[37]

Wynn was at that time thirty-one years of age, and had been in parliament for nine years. He remained intimately connected with lunacy reform until 1850, the year of his death, and was actually present in the House to hear Lord Ashley introduce the Lunatics Bill of 1845.[38] Wynn was not a brilliant man; his later career failed to fulfil its early promise, for he never became a major parliamentary figure. Canning described him as 'The worst man of business I ever saw', and even Southey, his life-long friend, thought him 'One of the most impracticable persons to deal with, taking crotchets in his head, and holding to them with invincible pertinacity.'[39] This latter charactersitic may have been an advantage in the circumstances. Wynn, with his lack of gifts of oratory or parliamentary vision, his capacity for detail and his single-track mind, was in some ways the ideal person to undertake the wearisome task of compiling a parliamentary report on an unpopular subject. The committee included members of both political parties, and some well-known names: George Rose, sponsor of the Friendly Societies Act of 1793, Romilly, Wilberforce, and Whitbread. The terms of reference 'to enquire into the State of Criminal and Pauper Lunatics in England' reflect the double interest in penal and Poor Law reform.

The report consisted of a brief survey of existing conditions together with several appendices containing valuable evidence. The committee found that the only law which might be construed to affect pauper lunatics was the Vagrancy Act of 1744, and referred to the evidence of Sir George Onesiphorus Paul in stating that the condition of those in workhouses was 'revolting to humanity'. It recommended that an asylum should be set up in each county, to which both pauper and criminal lunatics might be sent. Each asylum should have a committee of governors nominated by the local justices of the peace, and should be financed by means of a county rate: 'To this the public opinion appears so favourable that it may be sufficient at least in the first instance rather to recommend and assist than to enforce the execution of such a plan.'

In certain circumstances the new provision might be grafted on to the existing subscription hospital.

The first appendix to the report comprised the returns of pauper and criminal lunatics made to parliament in 1806. The Select Committee commented that these returns were 'so evidently deficient in several instances, that a very large addition must be made in any computation of the whole number.' This was one reason why it was necessary to make the new Act a permissive one: the total dimensions of the need could only be guessed at, and it was necessary for the scheme for county asylums to pass through an experimental stage.

The total number of lunatics in pauper institutions in England was given as 1,755,[40] but as the committee perceived, the omissions were considerable. Hampshire ignored the request for information. The authorities of the counties of Hereford, Stafford, Warwick, Hertford, Bedford, Cumberland and Cambridge replied that there were no pauper lunatics in their boundaries, though two of these counties— Staffordshire and Bedfordshire—were to find it necessary to construct county asylums only a few years later. The East Riding of Yorkshire found only three pauper lunatics, while the West Riding by contrast made a return of 424.

On behalf of the committee, Dr Andrew Halliday (see p. 100) personally investigated the position in Norfolk and Suffolk, in order to arrive at an approximate estimate of the proportion of pauper lunatics to population. In the workhouses of Suffolk, which had made a total return of 92, he found 47 'lunatics' and 67 'idiots', confined to 'damp, dark cells'. Thus there were 22 persons who had been over-looked by the county authorities in their return. In Norfolk, the position was worse. The official figure was 22; Halliday's figure was 112.

The same inaccuracies were apparent in the returns for criminal lunatics. It was clear that no one had any idea of the actual number of criminal and pauper lunatics in the country, and that under the existing administrative framework, it would be impossible to obtain an accurate picture of the situation.

The deficiencies of these returns might be explained in several ways. The most obvious cause is administrative inefficiency; when each parish controlled its own pauper institution, it was not easy to obtain information over the area of a whole county. Few counties possessed men of the calibre of John Howard or Sir George Onesiphorus Paul— men who would be willing to make protracted journeys by coach or on horseback, to risk the contagion of typhus or gaol-fever, solely in order to verify their facts. The desire for concealment may also have been an operative factor; if pauper lunatics were being kept in conditions 'revolting to humanity', parish overseers and local magistrates would have no desire to see those conditions publicized—especially when the only practicable alternative was to send all lunatics to expensive private madhouses. Probably many local officials had only the most elementary idea of what constituted insanity, and included in their returns only those in a state of ungovernable mania or complete idiocy. Some counties may have experienced a curious sort of local pride in proclaiming that all their inhabitants were in full possession of their faculties; but it seems likely that the chief cause of the inadequacy of these returns was a characteristic apathy concerning the condition of the mentally disordered.

The County Asylum Act, 1808[41]

The Ministry of All the Talents fell in 1807—partly, it is alleged, as a result of the Whigs' refusal to follow George Rose's system of paying 'hireling scribes' to praise the ministry in the Press[42]—and the Act of 1808 'for the better Care and Maintenance of Lunatics, being Paupers or Criminals, in England' was passed under the aegis of the Portland administration.[43] The measure was piloted through both Commons and Lords without difficulty, and became known as 'Wynn's Act'. It implemented the recommendations of the committee of the previous year by laying down detailed specifications for the construction and maintenance of county asylums.

In the first twenty years of its operation, only nine counties proceeded to erect asylums. This slow beginning might be attributed partly to the prevalent apathy, partly to flaws in the framing of the Act, and partly to a reluctance on the part of local magistrates to become involved in expenditure to an unforeseeable extent; but, in spite of its limited application, the Act was of considerable importance in the progress of reform. The county asylums so set up were the forerunners of the mental hospitals of to-day—some of which still occupy the original premises constructed under Wynn's Act. The importance of the Act lies primarily in the conception of treatment of a non-deterrent type as a public responsibility, and in the attempt to deal with the root cause rather than with the symptoms of anti-social behaviour.

The preamble of the Act stated:

> . . . the Practice of confining such Lunatics and other insane
> Persons as are chargeable to their respective Parishes in Gaols,
> Houses of Correction, Poor Houses and Houses of Industry
> is highly dangerous and inconvenient . . . it is expedient that
> further Provision should be made for the Care and Maintenance
> of such Persons, and for the erecting (*sic*) proper Houses for their
> Reception . . . it is also expedient that further Provision should
> be made for the Custody of insane Persons who shall commit
> Criminal Offences . . .

(*i*) *Initiation* (*sections 1–7*). Justices of the Peace might give notice at the Quarter Sessions of their intention to erect an asylum; two or more counties might combine for this purpose. A committee of visiting justices was to be appointed at the Quarter Sessions to be responsible both for the erection of the asylum, and for periodical inspection. They were authorized to contract, to purchase land, and to appoint a Clerk and a Surveyor.

(*ii*) *Finance* (*sections 4, 7, 8, 13 and 22*). The justices were empowered to raise a county rate for the purpose of building the asylum, and were given power to mortgage the rates for a period not exceeding fourteen years. No justice was to derive individual advantage from any asylum contract. Where two or more counties combined to erect an asylum, a calculation of the expense to be incurred by each was to be made on a population basis. An appeal for voluntary contributions might be made to meet part of the initial cost of the buildings.

(*iii*) *Site and accommodation* (*sections 16 and 26*).

> The said Visiting Justices, as well in the Choice of Ground and
> Situation as in determining on the Plans for building or for
> purchasing and altering Buildings for such Lunatic Asylums,
> shall as far as conveniently may be, fix upon an Airy and
> Healthy Situation, with a good Supply of Water, and which may
> afford a Probability of constant Medical Assistance, and pursue
> such Measures and adopt such Plans as shall provide separate
> and distinct Wards for Male and Female Lunatics, and also for
> the Convalescents and Incurables, and also separate and distinct

Day Rooms and Airing Grounds for the Male and Female Convalescents, and dry and airy Cells for Lunatics of every Description.

The buildings were to be exempt from the window-tax.

(*iv*) *Admission* (*sections 17–19*). Patients were to be admitted as 'dangerous to be at large' under the 1744 Act—on a warrant from two justices—or as criminal lunatics by the varied procedures outlined in the Criminal Lunatics Act of 1800. Furthermore, 'the Justices are hereby authorized and directed to issue Warrants on the Application of the Overseers of the Poor . . . for the Conveyance of any Lunatic, Insane Person, or dangerous Idiot who may be chargeable to such Parish, to such Asylum.'

The parish was to pay a charge laid down by the justices, this charge not to exceed 14s. weekly per patient.[44] If the overseer did not apply to the justices for a warrant to convey within seven days of receiving notice that there was an insane or mentally deficient person in the parish, he became liable to a penalty of not less than 40s., and not more than £10.

(*v*) *Discharge* (*section 23*). Patients were to be discharged by the committee of visiting justices upon recovery. A penalty of from 40s. to £10 was prescribed for any officer or servant of the asylum who made possible, either through neglect or connivance, the unauthorized departure of any patient.

(*vi*) *Appointment of Staff* (*section 24*). This visiting justices were to appoint a Treasurer, and 'such other Officers and Servants together with such Numbers of Assistants as they shall from Time to Time find necessary in Proportion to the Numbers of Persons confined in such Asylum'—and were to fix the weekly rate of payment at a sum which would defray 'the whole Expence of the Maintenance and Care, Medicines and Clothing, requisite for such Person, and the Salaries of the Officers and Attendants.'

Experience was to show that this first experiment in the public care of the insane was far from adequate. A mere comparison in length between the Act of 1808 and that of 1900 shows that the framers of the latter were aware of many possible abuses which Wynn and his associates did not envisage.

Amendments to the 1808 Act

The first asylum to be constructed under the new Act was that at Nottingham, which received patients from 1810, and was formally opened in 1811.[45] According to the returns of 1806, the county had only 35 pauper lunatics for whom provision was needed, and no criminal lunatics whatever. The asylum was built to accommodate 76–80 patients and yet this accommodation was found at once to be totally inadequate.[46] By the terms of the Act, there was no way in which the asylum staff or the visiting justices could exercise their discretion in admitting patients. Parish overseers were bound, on pain of heavy fines, to give information of all insane persons in the area, and the justices were equally bound to send those who were in poverty, or who exhibited criminal propensities, to the asylum. The new institution had already cost over £21,000,[47] and was badly over-crowded in the first year. An amendment passed in 1811 (51 Geo. III c. 79) remedied this situation, which not only severely handicapped the one asylum in operation, but also deterred justices in other counties from using their powers under the Act. Justices were given

> discretionary power as to issuing or not issuing warrants . . . particularly in cases where it shall be found that the number of applications on behalf of persons having just cause to be admitted does at any time exceed the number of those who can be properly accommodated in such an asylum, with a view to cure, comfort and safe custody.

An Amending Act of 1815 (55 Geo. III c. 46) dealt with questions of admission, certification and discharge of patients. Overseers of the poor were required to furnish returns of all lunatics and idiots within their parishes to the justices on request, and to provide a medical certificate[48] for each, whether admission to the county asylum was sought on behalf of the patient or not. This provided some guarantee that the overseers were carrying out their duties adequately. No attempt was made to define the status of the 'medical person' who was to give a certificate, nor was any provision made that he should receive payment for the exercise of this duty. The question of dis-charge arose out of the apathy of the visiting justices and the difficulty of inducing a quorum to be present at their meetings. Under the 1808 Act, patients could be discharged only by the visiting committee as a whole. In order to obviate any delay in procedure, the 1815 amendment carried a clause enabling any two visiting justices to discharge patients on their own responsibility at any time.

The 'Small Act' of 1819 (59 Geo. III c. 127) returned to the problem of certification; until this date, certificates stating merely that 'Mr —— is a suitable Object for your Place'[49] or, to quote a well-known example, that 'Hey Broadway, a Pot Carey' thought that 'A Blister and Bleeding and Meddeson' would be suitable for a gentleman who 'Wold not A Gree to be Done at Home'[50] were quite common. The new prescribed form of certification was as follows: 'I do hereby certify that by the direction of L.M. and N.O., Justices of the Peace for the County of H., I have personally examined C.D., and that the said C.D. appears to me to be of insane mind.'

The 1819 Act also gave the justices power to send patients to the county asylum on their own initiative, without the concurrence of the parish overseer.

The total effect of these three amending Acts was to place the responsibility for the admission of patients with the magistrates rather than with the overseers, thus weakening the connection of the county asylums with the Poor Law authorities.

4   The reform movement 1815–27

While the first developments in theory and practice were taking place in connection with the county asylums, the parliamentary group considered less satisfactory aspects of the lunacy problem. On 28 April 1815, parliament again proceeded to appoint a select committee on the subject, and this time public opinion was actively and vocally on the side of the reformers.

Samuel Tuke had published his *Description of the Retreat*—a book which told of the success of the new system of 'moral' management—in 1813, and the impact of the work of the Tukes on the national consciousness dates from that time. The book elevated the Retreat in the public estimation from a local experiment to something very like a national monument.

In the same year, a county magistrate named Godfrey Higgins uncovered a series of abuses at the York Asylum. Failing to obtain satisfaction from the authorities, he communicated his findings to the press. When an investigation seemed imminent, the staff resorted to panic-stricken measures, burning down part of the building in order to conceal the appalling conditions in which some of the patients were kept, and destroying records to remove the evidence of financial peculation. This not unnaturally had the effect of rousing rather than allaying public indignation, and Higgins sent his evidence to Earl Fitzwilliam, one of the leaders of the Whig party, who was then lord-lieutenant of the county.[1]

Another notable case of abuse which became public knowledge at this time was the discovery at Bethlem of William Norris, a patient who had been confined in a special apparatus of iron for nine years without respite. An iron collar several inches wide encircled his neck, and was fastened to a wall behind his head; his feet were manacled, and a harness fitted over his shoulders, pinioning his arms to his sides. It was just possible for him to stand, or lie on his back, but he was unable to shift his position when lying down, or to move more than one step away from the wall.[2] Six members of parliament visited Norris before his release; they found him quiet and rational, able to hold intelligent conversation on political matters, and to read with comprehension any matter which was put before him. He was in an advanced stage of tuberculosis, and died shortly after being set free.

The Select Committee of 1815

Armed with the evidence of these two cases, and strengthened by public opinion, the parliamentary group was able to press for the appointment of a new select committee with wider terms of reference. The committee set up in April 1815 represented a powerful body of parliamentary opinion. Wynn, George Rose, Lord Robert Seymour, the younger Peel and William Sturges-Bourne were among its members. Wynn was out of office, hovering uncertainly between the Whigs and the Tories. Between 1815 and 1819, he made an unsuccessful attempt to form a third party, and failing, joined the Tories.[3] Rose was over seventy, and had only three more years to live. The editor of his diaries states that 'during these three years, Mr Rose's activity was subsiding into the grave',[4] but the account in the 1815 report of the sessions at which he took the chair shows that he was still mentally alert, and an extremely competent chairman.

Throughout 1815 and 1816 the group issued a series of reports on the conditions of the insane in institutions of various kinds. They dealt with the York Asylum, Bethlem, St Luke's, the new county asylum at Nottingham, the Retreat, and the condition of pauper lunatics in workhouses. Upon being reappointed in 1816 they proceeded to consider private madhouses. The condition of criminal lunatics was no longer a separate consideration, since their numbers were very small, and they could usually be accommodated in one of the new county asylums, or in Bethlem. The reports thus covered all the main types of institutions in which the insane were then confined. This was the first attempt to provide a comprehensive survey of the situation.

It showed that both law and practice were in a state of unbelievable chaos. There were two types of lunacy law—that relating to county asylums, and that relating to private madhouses; in the latter case, the defective 1774 Act was still unamended. Subscription hospitals operated untrammelled by any considerations of legal powers and duties, and the thousands of pauper lunatics who remained in workhouses came under the Poor Law authorities. As a result, enormous varieties in practice were possible, from the humane treatment of the Retreat at one end of the scale to the inhumanity of Bethlem and the worst of the private madhouses at the other.

The rest of this chapter is based on the evidence given before the 1815–16 Committee. It has been amplified here in some respects, but was in itself enough to give a fairly comprehensive picture of the position.

York Asylum

In order to understand the full story of the events of 1813, it is necessary to go back to the early history of the Asylum.

An advertisement in the *York Courant* of 7 August 1772 first drew the attention of the citizens of York to 'the deplorable situation of many poor lunatics of the county, who have no support except what a needy parent can bestow, or a thrifty parish officer provide'. An appeal was made on the 27th of the same month for donations from 'such Noblemen, Gentlemen and Ladies as are desirous of promoting an Institution for the Relief of an Unhappy Part of the Community'. Unfortunately the institution built with such high ideals and excellent motives never lived up to its early promise. By 1790, when Hannah Mills died, its conditions were as bad as those of many a private madhouse, where the only motive involved was that of personal profit for the proprietor.

A local historian reports that 'the building, as an edifice, was worthy of the architects',[5] and the Asylum possessed an imposing list of Governors headed by the Archbishop of York;[6] but it appears that, as with Bethlem, the magnificence of the frontage and the social status of the Governors bore little relation to the conditions inside. A later Medical Superintendent of the Retreat, Dr Thurnam, tells us in his *Statistics of Insanity* (1845) that the building was originally designed for fifty-four inmates, and by 1815 it held 103. The patients were verminous and filthy, herded together in cells with an utter disregard for cleanliness or ventilation. The first physician, Dr Hunter, had his 'secret insane powders, green and grey' which were nothing more than powerful emetics and purges. 'Flogging and cudgelling were systematically resorted to,' writes Thurnam, ' . . . this indeed was denied at the time, but . . . several cases which were brought forward leave little doubt that these cruel practices of the Middle Ages, during which other methods of managing maniacal patients were unknown, were continued in the asylum with the concurrence of its officers.'[7]

All this was suspected, but there was no concrete proof. After

1792, the Retreat provided an alternative system for the care of the insane, but only on a small and restricted scale. Those who had no connection with the Society of Friends, and these were of course the majority, still went to the Asylum, where Dr Hunter and his successor, Dr Best, received patients, discouraged inquisitive visitors, and succeeded in evading public condemnation until 1813. In that year, Godfrey Higgins joined forces with the Tukes.

Higgins was then forty years of age, a quiet country gentleman who possessed a considerable estate, and who had a passion for the more abstruse forms of religion. A man of independent means, considerable leisure, with an objective and inquiring mind, he was admirably suited for the role which his duties as a justice of the peace thrust upon him.

The Vickers case

In the summer of 1813, a pauper named William Vickers or Vicars was brought before Higgins, being charged with assault. Higgins 'presently discovered he was insane', ordered the overseer of the parish to obtain the proper certificates, and issued a warrant to convey Vickers to the Asylum.

In October of the same year, the man's wife, Sarah Vickers, appeared before Higgins to ask for relief, and alleged that her husband, now discharged, had been ill-treated at the Asylum. Higgins sent the surgeon responsible for the paupers of the district to examine the man, and received the following report:

> He had the Itch very bad, was also extremely filthy, for I saw his
> wife not only comb several lice from his head, but take them
> from the folds of his shirt neck; his health was so much impaired
> that he was not able to stand by himself; his legs were very much
> swelled, and one of them in a state of mortification.

There were lash marks on Vickers' back, and he told Higgins that he had been flogged. His friends and relatives had been denied an opportunity of visiting him in the Asylum, being told on the occasion of one visit that he was 'insensible in an apoplexy'. Higgins commented, 'No doubt it must have disturbed him very much to be looked at in a state of insensibility.'

Higgins found on inquiry that it was the general belief that conditions at the Asylum were very bad, and that a previous attempt had been made to achieve reform. He corresponded with the physician,

Dr Best, but obtained no satisfaction from him, and at length, on 27 November 1813, he published a statement in the *York Herald*, together with extracts from the correspondence.

Attitude of the Asylum authorities

Dr Best's defence against the charges made by Higgins had consisted of a complete and unequivocal denial. He stated that Vickers' condition was 'the unavoidable consequence of the lamentable and dangerous illness under which he had recently laboured, and from which he was but then in an early stage of convalescence.' Vickers had had a fire in his room, a special attendant, 'assiduous medical treatment . . . nutritious food . . . mulled ale . . . everything conducive to his recovery.' Best urged Higgins to consider 'whether you are not lending your name as a magistrate to a purpose most foreign to your office as a magistrate, and giving effect . . . to a malicious conspiracy against myself and the Asylum.'

Best sustained this air of injured innocence throughout the subsequent revelations. When the Quarterly Court, or Governors' Meeting, was convened a week later, its members accepted his statement at its face value. A statement signed by Archbishop Venables-Vernon was issued:

> The Governors, having taken into consideration the statement published in the York and other newspapers respecting the condition of William Vickers, lately a patient in this Asylum, and having examined upon oath such witnesses as were competent to afford information of the same, are unanimously of the opinion that during the time the said William Vickers remained in the Asylum, he was treated with all possible care, attention and humanity.[9]

Higgins was less easily convinced: 'The Archbishop, the last minute before I came away, told me very politely that they would detain me no longer, they had not further occasion for me . . . I am very far from satisfied with what has been done.'[10]

The Quarterly Court had been adjourned for a week, and when it met again on 10 December it had forty-six new members. The foundation rule was that any person subscribing £20 to the work of the Asylum became a Governor, and forty-six citizens of York, including

Godfrey Higgins, William Tuke and Samuel Tuke, had availed themselves of this opportunity.[11] The old Governors, if not out-voted, were
certainly outflanked. The Archbishop bowed to the inevitable after
what Higgins called 'a warm debate',[12] and a committee of investigation was formed.

The fire

On 26 December the Asylum caught fire. A letter to the *York Herald*
of 4 April, 1814, signed 'A Governor of the Asylum' gives these details of the occurrence: conditions were unusually propitious for the
flames, for most of the staff were absent. Dr Best was thirty miles
away, attending a private patient, the apothecary and the housekeeper had 'gone out to keep Christmas'; two of the four male keepers
had Christmas leave, and of the two that remained, one was asthmatic,
and could not bear the smoke. Thus one keeper was left to deal with
the outbreak. 'Before the flames could be extinguished, damage was
done to the building and property amounting to £2392, and four
patients perished in the conflagration. This served to shut out from all
mortal eyes proofs of maladministration at which the imagination
shudders.'[13]

A plausible explanation was again forthcoming from Dr Best. The
fire was said to have been caused by sparks falling down a chimney
from an adjoining one, and 'setting fire to some flocks laid there to
dry in a room locked up.'[14]

Godfrey Higgins, in his new capacity as a Governor of the Asylum,
demanded to see the chimney in question, and found that it was
'built in a direction so far from the perpendicular' that it was almost
impossible for the outbreak to have originated in this way.[15]

The next turn of events is obscure. It appears that the old Governors
succeeded temporarily in their efforts to stifle criticism. By some
means, pressure was exerted on Higgins to induce him to withdraw
from further investigation, for the *York Herald* of 10 January 1814
contained a letter in which he expressed himself satisfied with conditions at the Asylum, and added unexpectedly, 'It gives me great
pleasure to be able to second a motion of thanks to his Grace the
Archbishop'; but if promises of reform were made, they were not
carried out. Nine weeks later, Higgins launched his second attack
through the medium of the press.

The second investigation

> Having suspicions in my mind that there were some parts of the
> Asylum which had not yet been seen, I went early in the
> morning, determined to examine every place. After ordering a
> a great number of doors to be opened, I came to one which was
> in a retired situation in the kitchen apartments, and which was
> was almost hid. I ordered this door to be opened . . . the
> keepers hesitated . . . I grew angry, and told them that I insisted
> on [the key] being found; and that, if they would not find it,
> I could find a key at the kitchen fireside, namely, the poker;
> upon that, the key was immediately brought.[16]

Higgins unlocked the door, and went in. He found a series of cells
about eight feet square

> in a very horrid and filthy condition . . . the walls were
> daubed with excrement; the air-holes, of which there was one in
> each cell, were partly filled with it . . . I then went upstairs, and
> (the keeper) showed me into a room . . . twelve feet by seven
> feet ten inches, in which there were thirteen women who, he told
> me, had all come out of those cells that morning. . . . I became
> very sick, and could not remain longer in the room. I vomited.

Higgins expressed in his letter to the press the hope that 'the public
will never rest until the Augean stable is swept clean from top to
bottom.' Five months were to elapse before this wish became realized
—five months of urbane explanations, recriminations, and constant
pressure to induce the reformers to give way. In a letter published in
the *York Herald* on 30 March Dr Best complained that 'Mr Higgins'
attack is personally and particularly levelled at me.' He behaved
throughout as though he were the victim of a monstrous conspiracy.
The cells mentioned by Higgins were, he stated, reserved for women
of unclean habits. They were cleaned out every morning, and it was
an extremely offensive undertaking. Chains and handcuffs found in
the Asylum had been examined by the Governors, and found to be
covered with rust, which proved that they had not been in use for a
considerable time. He then shifted to a defensive position. The place
was damp and low-lying, half the building had been destroyed by fire,
there were too few staff, and too many patients. 'If the servants
neglect to perform their duties . . . if the laws and constitution are
defective . . . I do not consider myself as responsible for any of these

circumstances, or for the evils which may naturally be expected to result from them.'

The *York Herald* of 4 April contained the first letter on the subject written by anyone other than Higgins and Best. It was signed 'A Governor of the Asylum' and contained a detailed point-by-point refutation of Best's letter of the previous week. The writer may have been one of the Tuke family, who would not wish his identity generally known, since the family was responsible for what was in some sense a rival establishment.

Best had stated that the women in the cells seen by Higgins had 'straw beds'. 'The expression,' commented 'A Governor of the Asylum' acidly, 'is scarcely applicable to loose straw covering the floor as in a stable.' On the question of the fire: 'It would certainly be unjust to blame any individual connected with the Asylum as answerable for the fire'; yet it was, to say the least, 'an unfortunate coincidence' that all the staff save one were absent or incapacitated. 'Thus it came about that four patients were burned to death—or, as the Steward's book records it, they died.' On Best's disclaimer of responsibility, the writer retorted that he was well paid for taking responsibility, since he received a large salary, and was permitted to take private patients in addition. The letter concluded: 'The public are convinced that if there be any prospect of a reformation of the defects and abuses which are now admitted to exist, they are chiefly indebted for it to the independent exertions and the firmness of Mr Godfrey Higgins.'

Mr Higgins' exertions continued. He had discovered other cases of cruelty, in which patients had been flogged or otherwise ill-treated by the keepers.

Some of these had been exposed at the first inquiry, but without result. One such was the case of 'the Rev. Mr Skorey', an elderly cleric suffering from a mild disorder, and having frequent lucid intervals. He had been 'inhumanly kicked downstairs' by the keepers, and told in the presence of his wife that he was 'no better than a dog.' To this complaint, Best made a typical reply: 'Mrs Skorey stated in evidence that she heard him knocked downstairs, which I conceive to be impossible . . . I mean, impossible that she could have distinguished by the ear alone whether her husband had been kicked downstairs or not.'

The male side of the Asylum was not completely separated from the female side. Two female patients had become pregnant while in the Asylum—one by a male patient, and one by a keeper named Backhouse. The latter openly admitted paternity, and paid regular sums to the overseers of the poor for the parish of Louth to maintain the child in the poorhouse. The keeper subsequently retired from the Asylum after twenty-six years' service, received a handsome present from the Governors—and opened a private madhouse. Higgins stated that he did not think the Governors knew of Backhouse's defection, but that Dr Hunter certainly knew, and kept silence.

Samuel Tuke also made use of his status as a Governor in order to investigate conditions. On one occasion, he found a mental defective in the wash-house: 'He was standing on a wet stone floor, apparently in the last stages of decay; he was a mere skeleton; his thighs were covered with excrement in a dry state, and those parts which were not so appeared excoriated . . . he was spoken of by all the attendants as a dying man.'

This patient was removed from the Asylum, and Higgins reported that he eventually made a physical recovery.

The reformers then turned their attention to the records, and found that they were false in many particulars. The number of deaths for 1813 was given as eleven, but comparison with the parish registers showed that there had been twenty-four funerals. The inference was that thirteen patients had died during the year, whose existence in the Asylum had never been recorded. When the fire took place, it was stated that four patients died in the flames; but the records were so inadequate that it would have been possible for several more to have died without trace.

Higgins went through the accounts, such as they were, and mercilessly exposed their discrepancies. 'One quarter's account was missing; of another quarter, two statements were transmitted, both apparently complete documents, but each in fact essentially differing from the other.'[17]

He proved that large sums of money had been appropriated by Dr Best and his predecessor; but again, the conspiracy of silence came into operation. The steward, when asked to produce the books for the inspection of the Quarterly Court, said lamely that he had burned them 'in a moment of irritation.'[18] It is difficult to ascertain exactly what happened, since the Court adopted a resolution against making the matter public. 'Another Y.Z.', in a letter to the *York Herald*, on

12 December 1814 wrote: 'The movers of the resolution against the freedom of the press discovered a fearful apprehension lest the burning of the books should find its way into the papers.'

Reform of conditions, 1814

The abuses came to an end in August 1814—nearly a year after the release of William Vickers. The Quarterly Court finally dismissed all the servants and officers of the Asylum. Dr Best was either asked or permitted to resign[19] though this of course did not affect his private practice, which was considerable. He apparently did not consider himself either condemned or defeated, since the *York Herald* published on 28 December of the same year a letter written by him to the editor:

I merely write this to give you notice, that if ONE SYLLABLE shall appear in any of your future papers in allusion to me, which may admit of an INJURIOUS or even an OFFENSIVE construction, my next communication with you will take place through my attorney.

The editor's comment on this letter was apt: 'It was . . . sent to intimidate me from that course which it is my duty as the Editor of a Public Paper to pursue. I give it, therefore, to the world.'

When the new staff was appointed, the Asylum was given a new constitution. The Quarterly Court of August 1814 laid down that two Governors were to visit the Asylum each month; that three ladies were to be asked to undertake the visitation of the female wards; that the physician was to receive £300 a year, but was not to undertake private practice or to receive gratuities; that a resident apothecary was to be appointed, whose duties would be those of superintending the issue of medicines, and also of supervising the work and conduct of the keepers; that the diet was to be revised regularly by the committee; and that an annual report was to be issued.[20]

A postscript was supplied by the declaration of the Quarterly Court of August 1815, from which the Archbishop of York was absent. The chairman was Earl Fitzwilliam, to whom Higgins' long letter of protest had been sent. It was resolved unanimously

that this Court feels with the highest degree of satisfaction the very great improvement which has taken place in every department of this institution, since the general meeting in August last, by which they have no doubt that in point of humane treatment of patients, and the general order and cleanliness of the house, the York Lunatic Asylum is scarcely excelled by any similar institution in the Kingdom. . . . This Court, contemplating the great improvement made in the state of the house, feels a pleasure in acknowledging its great obligation to Godfrey Higgins, Esq., to whose zeal and perseverance the origin of these improvements must in great measure be ascribed.[21]

The scandal was ended, as far as the city of York was concerned. From that time, the York Asylum stood comparison with any county asylum; but in 1815, the affair had repercussions on a national scale. Wynn, Rose and Seymour revived the Vickers case, the circumstances of the fire, the financial peculations, the destruction of the records. Higgins gave evidence, and so—less happily—did Dr Best. The attitude of the committee left no doubt as to which they believed to be telling the truth.

In this connection, mention should be made of the method of asylum-visiting initiated by Catherine Cappe, wife of the physician at the Retreat, who published her 'Thoughts on the Desirableness and Utility of Ladies Visiting the Female Wards of Hospitals and Lunatic Asylums' in 1816. Her system was in many ways analogous to the prison-visiting of Elizabeth Fry. After the reforms of 1814, she tells us, she began to visit the female patients of the York Asylum regularly, and she came to believe that such visits were a valuable safeguard against maladministration in asylums. Her standards were high: 'A lady visitor in an asylum or hospital should be to that institution what the kind, judicious Mistress of a family is to her household—the careful inspector of the economy, the integrity and the good moral conduct of the housekeeper and the other inferior servants.'

Mrs Cappe evidently had a low opinion of the capabilities and standards of asylum staff; but she had also a wide experience. She complained that the masters and matrons of institutions for the insane were often unsuited for the office which they held; that they were frequently appointed as a result of wire-pulling and nepotism. She pointed out that physicians and surgeons frequently served only in a part-time capacity, and that the 'father' of the 'family'—here we have the exact terminology used at the Retreat—was usually the resident apothecary, generally an unmarried man since the post carried with it limited accommodation in rooms on the premises. Consequently, unless the matron was an exceptional woman, there was often no woman to whom the female patients could turn. 'May there not be a variety of minute circumstances which may occasion great distress, and may retard, if not wholly prevent, recovery, but which could be communicated only to a female ear?'

We have no means of knowing how far Mrs Cappe's ideas were generally adopted, but the visitors' books of several county asylums mention frequent visits by the wives and adult daughters of the visiting justices; this suggests that these ladies may have attempted something more constructive than a mere sight-seeing tour; personal contact with the female patients, and supervision of the domestic arrangements of the asylums concerned.

Bethlem

The course of events at Bethlem in the year 1814–15 was in outline similar to that at York. Again a philanthropist visited the hospital in connection with a special case; again the circumstances of that case were sufficient to arouse public indignation; again, the medical and lay administrative officers did their best to excuse the inexcusable, and failing, tried each to shift the blame on to the shoulders of the others. It is possible that, since Bethlem was in London, the facts concerning the standards of treatment there were well known to the parliamentary reformers, but it was not until Edward Wakefield[22] visited the hospital in April 1814, and made known the condition of William Norris, that an opportunity presented itself for attacking the entire system.

Administration and medical treatment at Bethlem

The apothecary of Bethlem at that time was Mr John Haslam, and the physician Dr Thomas Monro. Haslam was responsible for administering medicines and directing the control of patients, and Monro for prescribing medicines and the form of treatment. The surgeon to both Bridewell and Bethlem until 1815—in which year he died—was Dr Bryan Crowther. This member of the College of Surgeons published in 1811 a treatise entitled *Practical Remarks on Insanity*, in which he described in detail the method of treatment employed at Bethlem.[23]

> The curable patients at Bethlem Hospital are regularly bled about the commencement of June, and the latter end of July . . . the lancet has been found a very communicative sort of instrument

... I have bled a hundred and fifty patients at one time, and have never found it requisite to adopt any other method of security against haemorrhage than that of sending the patient back to his *accustomed confinement.*

The last two words here reveal clearly Crowther's attitude to mechanical restraint. He believed firmly in the efficacy of purges and vomits in all cases of insanity. 'The servants at Bethlem have told me repeatedly of the quantity of phlegm evacuated.' He still believed in the cold bath, and used a notorious device known as the 'circular swing', in which the patient was rotated rapidly until he lost consciousness. His section on 'Management' has nothing to say about diet, clothing, occupations, or remedial measures of any kind, being solely concerned with the necessity for obtaining 'ascendancy' over the patients. It was the patient who was to be managed, not the institution.

It is easy to discredit Crowther, whose methods, even for his own time, were harsh. At best, he belonged to the old school of 'mad-doctors' and knew nothing of more enlightened methods of treating the insane. At worst, if Haslam's evidence before the 1815 Committee is to be believed, he was totally unfitted to have charge of patients. Haslam succeeded in discrediting Crowther most effectively when, less then a month after his death, he described him to the Select Committee as having been 'for ten years . . . generally insane and mostly drunk. . . . He was so insane as to have a strait waistcoat . . . he was so insane, that his hand was not obedient to his will.'

How far these charges were based on fact it is not easy to ascertain, for the dead man made a convenient scapegoat; searching cross-examination by Rose forced both Monro and Haslam into hesitation, contradiction and evasion. Haslam blamed Monro, Monro blamed Haslam, and both blamed Crowther. They were charged repeatedly with having ordered indiscriminate bleeding and purging of all patients at certain times in the year, and repeatedly, in the face of all evidence to the contrary, they denied it.[24] The following dialogue between Rose and Monro illustrates clearly the physician's attitude towards his Bethlem patients:

Would you treat a private individual patient in your own house in the same way as has been described in respect of Bethlem?
—No, certainly not.

What is the difference of management?

—In Bethlem, the restraint is by chains, there is no such thing as chains in my house.

What are your objections to chains and fetters as a mode of restraint?

—They are fit only for pauper lunatics; if a gentleman was put in irons, he would not like it.

The apothecary visited the hospital usually only for half an hour a day, and was sometimes absent for days at a time. Monro admitted that he 'seldom' went round the galleries to see the patients, but stated that they were sent to him if they were physically ill. Thus the patients —who at that time numbered nearly 150—were left almost entirely to the care of the keepers. There were five keepers—three men and two women: a ratio of one to thirty.

The Norris case

Both Monro and Haslam were called upon to account for the condition of William Norris. Haslam admitted the truth of the facts—that the man had been chained continually for nine years with his (Haslam's) knowledge and consent.

Do you mean he was never out of those irons for the whole nine years?

—They were never taken off, I believe. I do not know that they were ever taken off. If the keeper took them off, it was unknown to me.

Having made these admissions, Haslam put forward a series of statements in his own defence. He stated—and this was not contested —that Norris had at one time been homicidal, and had attacked a keeper and another patient with a knife. 'He was the most malignant and mischievous lunatic I ever saw.' Norris was, he said, a powerful man, who could free himself from any normal method of confinement, and could burst open a strait jacket with ease. He could not be secured by manacles, since his hands had an unusual bone formation, the circumference at the widest part being less than that of his wrists.

The Select Committee never attempted to prove that Norris had been wrongfully sent to Bethlem. He had undoubtedly been violently behaved at one time; but the length of his period of confinement, its method, and the fact that, when he was discovered, he was so physically weak from tuberculosis that he would have been unable to escape or to harm others even had he so desired—all these things far outweighed any explanation which Haslam could make. Accordingly, he fell back on his last line of defence—shifting the responsibility to others. He declared that the device had been constructed in accordance with the orders of a committee of the Governors, and that he himself would have preferred to have kept Norris in solitary confinement. This statement he partially contradicted by another—that Norris in his lucid moments had thanked him for restraining him from further crimes.

The Norris case at Bethlem was the equivalent of the Vickers case at York; it was not that either case was exceptional—rather that the ill-treatment involved was taken for granted by those concerned in the administration of the respective asylums. In each instance, it was only one case of cruelty among many.

The 'Blanket patients'

Edward Wakefield, in his initial visit to Bethlem, found a number of female patients chained to the wall by an arm or a leg, and completely unclothed save for a blanket apiece. Some of these women were quiet and coherent when he visited them, and fully able to comprehend the degradation to which they were being subjected.

By the time the Select Committee received evidence, the old matron had been pensioned off, and a younger woman named Mrs Forbes appointed. She obtained clothes for these women, freed all those who were not violent, washed and cleaned them, cut their hair. She related to the parliamentary reformers a typical response—that of a patient named Ann Stone.

> I asked the reason for her being always confined to the wall.
> I was told she was very troublesome, and tore her clothes; that
> she had a good many things sent her, but they were all torn.
> I said I would try to walk her about . . . I gave her a couple of
> caps, and she did not tear them. She looks better, and very
> comfortable and tidy; and every time I go round the gallery, she
> says, 'Accept my real thanks for allowing me my liberty.'

Nottingham County Asylum

By 1815, three county asylums were in operation—those at Nottingham, Bedford and Thorpe (Norfolk). These had been opened in 1811, 1812 and 1814 respectively, but were not yet sufficiently well established to be fairly judged. Evidence was given on the principles on which Nottingham Asylum had been founded by the Rev. J. T. Becher, a prominent member of the penal reform movement, who was also a member of the visiting committee of that asylum.[25]

Mr Becher was questioned by the members of the Select Committee about the cost of the Asylum, the maintenance charges for paupers, the system of classification of patients, the staff, the use of mechanical restraint in connection with violent or dangerous patients, and the amenities provided for those patients who were capable of appreciating them. The form which these questions took showed that the parliamentary group had evolved a series of criteria by which the administration of any institution for the insane could usefully be judged. This was a distinct step forward, for one of the great difficulties in the earlier days of reform had been the lack of definite standards.

The Asylum had been built by the county magistrates, and financed by a county rate and voluntary subscriptions. The total cost was £21,686, of which £16,651 was spent on the actual buildings, and the rest on the purchase of the site, furnishings and other considerations. The patients were divided into three groups, as at the Manchester Lunatic Hospital and the Retreat—the first and second classes being supported by their relatives, and the third, the pauper class, being paid for by the overseer of the parish concerned in each case. There were sixteen patients of the first and most privileged class, twenty of the second class, and forty paupers, for each of whom the charge was 9s. per week.

There was a rudimentary scheme of classification. Male and female patients were completely separated, and there was a special ward for the refractory cases of each sex.

Six keepers had charge of the patients—a male and female keeper for each class. This meant that each keeper had sole charge of a group of patients, though the others could be summoned, if needed, to quell an outbreak of violence.

The parliamentary reformers, considering this provision inadequate, inquired of Becher: 'Do you conceive that a keeper under any circumstances is equal to the due care of 20 patients?' The reply was: '20 patients are seldom found without some in a state nearly advancing to recovery, and with a disposition in the case of any emergency to assist the keeper.'

The system of restraint used was very mild, and the rules contained the provision that

> the assistants and servants . . . abstain from unnecessary acts of violence . . . that they do not use chains unless with the knowledge and consent of the director; and that they inflict neither blows nor stripes, but on the contrary that they behave with the utmost forbearance, tenderness, patience and humanity towards the unfortunate sufferers entrusted to their care and protection.

Some attempt was made to occupy the patients; there were gardens and airing courts for each class, and those patients who were sufficiently rational were encouraged to take up various forms of useful occupation.

The whole picture, as given by Becher, affords an interesting glimpse into the early development of county asylums. The old idea of deterrence had not quite been eliminated, but a real effort was being made to develop the new experiment on humanitarian lines. Comparison with the conditions in workhouses and private madhouses was to show how urgent was the necessity for extending the provision of county asylums.

Workhouses

One of the witnesses before the Select Committee was a banker named Henry Alexander, who had undertaken a self-imposed tour of forty-seven workhouses in order to discover the conditions under which pauper lunatics were confined.

Most of these workhouses were in the West Country. Nine had insane inmates, and of these only three had separate accommodation for them. One of the three was St Peter's, Bristol, where the inmates were 'comfortable' on the whole; but even there, Alexander found four incurable patients in wooden cells 'like pig-styes'—dark and lacking in ventilation and sanitation.

At Liskeard in Cornwall, Alexander found two women confined in the workhouse.

> In a fit place for them?
> —Very far from it. Indeed, I hardly know what to term the places, they were no better than dungeons.
> Were they underground?
> —No; they were buildings, but they were very damp and very

low. In one of them, there was no light admitted through the
door; neither light nor air. Both of them were chained down to
the damp stone floor, and one of them had only a little dirty
straw, which appeared to have been there for many weeks . . .
we asked if she was allowed water to wash herself, and found
she was not . . . the whole place was very filthy.
 Filled with excrement and very offensive?
 —Yes.

One of the women was apparently confined under section 20 of the
Act of 1744.

We enquired the reason of her confinement from the mistress of
the workhouse; and it appeared she had been confined many
months, both winter and summer; and the only cause they
assigned was, that she was troublesome, they could not keep her
within; she was roving about the country, and they had
complaints lodged against her from different persons.
 Not of any act of violence?
 —Not at all; we enquired particularly, and they gave us no
other reason than her being troublesome.

At Tavistock, Alexander and his companions experienced difficulty in gaining admission.

I am sorry my information will not be altogether satisfactory,
as we did not see the insane poor themselves . . . the situation
. . . was dreadful, indeed I could not stand up at all in some of
the lower rooms; the rooms were very small, and in one of the
bedrooms, 17 people slept; one man and his wife slept in the
room with 15 other people.
 We enquired if there were any insane persons; and upon
expressing a desire to see them, we were at first refused on the
ground that the place was not fit for us to go into; but we
persisted in our intreaties to see them, and went up the yard
where we understood the cells were, and upon entering them, we
found that the inmates had been removed. There were three of
them . . . they had been removed out that morning.
 For what purpose?
 —The cells had been washed and cleaned out.
 Who refused you?
 —The master of the house. He did not do it in a peremptory
manner at all, but told us it was unfit for us to go, and indeed
we found it so.

What was the state of the cells?

—I never smelt such a stench in my life, and it was so bad
that a friend who went with us said he could not enter the other.
After having entered one, I said I would go into the other; that
if they could survive there the night through, I could at least
inspect them . . . the stench was so great I felt almost suffocated;
and for hours after, if I ate anything, I still retained the same
smell; I could not get rid of it; and it should be remembered
that these cells had been washed out that morning, and the doors
had been opened some hours previous.

Alexander's further evidence reiterated the same story—filth, neglect,
and unthinking brutality.

The inference from the evidence was quite clear—that the Poor Law
authorities would not or could not make adequate provision for
pauper lunatics, and that any hope of bettering the condition of this
class lay in removing them to institutions of the county asylum type.

Private madhouses

In 1816, the Select Committee was reappointed to consider the condition of private madhouses, and the parliamentary reformers continued their accumulation of evidence of the abuses which were
possible under the 1774 Madhouses Act.

'Naval maniacs' at Hoxton

Mentally deranged seamen were commonly sent by the Navy to a
large private madhouse kept by Sir Jonathan Miles at Hoxton. In
1814, the house contained fourteen officers and 136 seamen, together
with other patients. Lengthy evidence was given by Dr John Weir,
the Inspector of Naval Hospitals, and other independent physicians,
who stated that the conditions there were extremely bad, but that,
although they were responsible for inspection, they had no power to
effect any improvements. The mortality rate was extremely high, and
there appeared to be no attempt at classification. Dr Weir was particularly indignant because in one case a naval captain shared a room
with a civilian grocer; but the confusion was not merely a matter of
social caste; clean and dirty patients, violent and peaceable, incurable
and convalescent officers and men—all were thrust together without
regard for their mental or physical condition. Male patients slept two

in a bed; the food consisted almost entirely of beef and beer—a diet which Weir thought 'too stimulating'—and there was no medical treatment.

Sir Jonathan Miles was cross-questioned by Rose, as chairman of the Committee:

> You do not consider yourself responsible for the medical treatment of the Government patients?
> —Yes, I am.
> Do the Government patients receive any medical treatment for the cure of their insanity?
> —I cannot say that they do, exactly.
> Is any medical attention particularly directed in your establishment to the cure of insanity?
> —None. Our house is open to all medical gentlemen who care to visit it.
> That is at the expense of the patient?
> —It is.
> How many are visited by their own medical men?
> —I cannot tell. . . .
> Do you suppose that there are twenty?
> —Yes, from twenty to thirty, probably.
> Is it your opinion, then, that there are above three hundred persons in your house, who receive no attention on account of the particular complaint for which they are confined?
> —Certainly.

Here was the policy of confinement at its worst.

There were in all 486 patients in this house, and the Commissioners had inspected it in the space of about two and a half hours. Dr Richard Powell[26] admitted that on this visit, he had not checked the number of patients, and that some might have been concealed in hidden rooms or cells. He had not seen samples of the patient's food, and he saw nothing harmful in male patients sleeping two in a bed: 'it cannot be expected that a man who pays only ten shillings a week should have a separate bed.' He considered the house 'in very excellent order.'

Warburton's houses

Thomas Warburton was the proprietor of four madhouses in the metropolitan area—Talbot's, the White House and Rhodes', all at

D

Bethnal Green, and Whitmore House at Hackney. Pauper lunatics from the parishes of Marylebone, St George, Hanover Square, and St Pancras were regularly sent to these houses, and in 1815, there were 300 patients in the White House alone.

The evidence given on these houses was highly contradictory. In the event, Warburton escaped censure; but the evidence given in 1827 (see page 102) suggested that the allegations were well-founded.

Other private madhouses: evidence of Edward Wakefield

Wakefield, who, it will be remembered, was responsible for the discovery of William Norris at Bethlem, explained in answer to the Committee's inquiry that his work as a land agent[27] took him to various parts of the country, and that he made a point, at each place he visited, of asking to see the gaols, Bridewells and madhouses in the vicinity. He was in the true tradition of the early nineteenth-century reformers. He knew the Retreat, and his standards, as far as madhouses were concerned, were roughly those of the Tukes. At Miles' house at Hoxton, he had been refused admission, a keeper telling him that 'an inspection of that house would be signing my death-warrant.' At Gore House, Kensington, he was also refused admission. At Thomas Monro's house at Hackney, he was told by the physician of Bethlem that he was welcome to visit—if he could secure the consent of the relatives of every patient; and he was refused a list of names of the patients, which made an improbable task impossible.

There were a few private madhouses in which conditions were good, as far as Wakefield could tell. As an unofficial visitor, he had of course no power to make a thorough inspection, and had to base his opinion on what the individual proprietor allowed him to see. At Talfourd's house at Fulham, there were fourteen ladies who appeared to be treated with the greatest kindness. They went to the local church, and were allowed out for walks—Wakefield met two who had just 'walked to Walham Green to see Louis XVIII.' London House, Hackney, also appeared to be excellently conducted. There, 'One lady, who conceives herself to be Mary, Queen of Scots, acts as preceptress to Mrs. Fox's little children, and takes great pains in teaching them French.'

Powers and duties of the Commissioners, 1816

It is significant that, while evidence of abuses had been forthcoming from other sources, the evidence of the Commissioners was almost entirely concerned with their own position. Dr Powell had been the secretary of the Metropolitan Commissioners since 1808. He testified that they visited all madhouses in the area, inquiring into the administration and the condition of the patients, but not into the form of medical treatment, which they considered outside their province— despite the fact that all the Commissioners were members of the College of Physicians.[28] The visitation lasted six days in the year; Powell himself had personally visited thirty-four houses—'some days, perhaps two; other days, six or eight'—over an area covering all central London, and as far out as Lewisham, Stockwell, Walham Green, Enfield and Plaistow. They suspected that some houses made false returns, but did not check the number of patients returned against those actually seen in the houses. The following scrap of dialogue concerning one house visited is illuminating:

How many patients were there?
—Three.
Men or women?
—Women, I think, but I am hardly certain.

In defence of the Commissioners, it may further be said that the state of the law was so defective that even had they applied themselves conscientiously to their duties, they could still have achieved very little in the way of reform. They had no power to refuse licences, and no power to liberate those whom they considered sane; the certificates of confinement could be signed by any 'medical man'—who need not even have examined the patient, but could give a certificate on what he had heard by repute. No medical certificate at all was necessary for pauper patients. A licence was issued for each separate madhouse, but without regard to the number of patients in it; the holder of the licence was not required to be resident in the house, so that it was possible to own several houses and leave them largely in the hands of untrained and unsupervised keepers. No licence was needed for single lunatics, and consequently it was perfectly possible for a madhouse proprietor to keep a number of small separate houses, or even single rooms in houses next door to each other, each containing one patient, and to evade the attention of the statutory authority completely.

The Select Committee presented its evidence to parliament, but it drew no conclusions, and made no recommendations. In this respect, it departed from the usual procedure of select committees. The 1807 Committee had, more conventionally, drawn up a brief report embodying concrete proposals, and included only what evidence was necessary to establish the point of Wynn's argument; but the reports of 1815–16 are simply verbatim accounts of evidence received, with no attempt to sift the true from the false, or the salient points from a mass of irrelevancies. The inference is that the Committee did not expect immediate legislative action to be taken. Perhaps, also, they thought that the facts spoke for themselves. All they could do was to publish the evidence, and to continue their agitation in parliament for a system of administration which would remedy the conditions they had uncovered.

Parry-Jones[29] has made the point that the madhouse system has tended to be judged by the evils of a few London houses, and that many madhouses offered reasonable care and treatment by the standards of the time. This may be the case; but the evils revealed in 1815–16 were sufficient to shock the House of Commons, and to bring an active reform movement into being.

The reform movement in parliament

From 1815 to 1819, repeated efforts were made by Wynn and his associates to introduce new and effective legislation. The reports of 1815–16 had shown clearly that a comprehensive lunacy law covering all types of institutions was necessary; but for that, the time was not yet ripe. The parliamentary group concentrated instead on a limited objective—that of reforming the private madhouses. The most pressing need was for a competent and powerful inspectorate; had this been achieved, it would have been a comparatively simple matter to extend the scope of its activities at a later date, and thus bring all the insane under a central control.

Bills designed to set up such an inspectorate were three times steered through the Commons—in 1816, 1817 and 1819. On each occasion the Bill was rejected by the Lords after many deferments. It was apparent that, even after the lapse of more than fifty years, the Upper House retained the stubborn opposition to lunacy reform which had characterized its approach to the subject in 1773. On the last of these occasions Lord Eldon made the famous remark which summed up the illiberal attitude of the House of Lords: 'There could not be a more false humanity than an over-humanity with regard to persons afflicted with insanity.'

After this final defeat of the reformers' hopes, there was no major parliamentary activity for some years.[30] The small group of reformers began to disintegrate. George Rose died in 1818; Wynn abandoned the Whigs and took office under the Liverpool administration in 1822; Romilly and Whitbread were dead—the latter dying while the Select Committee was still sitting, and the former committing suicide in 1818. Lord Robert Seymour was now too old to rouse himself from his habitual lethargy in order to take single-handed action. Perhaps he, like those of his colleagues who remained, recognized that under existing conditions, the battle was a hopeless one; but although the parliamentary group was temporarily inactive, the wider reform movement was gathering force. The Governors of Bethlem, shaken out of complacency by the revelations of 1815, took immediate action with regard to the management of that institution; as the county asylum movement developed, a distinct pattern of asylum administration gradually became apparent; and for the first time, new ideas on the treatment and care of the insane became widely current through the medium of the written word. Newspapers, periodicals and specialist publications spread the concepts of the small group of philanthropists and reformers to a larger public. All these factors facilitated the passage of the Bill when it was reintroduced in 1828. The earlier attempts to provide adequate legislation were part of the slow but necessary process of convincing the general public of the need for reform.

Reform at Bethlem

The publication of the Norris case and other evidence given before the Select Committee had a salutary effect on the Governors of Bethlem. While the inquiry was still pending, they dismissed the old steward and matron, appointing younger and more competent people to their posts. In 1816, with the full evidence of the Committee before them, they met to consider the future of their apothecary and their physician. Haslam was dismissed,[31] and returned to private practice until his death in 1844. His dismissal did not apparently cloud his reputation, for his biographer described him as 'long distinguished in private practice by his prudent treatment of the insane'.[32] The obituary notice in the *Gentleman's Magazine* more discreetly noted only his capabilities as 'reviewer, critic, epigrammatist, and author of witty and comic papers'.[33]

Dr Thomas Monro was also called before the Governors to justify himself, but he was more fortunate than Haslam. There was a long tradition of Monros at Bethlem, and the Governors seem to have been unwilling to proceed to extreme measures in his case. Moreover, he had taken the precaution of preparing an attempted rebuttal of the charges made against him, which he read aloud and subsequently had printed.[34]

In this address, he disposed of the Norris case by the simple method of saying that he had no wish 'to agitate it anew.' Of the case of Miss Stone, the blanket patient released by the matron, he said:

> The crowded state of the hospital afforded no means of classification . . . although one may deeply lament that an individual with such attainments as she possessed should be so degraded, it was difficult consistently with the general attention due to the other patients to place her in any other situation but that which she occupied.

Concerning the accusations levelled against him on the score of medical treatment, he stated baldly, 'With respect to the merits of the mode of treatment which I have practised, consisting chiefly of evacuants, as a general rule, I know no better.'

There is no record of the Governors' reaction to the defence, but it is significant that Monro resigned in July 1816—nominally of his own accord. He was replaced by his son, Dr Edward Thomas Monro.

Although it was many years before public control could be established over Bethlem, there was undoubtedly a considerable degree of reform in conditions after the disclosures made by the 1815 Committee. An anonymous publication in 1823 entitled *Sketches in Bedlam* suggested that great improvements had followed the removal to new premises in 1815. The work of the younger Dr Monro was mentioned with appreciation.

'Bedlam is well-conducted,' wrote Sir Andrew Halliday in 1828, 'and the patients are humanely and judiciously treated; but it has still too much of the leaven of the dark ages . . . for it ever to prove an efficient hospital.'[35]

The county asylums

By 1827, there were nine county asylums in operation.[36] Nottingham, Bedford and Norfolk were followed by Lancaster (1816), Stafford (1818), the West Riding of Yorkshire (at Wakefield, 1818), Cornwall (at Bodmin, 1820), Lincoln (1820), and Gloucester (1823). The cost of these asylums in relation to the accommodation provided was as follows:[37]

Asylum	Approx. total cost £	Accommodation	Initial cost per head £
Nottingham. . .	21,000	80	262
Bedford . . .	10,000	52	192
Norfolk . . .	35,000	102	343
Lancaster . . .	60,000	170	353
Stafford . . .	36,000	120	300
West Riding . .	55,000	250	220
Cornwall . . .	15,000	102	147
Lincoln . . .	12,000	50	240
Gloucester . . .	44,000	120	367

Sites of county asylums

Wynn's Act had specified that the new asylums were to be 'in an airy and healthy situation, with a good supply of water, and which may afford a probability of the vicinity of constant medical assistance.'[38] This posed some difficulty, since the only sites satisfying the last requirement were those in large towns, which at that period were neither healthy nor airy, and frequently had no public water supply.

In Lancashire, the magistrates met in 1810, and issued a statement proposing the erection of the new asylum at Liverpool for the rather curious reason that the patients would be able to enjoy 'the beneficial effects of sea air and sea bathing.'[39] The doctors of Liverpool, led by Dr James Gerard, protested strongly against the proposal. They reminded the magistrates that the Liverpool Royal Infirmary already had an asylum attached to it;[40] that, although they had not been consulted about the proposal prior to its publication, they would undoubtedly be expected to assume the responsibility for the extra work involved in prescribing care and treatment for the lunatics of the whole county; and they stated that, in their opinion, the situation should be 'exceedingly retired, and quite in the country'. This was an understandable sentiment. While admitting the necessity for an asylum, they were not pleased at the prospect of having it built in their own immediate vicinity. Another reason was more cogent.

Patients would be sent to the new asylum from all parts of the county, and it was therefore advisable that transportation costs should be equalized as far as possible by building the asylum in a central position. Some thirty or forty doctors wrote in support of Dr Gerard, many of them advancing Chorley or Wigan as suitably 'retired positions'.[41] The asylum was eventually constructed in the northern part of the county, about a mile from Lancaster. It had five acres of grounds and a dairy farm extending over a further ten acres.

In Stafford, the asylum was built next to the county gaol.[42] This arrangement permitted of some degree of common administration between the two institutions, thus minimizing expense. The Society for the Improvement of Prison Discipline reported in 1823 that 'as a source of hard labour, the treadmill is in full operation; it grinds corn for the consumption of the prison and the lunatic asylum, and also for sale.'[43] Stafford Asylum, in spite of its proximity to the prison, had an almost ideal site. It was built on rising ground, and although within a few minutes' walk of the centre of the town, was so enclosed in acres of park and woodland that the situation was both 'retired' and 'airy'.

The asylum at Wakefield was built within easy reach of the centre of the town, and enclosed in twenty-five acres of woodland.

The Cornwall Asylum was erected at Bodmin, on a low-lying and badly-drained site which caused dissatisfaction to the Lunacy Commissioners in the 1840s.[44] The view was 'cheerful' and the grounds were 'extensive', according to Halliday,[45] though a visiting Frenchman later in the century recorded 'les cours sont humides et sombres'.[46]

Most authorities settled the problem by building on the edge of a large town, or two or three miles out into the country. In the days before suburban living became popular, the boundary between the town and the surrounding country was usually sufficiently distinct for a building to be constructed in the latter while still within relatively easy reach of the former. The subsequent spread of the towns has meant that, where the buildings of the old asylums are still in use, they are generally well within the town boundaries.

Problems of administration

Since the visiting justices had no reliable precedents to follow, they inevitably made mistakes in these early days.

A frequent practice at this time was to appoint a superintendent who was paid on a capitation basis, and to leave him to provide out of that sum for the complete upkeep of the establishment. This practice was followed at Nottingham, where the physician was also allowed to accept gratuities from grateful relatives, and to take private patients.[47] At Bodmin, a study of the first minute book of the Cornwall Asylum shows that a particularly difficult series of situations arose. The first superintendent was a surgeon named James Duck, who received 14s. a week for each patient. There were constant disagreements with the visiting justices over matters of finance, he contending that the amount was inadequate, and they, that he was not providing necessities for the patients. Before the Asylum was fully established, Duck resigned, and claimed a large sum of money which he alleged he had spent on furnishing and provisions. The justices refused to meet his claims, and in February 1820 they appointed a Mr Kingdon on the same basis, with the title of 'Governor and Contractor'. This appears to have been a lay appointment. Within four years he too had found the tasks of satisfying the justices and making a profit irreconcilable. In June 1824 a third Governor was appointed, and the financial arrangements were reconsidered. He and his wife, who acted as matron, were given a joint salary of £200 a year, together with accommodation, full board, and all amenities. They were requested to visit Bethlem before taking up office in order to familiarize themselves with the nature of their duties.[48] The justices then proceeded to make five other appointments:

One Head Keeper (Baker & Shaver)	£25
One Keeper and Shoemaker	£20
One Female Head Keeper	£10
One Kitchenmaid	£6
One Labourer by the Week to work in the Garden	

This meant that the Governor was relieved of the responsibilities of engaging staff and of handling the duties usually assigned to a steward. It suggests that former Governors had either appointed no staff except for their own personal domestics, or that the justices had dismissed the previous holders of these posts.

Three years later, in 1827, the visiting justices became aware of another flaw in the terms of appointment of their chief officer. Since they visited the Asylum only at infrequent intervals, they had no real means of supervision, and it was possible for the Governor to absent himself from his duties without leave. On 8 August 1827 the third

Governor appeared before the committee, charged with being absent for ten days. He was allowed to resume his duties on giving a promise of better behaviour in the future, but apparently the humiliation involved was too much for him, as he resigned a few months afterwards.

The justices were then faced with the task of appointing their fourth Governor in seven years. Their experience appeared to have taught them four things about the office of Governor: that the man appointed should have a medical qualification; that he should have some knowledge of work among mental patients; that it was necessary to ensure at the outset that he would remain at his post; and that it was unwise to confuse clinical work with financial administration. Dr L. K. Potts of Bethlem was appointed, and paid a salary for his own use only. He was requested to sign a declaration to the effect that he would abide by the rules drawn up by the committee, including the proviso that he would not absent himself without leave.[49] It would seem that Dr Potts' rule was a beneficent one, since he stayed for some years, and subsequent resolutions concerning the welfare of the patients frequently bore the clause 'at the discretion of Dr Potts'.

At Stafford, the original minute book of the visiting justices shows that the arrangements with regard to senior staff were somewhat different. A physician was appointed on a part-time basis at a salary of £200 a year, and a lay administrative superintendent, who was to be resident, at a salary of £200 and maintenance. The other staff were:

One Matron at £40 and Maintenance.
One Porter with a Suit of Clothes and a Hat, £15.
One Keeper £25.
One Female Keeper £25.

The matron originally appointed was a Mrs White, but her term of office lasted only a few weeks. As soon as he was installed, the superintendent, Mr Garrett, asked permission to house his elderly mother in the asylum. This permission was granted on condition that she should provide all her own fuel and food; the condition was short-lived, for within a very short period Mrs White was dismissed, and the elderly Mrs Garrett installed in her stead. If there was any reason for the abrupt dismissal, apart from the discreet pressure of the superintendent, it was not noted in the minute book.

These cases are quoted as examples of incidents which were typical of many in the early history of the county asylums. They arose partly out of the inexperience of the visiting justices, and partly out of the fact that senior administrative officers were appointed without prescribed experience, qualifications, or a guarantee as to personal integrity.

There is no generic term, apart from the inaccurate and slightly invidious 'asylum doctors' which may be used to describe the small body of men experienced in the treatment of mental disorder at this time. They were not even necessarily medical practitioners. Their views and methods varied from those of Thomas Monro to those of William Tuke. Some of them were quacks, and some of them were highly enlightened men; and the people with whom their work brought them into contact—magistrates, Poor Law officials, clergy, general practitioners and others—rarely had sufficient knowledge to distinguish the one from the other.

These new specialists frequently published books in which they expounded their own systems, but showed no acquaintance with work being done in the same field in other parts of the country. This accounts in part for the extremely uneven development of the new methods.

Mechanical restraint

Since the staff of the average county asylum was so small, it is hardly surprising that both keepers and doctors tended to rely on mechanical restraint as the one method of keeping patients quiet and orderly.

The Act of 1808 laid down no regulations concerning treatment, but it provided statutory penalties against the keepers if patients escaped.[50] These penalties were high, being equivalent to at least one month's wages. The maximum penalty of £10 was a keeper's total wages for five months. As a result, the staffs of county asylums were unwilling to take the slightest risk in allowing a patient liberty of movement; mechanical restraint provided a way of preventing escapes without exercising unremitting supervision. At Bodmin, the visiting justices in 1819 requested one of their number, the Right Hon. Reginald Pole Carew, to apply to the Governors of Bethlem for 'patterns of the different securities necessary for patients' and subsequently ordered '12 padlocks for patients' belts'.[51] At Lancaster, which was a large asylum by contemporary standards, accommodating 150–200 patients,[52] the resident surgeon, Dr Paul Slade Knight, had his own methods of restraint. These he described in his treatise entitled 'Observations on the Causes, Symptoms and Treatment of Derangement of the Mind', which was illustrated with diagrams of the apparatus involved. One illustration shows a leather muff with iron wrist locks at each side in which a patient's hands could be confined, and a variant called the 'pocket muff' in which each hand could be encased separately. A more strict form of coercion was a device consisting of two strong leather sleeves terminating in 'pocket muffs'; the sleeves were fastened across the shoulders by a strap and a lock, and the whole apparatus was connected to leg-locks on the thighs, a chain joining the ankles. It is not known to what extent this crippling device was actually used, but Dr Knight advanced it in his treatise as being considerably more humane than the methods generally employed in asylums and madhouses.

Mention has already been made of the provisions concerning restraint laid down in the rules of the Nottingham Asylum.[53] Restraint at Stafford was also apparently kept to a minimum, since there are few records in the apothecary's day book of its being employed. When the Lunacy Commissioners made their first official visit to this establishment in 1842, they were gratified to find the patients 'tranquil and comfortable, and free from all restraint.'[54]

Diet

The food provided in the early county asylums was very much better than that in gaols and workhouses. A weekly order given at Stafford during this period for a total of sixty-nine persons has these items:

Meat, 264 lb.	£7 3s. 0d.
Cheese, 64 lb.	£2 2s. 8d.
Milk, 119 quarts	£1 9s. 9d.
Beer, 120 gallons, Ale, 5 gallons	£5 0s. 3d.

Bread was made at the county gaol, and therefore does not appear as an item of expenditure. This list of provisions—which was approximately repeated each week—would have supplied each patient and member of staff with a little less than 4 lb. of meat, 1 lb. of cheese, 2 pints of milk and 2 gallons of beer, at a cost of approximately 4s. 8d. per week.

The picture at Lancaster is less encouraging; though, since the asylum had its own farm, it is not possible to reconstruct a true picture of the actual diet from the account books; but the chief expenditure on food at the asylum was that on potatoes, which were ordered so frequently, and in such large quantities, that they must have formed the staple article of diet.

Dr Knight noted in his account book that the total cost of maintaining 176 patients in the first quarter of 1820 was £349—roughly 3s. 1d. a week per head.

Amenities

The patients at Lancaster slept on straw. There is no record of the purchase of beds and bedding prior to the year 1842, when the frequent indents for straw came to an end shortly before the first statutory visit made by the Metropolitan Commissions in Lunacy (see p. 134). The account books show occasional entries for tobacco or snuff, but in fairly small quantities. These may have been purchased for the keepers. Dr Knight's views on the management of patients coincided in the main with those of the Monros at Bethlem: 'I am quite of the opinion that one person only should have undivided authority over the lunatic . . . and that superior person should be his physician.'[55]

Patients were required to help in the kitchen or the garden when fit enough to do so;[56] Halliday noted that Lancaster did not possess a 'manufactory' for the occupation of the patients;[57] they were allowed in their spare time to play ninepins or knit, according to sex.[58]

At Wakefield, Halliday found that the patients were employed at various trades, approximating where possible to their trades in normal life. At Nottingham, Stafford and Gloucester, they worked in kitchen and garden, being 'useful to themselves, and beneficial to the establishment'. At Bodmin, the patients were 'not much employed in any regular manner', but in other respects, the general conditions appeared to Halliday to be above the average. Beds were supplied for all but the 'foul patients', who went to the 'straw room'. The bedsteads were three feet wide for men, and four feet wide for the women, who slept two in a bed. Blankets and sheets were supplied. This asylum, unlike most, had a form of central heating. In January 1817, when the building was in the course of construction, the surveyor was sent to London, 'to ascertain the best means of warming the asylum for £30'. Three years later, there is an entry in the minute book which refers to the pipes 'which circulate hot and cold air to regulate the temperature of the building'. These pipes seem to have been frequently in need of repair, and caused constant concern to the committee in the early days.

Visitation by the visiting justices

A study of the visitors' books of these asylums leaves the impression that official visitation was cursory in the extreme. The main criteria of the justices were cleanliness and quietude. 'Visited the asylum and found all in good order' . . . 'all going on well' . . . 'behaviour satisfactory' . . . 'everything regular and very cleanly'—phrases such as these recur constantly, and criticism or constructive suggestions are very rare. The justices had no complaints to make, provided only that the patients were kept quiet, washed and fed. They did not inquire into methods of treatment, and seem only belatedly to have become aware of deficiencies in such matters as ventilation, bedding, heating, clothing, diet and occupation for the patients when the Act of 1842 made inspection by an independent authority imminent. 'October 17 I saw the Asylum in Desent Order by me J. Hicks'[59] is a typical entry. The phrases used by the justices quickly developed into clichés which meant very little except that they were easily satisfied.

The early county asylums were experimental. Since their only precedents for administration and treatment were those of the prisons and workhouses, it was not to be expected that they would at once reach the status of hospitals. They were understaffed, overcrowded, and run by unqualified staffs under the guidance of generally apathetic and frequently inept local authorities. Nevertheless, they made possible an immense improvement in the conditions of the insane who came under their care, and indirectly influenced the administration of private madhouses, in many of which conditions were still far worse. Legislation did not as yet provide adequate safeguards for the well-being of the patients, and much depended on the ability and integrity of the chief medical officer; but the experiment had been abundantly justified. The principles of non-deterrent treatment and public responsibility had been conclusively established.

Public opinion

The following section deals briefly with the evidence of the written word as shown in the press, periodicals, and medical works on insanity. The picture is admittedly incomplete; but it cannot on that account be omitted, since it contributes something to an understanding of later developments in this field.

The press

London newspapers neither reflected nor developed public opinion to any great extent before 1830, and they therefore had little effect on lunacy reform. They contained only a small space devoted to news, most of their columns being filled with advertisements and trade notices. Their circulation was restricted; the stamp duty of 4d. imposed by the younger Pitt's government was raised in 1826 to 6d.;[60] but though the newspapers played so insignificant a part in the national life, their potentialities were feared by the ruling classes on the grounds that free circulation of information among the uneducated would lead to radicalism and demagogy. Cobbett, in his Tory days, stigmatized the daily journals as 'vehicles of falsehood and bad principles'.[61] Wynn seldom read them, and thought them of no importance.[62] George Rose paid them some attention, but only to ensure that they said what he wanted them to say. Reference has already been made to his employment of 'hireling scribes' in the interests of the Tory party.

The London newspapers were virtually controlled by the two political parties until the third decade of the nineteenth century; favoured papers, such as the *London Evening Post* or *The Times* received subsidies of £200 or £300 a year from the Tories.[63] The Whigs, who theoretically believed in a free press, retaliated by bribing the editor of the *Morning Post*.[64]

In the provinces, in spite of restrictive taxes and the mental limitations of the editors, local newspapers had a greater influence. They provided a forum for the debating of controversial issues, such as the site of a new county asylum, or the discovery of alleged abuses. The most outstanding example of the way in which the press could be used to mould public opinion is that shown in the controversy concerning York Asylum in 1813–15. The *York Herald*, even at a time of national crisis, when every inch of its columns could have been filled twice over with news of the war with France, opened its columns to Best and Higgins, printing the salient arguments on each side without comment and without bias. This was in the highest tradition of responsible journalism. Only once was the editor stung into personal comment—when Best threatened him with an action for libel. On that occasion, his attitude showed that he was proud of his independent position (see p. 73).

The position taken up by the editor of the *York Herald* was typical of a new trend in journalism. Editors realized gradually that they held a special position in the community—that they could influence the course of public action. Even *The Times*—that most conservative of all newspapers in its adherence to the eighteenth-century format—

introduced a leading article. Moreover, it regularly printed reports of parliamentary proceedings and legal cases, thus making the facts known to a wider public.

Periodicals

The foundation of the great nineteenth-century monthly and quarterly reviews provided a more direct means for the dissemination of facts and ideas connected with lunacy reform. Periodicals which dealt from time to time with topics of this nature included the *Gentleman's Magazine*, founded in 1731, the *Edinburgh Review* (1802), the *Quarterly Review* (1809), and the *Westminster Review* (1827). The *Edinburgh Review* in August 1817 published a lengthy article dealing with the progress of reform in the four previous years, concluding: 'It is the duty of every publication that has honestly obtained a great circulation on all occasions to give notoriety to these truths which are in danger of remaining unknown because they are . . . distressing in their details.'

These journals, although catering for a responsible and informed public, tended to stress revelations of neglect and cruelty rather than giving publicity to the unsensational and steady work of improvement. They contained much information about the worst of the private madhouses, but generally ignored the county asylums, where a social experiment of considerable importance was being carried out.

The *Lancet* was founded in 1823 by Thomas Wakley,[65] a member of the Royal College of Surgeons, who later became a member of parliament and Coroner for West Middlesex. Although Wakley later took some interest in lunacy questions, the columns of the *Lancet* in its early years were confined to subjects concerning physical sickness and disease. There was no periodical publication which could be used for discussion and for the dissemination of information about mental treatment on a professional basis.

Medical works on insanity

Works on the nature and treatment of insanity written during this period by members of the medical profession were many in number. John Ferriar's *Medical Histories and Reflections* was published in 1792, Haslam's *Observations on Insanity*—which presented a some-what idealized version of the treatment given at Bethlem—in 1794, and his *Considerations on the Moral Management of Insane Persons* in 1817. Bryan Crowther's *Practical Remarks on Insanity* appeared in 1811, and Paul Slade Knight's *Observations on the Causes, Treatment, etc., of Derangement of the Mind*, in 1827; but many of these works deserve Pinel's comment on Ferriar: 'A careful, impartial examination discloses nothing but vague dissertations, repetitions, compilations, scholastic formality.'[66] The material presented followed a stereotyped pattern, the ideas put forward had an unmistakable air of being second-hand. The publications which contributed most to the progress of mental treatment in the first quarter of the nineteenth century were those which were concerned with the human rather than the medical approach—Samuel Tuke's *Description of the Retreat* and Godfrey Higgins' *Letter to Earl Fitzwilliam*.

Three works written by members of the medical profession which in some degree combined the two approaches deserve special mention —the *Letter to Thomas Thompson, M.P.*[67] written in 1815 by William Ellis, Sir Andrew Halliday's *General View of Lunatics* published in 1828, and George Man Burrows' *Commentary on the Causes, etc., of Insanity*, which appeared in the same year.

Ellis devoted some space in his letter to a consideration of the different forms taken by insanity, recognizing that all mental patients did not exhibit the same symptoms, nor did they necessarily all require the same type of treatment. He also listed some of the factors which impeded the progress of mental treatment: the quackery of some medical men, who specialized in mental cases because the work was lucrative and unexacting; the helplessness of the patients, who were unable to fight their own battles; the insistence of wealthy friends and relatives upon secrecy, and their indifference to the mode of treatment, as long as the patient was kept closely confined; above all, the general belief that insanity necessarily involved an impairment of all the mental faculties: 'It must be observed that patients may be insane on one subject and perfectly sane on all others.' He recommended occupation, fresh air and exercise as the most beneficent factors in curative treatment, and warmly endorsed the system at the Retreat.

Burrows (1771–1846) held an MD from St Andrews, and was the prime mover in the passing of the Apothecaries' Act of 1815. He kept a private asylum at Clapham, significantly named 'The Retreat', at which the standards of care and treatment were high.[68] Though there is an echo of Burton in his statement 'Madness is one of the curses imposed by the wrath of Almighty God on his people for their sins', his attempt to chart the interaction of mental and bodily symptoms was one of the first tentative approaches to psychosomatic medicine. Like Ellis, he deprecated the low standards and high pretensions of certain sections of the medical profession in relation to insanity, and issued a stern injunction to the profession not to be led away by 'psychological disquisitions,[70] German mystifications,[71] and Bedlam sketches . . . calculated to gratify a romantic and prurient taste'.[72]

Burrows divided the causes of insanity into two groups—the 'moral' and the 'physical', and it becomes clear in his work that the former term as used by some writers on insanity at this time, had a specialized meaning. 'Moral' causes were emotional or affective causes, and 'moral treatment' was treatment through the emotions.[73] This was probably not the sense in which the Tukes used the word, since their method of treatment was indispensably bound up with religious and ethical teaching; but the two possible meanings should be borne in mind.

It will be remembered that Sir Andrew Halliday had undertaken an exhaustive statistical compilation on behalf of the Select Committee of 1807. His *General View of Lunatics*, written twenty years later, thus had the backing of a long semi-official association with the cause of lunacy reform, and had a great influence both in his own life-time and after. Halliday, despite his medical qualifications,[74] was associated rather with the parliamentary reformers than with the independent philanthropists or the asylum doctors; as he said of himself:

> I am neither the keeper of a madhouse nor do I practise this
> branch of the profession. . . . I have followed this inquiry from
> a desire to do all the good I could in my humble sphere. Accident
> brought me acquainted with some of the horrors of insanity when
> I had only commenced my medical studies . . . the impression
> made on my mind can never be obliterated.[75]

The fact that Halliday was possessed of high medical qualifications and had no financial association with the treatment of insanity strengthened his authority with the medical profession. Like Ellis, he wanted to break down the barriers of fear and secrecy which still separated the insane from the rest of society.

These three works struck a new note: an interest in insanity not merely from the clinical point of view, but as a social problem. They served to direct the attention of the medical profession away from 'vague dissertations' and 'repetitions', helping to establish a new and constructive approach to the subject.

5 The Metropolitan Commissioners

The Select Committee of 1827

On 13 June 1827 the lunacy question came to the fore again, when a Select Committee was appointed to consider the state of pauper lunatics from the metropolitan parishes. The immediate cause of this action was the renewed investigation by Lord Robert Seymour of the conditions of Warburton's madhouses.

Lord Robert was not a member of the Committee, having retired from parliamentary life some years previously. An old and sick man, he was unable to give evidence in person, but he submitted a written statement to which considerable importance was attached.

The Committee had thirty members, but a quorum of only five. The chairman was a Dorsetshire magistrate named Robert Gordon, who was renowned for his financial acumen,[1] and who appears to have been politically allied to Peel at this time. Gordon enjoyed a brief period of parliamentary prominence in 1827–8, when he was responsible not only for this Committee, and for the two Acts resulting from its report, but also for a committee on the ill-treatment of horses and cattle at Smithfield, which excited great public interest. He became a Lunacy Commissioner after the passing of the 1828 Act, and retained that office until his death in 1864;[2] but after 1828, he appears to have faded from the parliamentary scene, and the leadership of the parliamentary group devolved upon that capable and indefatigable reformer, Lord Ashley.[3] Gordon's speeches show him to have been a man of wide sympathies and a considerable command of language.

Though inexplicably brief, Gordon's period of leadership fulfilled a need. Wynn and Seymour were too old, Ashley too young, to lead the new group. Gordon bridged the gap. His purpose achieved, he seems to have returned after 1828 to less spectacular activities.

Ashley was only twenty-six years of age when he was appointed to this Committee, and had been in parliament for a mere matter of months. This was the first avenue of social reform which engaged his interest, and one in which he continued to work throughout his long life. As a member of the Marlborough family and the heir to an earldom, he was to possess a far greater influence than Gordon had at his command; but during this period of his inexperience, Gordon led, and Ashley followed.

This Select Committee thus provided a remarkable meeting-place for the old reformers and the new—the ageing men of experience and the young men of enthusiasm. For a few brief weeks, Lord Robert Seymour, one of the leaders in the first wave of reform, worked with the young Ashley, who was to bring about the second. The Select Committee was appointed on 13 June, and made its report on 29 June. The report contains a body of evidence concerning the state of pauper lunatics from the metropolis, a statement on the standards of inspection which the Committee thought desirable, and some concrete recommendations. It is thus a more satisfying document than the report of 1807, which contained recommendations with very little evidence, or the reports of 1815–16, which contained a wealth of evidence and no recommendations.

Pauper lunatics at the White House

Warburton had escaped definite censure in 1816; now his madhouses were investigated again, and the so-called 'crib-room cases of Bethnal Green' provided the most startling revelation of conditions since the investigations at Bethlem and York Asylum twelve years earlier.

Mr John Hall, a Guardian of the poor for the parish of St Marylebone, stated that he visited the White House in order to inspect the pauper lunatics from his own parish, whom the parish was maintaining at a cost of nine or ten shillings a week per patient.

There was a little hesitation in showing us the place . . . we found a considerable number of very disgusting objects, a description of pauper lunatics, I should conceive chiefly idiots, in a very small room: they were sitting on benches round the room, and several of them were chained to the wall. The air of the room was highly oppressive and offensive, insomuch that I could not draw my breath. . . .

These were 'the description of patients called the wet patients; they were chiefly in petticoats; the room was exceedingly oppressive from the excrement and the smell which existed there.'

Hall had been told by a discharged patient named William Solomon, who gave evidence separately, that patients were confined to cribs at a very early hour. To verify this, he called at the White House in company with Lord Robert Seymour, also a Guardian, about half-past seven in the evening.

> Mr Jennings (the keeper) refused to let us see the patients; he complained of the visit at such an unseasonable hour; he said he hoped the legislature would protect houses from visits of that sort. Lord Robert looked at his watch, and it was then a quarter before eight. Mr Jennings was pressed three or four times by Lord Robert, and at last he turned round and said, 'Surely you would not wish to see females in their beds at this time of night?' making use of the term 'night'. The answer of Lord Robert was, 'Show us the males.'

Jennings refused, and the Guardians were forced to withdraw. The Marylebone paupers were subsequently removed from the White House, and—for want of a better alternative—sent to Sir Jonathan Miles at Hoxton, with the condition that the house should be open to inspection by day or night.

The surgeon to the parish of St Pancras, who visited the pauper lunatics of that parish from time to time in the White House, stated that there was:

> No observance whatever as to regulation of diet . . . no observance of sending them back to bed when they are sick; I scarcely ever go there but I do not find someone that is lingering about the yard in a half-dying state that ought to be in bed. They are entirely at the mercy of the keepers; and my visit is of no use as a medical visit.

The overseers of St Pancras paid nine shillings per patient, and the surgeon was asked whether an increase in the amount would be likely to lead to better conditions. 'I do not think they would be a bit better off for the increase, the evil is in the system, and that evil begins in the parishes which send them off at once to a house for incurables.'

The Committee then turned its attention to the crib-room cases. Previous witnesses had heard of this room, but had not seen it; positive evidence was given by Mr Richard Roberts, the assistant to the overseers of St George's Hanover Square: 'A crib-room is a place where there are nothing but wooden cribs or bedsteads; cases, in fact, filled with straw and covered with a blanket, in which those unfortunate beings are placed at night; and they sleep most of them naked on the straw, covered with a blanket.'

The details of this type of accommodation were supplied by John Nettle, an ex-patient, who had personally experienced it. The unclean patients were placed in the cribs at three o'clock in the afternoon, their arms and legs secured, and left there until nine o'lock on the following morning. At the week-ends, they were secured at three o'clock on Saturday afternoon, and left there until nine o'clock on Monday. Food was brought to them, and their arms were freed just sufficiently to enable them to eat it. On Monday, they were taken out into the yard, and the accumulated excrement was washed from them with a mop dipped in cold water. When Nettle was convalescent, and freed from the crib-room, he went back to examine the cribs. 'I turned the straw out of some of the cribs, and there were maggots in the bottom of them where the sick men had laid.'

John Dunston, who had testified in 1816, was called to give evidence. He stated that he was a surgeon, and that he attended the White House every other day; Warburton stated that an apothecary lived within three or four hundred yards of the house, and had been repeatedly called in when John Dunston was not available; on closer questioning, however, he was unable to recall the apothecary's name. When he was questioned on the crib-room cases by Robert Gordon, the following dialogue ensued:

If all the violent cases in your establishment are confined from Saturday to Monday, do you consider that an unnecessary confinement?
—I consider it necessary to confine them.
Do you consider it necessary to confine all violent crib patients in your establishment from Saturday night to Monday every week?
—They were not confined under my direction, certainly.
Do you consider it necessary?
(The witness hesitated.)
Do you decline answering the question?
—I do.

The most striking instance of evasion and falsehood was that provided by Mr Cordell, John Dunston's 'occasional assistant', best told in Gordon's subsequent speech to the House of Commons:

> This person was asked whether any register was kept of the state
> of the patients. He replied, 'Yes, we have the most perfect
> register you can conceive, it is an account of the treatment and
> condition of every patient, moral and medical: it is, for accuracy
> neatness, a perfect . . . pattern. We can trace the illness of every
> patient for six or seven years, and we can find a statement of
> every prescription written for him, and every circumstance
> attending the progress of his malady.' Would the House believe
> that there was not one word of truth in this statement? Could
> they believe that it was wholly false? Yet so it was.[4]

After making the statement mentioned, Cordell was sent for by the
Committee a second time.

> Are we to understand that all you have said to us is correct?
> —Yes, very probably. (A laugh).
> Is the story of the book?
> —No.
> Which are we to believe—what you have to-day told us, or
> your previous statement?
> —Take your choice. (A laugh).
> He then admitted that it was all false.'[5]

Standards of the Commissioners, 1827

A footnote to the conditions at the White House is provided by the
evidence of two Commissioners who were still operating under the
defective Act of 1774. Dr Grant David Yates said that he understood
the mode of management to be merely for confinement, not cure. Dr
Alexander Frampton considered the White House to be 'excellently
regulated . . . a very good house'. He agreed that there was no glass in
the windows, but that was 'usual' in institutions of this kind. He had
no objection to the establishment.

> Have you ever seen any county lunatic asylum?
> —I have not.
> You have not thought it part of your duty . . . either to
> examine New Bedlam or to examine any lunatic asylum in order
> to form a comparative view of the treatment at Mr Warburton's
> and those other establishments near London?
> —I have not examined any of those asylums.

How many visitations do you make to each (madhouse) in the course of a year?

—Seldom more than one.

Standards of the parliamentary reformers, 1827

Appendix III of the report was particularly valuable. It consisted of a detailed list of 'Inquiries relative to Lunatic Asylums and the Treatment of the Insane', tabulated by the parliamentary reformers, which showed how far the theory of lunacy administration had advanced in more enlightened circles than those frequented by the Commissioners. The suggested inquiries are here given at some length because they give a clear picture of the kind of asylum people like Gordon and Ashley had in mind as the ideal:

On accommodation:
Is the separation of the sexes complete?
Are the dormitories properly ventilated?
Are the courtyards airy and dry . . . do they afford some prospect over the walls?
Are there complete baths for hot and cold water?
On physical care of the patients:
What steps are taken to ensure the personal cleanliness of the patients, particularly of the most unclean?
How often is bathing insisted on generally?
Is the practice of daily exercise . . . insisted on with all patients able to partake of it?
On occupation:
How far has manual labour been adopted with advantage, and with what description of patients?
Has the active engagement of the mind to the sciences, fine arts, literature or mechanical arts been attempted with patients of a superior description, and what has been the result?
Where graver studies would be unsuitable, has it been found beneficial to afford patients such employments as are calculated to engage the attention to external objects . . . such, for example, as drawing, painting, designs, models, gardening, etc.?
Where the mind is so diseased as to be evidently unfit for the foregoing exercises, has benefit been experienced by furnish-

ing the patients in their courtyards with means of innocent amusement, from music, domestic animals, poultry, birds, flowers, and objects of a similar nature?

Is it the opinion of the superintendent that a state of entire indolence and mental inertness is decidedly prejudicial to the patient?

On moral treatment:

In the moral treatment of the patients, is it considered an object of importance to encourage their own efforts of self-restraint in every possible way, by exciting and cherishing in them feelings of self-respect, by treating them with delicacy, more especially in avoiding any improper exposure of their cases before strangers in their own presence; and generally by maintaining towards them a treatment uniformly judicious and kind, sympathizing with them, and at the same time diverting their minds from painful and injurious associations?

This questionnaire was apparently sent to asylum authorities, though there was at that time no statutory power to compel them to answer. Dr E. P. Charlesworth's book, *Considerations on the Moral Management of Insane Persons*, published in 1828, consists of the answers given at the Lincoln Asylum, where he was then a physician.

The influence of the Retreat is clearly to be seen in the formulation of these questions; however difficult it might be to universalize the Tukes' system of treatment, it was set as the ideal towards which institutions of every type must strive. The reformers were no longer concerned only with material standards of well-being—cleanliness, order, and quietude; though the second part of the report showed that even these minimum requirements were lacking in Warburton's treatment of the lunatic poor at Bethnal Green.

Results of the investigation

The conclusions to be drawn from this mass of evidence were clear: 'If the White House is to be taken as a fair specimen of similar establishments, your committee cannot too strongly or too anxiously express their conviction that the greatest possible benefit will accrue to pauper patients by the erection of a County Lunatic Asylum.'

The result was the construction of the large Middlesex Asylum at

Hanwell, which afterwards absorbed most of the insane poor from the metropolitan area.

It was also clearly necessary that legal provision should be made for more stringent inspection, and above all for more efficient and experienced inspectors. The parliamentary reformers were determined to remove the inspectorate from the sphere of the Royal College of Physicians, which had proved incompetent, and to assume the responsibility themselves. These aims were achieved in the following year.

The Acts of 1828

The Acts dealt respectively with private madhouses and with county asylums. The County Asylums Act (9 Geo. IV c. 40), was largely a consolidating measure, but it provided in addition for a certain degree of centralization. Visiting justices were to send annual returns of admissions, discharges and deaths to the Secretary of State for the Home Department, who acquired the power to send any visitor he chose to inspect any asylum. Such visitors were to be paid a fee out of the asylum funds. This link with the Home Department was the first step towards bringing all institutions for the insane under one form of administration.

The Madhouse Act (9 Geo. IV c. 41) also simplified the administrative structure, since it covered not only private madhouses, but also all subscription hospitals with the exception of Bethlem.

The Act did not abolish the distinction between metropolitan and provincial houses, but it removed the power of inspecting the former from the jurisdiction of the medical profession and placed it under that of a statutory authority. The number of Commissioners was increased to fifteen. Five of these were to be physicians who were to be paid at the rate of £1 per hour; the others were to be unpaid. All were to be appointed by the Secretary of State for the Home Department, and were to make an annual report to him. They were to visit each asylum four times a year. They could visit at night if malpractice had been alleged on oath. They were to meet quarterly for the purpose of granting licences, and were given power to recommend to the Secretary of State for the Home Department that certain licences should be revoked or refused. They could release any person who was in their estimation improperly confined.

Similar provisions applied to the visiting justices in the provinces, where two justices and a medical visitor appointed at Quarter

Sessions were to visit each house four times yearly, and to submit a report to the Home Department.

The Act also provided for a more detailed form of certification of patients, designed to obviate the possibility of illegal detention.

Pauper patients were to be admitted on the signature of two justices or of the parish overseer, the incumbent of the parish, and one medical practitioner.

The Act did not introduce any specific provisions with regard to treatment, save that it ensured that each house should have regular medical attention. All establishments containing more than one hundred patients were to have a resident medical officer. Those containing less than a hundred patients were to be visited by a medical practitioner not less than twice a week. Proprietors were to keep records which could be inspected by the visitors (i.e., the Commissioners or the visiting justices). Schedule B of the Act gives the details of the returns which were required. They included the number of curable patients in the house, differentiated by sex, the number of those judged to be incurable, details of those under restraint, and general remarks on patients' conditions. Restraint was only to be imposed by the order of the medical attendant, who might be a physician, a surgeon, or an apothecary.

Divine service was to be performed every Sunday in the presence of the patients[6] and the relative or friend on whose authority the proceedings for certification had been initiated was obliged to visit the patient twice a year, or to appoint someone to carry out this duty for him. Records of certification, admission, and death or discharge of patients were to be kept, and to be forwarded annually to the Commissioners or the justices in metropolitan and provincial areas respectively.

The new commissioners at work

The first Commissioners appointed under the 1828 Madhouse Act took office in the same year. Eleven of them were members or ex-members of parliament, and five were medical practitioners. The chairman was Lord Granville Somerset, and other members included Robert Gordon, Lord Ashley, Lord Robert Seymour, Charles Williams-Wynn, and Sir George Henry Rose. As might be expected, they took their duties seriously. The reports made by them to the Secretary of State in 1830 show that even in the space of two years their vigilant inspection had brought about a great change in conditions. Of the notorious White House, they were able to report that they were 'much gratified with the general condition of the House . . . Mr Warburton has devoted much pains to the improvement of this establishment, and the result is highly creditable.'

A study of the Commissioners' first reports shows that they did in fact abide by the standards laid down in the 1827 Report, and that their inspection was highly effective. Madhouse proprietors who had flouted the spirit, if not the letter, of the law since 1774, seem to have recognized that they could no longer do so, and that the only alternative to compliance with the Commissioners' demands was a total loss of livelihood.

Although the system worked well, and resulted in an improvement of standards inside the metropolitan madhouses, the reformers were not satisfied that it dealt adequately with the question of possible illegal detention. Medical representation among the Commissioners had been safeguarded, but legal representation had not, and the legal aspects of insanity had been largely ignored. An Act passed in 1832 (2 and 3 Will. IV c. 107) redressed the balance by stating that at least two of the Commissioners must be barristers, and by removing the inspectorate from the jurisdiction of the Secretary of State to that of the Lord Chancellor. This last was in some ways a retrogressive step, since it decreased the immediate possibility of a centralized and uniform control. County asylums continued to be under the supervisory authority of the Secretary of State.

After 1832, there were still five separate ways in which insane people might be confined, and it may be useful at this point to recapitulate them:

1. In private madhouses under Gordon's Act and the Act of 1832. The departmental authority was the Lord Chancellor's Office.
2. In county asylums under the second of Gordon's Acts, the ultimate control being that of the Home Department.
3. In workhouses, controlled until 1834 by the local authorities, and after that date by the Poor Law Commissioners.
4. In Bethlem, which was still exempt from all legal supervision.
5. As single lunatics. The Madhouse Act of 1828 contained provision for the compilation of a list of single lunatics, but this clause was so hedged about with precautions and restrictions to ensure secrecy that it remained virtually a dead letter.

Thus, even as late as 1842, we still have to deal with five distinct systems of administration, the possible relationship between which was only dimly recognized. Before turning to the final movement which led to the establishment of a central control, it is necessary to discuss briefly the developments which took place in each category between 1832 and 1842.

Private madhouses

Although private madhouses in the London area had greatly improved in character, the situation, especially with regard to problems of illegal detention, was still far from satisfactory. Mention can only be made here of a few of the outstanding cases which excited the public attention during this period.

John Mitford, Esq., of London produced about 1830 two pamphlets—*The Crimes and Horrors of Warburton's Private Madhouse* and *The Crimes and Horrors of Kelly House*. These publications, couched in lurid and unrestrained language, clearly catered for the sensation-seeking public. It is significant that the details given by the author were almost entirely sexual in character.

A more serious publication was Richard Paternoster's *The Madhouse System*—a series of sketches published in pamphlet form in 1841. Paternoster was a man of good education—he claimed to have been a civil servant in Madras—and the sketches are peppered with classical allusions. The work is bitter, sometimes abusive, and clearly biased, but it shows a vehement preoccupation with the subject of civil liberty which lifts it out of the class of merely sensational literature.

Paternoster was confined in Finch's madhouse in London in 1838 on the representation of his father, who wished to defraud him of a sum of money. Having some apprehension of this, he had taken the precaution of depositing the money with an attorney in Chancery Lane, some time before his seizure. He was captured by violence, and deprived of any contact with the outside world. The keeper in whose charge he was placed was a man who had been convicted five years previously for homosexual offences. Paternoster had journalistic connections; his friends notified the police, the Commissioners and the press. Nevertheless, it took six full weeks for him to be freed according to the due process of law.

The picture of conditions in the London madhouses given in this pamphlet is very different from that give by the Commissioners. At Finch's house, he alleged, the linen was foul, the food revolting, restraint and cold baths were commonly used as methods of intimidation, and the answer to every complaint was: 'It's your delusion.' At Brooke House, Clapton, which was owned by Thomas Monro,[7] Paternoster reported that 'the coercive system is in full force, as might be expected from the cruel, brutal system of the owner, whose conduct to the patients in Bedlam had so often been a matter of enquiry and comment.'

Warburton had a thousand patients in all, and personally supervised none of them. Even George Man Burrows, owner of the Clapham Retreat, was an absentee proprietor (see pp. 99-100).

How can Paternoster's account be reconciled with the Commissioners' reports? The Commissioners were men skilled in the detection of abuse, and long experienced in the possibility of malpractice so that it is hard to believe that they were so fully deceived as Paternoster would imply. He was, of course, a man embittered by his own experience; and he was a journalist. Moreover, having no previous experience of the subject of mental illness, he was probably unprepared for the manifestations which frequently accompany it. Nevertheless, his pamphlet pointed to the need for continuous and unceasing vigilance on the part of the Commissioners.

The case of Lewis Phillips is a more fully authenticated instance of abuse, since it was recounted in the House of Commons by Thomas Duncombe,[8] and uncontested.

Phillips was a prosperous London business man, a partner in a firm of glass and lamp manufacturers. On 16 March 1838, at the suggestion of one of his patrons (whose name is not revealed) he presented himself at Buckingham Palace in an attempt to secure the patronage of the young Queen Victoria. There had been an attempt on the life of the Queen a few weeks before, and the palace guards were suspicious. Phillips, who was evidently a hot-tempered man, expostulated with them, and was finally arrested on a charge of attempting to force an entry to the royal quarters.

His lawyer, hastily summoned, was able to convince the authorities of his client's respectable standing, and Phillips was released; at this juncture he made the fundamental mistake of returning to the palace in order to make trouble for the person who had caused his arrest. He was again arrested on the same charge, taken to Bow Street, and thence removed on a magistrate's warrant 'in a hackney coach, closely guarded' to one of Warburton's houses.

He remained at Bethnal Green for six months. He had no knowledge of why he had been sent to the palace on a false pretext, who was responsible for his arrest, or why he had been sent to an asylum. Although the law required that his order of committal should be signed by at least one doctor who had no financial connection in the establishment concerned, he had been examined only by Warburton. He received no visitors, and was allowed no communication with the outside world.

The Lunacy Commissioners made their statutory round of inspection, but the patients were intimidated in advance. Phillips alleged that a woman who ventured a complaint was subsequently beaten severely by the head attendant, who afterwards reappeared with the words 'That has cured her of complaining.'

Moreover, Phillips claimed that the staff of the madhouse went to extraordinary lengths to turn his brain. On the day of the Queen's coronation, he stated.

> some strange female was actually introduced to your
> petitioner dressed in paltry imitation of our Sovereign, to induce
> your petitioner to believe that it was her Gracious Majesty . . . the
> officers, both medical and otherwise, assisted in this nefarious
> scheme . . . your petitioner has suffered the torture of mind and
> body through the acts and filthy observations and questions, too
> disgusting to be mentioned. . . .

At this juncture, the motive force behind his confinement became clear. Lewis Phillips received a visit from his cousins and partners in the firm—Ralph and Samuel Phillips. They offered to secure his release, arrange his passage to Antwerp, and to provide him with a small allowance—all on condition that he signed away his interest in the family business. Evidently they had been responsible for the entire sequence of events.

Rather than remain indefinitely in the hands of Dr Warburton, Phillips signed, and took the passage to Antwerp; but within a few days he was back in London, determined to have his legal rights. Dr Warburton was hastily notified, and at night two keepers arrived at Phillips' house to take him back to the madhouse:

> Your petitioner, having endured so much misery, was fully
> prepared for any design that might show itself, and seeing the
> manoeuvres, immediately forced his way out of the house, crying
> 'Murder', the keepers hallooing out 'Stop, thief!'

Phillips escaped—by what means, he does not say—and succeeded eventually in indicting all the parties concerned in his detention for conspiracy. The matter was finally settled out of court for £170.

The Phillips case, more than any other, proved that in spite of the new safeguards which looked so effective on paper, cases of illegal detention could and did still occur. Both Phillips and Paternoster were men of resourcefulness and good education who succeeded in making their wrongs public knowledge; but it was disquieting to reflect that there might be many other cases in which the victim was not able to conduct his own defence. Improved methods of certification and inspection were still an urgent necessity.

County asylums

After 1828, the county asylums, which had hitherto been few in number and widely misunderstood as to purpose, gradually emerged as the most significant factor in the development of lunacy reform. Hitherto, pioneer work had been done by voluntary effort—at the Manchester Lunatic Hospital, at the Retreat. Now the impetus came from Lincoln and Hanwell.

The non-restraint movement

In these two asylums developed the theory and practice of non-restraint, which carried 'moral management' to the logical extreme of stating that no patient should be subject to mechanical restraint at any time, whatever his condition. The system was never adopted at the Retreat, where the Tukes always insisted on a minimum of restraint in violent cases in order to protect the patient himself and those around him; but at Lincoln and Hanwell, the system was carried out in full, and enjoyed for some years the attention of those who were seeking more enlightened methods of treatment for insanity.

During the period 1828–42, eight further asylums were constructed in England, as follows:[9]

Asylum	Accommodation
Chester	110
Dorset	113
Kent	300
Middlesex	1000
Norfolk	470
Suffolk	591
Surrey	—
Leicester	104

The Middlesex Asylum at Hanwell was thus the largest in the country, being nearly twice the size of the next largest, those at Lancaster (now accommodating 600 patients) and Suffolk (591). The experiment in non-restraint began at Lincoln, which was comparatively small, treating only 72 patients in 1829 and 130 in 1837,[10] when the total abolition of restraint was finally achieved. The subsequent adoption of the system at Hanwell, which served the metropolitan area and now took most of those pauper patients who had formerly been confined in Warburton's madhouses, thus meant the development of the experiment on a much wider scale, and attracted a proportionate amount of public attention.

D. H. Tuke makes the point that to speak of 'non-restraint' in this context is inaccurate, since confinement in an asylum is always restraint of a kind.[11] Moreover, in those asylums where 'non-restraint' was practised, it was permissible for the attendants to hold down violent patients with their hands, or to place them in solitary confinement.[12] 'Non-restraint' is therefore used here only in the limited sense in which it was used at Lincoln and Hanwell—to imply the non-use of mechanical devices which hindered the patients' bodily movements.

This policy was commenced at Lincoln by one of the three visiting physicians, Dr Charlesworth, who gradually reduced the instances of the use of restraint between 1829 and 1835. Restraint was totally abolished by the house surgeon, Mr Robert Gardiner Hill, between 1835 and 1838. Since much time and energy were wasted by these two officials in fruitless argument as to which should claim the merit of having introduced the system, it is necessary to set out here the basis on which their respective claims were made:[13]

1829–35: Under the supervision of Dr Charlesworth

Year	Patients	No. restrained	Total instances of restraint
1829	72	39	1727
1830	92	54	2364
1831	70	40	1004
1832	81	55	1401
1833	87	44	1109
1834	109	45	447
1835	108	28	323

These figures, taken together, show that the real move towards the

E

substantial reduction of the use of restraint started in 1834, when the number of patients restrained was for the first time less than 50% of the total number of patients, and the number of instances of restraint per patient restrained fell by one-half.

In the first three years of Gardiner Hill's work at Lincoln, the figures were as follows:

1836–38: Under the supervision of Mr Gardiner Hill

Year	Patients	No. restrained	Total instances of restraint
1836	115	12	39
1837	130	2	3
1838	———————— all restraint abolished ————————		

Thus, within twelve months of taking up his position, Gardiner Hill improved on Charlesworth's work, and within three years he carried it to its logical, though possibly unforeseen, conclusion.

When Gardiner Hill arrived at Lincoln in 1836, the methods of restraint still in use included boot hobbles, which fastened the feet to the end of the bed and prevented the patient from shifting his position; and a belt and wristlocks similar to those designed by Dr Slade Knight for use at Lancaster.

Gardiner Hill realized that it was impossible merely to abolish all restraint without providing other means for quieting noisy or violent patients. He induced the Governors to increase the staff, and also to increase the remuneration, so that it would be possible to recruit relatively intelligent and well-trained nurses. He looked especially for tall, strong attendants whose physique would in itself deter patients from violence. He instituted a continuous night watch on the dormitories, and decreed that all patients should have abundant exercise, with the object of reducing violence by the effect of sheer exhaustion. All fermented liquor was banned from the institution—in opposition to the practice at the Retreat, where copious draughts of porter were held to have a calming influence.

This system undoubtedly helped the patients. Experience at Bethlem after 1815 and at the Retreat had already shown that many patients could be restored to quietude and cleanliness by sudden freedom from restraint. Pinel found the same thing in France. Gardiner Hill's real departure from precedent lay in the fact that he openly abolished restraint even for suicidal and homicidal patients, and worked without the threat of restraint to reinforce discipline as a last resort.

One alternative to the use of mechanical restraint was, of course, the use of drugs to quiet patients, but this too was avoided at Lincoln after 1835: 'Every deviation from this principle should be immediately checked,' wrote Gardiner Hill, 'that neither unnecessary force nor drugs nor the douche nor the bath of surprise nor prolonged shower nor other baths be employed as substitutes . . . they form no part of the system of non-restraint.'

He published in his book a letter said to have been written by a female patient to a friend, which gave an encouraging picture of the conditions at Lincoln:

> I am in the wards up and down, where there are 33 female patients. I have not seen a strait-waistcoat nor yet leather sleeves, nor leg-locks nor muzzles nor other sorts of confinements. Say or do what you will, there is no fault found. The nurses all seem very loving and dutiful to the patients. If your finger only aches, the House Surgeon attends several times a day; and at night, if he sees any of them unruly, he orders a nurse to sit up with them. The bedrooms are carpeted (feather beds, most of them with hangings), wash-stands, basins, towels, looking-glass, comb and brush, and a nurse to attend us. We have tea twice a day, and as much toast as we can eat—milk and bread for our supper, meat dinners every day, and different sorts of puddings. The Matron of the Asylum stands at the table, and asks whether we are all satisfied, and if anyone wants more, she orders a nurse to bring it. She wishes to see us all comfortable. We go to bed at eight o'clock; we have nothing to do only to walk in the gardens twice a day, and cards to play, and other sorts of exercises. I never was better off since I left my parents.

This system, while ideal for the average patient, imposed a tremendous strain on the attendants, who ran some physical risk and were responsible for a continuous and uninterrupted surveillance of all patients; but it had one great advantage: the removal of the pressure of fear.

The Charlesworth-Gardiner Hill controversy

It would be unnecessary to recall the facts of this unresolved and protracted argument were it not for the fact that the dispute reached far beyond the bounds of Lincoln, and thus gave the new system more publicity than it would otherwise have received. It continued until 1853, and ended in the collection of rival subscriptions for Gardiner Hill and Charlesworth. The former was presented with a silver épergne, the centre-piece being engraved with the statement that he alone was responsible for the introduction of the system of non-restraint. Dr Charlesworth's supporters contented themselves with the erection in the grounds of Lincoln Asylum of a statue bearing a similar inscription.

Many medical men were involved in the controversy, and Sir Alexander Morison, physician of Bethlem, and former physician to the Surrey Asylum, earned general opprobrium by contributing to both funds. A lengthy controversy raged in the *Lancet* from 1850 to 1853; the *Medical Circular* accused the *Lancet* of receiving bribes, alleging that an article written by the Charlesworth faction had been published on receipt of a monetary payment. The *Lancet* referred to the *Medical Circular* as a 'scurrilous medical print', and stated that the charges were 'base and unfounded'. The *Medical Circular* then accused the editor of the *Lancet* of 'a career of habitual corruption.'

Most of the events here referred to fall outside the period immediately under review, but it is necessary to mention them in order to illustrate the widespread stir which the matter caused. Gardiner Hill delivered a lecture on 'The total abolition of personal restraint in the treatment of the insane' to a lay and medical audience at the Mechanics' Institute in Lincoln in June 1838, and the lecture was afterwards published, forming the basis of his book. To quote Gardiner Hill's account of the subsequent furore:

> Public attention was soon aroused, as well it might be, to the subject . . . indeed for many years I was stigmatized as one bereft of reason myself, a speculator, peculator, and a practical breaker of the sixth commandment by exposing the lives of the attendants to the fury of the patients.

The system was called 'a piece of contemptible quackery, a mere bait for the public ear'. Opposition grew in fact even among the Asylum Governors, so that Gardiner Hill was ultimately compelled to resign his appointment. 'In fact, it was impossible to remain. The attendants were encouraged in acts of disobedience, and all control was lost. Had I retained my appointment, I must have sacrificed my principles.'

Gardiner Hill returned to private practice. He remained in the vicinity of Lincoln, and in 1852 became Mayor of the city.

Non-restraint at Hanwell

Dr John Conolly went to Hanwell Asylum in 1839. Hanwell was by far the largest establishment for the insane in the country, and Conolly already possessed a great reputation in medical circles. He had studied in Edinburgh, practised in general medicine at Chichester and Stratford-on-Avon, becoming Mayor of Stratford. He had also been appointed Professor of the Practice of Medicine in the University of London, but relinquished this post after two years for private practice.

His acceptance of the Hanwell appointment may be explained in various ways. The human reaction is that he disliked academic circles in London and preferred to live in the Stratford area, where he was well-known and appreciated. Sir George Thane, of University College Hospital, London, had another theory:[14] 'In spite of the friendship of Lord Brougham, Lord John Russell, and other very influential men, John Conolly failed in practice as a London physician, nor does it appear that his duties were performed with any distinguished ability.' Thane judged him as 'essentially unscientific'— a good administrator, but a sentimental humanist unfitted for the detached and painstaking work of medical research.

Thane was speaking from the viewpoint of the fashionable physician and the medical research worker, so that his prejudice against Conolly, who deserted this desirable post for a branch of medicine only partially accepted and of doubtful antecedents, is perhaps only to be expected; but Conolly's interest in the treatment of the insane was not a new factor in his life, nor was it, as Thane implied, an avenue of escape from a sphere in which he had been proved a failure. Conolly's MD thesis, presented at Edinburgh in 1821, bore the title 'De statu mentis in Insania et Melancholia', and he had published his *Inquiry Concerning the Indications of Insanity* in 1830, the year in which he abandoned his academic post. The very qualities which made him unsuitable, in Thane's eyes, for the practice of general medicine, were admirably suited to the work of a medical administrator in a large asylum.

Before taking up his appointment at Hanwell, Conolly visited Lincoln and undertook a thorough investigation of the methods used there, and their results.[15] This apparently convinced him that the system was workable on a large scale. In his book *On the Treatment of Insanity*, he described the steps he took to translate Lincoln's experience at Hanwell. On 1 July he required from the officials at Hanwell a daily return of all patients kept under restraint, and within seven weeks from that time, he had totally abolished restraint:

> The coercion-chairs (forty in number) have been altogether removed from the walls . . . several patients formerly consigned to them, silent, stupid and sinking into fatuity, may now be seen cheerfully moving about the walls or airing-courts; and there can be no question that they have been happily set free from a thraldom of which one constant and lamentable consequence was the acquisition of uncleanly habits.[16]

Conolly, like Gardiner Hill, realized that the abolition of restraint was only one factor in a new approach to the insane. If it was to be carried out successfully, it demanded a high standard of nursing and administrative staff, and the development of new ways of occupying the patients. Working in conjunction with the asylum chaplain, the Rev. John May, he established classes in reading and writing for the illiterate, and in drawing, singing and geography for the literate. This was the first experiment in England in the organized education of patients as part of their treatment and rehabilitation. Unfortunately, the wishes of Conolly and May were frustrated by the visiting committee, which—some forty years before the introduction of universal education—considered such a measure an unnecessary expense. 'Many sources of happiness, of mental composure and, as I believe, of means auxiliary to recovery, were . . . arbitrarily cut off,' wrote Conolly.[17]

Conolly was in many ways ahead of his time. Among the suggestions made by him to his committee were two which have only come into universal application in the twentieth century. These were:

1. Clinical instruction in the treatment of mental abnormality to be carried out in the asylum for qualified medical practitioners intending to specialize in this type of work. Instruction of this kind was already carried out at St Luke's, but the stream of St Luke's-trained men was totally inadequate to meet the needs of a developing service. Most asylum doctors took up their appointments with no more than a training in general medicine, which did not include any work in the rapidly-developing science of psychiatry. Hanwell, with its large number of beds, would have provided an admirable

place for a training-school, especially in view of the fact that Conolly himself had experience in university teaching.

2. A 'place of education' for male and female keepers. Conolly was among the first to propound the view that the possession of a powerful physique and good intentions was not enough, and that the nursing of the mentally ill should be a skilled profession.

The committee negatived these suggestions, presumably on the grounds of expense, and Conolly was forced to work within the framework dictated by them.

Staff problems in county asylums

Not all asylums were as fortunate as Hanwell in their medical superintendent. Caleb Crowther, in his *Observations on the Management of Madhouses*[18] raised an important question: were the prevailing conditions of appointment such that superintendents were encouraged to exercise their powers in a responsible manner? He came to the conclusion that they were not—that in most cases the superintendents were so well paid and their duties so loosely defined that they tended to mix socially with the landed gentry and to ignore their real duties.

The election of the superintendent was in the hands of the visiting committee, which was of course drawn mainly from the landed gentry of the neighbourhood. It was therefore natural that they should appoint one of their own kind where possible, and that the superintendent should exert himself to remain in social contact with them. The conditions of his appointment in many cases made this only too easy. He was commonly required to be resident in the asylum, and was provided with everything he could need for normal living—food, light, fuel, servants and furniture. He could entertain on a large scale out of the asylum funds, and received in addition a generous salary. The resident director of the Wakefield Asylum received £550 a year for himself and his wife, plus services valued at not less than £400 a year. He was thus in receipt of a gross salary of nearly £1000 per annum at a time when a living wage was well under £1 per week.

The visiting committee of the Cornwall Asylum had exerted itself to prevent its chief officer from absenting himself without authority, but in other asylums the superintendent was frequently away from duty. Crowther cited a case at the Wakefield Asylum in 1833. A suicidal patient named Ackroyd seized a razor and killed himself; it was stated at the inquest that the director had been away at the time, and that no orders had been given to the staff for the supervision of suicidal patients. When the coroner inquired whether such absences were usual, he was told that the director was '. . . very often from home, sometimes for weeks together . . . sometimes on the Rhine, sometimes with the fox-hounds, and very often in the streets of Leeds or Wakefield.'

It was still the common practice for the matron to be the wife of the superintendent. While this made for simplicity of administration, it was from other points of view highly undesirable. It meant that experienced female staff were controlled by an inexperienced woman who combined a nominal post with marriage and the begetting and rearing of children, and who also shared the social round to which her husband's social position entitled her. Unless she was a very exceptional woman, she was likely to have neither the aptitude nor the inclination to exercise efficient supervision over the female side of the asylum.

Crowther wrote in 1838; it may have been partly as a result of his work that when the Surrey Asylum was opened in 1841, the visiting committee drew up rules which attempted to define the duties of the superintendent and the matron, and to ensure that those duties were fully carried out.[19] The superintendent was to be a qualified medical man—a surgeon or an apothecary; he was to be resident in the asylum, and to absent himself only with the consent of the visiting committee. His post was to be a full-time one, and he was forbidden to undertake private practice. He was to visit all the patients (there were 350 when the asylum opened) every day; to keep case-books; to report to the committee on every case of the use of restraint or seclusion; to control the attendants and staff; and to read prayers without fail morning and evening. His salary was £150 a year.

No qualifications were prescribed for the matron, since there was of course no appropriate qualification that a woman might possess; but she was preserved to some extent from the pitfalls of a life of luxury by the provision that she must visit all the female wards before ten o'clock in the morning, attend prayers morning and evening, and be responsible for the employment and conduct of the female staff. Her salary was £80 a year.

The problem of ensuring that the keepers fulfilled their duties adequately was also a difficult one. Crowther stated that dysentery was general in asylums because the cleaning of dirty patients was left to other patients, who ignored the most elementary principles of hygiene. There were many ways in which the attendants could avoid the more unpleasant aspects of their duties—by employing the quieter patients to do the work for them, by using intimidation, mechanical restraint or seclusion, or by simply putting troublesome patients to bed for long periods. This last practice had been exposed in Bethlem and the private madhouses, but it apparently continued to some degree in the county asylums. Dr Browne, in his book, *What Asylums Were, Are, and Ought to Be*, published in 1837, pointed out that the generally-accepted proportion was that of one keeper to thirty patients, and that it was impossible under such circumstances for the patients to be adequately cared for. He related a case in which a visitor inquired after a certain patient, and received from the keeper the reply: 'Oh, Mr D. is perfectly quiet, he has been standing on his head for the last half hour.' He also made the point that while keepers were so few in number, they naturally tended to remain together for company and safety rather than walking singly about the wards. He referred to the keepers as 'the unemployed of other professions . . . if they possess physical strength and a tolerable reputation for sobriety, it is enough and the latter quality is frequently dispensed with. They enter upon their duties altogether ignorant of what insanity is.'

Again the Surrey Asylum's committee provided detailed rules to overcome the worst of these abuses. The attendants were to rise at 6 a.m., to 'wash and comb' the patients, to report any illness, and to attend prayers. At 8 a.m., they were to serve breakfast, and to proceed to clean the sleeping-rooms, personally removing any foul straw or linen. They were to serve other meals at specified times, to attend the patients at intervals during the day, and to attend evening prayers at 9.30 p.m. 'The attendants are forbidden to strike or otherwise ill-treat the patients . . . on pain of IMMEDIATE DISMISSAL.'

In 1844, Sir Alexander Morison, the visiting physician, succeeded in instituting lectures for male and female attendants, in which he 'endeavoured to communicate in a familiar and . . . intelligible manner, the principles on which our conduct towards the insane ought to be regulated.'[29]

Morison was thus the first to carry Conolly's idea into effect. Prizes were awarded to attendants whose conduct was judged meritorious, in order to provide them with an incentive for carrying out their duties well. The first steps were being taken to overcome the abuses of the existing staffing system, and to raise the status of mental nursing to that of a profession.

Lunatics under the Poor Law

The position of the pauper lunatic in a workhouse was in many cases an increasingly unhappy one. After 1834, the parish poorhouse—that relic of the old Elizabethan Poor Law—was gradually superseded. With it went diversity of administration, and the last vestiges of that medieval ideal of charity which was akin to love. From the passing of the Poor Law Amendment Act of 1834, the twin watchwords were uniformity and deterrence. It is significant that the Report of the Poor Law Commissioners which preceded the framing of the Act dealt almost entirely with the problem presented by the able-bodied pauper who would not work, largely ignoring the plight of those who could not. The Commissioners complained that 'the diet of the workhouse almost always exceeds that of the cottage'[21] and claimed that 'by the means which we propose, the line between those who do and those who do not need relief is drawn perfectly.'[22] The means proposed, and carried into effect with efficiency, were those which have been summed up in the principle of 'less eligibility.'

The number of lunatics and idiots in workhouses in 1828 was estimated at 9000.[23] In 1845, despite the increase in the provision of county asylums and the growth of the practice of 'contracting out', there were still 4080.[24] Thus developed the anomalous position of a law framed to deter the able-bodied from seeking relief being applied in all its stringency to some thousands of people who were totally unable to support themselves, and who were in some cases subject to coercion.

Classification of paupers after 1834

Under the direction of the Poor Law Commissioners, the inmates of pauper institutions were classified as follows:

1. Aged and infirm men.
2. Able-bodied men, and boys over 13.
3. Boys from 7 to 13.
4. Aged and infirm women.
5. Able-bodied women, and girls over 13.
6. Girls from 7 to 13.
7. Children under 7.[25]

As the Webbs comment: 'the modern student is struck at once by the omissions in this compulsory classification scheme. There is no class for the sick, either those suffering from infectious or contagious disease, or from others. There is no class for the lying-in cases. There is no class for the lunatics, idiots, or imbeciles.[26] They point out that 'it was no part of the policy of the central authority that the sick should be received into the workhouse at all', but while outdoor relief was practicable in most cases of bodily illness, it was clearly not so in cases of acute mental illness.

The Poor Law Amendment Act of 1834 contained only one clause in which the insane were mentioned. Section 45 ran:

> nothing in this Act contained shall authorise the detention in any workhouse, of any dangerous Lunatic, insane Person, or Idiot for any longer period than 14 days and every Person wilfully detaining in any Workhouse any such Lunatic, insane Person or Idiot for more than 14 days shall be deemed guilty of a misdemeanour.

The operative word was 'dangerous'; it became the practice for boards of guardians to pass on to the county asylum the violent patient, whose condition might be incurable, while retaining in the workhouse the milder or quieter cases, which were perhaps in the early stages of the disease, and more readily susceptible to treatment. The county asylum authorities were given no choice in the matter, for there was no machinery by which they might select suitable cases for treatment and reject the others. It is clear that at this time the Poor Law Commissioners regarded the county asylums as no more than a place of confinement.

In 1842, the clerk of the Chesterton Union wrote to ask the Commissioners whether the relieving officer of that union had acted rightly in sending a lunatic pauper to the workhouse until the next board day. He received the following reply:

> The Commissioners think as a rule, that the workhouse is not the proper place for lunatic paupers. The 9th George IV, c. 40, s. 38[27] points out the course which ought to be taken for the care and safe custody of insane persons who become chargeable to the parish, viz., by causing them to be conveyed to an asylum or licensed house under the order of the justices.
>
> But there may be cases in which some short delay must occur before the necessary order of justices can be procured, and the other arrangements made for the conveyance of such lunatics to an asylum. In these instances, it may be desirable for the security

as well of the public as of the insane person, that the temporary admission of the latter into the workhouse should be resorted to. The 45th section of the Poor Law Amendment Act, however, forbids the detention of a dangerous lunatic in a workhouse for any longer period than 14 days: and the Commissioners on every ground, both as regards the lunatic and the other inmates of the workhouse, disapprove of the detention for any longer period than absolute necessity may warrant.[28]

It may be asked why, in view of this statement, over 4000 pauper lunatics were still in workhouses eleven years after the Act came into force. The answer lies partly in the insufficient number of county asylums, and partly in the reluctance of individual boards of guardians to pay the cost of maintenance in these relatively expensive institutions; but the Commissioners' statement gives the key to the lack of provision for the insane in workhouses. It was clearly not envisaged that they should remain in these institutions for any length of time.

Accommodation for pauper lunatics

The 'ward for lunatics and idiots' is mentioned several times in the orders and reports published by the Poor Law authorities during this period, and the implication is that most, if not all, workhouses possessed such a ward. In fact, there had never been a statutory provision to this effect, nor had the provision of such accommodation ever been officially suggested. Yet according to the Lunacy Commissioners, accommodation of this kind certainly existed in the large towns by 1844:

> there are numerous workhouses belonging to Parishes and Unions, which are not licensed for the reception of the insane, but which nevertheless contain certain wards exclusively appropriated to lunatics, and receive large numbers of insane persons, dangerous as well as harmless; such as the workhouses at Birmingham, Manchester, Sheffield, Bath, Leicester, Redruth in Cornwall, the Infirmary Bethel at Norwich, and others.[29]

Here was a clear contradiction of both the letter and the spirit of 1834; yet it was obviously a matter of official policy. The iron control of the Commissioners over the activities of the individual unions was such that the possibility of a procedure involving extra expense being initiated spontaneously in a number of different areas without official approval or official comment is remote.

The probability is that where such lunatic wards existed, they had been in existence before 1834, and that although they were to be met with in the larger towns, the provision of such accommodation was by no means universal. Why, then, did the Poor Law Commissioners, who must have been aware of these facts, suddenly assume the existence of a lunatic ward in every workhouse? The answer seems to lie in a curious episode in Poor Law policy which occurred in 1838.

Select Committee on the Poor Law Amendment Act, 1838

Among those who gave evidence before this Select Committee was Edward Gulson, the Assistant Poor Law Commissioner. His evidence, like that of his colleagues, was mainly concerned with the effect of the operation of the Act on the able-bodied pauper who was to be forced back into self-maintenance; but in the minutes of this Committee there occurs a remarkable passage[30] in which Gulson attacked the administration of the county asylums, and made a plea for the transfer of power over lunatics to the Poor Law Commissioners.

> I conceive a very great evil exists in the law with regard to pauper lunatics. It has always appeared to me that a great improvement might be effected relating to them; at the present time, the expenses of maintaining pauper lunatics in places pointed out by law for lunatic asylums is very great indeed, varying from 8s. to 12s. a week for each person . . . that circumstance operates to a very great degree in keeping individuals in the parishes who ought to be taken care of in a lunatic asylum.

He recommended

> in a given group of Unions, a regular lunatic asylum solely for paupers, to which all those Unions should send their paupers, and where they would be kept at one-half or a third or a fourth of the expense at which they are now kept.

The chairman of the Select Committee[31] seems to have regarded this proposal as both retrogressive and administratively unworkable:

> Are you aware when you speak of the expense per head in those establishments (county asylums) that those establishments can scarcely be maintained even with that revenue?

—I am not aware of the fact, but taking it to be so, I am
stating distinctly what I conceive to be the best for the paupers,
and for the parish purse.

Then you are aware that the lunatic asylums already established have been built by contributions from the poor rate?

—I am aware that in a great many instances that is the case,
and I am aware that very great jobs have been made of such
establishments.

Are you of the opinion that it would relieve the poor rate to
tax them again to build other asylums? . . . are you of the
opinion that the houses already established should be suffered to
become empty and of no use?

—As far as paupers I am, unless they were converted to such
a purpose as this.

Are you aware that they have been built specially for the
reception of paupers?

—Yes I am, in some instances.

Should you think it a wise and prudent policy to abandon
those houses and to build others?

The chairman was evidently treating **Gulson** as a hostile witness,
and was driving him into a position from which it was impossible to
retreat. Gulson's reply to the last question was:

If those houses could be converted to such a purpose, and
placed under the entire control of the Board of Guardians . . .
I think the change would be very much for the general benefit of
the people.

—Then your impression appears to be, that abuses and unnecessary expenditure exist in those houses at present?

—That is distinctly my impression.

Are you aware what any of those asylums have cost in the
erection?

—I am aware that a vast sum of money has been thrown
away in the erection of some of them, and that very great jobs
have been perpetrated in the erection of lunatic asylums.

The real author of this proposal to bring the county asylums
within the scope of the Poor Law was almost certainly Edwin
Chadwick. In the hostilities which divided the Poor Law Commissioners from their secretary at this time, Gulson was always Chadwick's loyal adherent and close friend.[32] Chadwick was engrossed in
plans of administrative simplification in which the Poor Law Union

would become the primary unit of local authority; he detested administrative complexity, financial waste, and curative medicine. Ashley, now emerging as the leader of the lunacy reformers, was at this time Chadwick's 'arch-enemy.[33] Moreover, as a Benthamite, Chadwick was bitterly opposed to the humanist approach to social problems, the paternalistic interest in oppressed minorities. The 'greatest happiness of the greatest number' in this instance lay in sparing the pockets of the sane.

Chadwick led, Gulson followed; but by 1838, both were fighting a losing battle against hostile interests. Although Chadwick nominally held office as Secretary to the Commissioners until 1847, the days of his power and prestige in this sphere were over, and this proposal, like so many others which he initiated in those nine years, failed to gain influential support. The visiting justices and the Metropolitan Commissioners in Lunacy continued their work unhampered by the claims of Somerset House.

Summary: costs and accommodation

The real point at issue between the Poor Law authorities and the Lunacy authorities was the old one of cure or detention. If the county asylums were looked upon as curative institutions, then their high cost was justified, and they had a legitimate grievance against the Poor Law authorities for refusing to send them pauper lunatics who were susceptible to treatment. If, on the other hand, they were regarded merely as places of detention, the Poor Law authorities could rightly claim that they could do this work much more cheaply.

County asylums were certainly much more expensive to operate than workhouses. A comparison of costs in 1845 shows that the cost of board and clothing alone in county asylums averaged 7s. 3½d. a week for each patient. The highest was Hereford, with a figure of 12s. per week. The figures for workhouses, on the other hand, were still very low, being in many cases little more than they had been a century earlier, in spite of a considerable rise in the cost of living.[34] The average was 2s. 7d. a week, the highest figure of 4s. 1d. being that for Rutland, and the lowest being that for Cornwall—2s. 0¼d. The cost of maintenance in the Cornwall Asylum was 5s. 11½d. a week, so that Gulson was strictly accurate when he said that it was possible to maintain lunatics for one-third of the cost under workhouse conditions; but the justification of the county asylums lay not in the fact that they kept costs down, but that they cured their patients. The old argument of the subscribers to the Manchester Lunatic Hospital still held good: that it was better to pay a higher amount for a few months, and restore a patient to self-maintenance, than to pay a lower amount for his entire life-time.

A statement which underlined the unsatisfactory division of functions between workhouses and county asylums was contained in a report published in 1844 by Dr Boyd, the parish doctor of St Marylebone.[35] He pointed out that there were seventy-nine patients from that parish in the Middlesex Asylum at Hanwell, all of whom were incurable save four. Among them were twenty-two quiet chronic cases—patients who would be capable of living the normal restricted life of the workhouse without causing alarm or annoyance to the other inmates. At the same time, there were many patients in urgent need of treatment who remained in the Marylebone workhouse because there was no accommodation for them in Hanwell. Some clarification of function and practice, involving close co-operation between the asylum and the workhouse, seemed an obvious necessity.

By 1842, it seems, the Poor Law Commissioners were anxious to be rid of the whole problem of the pauper lunatic. The attitude expressed in Gulson's statements—if indeed it was ever more than a piece of wishful thinking on the part of the Chadwick faction—was short-lived. In 1842, the Commissioners issued the following directive to boards of guardians:

> From the express prohibition of the detention of dangerous
> persons of unsound mind in a workhouse . . . coupled with the
> prevalent practice of keeping insane persons in a workhouse
> before the passing of the Poor Law Amendment Act, it may be
> inferred that persons of unsound mind, not being dangerous, may
> be legally kept in a workhouse. It must, however, be remembered
> that with lunatics, the first object ought to be their cure by means
> of proper medical treatment. This can only be obtained in a well-
> regulated asylum; and therefore the detention of any curable
> lunatic in a workhouse is highly objectionable on the score both
> of humanity and economy.[36]

This statement implied a neat division of functions between the Lunacy Commissioners and the Poor Law Commissioners; but the issues involved were to be fought over both nationally and locally for many years. Even today, the difficulties of transfer from a psychiatric hospital to Part IV Accommodation and vice versa reflect this struggle.

Bethlem

After 1828 the authorities at Bethlem seem to have shunned publicity as much as possible. Growing central control constituted a threat to their independence, and incidents which might throw an unfavourable light on the hospital were avoided at all costs. Consequently, very little is known about the conditions in Bethlem from 1828 to 1853, when the Lunacy Commissioners at last assumed control. We know that many patients died in the cholera epidemic of 1832, and that the diet was subsequently improved in order to strengthen the bodily resistance of those who survived.[37] The building which had met with the disapproval of the Select Committee of 1815 was still in use during this period.

Single lunatics

Despite the provisions of the 1828 Madhouse Act and the constant efforts of the parliamentary reformers, no improvement whatever had taken place in the condition of single lunatics. It was still possible for any person to be confined alone with great secrecy and no public supervision, on the unsupported word of a relative. This constituted the greatest gap in existing lunacy legislation when the reformers again brought the matter before parliament in 1842.

6   Ashley and the achievement of reform

The reports which the Metropolitan Commissioners in Lunacy issued between 1829 and 1842 make impressive reading. They show a constant attention to detail, and an increasingly stringent view of their duties. The Commissioners began to inquire as to the character and conduct of the attendants and nurses; they broke with tradition in listening to the patients' grievances and investigating them; they experimented with a system of liberating recovered patients on trial, so that the transition from the sheltered world of the asylum to the world outside could be carefully supervised. The work which the Commissioners did at this time did much to impress the importance of the whole subject on the minds of thinking people. 'The subject of insanity has lately excited much attention,' wrote Ashley in his report of 1839–40; but the whole position of divided authority and divided responsibility was manifestly unsatisfactory. It was clearly necessary to deal with this problem before attempting further internal reforms.

With the events of 1842–5, the story of lunacy reform enters on a new phase. Ashley was now the acknowledged leader of the reform group.

By 1842, Ashley's reputation as a social reformer was decisively established. He was forty-one years of age; he had been a member of parliament for sixteen years, and a Lunacy Commissioner for fourteen. His unremitting work to improve conditions in the factories and the mines had earned him a place in the minds of the general public. He had become something of a national figure, and to the initial advantage of aristocratic connections had added those of detailed knowledge and practical experience.

The Act of 1842

On 17 March 1842 Lord Granville Somerset rose in the House to propose that the Commissioners be empowered to carry out an inspection of all asylums and madhouses in the country, whatever their legal status. Somerset stressed that his proposal was only the

132

first stage in the movement to secure a national system of inspection and supervision. After some discussion, in which Ashley's comment that 'a man of common-sense could give as good an opinion as any medical man he knew' lost him some medical support, a Bill was prepared and became law on 5 August 1842. The Act (5 and 6 Vict., c. 87) was to operate for three years in the first instance. Doubtless the supporters of lunacy reform had in mind the substitution of comprehensive legislation within that period, and this was actually achieved by the passing of the 1845 Act at the expiry of the earlier one. There was less finality about a three-year Act; yet at the same time, it gave the Commissioners time in which to carry out their tour and to set their own standards.

The number of Commissioners was increased. There were to be fifteen to twenty, of whom four were legal Commissioners, and six or seven 'Physicians or Surgeons not practising in Midwifery or Surgery.'[1] They were to carry out a detailed national tour of inspection and to record their findings.

Sections 8–11 provided that they were to report on the efficacy of the non-restraint system in any place where it was practised; on the method of classification adopted; on the effect of occupation and amusements, and especially on the conditions of the pauper patients.

The 1832 Act had removed the work of the Commissioners from the jurisdiction of the Secretary of State for the Home Department, and placed it within the jurisdiction of the Lord Chancellor. The interests of the Home Department were now safeguarded by a provision (section 38) that the Secretary of State, like the Lord Chancellor, might require the Commissioners to make a special visit to any institution for the insane except Bethlem.

The Commissioners continued to receive £1 an hour for their work in the metropolitan area; outside it, they were now to be paid at the rate of five guineas a day. In spite of the arduous nature of the projected tour, the position of legal or medical Commissioner remained a part-time one, to be undertaken by a professional man in his spare time.

The tour of inspection

How the asylums and madhouses which had hitherto been exempt from any real inspection greeted the prospect of the Commissioners' visits, we may only guess in most cases. The only reliable records available relate to certain asylums and hospitals; no documents relating to private madhouses appear to be in existence. In most cases, it does not appear that any very great effort was made to improve conditions especially for the Commissioners' eyes. The rate of purchase for staple commodities remains steady. The outstanding exception is the Lancaster Asylum, where a great change took place as soon as the 1842 Bill was introduced. The cash book shows a sudden rush of buying; hardware, kitchen utensils, soap, candles and 'scouring liquors' were bought in large quantities. From May to September 1842, £243 was spent on blankets alone, and the former frequent indents for straw stopped completely. Evidently most of the patients had previously slept on straw, and were now given proper bedding for the first time.

The sudden change in policy was due not only to panic on the part of the visiting justices, but also to the effects of the appointment two years previously of a new and enlightened medical superintendent, Mr Gaskell. The use of mechanical restraint had been abolished in June, 1841, on his orders, and we may conclude that he probably used the threat of inspection as a means to induce the justices to provide the money for a thorough overhaul of living conditions.

The Commissioners reached Lancaster in October 1842—only two months after the passing of the Act. It must have been gratifying to Gaskell, in view of his strenuous efforts, to read the Commissioners' report, written in the visitors' book; this expressed 'unqualified approbation', commented on the 'skill, zeal and attention' of the staff, and remarked that 'the bedding is good and sufficient, and is arranged with neatness on the bedsteads during the day.'

The significance of the Lancaster episode lies in the fact that it illustrates the double standard which had previously existed in lunacy administration. The Lancaster authorities must have been well aware that the conditions for which they were responsible were well below the standards demanded in the metropolitan area; but it was not until the new Bill was proposed and inspection became imminent that they took steps to remedy this situation. If this could happen in the second largest county asylum in the country, we may readily imagine that it also happened in many provincial private madhouses. The mere threat of inspection was a valuable corrective.

The lay Commissioners, such as Ashley and Somerset, did not take part in the tour; but the actual sifting of the information received and the writing of the final report, published in 1844, was Ashley's work (with the exception of two sections—those on restraint and medical classification. See pp. 140–1). The tour had two distinct results; it enabled the professional Commissioners to visit institutions formerly outside their control, and to remedy individual cases of abuse; and the mass of raw material received enabled Ashley to draw up a comprehensive picture from the national view-point, and to make recommendations on matters of general policy.

The report of the Metropolitan Commissioners, 1844

The report dealt first with county asylums, giving details of conditions in individual asylums, and paying some attention to matters of internal administration, such as heating, diet, and the employment of patients. Other institutions were subsequently dealt with in the same way. There was a section on the nature of insanity, and a classification of its forms; a section on the non-restraint system; and a section on the admission of paupers from workhouses.

From the reader's point of view, this is a muddled report in which details obtrude and the overall picture is not easily grasped. Ashley had little literary ability; but the patient piling of fact on fact provided a sound basis for the recommendations which concluded the report.

County asylums

The section of the report which dealt with county asylums consisted largely of a mass of domestic detail. There were apparently no outstanding abuses by the time the Commissioners undertook their inspection, but there were many points which they desired to bring to the attention of the visiting committees.

There were twelve county asylums which provided accommodation only for criminal and pauper lunatics, and five 'county asylums united with subscription asylums'—institutions such as those at Stafford and Nottingham, where the cost of construction and maintenance had been raised partly from the county rate, and partly from public subscription. In these latter institutions, paying patients were admitted to offset in part the cost of maintaining paupers.

The Commissioners were disturbed by the sites chosen for many county asylums; in spite of the specific provisions of the 1808 Act, these were often in crowded areas, and without a satisfactory water supply. Bodmin Asylum was frequently short of water, and when visited by the Commissioners, had been totally without water for a whole week. Hanwell had an inadequate supply, and the visiting justices had been forced to sanction the expense of boring a new well. At Nottingham and Lancaster the asylums were in populous areas, and there was little space where the patients could take exercise. The most serious result of building in towns was that when the asylum became overcrowded, additional accommodation could only be provided at the expense of the gardens and airing courts.

The cost of county asylums was still very high, and the Commissioners had a cautious word to say about excessive costs:

> Although county magistrates have properly the control of funds
> to be raised in their own districts, it can scarcely be expected
> that they should devote so much attention as is really necessary
> to make them conversant with the various points which involve
> the convenience, comfort and security necessary to be provided
> for in large asylums for the insane, and they are therefore liable
> to be misled as to their proper cost and construction.[2]

Again, they stated: 'While we have no wish to advocate the erection of unsightly buildings, we think that no unnecessary costs should be incurred for architectural decoration; especially as these asylums are erected for persons who, when in health, are accustomed to dwell in cottages.'[3]

This emphasis on inexperience and architecture was a polite way of endorsing Gulson's opinion that 'very great jobs have been perpetrated in the erection of county asylums.' At all events, it made a sound basis for Ashley's plan for a central administrative structure to control the design and construction of new asylums:

> It is apparent . . . that although a few of the existing county
> asylums are well adapted to their purpose, and a very large
> proportion of them are extremely well-conducted; yet some of
> them are quite unfit for the reception of the insane, some are
> placed in ineligible sites, some are deficient in the necessary
> means of providing out-door employment for their paupers,
> some are ill-contrived and defective in their internal construction,
> some are cheerless and confined in their yards and airing-
> grounds . . . it appears to be deserving the attention of the legis-
> lature, whether the erection of public asylums for the insane
> poor may not advantageously be regulated by some independent
> authority . . . pauper lunatics have unfortunately become so
> numerous throughout the whole kingdom, that the proper

construction and cost of asylums for their use has ceased to be a subject which affects a few counties only, and has become a matter of national interest and importance.[4]

Public lunatic hospitals

Some public lunatic hospitals, notably the Warneford Asylum[5] and the Exeter Asylum, had followed Bethlem's example in claiming exemption from visitation. This exemption was granted in 1832.[6] For these asylums, Ashley had a word of reproof: 'We cannot . . . but think that all places receiving and detaining in custody any class of Her Majesty's subjects, should be open to inspection by proper authority.'[7]

The Commissioners commended the administration of the Retreat; St Luke's they found ill-placed, and deficient in most of the necessary amenities. They were particularly severe about two old pioneer institutions—the Bethel Hospital at Norwich and the Manchester Lunatic Hospital, which were 'very ill-adapted for receptacles for the insane.'[8]

Licensed madhouses

There were thirty-seven licensed madhouses in the metropolitan area; these had, of course, been within the jurisdiction of the Metropolitan Commissioners for the past fourteen years, and so were familiar to them; but there were ninety-nine houses in the provinces which the Commissioners visited for the first time on their tour of inspection. Their chief impression was not of widespread cruelty and neglect, but of a common evasion of the law. In many houses, the law relating to the registration of certified persons was evaded by declaring that the patient was merely suffering from 'nerves', and did not therefore require certification. Some houses took 'low-spirited or desponding' patients as 'boarders'. It should be said here that these patients were probably equivalent to the 'voluntary' patients suffering from psycho-neuroses who now form a large part of the admissions to mental hospitals. The fault may have been in the law, which made no provision for the treatment of those who were not certifiable. The licensing laws were also evaded; it frequently happened that a proprietor would keep patients in several different houses, although he had a licence only for one. This increased the difficulties of inspection.

Proprietors of private madhouses often took their responsibilities lightly. At Cranbourne, in Dorset, two Commissioners visited a house on three separate occasions, and the proprietor was away each time, the house being left to the care of a solitary female servant. At Belle Grove House, Newcastle, there was a repetition of an incident which the Commissioners had encountered during their first year of office: the house was being administered by a man who knew nothing whatever about the treatment of insanity, merely because he happened to be the chief creditor of the former owner.

The effect of some years' systematic and thorough inspection in the metropolitan area had been wholly good; the Commissioners were especially pleased to report that Warburton's houses were greatly improved:

> We have visited few, if any, receptacles for the insane in which the patients are more kindly or more judiciously treated . . . the abuses which existed in this and some other asylums previously to the year 1828 led to the introduction of the system of visitation by commissioners in the metropolitan district. The houses at Bethnal Green, which were among the worst, now rank with the best receptacles for the insane.[9]

There were three houses on which the Commissioners felt themselves bound to pass 'almost unqualified censure'. These were the asylums at Haverfordwest, where patients existed in an almost unbelievable state of filth and neglect, a house at West Auckland in similar conditions, and St Peter's, Bristol. There was no doubt that, like most of the other old pioneer institutions, St Peter's was now totally out of date. The airing ground was 'utterly unfit', the site 'totally unfit for an asylum'; there was no system of classification of patients, no plan for exercising them, and no arrangements for employing them. The Commissioners who visited this institution concluded roundly, 'the entire body of lunatics ought to be removed to more spacious premises, and to a more airy and healthy situation.'[10]

Previous suspicions that the local magistrates were not in all cases taking their duties under the Lunacy Acts seriously were now confirmed. In four cases, the Commissioners found that the magistrates did not visit at all; in one, they invariably sent for the visitors' book beforehand, so that the proprietor was forewarned of their intentions.

Where the Commissioners found grounds for complaint in the conduct of an asylum, they communicated with the chairman of the Quarter Sessions, calling his attention to the abuses which they had in mind; in almost every case, a subsequent visit showed that no action had been taken. On the very day on which the Commissioners visited the house at West Auckland, the local magistrates also visited. The Commissioners found the house 'utterly unfit'; the magistrates, only an hour or two before, had recorded 'everything in good order'.

Some magistrates did attempt to carry out their duties conscientiously, but in almost all cases they were content to inspect the bodily condition and cleanliness of the patients, and made no inquiries concerning diet, medical treatment, employment of patients, or whether any of them were fit to be released.

Again Ashley returned to his main theme: the only remedy for these diverse and unsatisfactory conditions was the creation of a powerful national inspectorate on a permanent basis. He quoted Samuel Tuke: 'We shall not secure efficient visitation until we have an appointment of a number of competent persons to visit, under the authority of Government, all the places of whatever description, chartered or unchartered, in which the insane are confined.'[11]

Workhouses

Since they were under the control of the Poor Law Commissioners, workhouses lay outside the Lunacy Commissioners' terms of reference; at the same time, a consideration of the relations between the two branches of administration made it imperative that they should form a picture of the state of pauper lunatics as a whole. They contented themselves with visiting 'such as lay in our road'—the workhouses at Redruth, Bath, Leicester, Portsea and Birmingham. All these were large workhouses possessing a special lunatic ward; there is no information about those which did not.

There were 21 insane persons—this term still including the mentally subnormal—at Redruth, 21 at Bath, 20 at Leicester, 26 at Portsea and 71 at Birmingham. Many of them were dangerous. At Leicester alone, the lunatic ward included 'a noisy maniac, very cunning', a man 'subject to maniacal attacks . . . raving mad . . . constantly fastened to his bed at night', another 'violent and passionate and tried to cut others with knives', 'a destructive and dangerous idiot', and 'an abusive and dangerous lunatic.'

In spite of the injunctions of the Poor Law Commissioners, section 45 of the Poor Law Amendment Act was still apparently not being observed in many places. The Metropolitan Commissioners found, as might have been expected from previous evidence, that some patients whose condition would have been curable had they been passed to the county asylum within the statutory fourteen days were still being detained in workhouses. In Cornwall, they noted: 'it had been the custom . . . not to send a patient to the asylum until he had become, either from dirty habits or dangerous propensities, unmanageable in a workhouse or in lodgings.'[12]

At Nottingham:

> The result of our latest enquiries . . . has been that, since the new Poor Law came into operation, an increased reluctance has been exhibited on the part of the parish authorities to send their poor to an asylum, and the patients frequently come in a very debilitated and exhausted state. Great advantage is said to be taken of the use of the word 'dangerous' in the 45th section of the Poor Law Amendment Act, and many curable cases are detained in Union workhouses in the rural districts.[13]

In Surrey, the Poor Law authorities were responsible for the patients being 'sent into the asylum in some cases to die.'

Ashley concluded his general consideration of this problem by attacking the implications of section 45: 'The clause which is supposed to sanction the confinement in workhouses of lunatics, without advertising to the probability of their being curable or not, is, in our opinion, impolitic and open to serious objection.'[14] He was probably understating the case when he said that the Poor Law Commissioners were 'under some misconception as to the condition of lunatics in workhouses.'

Mechanical restraint

The section of the report which deals with experiments in non-restraint was not Ashley's work. Ashley was known to be a firm supporter of the non-restraint system, and as early as 1842 had publicly praised the work done in this connection at Hanwell. He 'could not speak too highly either of the system itself, or of the manner in which it was carried out by the talented superintendent, Dr Conolly.'[15]

The report did not reflect that attitude. It summarized the main arguments for and against restraint with a show of fairness, but it is quite clear that the writer was actually in favour of coercion, though only as a last resort.

The main arguments for absolute non-coercion were that it soothed the patient, and was thus more humane than mechanical restraint, which tended to degrade and humiliate him; that the use of restraint gave the keepers an opportunity of abusing and neglecting their charges; that the only requisite was an increase of staff, which ought not to be refused merely on the grounds of expense; and that experience showed that the general tone of the asylum improved when restraint was abolished.

The arguments in favour of moderate coercion involved diametrically opposed claims: that slight restraint frequently induced tranquillity in an otherwise restless patient; that the only real alternative to restraint in the case of an excited or dangerous patient was solitary confinement, which could be even more degrading; that it was impossible for the staff, however great their devotion to duty, to exercise an unwearying surveillance; and finally, that experience showed that the best approach to the insane was that in which kindness was mingled with a show of authority.

The Commissioners' experience at Lincoln and Hanwell evidently led them to support the latter view; they found that the non-restraint system did not always produce the tranquillity and high moral tone claimed by its advocates. In fact, they took more or less the view of a patient at Hanwell who addressed the following lines to his member of parliament:

> We have in this asylum, sir,
> Some doctors of renown,
> With a plan of non-restraint
> Which they seem to think their own. . . .
> All well-meaning men, sir,
> But troubled with a complaint
> Called the monomania
> Of total non-restraint. . . .[16]

Suggestion for the amendment of the law

The Commissioners' recommendations had two primary aims: to secure the unification of the forms of statutory control exercised over asylums and madhouses, and to extend the lunacy laws to all institutions of whatever character in which the insane were detained. They recommended that:

1. Each county should be required to build a county asylum for its own pauper lunatics. (The previous Acts were of course permissive.)

2. All asylums and hospitals for the insane should be subject to inspection by the statutory authority; they should also be required to keep records and case-books of a prescribed type, which should be the same for all institutions.

3. All authorities responsible for the care of the insane should be required to furnish certificates of the admission, discharge or death of a patient within two days of the event. These should be forwarded in all cases to the statutory authority.

4. A new, more detailed, and standardized form of medical certification should be devised.

5. The person who certified a patient's insanity should not be allowed also to sign the certificate of consignment. (This was to obviate the situation which arose when a patient was certified by a medical practitioner who was also a relative, and thus in a position to sign both documents. The 1828 Madhouse Act had provided safeguards against collusion between the certifying doctor and the madhouse proprietor; this recommendation was designed to prevent collusion between the certifying doctor and the relatives.)

Recommendations which concerned the relation between workhouses and county asylums may be classified under three heads:

6. County asylum authorities should be empowered and encouraged to make separate provision for incurable lunatics who were paupers, in order to make room for a greater number of curable cases in the asylum.

7. Pauper patients should not be sent to workhouses unless their condition was definitely incurable; in that case, they should be sent only to certain specified workhouses which could make special provision for them.

8. The lunacy authority should be responsible for visiting and reporting on the condition of all pauper patients, whether in workhouses or county asylums.

These measures would have the effect of giving the Lunacy Commissioners a power of supervision, and therefore to some extent of removing pauper lunatics from the grip of the Poor Law.

9. A board or authority should be set up, to be responsible for the approval of sites, plans and estimates for all new asylums to be built at the public expense. This proposal broke new ground, since it proposed an entirely new kind of function for the central

authority. It was designed as the final answer to critics of the financial policy of visiting justices.

Effect of the 1844 Report

'July 2nd, finished at last, Report of the Commission in Lunacy. Good thing over. Sat for many days in review. God prosper it! It contains much for the alleviation of physical and moral suffering.'[17]

Thus wrote Ashley at the conclusion of his task. The writing of the report, however, was only the first stage in the process which was to culminate in legislative action. From the first, it was apparent that there would be action within a relatively short space of time. Peel, who had consistently supported the reformers, was now Prime Minister of an administration which, though Tory in name, was Liberal in social policy. Social reform was in the air, and the reformers were no longer handicapped by the necessity of struggling against the weight of public indifference.

The Lunacy Report, in spite of its turgid and unimaginative form, attracted a good deal of attention. The *Westminster Review* in particular published a detailed analysis in which the new note of social responsibility was sounded.[18] The writer stated that the report was highly creditable to the Commissioners, but 'at the same time humiliating to us as a nation. Our feeling of humiliation, however, ought to give way to thankfulness that such facts are brought to light.' This correspondent felt strongly that the welfare of the patients was not, as it should be, the focal point of the Lunacy Laws. Confinement in the interests of the sane was still the ruling motive.

Do we not discover the protection to the public rather than the cure of the sufferer is the predominating principle inculcated in our Acts of Parliament? The guardians of the poor are instructed to send patients to the county asylum when they become dangerous . . . our county asylums have thus become, and the evil is daily increasing, places of security rather than curative establishments.

All this covered relatively familiar ground; but the writer then proceeded to an analogy which, though common to-day, must have been novel to his readers. He inquired of them what would be the reaction of the general public if patients suffering from acute physical ailments, such as inflammation of the lungs, were commonly sent to workhouses, and allowed to remain there until the disease was incurable before being sent to hospital; and stressed that the insane person was a sick person, urgently in need of specialized treatment. The questions which the Poor Law authorities commonly asked themselves in cases of insanity—is he dangerous? and, how much will it cost?—were irrelevant and anti-social. The true interest of the community lay in the achievement of a speedy cure.

The similarity between mental and physical illness was repeatedly stressed by reference to 'patients', 'hospitals', and 'nurses', avoiding the derogatory and emotionally-coloured terms then still in common use. With reference to such official phrases as 'order for admission', 'commitment papers' and 'keepers', the writer commented: 'Does not this savour of transport to prison rather than of removal to hospital? We recommend the total disuse of these terms.'

This humane and enlightened study of the subject surpassed even Ashley's aims and standards. The attitude expressed evidently found a response in the minds of the educated public, for the article was reprinted and subsequently sold as a pamphlet.

Ashley in parliament, 1844–5

Meanwhile, Ashley was attempting to translate sentiment into action. On 23 July 1844 he brought forward in the House of Commons a motion praying that the Lunacy Report might be taken into consideration. In a lengthy speech, he recapitulated the findings of the Report, and ended:

> These unhappy persons are outcasts from all the social and domestic affections of private life . . . and have no refuge but in the laws. You can prevent, by the agency which you shall appoint as you have in so many instances prevented, the recurrence of frightful cruelties; you can soothe the days of the incurable, and restore many sufferers to health and usefulness . . I trust, therefore, that I shall stand excused, though I have consumed so much of your valuable time, when you call to mind that the motion is made on behalf of the most helpless, if not the most afflicted, portion of the human race.

It was unfortunate that this undeniably moving speech should have been made at an inopportune moment. Ashley appears to have known little about parliamentary tactics, and not to have realized that he had committed a blunder in bringing the matter forward at the end of a session. He had evidently not consulted the administration before acting, for the Home Secretary rose in answer to urge him not to press the motion at that stage, and to promise Government support at a later date. Ashley agreed, and the whole matter was allowed to lapse until the following session. On 6 June 1845 the motion for the ordering of the Bill was at last brought forward. 'Sir,' said Ashley in his opening speech, 'it is remarkable and very humiliating, the long and tedious process by which we have arrived at the sound practice of the treatment of the insane, which now appears to be the suggestion of common sense and ordinary humanity.'

He dwelt at some length on the work of Pinel in France:

This was indeed a man to be honoured by every nation under heaven . . . the system passed from France to this country[19] . . . we are mainly indebted for it to the Society of Friends, and that remarkable family of Tukes who founded the Retreat at York soon after the victories of Pinel in France.

and he spoke vehemently on the subject of the plight of the single lunatic: 'I have said it before, and I say it again, that should it please God to afflict me with such a visitation, I would greatly prefer the treatment of paupers . . . to the treatment of the rich.'

Graham seconded the motion on behalf of the Government, giving it his full support and approval. 'I have the satisfaction of stating that the measures which my noble friend wishes to introduce are introduced with the Lord Chancellor's entire approbation . . . we determined to give the Bill, as a Government, our most cordial support.'

The Lunatics Bill passed the Commons on 23 July and went to the Lords; the Lords returned it on 1 August with several amendments, the chief of which was a clause exempting Bethlem from all its provisions. These amendments were agreed to, and the Bill became law on 4 August as 8 and 9 Vict. c. 100.

A subsidiary Bill, dealing with the erection and management of county asylums, was introduced at the same time; this suffered only minor amendments by the Lords, and received the Royal Assent on 8 August (8 and 9 Vict. c. 126).

The Lunatics Act of 1845

The new Lunacy Commissioners—formerly the Metropolitan Commissioners in Lunacy—were named by the Act. They included five laymen—Lord Ashley, Lord Seymour, Vernon Smith, Robert

Gordon and Francis Barlow. In addition there were nominated three medical Commissioners—Thomas Turner, H. H. Southey, and J. R. Hume; and three legal Commissioners—James Mylne, John Hancock Hall, and Bryan Procter, better known as 'Barry Cornwall', the writer. These constituted a permanent full-time inspectorate. The medical and legal Commissioners were to receive a salary of £1500 a year, and were debarred from holding any other office. The lay Commissioners were unpaid. All held their positions during good behaviour, and were bound by an oath of secrecy unless called upon to divulge information by legal authority. In the case of death, dismissal or resignation, the Lord Chancellor was to make further appointments, which must maintain the existing proportion of lay, legal and medical Commissioners.

The chairman was to be a lay member, elected by the other Commissioners. A small secretariat was provided for by the appointment of a secretary—the stipulated salary of £800 a year suggests that this was a post carrying responsibility—and two clerks.

The work of the Commissioners was an extension of that of the old Metropolitan Commissioners—that is to say, it consisted of three main functions—inspecting, licensing, and reporting.

The duty of inspection was now extended permanently to cover all hospitals and licensed houses in the country. A legal and a medical Commissioner were to visit each hospital once a year, each licensed house in the metropolis four times a year, and each licensed house in the provinces—where the justices would also continue to visit—twice a year. They also had power to visit single lunatics under certain circumstances. They could visit by night, and inspect all buildings and outhouses; they were to inquire about each patient under restraint, and to inspect all the prescribed records; they could discharge patients (apart from criminal or Chancery cases) on their own authority after two visits at an interval of seven days.

Thus far, the powers granted to the Commissioners were mainly a ratification of those granted on a three-year basis in 1842; but three other clauses extended the right of inspection in such a way that it covered all the insane in whatever type of institution they might be confined. The Commissioners were specifically empowered to visit gaols and workhouses—making a separate report to the Poor Law Commissioners in the latter case—and were also given a general power to visit any other institution not named in the foregoing clauses. In addition, the Home Secretary and the Lord Chancellor retained the right to order a special visitation in any circumstances in which they saw fit. Bethlem was not exempted from this last clause.

The Commissioners retained their licensing function in the metropolitan area; licensing in the provinces remained in the hands of the magistrates, but a copy of every provincial licence was to be sent to the Commissioners for their information.

The reporting function of the Commissioners formed a permanent link between their work and that of the Lord Chancellor's office. They were to report in all three times in the year: once every six months to furnish routine particulars of the number of visits undertaken and the establishments visited, and annually in June to supply details of the state of institutions visited in the foregoing year.

The new Commission was, then, a development of the old—the chief differences being the extension of the inspectorate to cover the entire country and all types of institutions, and the appointment of full-time salaried Commissioners.

Certification

A more detailed form of certification was devised, which while not abolishing the distinction between pauper and private patients, increased the legal safeguards against wrongful detention in each case. The form of petition for private patients given in Schedule B of the Act was as follows:

I, the undersigned, hereby request you to receive A.B., a lunatic (or insane person or idiot or person of unsound mind) as a patient in your house (or hospital). Sub-joined is a statement concerning the said A.B.

The person making the petition was required to append his signature, details of his occupation, address, and the degree of relationship with, or other circumstances connected with, the patient; this was followed by a list of requirements designed to furnish a rudimentary medical and social history of the patient. The two medical certificates were to be signed in a form prescribed in Schedule C:

I . . . hereby certify that I have this day, separately from any other medical practitioner, visited and personally examined A.B., the person named in the accompanying statement, and that the said A.B. is a lunatic (or an insane person or an idiot or a person of unsound mind) and a proper person to be confined, and that I have formed this opinion from the following fact or facts, viz.:

(signed)

F

The form of petition for a pauper patient, which had, as before, to be signed by a justice of the peace or officiating clergyman of the parish, and also by the relieving officer or overseer (Schedule D), was similar in form, and required the same detailed statement.

Records

All institutions for the treatment of the insane were now required to possess an admission book, in which the name of the patient had to be entered within two days of his reception, and the diagnosis of his complaint within seven; a book in which to enter the cause of a patient's removal from the institution, whether by death, discharge, transfer or escape; a medical visitation book 'to include details of restraint, seclusion, medical treatment, injuries and acts of violence'; a medical case-book, a visitors' book, which was to contain the reports of those who had made an official or unofficial inspection; and a patients' book, in which the visitors or Commissioners might make observation on the condition of individual patients.

In addition, the proprietor or superintendent was made legally responsible for forwarding notice of each individual reception, death, discharge, escape or transfer to the Commissioners within seven days of the occurrence, and if the institution was outside the metropolitan area, to the justices in addition. Thus there were five different sets of documents to be dealt with, and five sets of records to be kept. This was all in addition to the documents required for the original consigning procedure, which had to be seen by the superintendent, though not actually completed by him.

It might be asked whether such an insistence on record-keeping was either necessary or effective. Unnecessary complication of paperwork tends to defeat its own ends, for when the law becomes so complex that it may be transgressed unwittingly, deliberate evasion is easily explained away. Ashley, however, in the light of his experience in the metropolitan area, believed implicitly in the value of documentation as a safeguard against irregular practice.

So ended the first stage of reform.

'One of the minor, but not the least valuable, fruits of the session' was the comment of the *Annual Register* on the Act. The writer added that 'the feeling of the House was strongly in favour.'

Legislation for a minority—particularly an anti-social minority—is not usually of great import to the majority; and it is in some ways surprising that so great a degree of public interest was aroused and maintained on behalf of the insane. There was, it is true, some opposition to the Act; but this came almost entirely from people who believed that its terms did not go far enough. The dead weight of apathy and reaction which defeated earlier attempts at reform was now fully overcome.

Ashley and his colleagues had roused the conscience of mid-Victorian society, and had set a new standard of public morality by which the care of the helpless and degraded classes of the community was to be seen as a social responsibility.

The victory was unquestionably Ashley's, and is commonly associated with his name; but the reform which had taken place in the care and treatment of the insane was not merely one man's work. The 1845 Act marked the culmination of a slow process of social revolution which transformed the 'Lunatick or mad Person' of 1744 into the 'person of unsound mind' of 1845.

Part Two

1845–1946

The triumph of legalism

After the passing of the 1845 Act, there were three possible channels for further reform. It could develop along the social and humanitarian lines laid down at the Retreat and Hanwell and the Surrey Asylum; it could develop along purely medical lines, blurring the distinction between mental and physical disorders, sharing in the great developments which characterized general medicine in the second half of the nineteenth century; or it could proceed along legal lines, piling safeguard on safeguard to protect the sane against illegal detention, delaying certification and treatment until the person genuinely in need of care was obviously (and probably incurably) insane. In the social approach, the emphasis was on human relations; in the medical approach, it was on physical treatment, in the legal approach, it was on procedure.

The movement for further reform of the law became an affair of pressure-groups—and the pressure-groups were unequal. The legal profession had been fully established for centuries. Medicine was engaged in throwing off the shackles of a long association with barbering and charlatanism, and did not achieve full status until the passing of the Medical Registration Act of 1858, which set up a register of doctors who had passed prescribed examinations. Social work and social therapy were to remain occupations for the compassionate amateur until well into the twentieth century. It is therefore not surprising that the legal approach took precedence, to be followed after 1890 by the medical approach. It is only now, when the social services have developed a comparable professional status, that the social approach is coming into its own again.

The 'liberty of the subject'

It is ironic that the major outbreaks of public concern on the matter of the liberty of the subject came after, and not before, 1845. In the earlier part of the century, there had been many cases of illegal detention, of people who were 'put away' on doubtful evidence, and kept in secrecy and personal degradation. Patients' names were

changed, they were forbidden to correspond with the outside world
or to receive visitors, and the conditions under which they were
imprisoned were enough to make a sane man mad. Often such
patients were wealthy people, and the initiative came from grasping
relatives, who were able to seize the patients' money. The madhouse-
keeper had a vested interest in the continuation of the 'illness', since
he was able to charge a high fee for his doubtful 'care'; it was
scarcely in his interest to discharge a patient while the relatives were
willing to pay for his confinement.

Ashley and his small group of parliamentary reformers had done
their work only too well. They had aroused public indignation in
order to press for legal control over the private madhouses. By the
1845 Act they obtained it, and the worst evils of the 'conspiracy of
silence' disappeared; but public opinion was now fully aroused, and
would not be quieted.

It should perhaps be stressed that public indignation was not
directed at the conditions under which the genuine 'lunatic' lived,
and did not arise from sympathy with mental disorder. Rather, it
sprang from fear; and gradually, the phrase 'lunacy reform' came to
connote the protection of the sane against conditions which were
considered suitable for the insane. This was a connotation with which
Shaftesbury and his associates were totally out of sympathy. The
Commissioners, previously the spearhead of reform, were now
forced into a defensive position, and a great deal of obloquy was
heaped upon them.

A body which played a prominent role in creating this hysteria
was the Alleged Lunatics Friend Society, founded by Luke James
Hansard, son of the original printer to the House of Commons. The
Society was formed in 1845 'for the protection of the British subject
from unjust confinement on the grounds of mental derangement,
and for the redress of persons so confined'.[1] There was no president.
By 1851 ten members of parliament were vice-presidents, including
Thomas Duncombe, who had strenuously opposed the passing of
the 1845 Act.[2]

The Society's Annual Report of 1851 complained that 'the alleged
lunatic may be confined, cut off from all communication with his
friends, and placed in circumstances most calculated to render him
insane, for thirteen weeks or more before the quarterly visit of the
magistrates or Commissioners can afford him any opportunity of
appeal'. It admitted that the Commissioners acted 'with praise-
worthy vigour' in pursuance of their duties, but quoted Ashley

himself as saying that the system of inspection was 'both irregular and imperfect'. It would appear from the tenor of the report that the Society was not on good terms with Ashley, who must have found its activities decidedly embarrassing. Its members visited asylums and investigated individual cases, taking the view that any patient who was not obviously deranged at the time of the visit should be released immediately.

The 'asylum doctors' gradually organized themselves into a pressure-group. In 1853, Dr Bucknill, medical superintendent of the Devon County Asylum,[3] founded the *Asylum Journal*. A year later, this publication became the *Asylum Journal of Mental Science*, and in its sixth year, the word 'asylum' was dropped from the title. The journal was the organ of the 'Association of Medical Officers of Asylums and Hospitals for the Insane', formed in 1841. In 1865, this body changed its title to the shorter, but scarcely less cumbrous one of the Medico-Psychological Association. There was a considerable amount of discussion in the journal on the subject of terminology. In 1861, the terms 'administrative psychiatry' and 'psychological physicians' were used. The subject of study was variously described as 'medical psychology' and 'physiological psychology'. Behind this play with words was a real attempt to find verbal formulae which would describe a new professional group, and a new academic discipline.

The *Asylum Journal*, being the official organ of the asylum doctors, was strongly pro-medical, inclined to resent any lay intervention in their field. 'Insanity is purely a disease of the brain' wrote the editor in the second issue. 'The physician is now the responsible guardian of the lunatic, and must ever remain so.'[4]

In 1859, Dr Bucknill complained of the activities of the press: 'The mob of newspaper writers in the dullest season have suddenly started game . . . and like a scratch pack, they have opened their sweet melodious voices on the poor mad-doctor . . . it is a wonderful thing, this newspaper press of ours.'

He was afraid that any legislative action resulting from this action would be 'a sop to the Cerberus of public opinion'.[5]

The amending Acts of 1853

Three amending Acts, initiated in the House of Lords by Ashley (who had become the Earl of Shaftesbury on the death of his father in 1851) were passed in 1853. They were largely uncontroversial, and did little to allay public alarm. One related to private madhouses and subscription hospitals—now known as 'private asylums and hospitals'—and provided for a closer check on the certification of patients. The second was concerned with the provision of county asylums (now 'public asylums') and the admission of patients to them. It clarified the various means by which an asylum might be set up—by the formation of a joint authority by two counties, or by a combination of public financing and private subscription. The parish medical officer was required to visit all paupers in his area four times a year, and to notify the guardians or the overseer of those who seemed in need of mental treatment.

The third Act was concerned with Chancery lunatics—that small group of persons who had originally been specified by an Act of Edward II, and for whom a special procedure existed. This involved the trial by jury of the case of an allegedly insane person whose relatives petitioned for a declaration of insanity to prevent him from dissipating a considerable fortune. The procedure had been simplified in 1833 and 1842 by Acts which abolished the trial by jury and created special Commissioners (known after 1845 as the Masters in Lunacy) to determine the question of sanity in these cases, and to visit lunatics and idiots so found. The cost of an inquisition was still high, however, and the Act of 1853 was designed to prevent the fortune which was at stake from being consumed by legal expenses. It made possible the holding of an inquisition by a Master in Lunacy alone in cases where the petition was unopposed.

The Select Committee of 1859

Despite the provisions of these Acts, public agitation concerning the inefficacy of the lunacy laws continued. There were rumours of ill-treatment at Hanwell, complaints from released patients, a constant flow of indignant letters and articles in the national newspapers. Among those vilified was Daniel Hack Tuke (1827–95)—great-grandson of William Tuke of the Retreat, and a consultant physician of some standing. He writes:

> The author himself did not escape animadversion, and was represented in a newspaper as a brutal mad-doctor using a whip upon an unfortunate patient. The charge was the offspring of a bewildered editor who was obliged to acknowledge that he had been the victim of his own imagination.[6]

The second Derby administration, in which Spencer Walpole was Home Secretary, appointed a Select Committee of the House of Commons in February 1859. Both Walpole and his predecessor in office, Sir George Grey, were members of this Committee. The Committee continued to sit during the subsequent Palmerston administration. The question of reform of the lunacy laws was not a party issue.

Shaftesbury gave a clear and concise picture of the working of his Act in his evidence before this commission. He considered that the law was defective, but for a series of rather unexpected reasons. The authority of the Commissioners was too limited: they had no jurisdiction over Scotland, none over patients taken abroad—he considered foreign asylums 'wonderfully inferior to our own'—and little over Chancery lunatics. He thought that the greatest single cause of insanity was alcoholism, and that the most effective measure of prevention was the formation of temperance societies. He had a sharp exchange with Mr Tite, a member who thought that religious preoccupations led to mental instability. Shaftesbury was a power in the Church of England. 'Am I to understand the Honourable Member to ask whether religion is a cause of madness?' he retorted on one occasion.

Shaftesbury considered that the quality of the nursing and medical staff was one of the most important factors in the development of lunacy treatment. Most urgent was the problem of recruiting male and female nurses of the right type. Wages were low—in many hospitals no more than twelve guineas a year—'the wages of a house-maid'. The hours were extremely long, and the work was exacting. There was no great shortage of female nurses, because 'the tendency of woman's nature is to nurse'; few other professions were open to women and the work suited them. Good male attendants were far more difficult to recruit. Commissioner W. G. Campbell, another witness, said of male asylum attendants, 'They are all of too low a class. They are an uneducated class.' He considered that there was truth in the assertion that they frequently used force against their patients when they could do so undetected by authority. The development of professional standards could, he thought, best be assured by the institution of formal qualifications and a higher wage-scale.

Shaftesbury urged also the importance of medical specialization—'a school for students of lunacy'. At this time, only St Luke's Hospital in London received medical students and gave them systematic instruction in the treatment of mental disorder, since Conolly's attempts to set up a similar school at Hanwell had failed. The consideration of this question had now been made easier by the Medical Registration Act, passed in the previous year, 1858. A professional medical council had at last been set up, with power to fix an examination standard, and to make legal recognition as a 'qualified medical practitioner' dependent on reaching this standard. The terms 'doctor', 'physician' and 'surgeon' now had a clear meaning, and the way was open for further specialization. Shaftesbury pointed out that even a trained and qualified medical man often knew no more about lunacy than a layman, and based his judgment of a patient's condition not on his medical knowledge, but on his general experience of human behaviour.

He considered that the salary scales for asylum doctors also needed revision. Conolly when medical superintendent at Hanwell, received only £200 a year and a house. A fair salary would be £500 or £600 in addition to residential emoluments.

Public asylums had now been provided for almost every county in England and Wales—some by joint contracting arrangements. The larger and more populous counties, such as Lancashire and Middlesex, had built more than one.

Private asylums were decreasing in number; Bethlem had finally been brought under the supervision of the Commissioners following an inspection and inquiry ordered by the Lord Chancellor in 1853; the public asylum was now the normal channel of treatment both for fee-paying patients—and for paupers.[7]

There were still many chronic patients in workhouses, and their treatment was a matter of some concern. Mr Andrew Doyle, an inspector of the Poor Law Board, stated that of 126,000 workhouse inmates, 6,947 were known to be insane.[8] Mechanical restraint was still in general use. Doyle denied any knowledge of cruelty against pauper lunatics, but with hesitation and little conviction. The attitude of the Select Committee made it clear that they believed lunatics in workhouses to be subjected to restraint, cruel treatment, poor and insufficient diet, and general neglect.

The treatment of criminal lunatics was still a subject of great difficulty, but Broadmoor was already under construction, and it was hoped that this new institution would greatly relieve the pressure on Bethlem and some public asylums.

On the question of private asylums (formerly private or licensed madhouses), Shaftesbury thought that the association of the profit motive with the care of mental patients was unfortunate. 'If patients who could pay £500 or £600 a year were so plentiful that, when one was cured, another would come, the doctor would be willing to discharge as evidence of his skill. But . . . years may go by before he gets another of the same stamp.' Since he made his living out of them, the doctor was inclined to keep his paying patients as long as possible.

The position was particularly bad in relation to single patients. Shaftesbury confessed that the Commissioners had no idea how many singly confined patients existed—'and we have spent years trying to learn it.' The Commissioners could only visit a house where they suspected that a single lunatic was detained after obtaining the authority of the Lord Chancellor. The Commissioners had no assurance that the Lord Chancellor's list was accurate or up-to-date, and they were not allowed to see it, though they might ask for specific information from it. This list did not include the names of patients confined in their own homes, where no payment was involved.

The tenor of Shaftesbury's evidence, and that of the other Commissioners and Masters in Lunacy, was in direct contrast to the evidence given by the chairman and secretary of the Alleged Lunatics Friend Society. The chairman, Admiral Saumarez, was a member of a well-known Guernsey family, and had a distinguished naval record. He was a surgeon's son and a peer's nephew. At this time he was sixty-eight years of age, and the managing of this Society seems to have been one of his primary interests in his retirement. The secretary, Gilbert Bolden, was a solicitor.

Both were at pains to placate Shaftesbury by paying tribute to the work done by the Commissioners; but they made great play of Shaftesbury's admission that the system was not yet perfect, and of Commissioner Campbell's opinion that attendants still used violence against their patients. Every safeguard against illegal confinement must be devised, even though the complex mechanism involved might sometimes delay treatment in a curable case. They complained that the Commissioners would not give them power to visit alleged lunatics and asked that any justice of the peace might be empowered to grant the right to make visits.

The Report of this Committee published some figures on the incidence of insanity. At first sight, it appeared that there was a distinct increase. The total number of patients known to the Commissioners had risen from 20,611 in 1844 to 35,982 in 1858; but the report pointed out that this higher figure was due partly to the increase in asylum accommodation, and partly to the work of the Commissioners in discovering previously un-notified cases. In addition, the population was rising rapidly, and the expectation of life had lengthened as a result of increased prosperity and medical advances in the field of public health. When all these considerations were borne in mind, the increase in numbers was a reasonable one. Shaftesbury even considered that the incidence of insanity was dropping. There were certainly no grounds for believing that it was rising.

The Committee produced, in their Report of July 1860, a series of detailed recommendations, of which the most controversial was the proposal to introduce the intervention of a magistrate in private cases of certification.[9] This originated in the suggestion of Gilbert Bolden, the secretary of the Alleged Lunatics Friend Society, and was to form a point of debate and bitter recrimination for the next thirty years. Shaftesbury opposed it with all the force at his command, and was successful in preventing it from becoming law in his own life-time, though the proposal was revived after his death in 1885.[10]

In theory, the Committee thought that it was better to lessen the legal procedures of certification and to make early treatment possible. The danger that those who needed treatment would not get it in time was greater than the danger of illegal detention; but in practice most of their recommendations were for changes of procedure which would lessen this latter danger, and thereby increase the former. They considered that the first certificate should be valid only for three months, the case being reviewed at the end of that time; the order confining the patient should be sent to the Commissioners within twenty-four hours (the period allowed was then seven days) and the Commissioners should visit the patient 'as soon as possible'. Section 36 of Gordon's Act (the Madhouse Act 1828), which required the petitioning relative to visit the patient every six months, was to be renewed. These last recommendations were embodied in an Act of 1862, which also consolidated previous legislation.

Grant-in-aid of pauper lunatics, 1874

The Committee's expressed dissatisfaction with the plight of pauper lunatics produced no immediate national result, but eventually, in 1874, an improvement in the situation was produced by the device of a grant-in-aid from the Consolidated Fund.[11] This method had already been employed in 1846 by the Peel administration to ensure the provision of parish medical officers and workhouse teachers, following the first grants-in-aid in 1833 for educational purposes. The sum now involved was 4s. per head for each pauper lunatic removed to an asylum. This gave an incentive to Boards of Guardians to get their paupers out of the workhouse and into a centre for curative treatment.

The Lunacy Commissioners, in their Annual Report for 1875, commented that this measure:

> might be beneficial in promoting the removal to asylums of patients requiring such treatment . . . it remains to be seen whether the alteration . . . will not also have the effect of causing unnecessarily the transfer to asylums of chronic cases . . . thus rendering necessary . . . a still larger outlay than heretofore in providing additional asylum accommodation. The returns for the 1st of January tend to show that such results are not unlikely to accompany the working of this new financial arrangement.

The introduction of this grant-in-aid marked a departure from previous practice in lunacy administration. Hitherto, although the salaries of the Commissioners (paid largely out of the monies received from licensing) were backed by the Consolidated Fund, and authorities were empowered to borrow from the Fund, no central responsibility had been taken for the maintenance of any section of the insane. The grant-in-aid led inevitably to a tightening of central control.

The Lunacy Commissioners' forebodings were fulfilled to some extent. Numbers of chronic patients were transferred to county asylums, which increased their custodial role and diminished their function as centres of treatment; but the frontier between asylum and Poor Law care was to remain blurred for many years.

Public opinion and the 'sensation novelist'

In 1877, the public preoccupation with the danger of illegal detention came to a head again. Among those instrumental in fostering this agitation was Charles Reade, who published his novel *Hard Cash* in 1863.

Reade later defended himself against the charge of being 'a sensation novelist' and claimed that the novel was the result of 'long, severe, systematic labour, from a multitude of volumes, journals, pamphlets, reports, blue-books, manuscript narratives, letters and people whom I have sought out'.

This was probably true; but he set the book in the post-1845 period (the details of methods of admission and discharge of an alleged lunatic are those laid down in the 1845 Act) and neglected to add that most of his sources referred to the scandals and revelations of the early part of the century.[12]

The book tells the story of a young man, Alfred Hardie, wrongfully confined at the instance of his father, who wished to gain control of his money. He is captured by violence, beaten, intimidated and drugged, subjected to the unwelcome attentions of the matron. When at length he manages to convince a visiting magistrate of his sanity, the process of regaining his freedom involves lengthy correspondence and legal delays. This is in every respect the story recounted in 1838 by Richard Paternoster, who was confined for six weeks, and subsequently published his experiences in a series of articles and a book entitled *The Madhouse System* (see p. 111). The similarities are too strong to be merely coincidental; but much of Reade's material comes from even earlier sources.

In one scene, Alfred tells the visiting magistrate that instruments of restraint are hidden in a locked room:

> Baker had not the key; no more had Cooper. The latter was sent for it: he returned, saying that the key was mislaid.
> 'That I expected,' said Alfred. 'Send for the kitchen poker, sir. I'll soon unlock it.'
> 'Fetch the kitchen poker,' said Vane.
> Cooper went for it, and came back with the key instead.

This echoes a passage in the evidence of Godfrey Higgins, fifty years earlier, before the Select Committee of 1815. Higgins also came upon a locked door:

> 'I ordered this door to be opened . . . the keepers hesitated . . . I grew angry, and told them that I insisted on [the key] being found; and that if they would not find it, I could find a key at the kitchen fireside, namely, the poker; upon that, the key was immediately brought.'

At another point, Alfred is made to say: 'one or two gentlemanly madmen . . . have complained to me that the attendants wash them too much like hansom cabs; strip them naked and mop them on the flagstones.'

In the 1827 Report on the Condition of Pauper Lunatics in the Metropolis, evidence given on the notorious 'crib-room cases of Bethnal Green' by an ex-patient, John Nettle, described this process in very similar words. This single instance had raised a considerable public outcry a quarter of a century before Reade wrote his novel.[13]

Reade had certainly studied the available literature, and to this extent he could claim that his account was 'based on fact'. Most of his information referred to isolated cases of abuse—not normal practice—discovered and rectified many years before *Hard Cash* was written. He took the framework of the law as it was in 1863, but fitted into it incidents from sensational cases of the past.

The book was probably inspired by the Report of the Select Committee of 1859–60. It was published at a time when public feeling on these issues ran high; and it enjoyed considerable financial success.

Another novel dealing with the subject of insanity which was widely read at this time was Charlotte Brontë's *Jane Eyre,* first published in 1847. Here is the reverse of the picture—the lack of public under-standing as to the real issues involved in insanity. No appeal for sympathy is made on behalf of the first Mrs Rochester. She remains 'the monster', 'the maniac'—a grim and hated figure locked in a tower with a gin-sodden attendant. No Commissioner visits her—for, as a lunatic confined in her own home, she is outside their jurisdiction. Even those living in the same house only suspect her existence. The blanket of secrecy is complete.

Charlotte Brontë, the most 'moral' of Victorian writers, directs her sympathies elsewhere—to Jane and Mr Rochester. It is with the greatest satisfaction, that author and reader reach the final dénoue-ment—the fire, the death of the 'maniac' as she hurls herself from the burning building, and Rochester's freedom to marry Jane. There was some contemporary criticism of Rochester's character directed against the fact that he was a potential bigamist; but apparently not of his failure to take adequate care of his first wife.

There is no evidence in the Brontë biographies that Charlotte had ever come into close personal contact with the problem of insanity, and the character of the 'maniac' seems to be merely a figment of the imagination stimulated by the horror novels of the late eighteenth century. Mrs Rochester is a figure from *The Castle of Otranto* or the later 'penny dreadfuls'—not a personification of an existing social problem; but when all this has been said, the fact remains that not only the author but apparently the readers also found this present-ation of an insane person acceptable. Even Swinburne, writing in the 1890s, had no fault to find on this score.[14]

We may contrast with this grim picture the gentle sketch of Anne

Catherick drawn by Wilkie Collins in *The Woman in White*, first published in 1869. 'Poor, dazed Anne Catherick' is mentally retarded, a little confused, but wholly an object of pity. When the hero assists 'the victim of the most horrible of all false imprisonments' to escape from an asylum by refusing to give information to the pursuing keepers, he carries the reader's sympathy with him. Later in the novel, when Laura, Lady Glyde, who physically resembles her, is locked in the asylum in her place, the author comments almost casually that 'any attempt . . . to rescue her by legal means would, even if successful, involve a delay which might be fatal to her. . . . intellects, which were shaken already by the horror of the situation to which she had been consigned'. There is no sensational suggestion of ill-treatment; but the calm acceptance of the belief that asylums are places which would shake the mental balance of a sane person, and from which release is almost impossible, is more telling than the vivid imaginings of Reade or Charlotte Brontë.

Fear and hatred of the insane, fear of those who cared for them: both were strong in the second half of the nineteenth century. All the uninformed public agitation centred on the border-line cases, where the issue of illegal detention could be raised. The activities of the Dillwyn Committee of 1877 are a case in point.

The Select Committee of 1877

On 12 February 1877 a Select Committee of the House of Commons was appointed under the chairmanship of Thomas Dillwyn 'to inquire into the operations of Lunacy Law *so far as regards security afforded for it against violations of personal liberty*' (italics added).

Both Dillwyn and his associate, Stephen Cave, showed in their questions a remarkable lack of knowledge of any issues other than the legal ones involved.

'Do you consider', asked Cave of Shaftesbury, 'that the facility with which patients are admitted to asylums is not too great at the present day?'

Shaftesbury's retort was, 'No, certainly not . . . we stated so in 1859, and we state it still more emphatically now.'

His patience was wearing thin under the strain of constant ill-informed attacks on his work. Now seventy-six years of age, he was nervous and depressed, uncertain of how long his failing power would enable him to carry on his public work. On 11 March 1877, shortly before he was called to give evidence before this Select

Committee, he noted in his diary, 'My hour of trial is near; cannot, I should think, be delayed beyond the coming week. Half a century, all but one week, has been devoted to this cause of the lunatics; and . . . the state now, as compared with the state then, would baffle description.' Now he undertook the laborious task of educating the Select Committee.

'It sounds very well,' said Shaftesbury, 'to say that persons acquainted with lunacy should be the only ones to sign certificates.' It was plausible to insist that a lengthy and detailed inquiry should take place before any citizen was forcibly deprived of his liberty; but by the time this step was finally taken, the symptoms would have to be so pronounced that a clear and unequivocal statement of insanity could be made. 'What follows from this course? Why, that the cases are very far advanced, and have got pretty nearly into the category of the incurable.'

The *Journal of Mental Science*, reporting his evidence, stated that 'His lordship spoke with a thorough mastery of every lunacy question about which he was asked'. Shaftesbury himself was pessimistic—in one of his self-doubting moods. 'Beyond the circle of my own Commissioners and the lunatics I visit,' runs an entry in his diary, 'not a soul . . . has any notion of the years of toil and care that, under God, I have bestowed on this melancholy and awful question.'

But the Select Committee was apparently won over. The Report stated that 'allegations of mala fides or of serious abuse were not substantiated. Much of the evidence . . . amounted to little more than differences of opinion among medical men'.

> The Committee cannot help observing here, that the jealousy
> with which the treatment of lunatics is watched at the present
> day, and the comparatively trifling nature of the abuses alleged,
> present a remarkable contrast to the horrible cruelty . . .
> apathy . . . and indifference of half a century earlier.

Shaftesbury's lesson in the history of reform had apparently not been in vain.

On the vexed question of a magistrate's order, the Committee did not 'attach any special importance to the order emanating from a magistrate'. Moreover, they felt that it was permissible for voluntary boarders, i.e. non-certified and possibly non-certifiable cases—to continue to be allowed in small licensed houses, provided that the Lunacy Commissioners were informed within twenty-four hours of reception. 'Nervous' cases had been admitted without formality to licensed houses since 1862, though their numbers were comparatively small; but a beginning had been made which would lead ultimately to the provisions for voluntary status under the Mental Treatment Act of 1930 and for informal status under the Mental Health Act of 1959.

The *Lancet* commission of 1877

In the same year in which the Select Committee made its report, the *Lancet* sponsored a fact-finding commission on 'The Care and Cure of the Insane' under the direction of Dr Mortimer Granville, which was to take this idea a stage further. Dr Granville personally visited a number of asylums, both public and private, in London and the Home Counties, and produced a voluminous report which is notable for its sober judgment and unusually progressive views.

The general tone of the report expresses the author's belief that, after a period of unusual activity in which the worst abuses of the 'madhouse' system had been remedied, asylums were marking time, and in some cases regressing from the standards of 1845. At Hanwell, he found that Conolly's work had 'languished'. 'There was no open retrogression at Hanwell, but it is difficult to believe that there was any progress. Things went on very much in the humdrum way which might have been expected to succeed a period of energetic reform.'

At Wandsworth, (the Surrey Asylum, p. 122) Dr Granville noted with approval the 'judicious practice' of visiting the wards unexpectedly by day and night, employed by the medical officers. He added, 'Everywhere attendants, we are convinced, maltreat, abuse and terrify patients when the backs of the medical officers are turned. Humanity is only to be secured by watching officials.' At the same hospital, he was distressed to find that the old system of providing incontinent patients with straw palliasses instead of mattresses had been revived: 'Such a provision could only be advocated on the hypothesis—so mischievous in lunacy—that the bad and dirty habits of patients are to be regarded as incurable, instead of being eradicated by proper training.'

At Dartford, (the City Asylum, Stone House) he wrote acidly of the 'outside show' and the contrast with the 'spirit of parsimony' within. 'It appears strange ... to charge a representative committee of the City of London with cheese-paring. Unfortunately, the evil is evident at every turn in this establishment.'

The staircases were 'cramped and draughty', the patients' clothing 'torn and dirty', the corridors 'meagre', the lavatories 'very defective'.

Bethlem and St Luke's, the two great curative establishments of the metropolis, were both doing outstanding work; but both were 'singularly ill-adapted for the residence of large bodies of patients'; and though Bethlem was well endowed, St Luke's was 'starved and crippled in its work in a fashion that reflects dishonour on the philanthropy of our great City firms and the wealthy classes of the metropolis'.

Lack of the personal touch, lack of money—these were the real evils of the system. The remedy was to be found in a radical change of attitude to the insane; and here Dr Granville's words are so strikingly in harmony with the recommendations of the Royal Commission on Mental Illness and Mental Deficiency of 1957 that it is difficult to believe that they were written eighty years earlier:

> Patients labouring under mental derangement should be removable
> to a public or private asylum as to a hospital for ordinary
> diseases, *without certificate* . . . the power of signing certificates
> of lunacy should be withdrawn from . . . magistrates.[15]

This was the enlightened medical opinion of 1877; it was to take the general public a very long time to learn from it.

Despite the work of the Lunacy Commissioners, the Report of the Select Committee, and the *Lancet* report, there was no public support for early and humane treatment, and the constant allegations of illegal detention continued. The columns of *The Times* exhibit all the old fear and prejudice against the insane. On 5 April 1877 a leading article commented that 'if lunacy continues to increase as at present, the insane will be in the majority, and, freeing themselves, will put the sane in asylums'. This bogey of the supposed increase of insanity, though officially denied, occurs again and again. On 23 May there was a letter signed 'A Lunatic's Victim' which deplored the tendency of the present laws 'to protect the liberty of the lunatic at the expense of the lives, limbs and comfort of the same'. Two days later came a complaint from an attendant: 'I have been cut down with a hatchet once, and shut up for three hours in the strong room of a private asylum with a patient suffering from delirium tremens, who stood 6 ft. 2 ins., hanging at my throat . . . and all for £25 a year.'

The case of Mrs Georgiana Weldon

These two public prejudices—the fear of the insane and the fear of illegal detention of the sane—reached a new height in 1884, through the much-publicized activities of Mrs Georgiana Weldon.[16]

Mrs Weldon was an extremely eccentric lady of considerable means and some social position. Her husband, who held the position of Windsor Herald, deserted her in 1875, leaving her with a house and an income of £1,000 a year. She was a strong believer in psychical forces—it later transpired in legal proceedings that she believed the spirit of her deceased mother to have entered into her pet rabbit—and was associated with the editorial board of a journal called the *Spiritualist*. She had a favourite medium, Madame Nenier, under whose influence she frequently acted. She was said by a specialist in mental disorder to 'have peculiar ideas on the education of young children and the simplification of ladies' dress'. This was not in itself proof of insanity; the wealthy, eccentric Englishwoman is a common-place of nineteenth-century fact and fiction. Mrs Weldon's behaviour was undoubtedly abnormal in that it did not conform to the conventions of the society in which she lived; but the question at issue was whether it was so strongly anti-social that she should be removed from that society.

Mr Weldon, as the petitioning relative, requested Dr Forbes Winslow,[17] a specialist in mental disorder, to take Mrs Weldon into his private asylum at Hammersmith. Dr Winslow was an eminent man in his profession—what we would now call a forensic psychiatrist—who had given evidence in many murder cases on the issue of criminal insanity.

The ensuing proceedings were almost farcical. Dr Winlsow and an attendant went to Mrs Weldon's house. Mrs Weldon bolted the door. A *dea ex machina* appeared, presumably through the back entrance, in the shape of a Mrs Lowe, a discharged mental patient who was secretary of the Lunacy Laws Amendment Association.[18] As Dr Winslow and his attendant forced an entry, Mrs Weldon, disguised in the habit of a Sister of Mercy, left by another door in the company of Mrs Lowe.

Here were all the ingredients of a popular *cause celèbre*: the society background, the wealthy and beautiful lady under threat of duress, the dramatic escape in disguise. Mrs Weldon, who was undoubtedly an exhibitionist, then started a number of law-suits, with the support of the Lunacy Laws Amendment Association and the editor of the *Spiritualist*. She sued Dr Forbes Winslow for alleged libel, assault, wrongful arrest, false imprisonment (in that she was under duress in her own house before she made her escape) and trespass. An interesting legal side-line arose from the fact that these events took place in 1877, five years before the passing of the Married Woman's Property Act. The house therefore legally belonged to Mr Weldon. Mrs Weldon was suing for trepass in a house belonging to her husband a person who had entered with her husband's consent; and if she were successful any damages awarded to her would become the property of her husband.

Mrs Weldon also sued her husband—for the restitution of conjugal rights; she sued a Mr Betts, editor of *Figaro*, for alleged libel, in that he had published a statement to the effect that a pamphlet written by her 'could excite in the minds of decent people no other feeling than disgust'. She sued the editor of the *Daily Chronicle* for a similar libel. She sued the two doctors who signed the certificates. She hired the Covent Garden Opera House for a meeting on her own behalf, at which she distributed many copies of her own pamphlet, and sang from a box at the side of the stage. She subsequently disagreed with the management over the cost of hire of the hall, and sued an impresario named Rivière and the composer Gounod, who was associated with him, for breach of contract.

The multiplicity of these legal actions seems in itself *prima facie* evidence that Mrs Weldon was not a balanced person. Nevertheless, there was a strong public feeling that she was a very much wronged woman. Specialists in mental disorder disagreed in court concerning her mental condition. A Dr Edmonds considered that she was an unconventional person, but sane; the unhappy Dr Forbes Winslow considered that she was incoherent and deluded, decidedly in need of treatment.

There was never a clear judgement in this case. There were trials, re-trials and appeals. For months, the legal columns of *The Times* were filled with accounts of Mrs Weldon's protests and eccentricities. In the end, she won some of her cases—in particular those against Dr Forbes Winslow and the two certifying doctors; but the damages awarded must have been swallowed up in the costs.[19] The discussions on the principle of the liberty of the subject degenerated into squabbles on minor legal issues.

The Weldon issue brought the whole question of the amendment of the lunacy laws into the public eye in an atmosphere of heated debate and partisanship. The asylum doctors were the villains of the piece— the infringers of personal liberty. The editorial in the *Journal of Mental Science* in October 1884, written by Daniel Hack Tuke, states, 'It is so easy to talk glibly about the liberty of the subject, and so difficult to guard against the licence into which that too often degenerates'. Tuke continues with a reference to 'the crude views which are entertained upon this subject in some quarters . . . we think it right to ask that we may be generally credited with ordinary honesty and integrity'. This probably referred to Baron Huddleston's celebrated 'crossing-sweeper judgement' in which he stated after Mrs Weldon's first trial:

> It is somewhat startling—it is positively shocking—that if a pauper, or as Mrs Weldon put it, a crossing-sweeper should sign an order, and another crossing-sweeper should make a statement, and then that two medical men, who had never had a day's practice in their lives, should for a small sum of money grant their certificates, a person may be lodged in a private lunatic asylum, and that this order, and the statement, and these certificates are a perfect answer to any action.[20]

The doctors were only too well aware of the difficulties of their own position, and of the weight of public sentiment which was mounting against them. Hack Tuke's editorial sounded a sombre note:

> Of one thing we are sure, and that is that troublous times are before those entrusted with the care of the insane. Already we know of several threatened proceedings by former patients . . . Lunacy Law will be amended, or probably re-made, and the foundations will be laid at the cost of some martyrs.[21]

Following the Weldon cases, there developed a strong movement for a major revision of the lunacy laws; this brought together diverse groups and personalities—the Lord Chancellor and the legal profession working for the same ends as the Lunacy Laws Amendment Association and a variety of ex-patients with real or fancied grudges against the existing system. Shaftesbury's plea and Granville's recommendations for early treatment and easier methods of admission and discharge were swept aside. The tide of public opinion was against them.

Selborne and Shaftesbury

The leader of the movement for tightening up the legal procedure was the Lord Chancellor, Lord Selborne, a man of outstanding personality and ability who, at seventy-two, had a subtle intellect unimpaired by age. His biographer credits him with 'a rare power of easy and persuasive speech, a learning and knowledge of affairs equally wide, profound and exact, the abstemiousness of an ascetic, a vigorous constitution and untiring energy'.[22] A less reverent contemporary, Lord Bowen, described Selborne as 'a pious cricket on the hearth'.[23] Shaftesbury could match him in abstemiousness and piety, but in little else.

Shaftesbury was now a very old man, in his eighties. He noted in his diary at this time 'the sensible decline of mental application and vigour'. He was afraid that 'body and mind are falling to pieces'. His diary shows an almost incredible pressure of work—constant meetings, deputations and public dinners, a voluminous correspondence on many issues, frequent interviews with both group representatives and individuals. His days were overloaded and these engagements took their toll in mental and nervous exhaustion. Between public functions, he would collapse, afraid that the next would be his last: and one comment in conversation, quoted by Hodder, comes from the heart—'I cannot bear to leave the world with all the misery in it.'[24]

These were the antagonists in the struggle ahead. The contrast could scarcely have been greater. Selborne described Shaftesbury in his memoirs[25] as 'my excellent antagonist', but the general tone of his references is one of patronage. He saw Shaftesbury as honest and well-meaning, but tiresome and politically inept. They had clashed frequently in the past over religious issues: there is a slightly acrimonious correspondence between them in *The Times* as early as 1842. Selborne, though not a Puseyite, was a convinced High-Churchman. Shaftesbury had broken with his cousin Pusey over the Oxford Movement and was an equally convinced Evangelical. Under the Palmerston administration Shaftesbury, as the Prime Minister's son-in-law, had been instrumental in securing the appointment of exclusively Evangelical bishops—a fact of which Selborne frequently complained in the press and in the House of Lords.

Parliamentary procedure 1884–9

In 1883, even before the publicity accorded to the Weldon case, Selborne had introduced a Lunacy Bill in the House of Lords. This was withdrawn owing to the lack of support at the time; but on 5 May 1884 Lord Milltown, an Irish peer and a barrister, put forward a motion that 'in the opinion of this House, the existing state of the Lunacy Laws is unsatisfactory, and constitutes a serious danger to the liberty of the subject'. He referred in his speech to Baron Huddleston's statement in Weldon *v.* Winslow that 'a person could be confined in an asylum by anybody, on the statement of anybody, provided certain formalities were gone through . . . it was positively shocking that such a state of things should exist'.

It should be noted here that the Weldon case never came to the direct attention of the Lunacy Commissioners, since they would only have been officially notified of Mrs Weldon's certification after her reception into Dr Winslow's house. Since she 'escaped', this eventuality never occurred. However, Mrs Weldon subpoenaed them in her case against Dr Semple, one of the certifying doctors, and later commented that 'Lord Shaftesbury . . . seemed not to care much for the judge's opinions'.[26]

Milltown described the state of the lunacy laws as 'intolerable . . . a damning blot . . . (on) the Statute Book'.[27]

Shaftesbury rose to reply. He 'thought it necessary, and almost a point of duty, to explain the state of things and calm the public mind'. He deprecated Baron Huddleston's strictures, and declared that, although some revision in the law respecting private asylums was necessary, an increase in legal formality—particularly by the device of a magistrate's order—was undesirable.

Milltown's motion was carried—to Shaftesbury's great distress. A long correspondence between Shaftesbury and Selborne ensued, but there was no possibility of compromise between them. In 1885, Selborne introduced a Lunacy Amendment Bill into the Lords, and Shaftesbury thereupon tendered his resignation from the chairmanship of the Lunacy Commission.

In June, the Bill was shelved and Shaftesbury was persuaded to remain in office. The shelving of the Bill may have been due to genuine pressure of parliamentary business; to the obstruction of the Irish members—who at this time were blocking all legislation to the point where it was almost impossible to get a Bill through the Lower House; to Shaftesbury's great reputation with the general public; or to a combination of all three.

In July, Shaftesbury moved to Folkstone, and it became clear that his life would end there. He died on 1 October. Over two hundred philanthropic organizations sent deputations to the memorial service at Westminster Abbey; but the Lunacy Laws Amendment Association does not appear to have been represented.

In the session 1885–6, political conditions were unsettled, and there was no opportunity for the re-presentation of the Bill; but in August 1886, the position was more favourable. The Salisbury administration was formed, with Lord Halsbury securely on the Woolsack. Halsbury had practised before Selborne as an advocate, and sat with him as a judge. The link between them was a strong one.

Now that Shaftesbury was gone, the way was open for the introduction of the measures he had so long opposed. On 31 January 1887 two Bills were introduced in the House of Lords by Lord Halsbury. They represented considered legal opinion on the subject, and the Lord Chancellor paid tribute to the work done by his predecessors in office, Lord Selborne and Lord Herschell.[28] The first Bill was a consolidating measure, designed to draw existing legislation into a coherent whole. The second was the Lunacy Acts Amendment Bill, which included a number of points raised by the Dillwyn Committee, ten years before, and introduced again in an amended form the highly controversial clause requiring a magistrate's order in non-pauper cases. The Commissioners, faithful to the Shaftesbury tradition, opposed the clause; but the Lord Chancellor felt that 'no alteration of the law would be satisfactory that did not make further provision for the liberty of the subject'. He proposed a compromise, whereby a magistrate's order would not be required in every case, but the alleged lunatic could require the presence of a justice if he wished to defend his sanity.

Both Bills were passed by the Lords and sent to the Commons. The Lunacy Bill survived its third reading, but the Lunacy Acts Amendment Bill was withdrawn in August by the Solicitor-General after the first reading. No reason was given for this action, and after this, both Bills disappeared from the parliamentary scene. It was apparently not the intention of the Lord Chancellor and his supporters that one Bill should pass without the other.

In February 1888, the Lunacy Acts Amendment Bill appeared once more in the Lords. This time, it contained the provisions of both the previous Bills. The Lord Chancellor summarized the intentions of the new Bill as follows:

1. The introduction of a judicial authority for ordering the detention of a person as a lunatic. (The previous compromise had apparently been withdrawn.)

2. The provision that all orders of detention should cease to have effect unless renewed at the stated time. This placed the onus of continued detention on the shoulders of the medical profession,

rather than leaving the question of discharge to their initiative.

3. Protection to medical men and others 'against vexatious actions where they have acted in good faith'. This was a gesture to the medical profession following the widespread alarm aroused by the case of Weldon *v*. Winslow. This clause conciliated a powerful pressure group—the asylum doctors—who might have wrecked the Act.[29]

4. Restrictions on the opening of new private asylums. This was a means of winning over the Shaftesburyites. Shaftesbury had written to Lord Milltown only six months before his death to say that he had not changed by one hair's-breadth his opinions of 'the danger which beset all private asylums, and of the necessity of placing the whole care of lunacy on a public basis'.

5. Consolidating clauses.[30]

The Lord Chancellor was in fact saying to the doctors, 'If you want legal protection, you must take the magistrates clause,' and to the Shaftesburyites, 'If you want to reduce the number of private asylums, you must take the magistrates clause.' He concluded with an appeal to the Lower House. The Bill 'had already received very full and careful consideration in their Lordships' House; and having been adopted at some stage in its history by each party represented in "another place", it might be expected to be received in a like spirit there'.

The Bill was introduced in the Commons by Salisbury's Home Secretary, Henry Matthews, on 24 April. Two days later, the second reading was deferred on a motion by Arthur O'Connor and Dillwyn on the grounds that it was very long, and that the House had not yet had time to digest it.

On 8 May, the Earl of Milltown asked with some irritation what had happened to the Bill; and the Lord Chancellor confessed, with equal irritation, that he did not know. By June, it appeared that the Government no longer had any serious intention of proceeding with the Bill in the face of continued opposition; and in July, it was withdrawn by common agreement.

The Lord Chancellor's determination did not slacken; and in February 1889, the Bill was introduced for the third time. It reached the Commons in April, and a close debate followed the report of the Standing Committee in July.[31]

The clause relating to the justice's order was apparently no longer a matter of controversy. Instead, discussion centred on the proposal that all letters written by patients to certain persons in authority, including the Lunacy Commissioners and the Lord Chancellor, should be forwarded to them, and that notices should be placed prominently in every asylum informing patients that they had this right of access to higher authority. Dr Farquharson, member of parliament for Aberdeen, who had welcomed the clauses relating to the protection of the medical profession, was very much opposed to this provision. He stated that 'hanging these notices all over lunatic asylums will tend very greatly to retard the recovery of the patients, by unsettling their minds and leading them to brood over fancied grievances'. Arthur O'Connor supported him: 'Many patients spend most of their time in writing letters to the Lord Chancellor. I know of a case in which two sisters spent every day from morning to night in writing letters to the Lord Chancellor, and another in which a person was continually writing to Satan . . . .'

The Bill was eventually passed, after some reference back to the Lords, and received the Royal Assent on 26 August.

By now, the battle was over. A Lunacy Bill to consolidate all previous enactments was introduced in the Lords in the same month, but dropped because of the pressure of parliamentary business. It was revived in the next session as the Lunacy (Consolidation) Bill. The administration was weary of the whole issue, and one can detect in the speeches of the Bill's adherents an almost pleading note, a hope that the protracted controversy over a difficult issue had been ended once and for all.

'It is simply a measure of consolidation,' placated Lord Halsbury in the Lords, 'and it is hoped that every facility will be given for its passing.'[32]

'It is a consolidation Bill only,' explained W. H. Smith, the First Lord of the Treasury, in the Commons, 'and it is to the interest of the entire community that the consolidation of statutes should be effected as speedily as possible.'[33]

The long-drawn-out controversy ended on 27 March 1890, on a note of weary facetiousness:

> Mr. J. Morley. 'I hope the First Lord of the Treasury will . . .
> draw attention to the fact that the Opposition have afforded
> great facilities for the passing of this Bill.'
> Mr W. H. Smith. 'I shall certainly have great pleasure in
> calling . . . attention to the fact that the Opposition have given
> the greatest possible facilities for the passing of a Lunacy Bill.'

The Lunacy Act of 1890

The Act itself is an extremely long and intricate document, which expresses few general principles, and provides in detail for almost every known contingency. Nothing was left to chance, and very little to future development. The following summary gives only the main provisions.

Administration

(*i*) *Central.* The Lord Chancellor was still the ultimate authority. He continued to be responsible for the appointment of the Lunacy Commissioners, and to receive their reports (sections 150–62). He appointed the Chancery Visitors (sections 163–8, 183–6) and possessed direct powers of intervention, through the agency of the Lunacy Commissioners, in the affairs of single patients (sections 198–200, 206).

The Lunacy Commissioners and their secretariat continued to exercise powers of visitation and inspection over all institutions (sections 187–206) and all patients except Chancery lunatics (sections 183–6).

The Judge and Masters in Lunacy and the Chancery Visitors continued to be responsible for Chancery cases, i.e. lunatics so found by inquisition (sections 163–8, 183–6).

(*ii*) *Local.* The local authority responsible for public asylums was now the county or county borough council, as constituted under the Local Government Act of 1888 (section 240). They were compelled to build and maintain an asylum, either alone or under a joint agreement with a neighbouring authority (sections 238, 241–52). The local authority appointed the Visiting Committee of an asylum. This Committee was to be formed of not less than seven members, but there were no specifications concerning their interests or qualifications (sections 169–76).

Admission

There were four methods of admission to an asylum or a licensed house:

  (i) by reception order (sections 4–8)
  (ii) by urgency order (section 11)

(iii) by summary reception order (sections 13–22)
(iv) by inquisition (sections 12 and 90–107)

A reception order on petition involved a near relative or other person stating his connection with the patient in making a statement before a justice of the peace supported by two medical certificates. It was necessary for the petitioner to be over twenty-one years of age, to have seen the patient within the previous fourteen days, and to undertake to visit the patient (in person or by proxy) every six months. This applied only to non-pauper cases.

An urgency order applied in those private cases where there was no time for a lengthy procedure of certification. The procedure involved a relative's petition and one medical certificate only, and a magistrate's intervention was not necessary. The total duration of an urgency order was seven days, during which time a normal reception order on petition had to be completed, or the patient discharged.

A summary reception order was the normal method of admission for pauper patients. The initiative here rested with the Poor Law Relieving Officer or the police, who were responsible for notifying a justice of the peace. One medical certificate was necessary in addition to the justice's order.

In the case of a patient found wandering at large, the relieving officer or constable could detain him and bring him before a justice (section 15) or remove him to a workhouse until proceedings could be taken (section 20). The period of detention without legal certification under this clause was not to exceed three days.

Admission by inquisition applied only to Chancery lunatics. There were several forms of procedure, varying in elaboration and expense. The simplest was that whereby, in an uncontested case, the Judge in Lunacy could direct the Masters in Lunacy to examine an alleged lunatic and to receive evidence on his state of mind. If they considered the patient to be of unsound mind, they would issue a certificate to this effect. A 'committee of the person' would then be appointed[35] under their direction to administer the estate; and the patient could be received into an asylum, or confined singly, on an order either from the Masters or from the committee of the person. If the alleged lunatic wished to contest the issue of his sanity, he could request a trial by jury. This often meant protracted litigation, and a more costly procedure.

These methods of admission had grown out of existing legislation. The procedure for reception on petition had developed from the Madhouse Act of 1828—one of Gordon's Acts: the summary reception order, involving the Poor Law relieving officer or the constable, had grown out of the historic section 20 of the Vagrancy Act of 1744. The procedure for Chancery lunatics had the longest heritage of all, being derived from that *Praerogativa Regis* of Edward II which is often taken as the starting-point of lunacy legislation.

Reception orders and certificates. (*i*) *Prohibited relationships* (*sections 30–3*). There were detailed regulations to prevent collusion between the parties responsible for the process of certification. Prohibited relationships were: first degree relatives or relatives-in-law (i.e., father, father-in-law, brother, brother-in-law, son, son-in-law, and so on); professional or business associates (i.e. partners, assistants, employers, employees); and financially-interested parties.

These relationships were prohibited between petitioner and doctor, doctor and doctor, where two medical certificates were required; doctor and manager of the institution to which the patient was sent; petitioner and manager of the institution. It is typical of the framing of this Act that the relationships are set out at considerable length. Each case is dealt with separately, and there is no attempt to frame a general principle of non-collusion.

(*ii*) *Duration* (*sections 29 and 38*). The medical certificates were to be signed not more than seven days before the date of the petition, or two days in the case of an urgency order.

The duration of a reception order on petition or a summary reception order was one year. It was then renewable after periods of two years, three years, five years, and successive periods of five years, on the report of the medical officer of the asylum to the Lunacy Commissioners.

Care and treatment

(*i*) *Reports and visitation* (*sections 39, 163–82, 187–206*). A complicated system of documentation and inspection was laid down. This was an elaboration of the system evolved by Shaftesbury and his colleagues for the 1845 Act. The Lunacy Commissioners were to send two of their number—one a medical practitioner and one a barrister—to every public asylum at least once a year; to every licensed house in the metropolis four times a year, with two additional visits by a single Commissioner; to licensed houses outside the metropolitan area twice a year; to registered hospitals—i.e., subscription hospitals such as the Retreat which were not run for profit—once a year. The Commissioners were to visit without previous notice, at any hour of the day or night as they saw fit. They were to make detailed enquiries concerning the construction of the building, the classification, occupation and recreation of the patients, the physical condition and diet of pauper patients, the admission, discharge and visitation of all patients, the performance of Divine Service and its effect on the congregation, and the use or non-use of mechanical restraint. The Commissioners were to lay a report giving the number of visits made and the number of patients seen before the Lord Chancellor every six months, and were to make a detailed report of their inspection, to be laid before Parliament, once a year.

In public asylums, two members of the visiting committee (i.e., in this case the committee of management) were to make a statutory visit to the asylum every two months,[36] and to lay an annual report before the local authority of the area.

In licensed houses and registered hospitals, the justices' visitors were to inspect as follows: two, one of whom was a medical practitioner, twice a year; one, twice a year. They were to be appointed by the justices at Quarter Sessions (sections 177–81).

(*ii*) *Mechanical restraint* (*section 40*). Restraint by instruments and appliances was only to be used for the purposes of surgical or medical treatment, or to prevent the patient from injuring himself or his fellow-patients. A medical certificate was necessary for each instance of restraint, and a report book was to be kept; a copy of the records was to be sent to the Commissioners once a quarter.

(*iii*) *Correspondence and interviews* (*section 41–2*). All letters written by patients to certain persons in authority, including the Lord Chancellor, a Judge in Lunacy, a Secretary of State, a Lunacy Commissioner or a Chancery Visitor, were to be forwarded unopened. The Commissioners could direct that notices explaining this clause should be placed in an asylum, and could choose the actual site of the notice, to ensure that it should be seen by all private patients. Pauper patients possessed the same right of having letters to persons in authority forwarded unopened, but there was no obligation on the Commissioners to ensure that they were aware of this right. This may

G

have been because paupers' complaints were likely to be more frivolous than those of private patients; because, in the eyes of the law, they were rather less important; because there was less need for safeguards where no property was involved; or simply because in 1890 a high proportion of pauper patients could neither read nor write. (In practice, of course, most letters written by patients were forwarded unopened.)

Discharge

(*i*)*Absence on trial* (*section 55*). Any two visitors of an asylum were empowered to consent to the absence of a patient on trial for as long as they thought fit. During the period of trial, an allowance not exceeding the cost of his board in the asylum might be made to a pauper lunatic. In the case of a private patient, the written consent of the person on whose petition the original reception order was made was required.

(*ii*) *Boarding out* (*section 57*). This clause applied only to pauper lunatics, who might be boarded out with a relative or friend if the visiting committee and the guardians of the union agreed. An allowance might be made as for a patient on trial.

(*iii*) *Full discharge*. A private patient might be discharged on the direction of the person who signed the petition for a reception order (section 72). A pauper patient might be discharged on the direction of the authority responsible for his maintenance (section 73). In either case, the medical officer of the asylum possessed a right of veto. If he considered that the patient was 'dangerous and unfit to be at large', he could issue a barring certificate (section 74).

Two Commissioners, one legal and one medical, might discharge a patient after giving seven days' notice of their intention to do so. Any three members of the visiting committee could order a discharge, or any two with the advice and consent of the medical officer; or in the case of a pauper, any two visitors, if a friend or relative was willing to be responsible for the patient (sections 75–9).

(*iv*) *Escape*. Any patient escaping from an institution might be recaptured within fourteen days. After the expiry of that period, he could not be returned to the asylum unless fresh proceedings for certification were completed (section 85).

Miscellaneous provisions

(*i*) *Single lunatics*. The procedure for visitation and inspection of single lunatics received for profit continued as under the Act of 1845. It will be remembered that one of the defects of that Act was the lack of provision for single patients confined in their own homes, or in charitable institutions—the 'Mrs Rochesters' of society. Section 206 of the 1890 Act made it possible for the Commissioners to visit such a patient, and to require periodical medical reports on the patient's mental and physical condition. The Commissioner might, if they thought fit, pass on their findings to the Lord Chancellor, who was empowered to remove the patient from custody, or to secure his transfer to an asylum.

(*ii*) *'Penalties, misdemeanor and proceedings'*. Part XI of the Act set forth at some length the penalties for non-compliance with its terms. 'Misdemeanors' ranged from obstructing a Commissioner in the course of his duty to connivance at a patient's escape. The range of penalties for each offence was laid down in terms of fines and imprisonment.

The very length of this Act singles it out from all previous attempts at lunacy legislation, and it bears the heavy impress of the legal mind. Every safeguard which could possibly be devised against illegal confinement is there. Dillwyn's suspicions, Mrs Weldon's accusations, Shaftesbury's doubts, Hack Tuke's fears, Milltown's wrath, and the determination of three successive Lord Chancellors helped to shape it. The result, from the legal point of view, was very nearly perfect. From the medical and social view-point, it was to hamper the progress of the mental health movement for nearly seventy years.

Mental defectives

When the Lunacy Act of 1890 came into force, it applied also to mental defectives. The Act stated (section 341): ' "Lunatic" means an idiot or person of unsound mind.'

No distinction was made between the two conditions. This was surprising in view of the fact that the movement for the recognition of mental deficiency as a separate condition was then nearly fifty years old; and a permissive Idiots Act which recognized the special asylums for 'idiots' (the terms 'idiots', 'feeble-minded persons' and 'mental defectives' were often used interchangeably during this period) had been passed in 1886. It was probably a recognition of the fact that, for many years to come, mental defectives would have to be sent to asylums for the insane, because there would be insufficient specialized accommodation for them.

The pioneer work in this field had been undertaken in France, where Dr Itard attempted the education of a wild boy discovered by hunters in the woods. Itard was at first confident that, by creating suitable environmental conditions, it was possible to turn the boy into a normally socialized being. In 1801 he published his first pamphlet, *L'Education du Sauvage d'Aveyron*; but by 1807 he had to confess at least partial failure.

This experiment led Itard to two conclusions: that there was a condition of innate defect which could be minimized, but not eradicated, by suitable training; and that some kind of special provision for cases of this kind was necessary.

In 1828, the first institute for the education and training of the mentally defective was set up in Paris. Its work quickly gained recognition, and was followed by the foundation of similar institutions in Switzerland and Germany. From 1837, Dr Séguin undertook the development of Itard's work in Paris, working at two large hospitals, the Paris Hospital for Incurables, and Bicêtre. Professor J. C. Flügel states categorically that 'By the middle of the (nineteenth) century, it may be said that the principle of a special training for the mentally defective was well on the way to recognition'.[1]

182

Early 'idiot asylums' in England

Development in England was comparatively slow. A small 'School for Idiots' was started in Bath in 1846 by the Misses White, but this took only four patients. The real beginning of the work in England dates from 1847, when an 'asylum for idiots' was founded at Park House, Highgate, under the patronage of the Duke of Cambridge and the Duchess of Gloucester.

'We have laboured under the appalling conviction that idiocy is without remedy, and therefore we have left it without help. It may now be pronounced,' runs the somewhat floridly written brochure, 'not as an opinion, but as a fact, a delightful fact, that THE IDIOT MAY BE EDUCATED.' The institution was supported by charitable donations, 'moderate payments' being received from those with means. 'Idiots' of both sexes and any age were received, but preference was given to those who were young and suffering from the lesser forms of defect: what we would now call 'subnormal', but probably not 'severely subnormal'. The institution moved in 1855 to Redhill in Surrey, where the new building was opened by the Prince Consort, and became known as the Earlswood Asylum.[2] By 1881, it had 561 inmates.

In 1864, a similar institution, the Starcross Asylum, opened at Exeter, and four years later, the foundation stone of the Northern Counties Asylum for Idiots and Imbeciles[3] was laid at Lancaster. The Northern Counties Asylum had the Queen as its patron, and the Archbishop of York as its president. The first medical officer came from Earlswood. It accommodated 600 patients, all male, and cost £50,000 to build. Payment for patients ranged from 50 guineas per annum to 200 guineas, though a certain number of 'children of persons in narrow circumstances' were accommodated for only twenty guineas. The first patients were admitted in 1870. The Lunacy Commissioners visited in 1871, and were pleased with what they saw—though they commented characteristically that the meat was cold, and the pipes in need of lagging.

Earlswood, Starcross and the Northern Counties Asylum were subscription hospitals. The first large-scale provision by a public authority was the building of the Darenth Training Schools by the Metropolitan Asylums Board in the 1870s.

By 1881, a return of idiots (i.e. mental defectives of any grade) in public institutions totalled 29,452. Only three per cent were receiving care and treatment in institutions specifically designed for them. The rest were scattered in workhouses, lunatic asylums and prisons. Daniel Hack Tuke, writing in 1882,[4] believed that the real total was much higher—that there were many defectives whose existence was unknown to the public authorities.

In fact, history was repeating itself. Similar factors had been present when the insane as a whole were first recognized as a separate class—the personal secrecy, the public apathy, the submerged nature of the whole problem.

Sub-committee of the Charity Organisation Society, 1877

The Charity Organisation Society, founded in 1868 for the co-ordination of charitable effort of all kinds, and the suppression of mendicity, was a body of some power and prestige. One member of its original council was Sir Charles Trevelyan, a former Governor of Madras, who had two great assets: a sympathy for oppressed peoples, and a knowledge of administration both from the voluntary and the statutory viewpoint. In 1875, he placed before the council his view that the Government should intervene in the field of provision for 'improvable idiots'—and backed his opinion with a pamphlet written by himself, and a letter from the Lunacy Commissioners expressing their agreement.

A special sub-committee of the Charity Organisation Society debated the question throughout the winter of 1876–7. The members concluded that special provision for this class—it was Sir Charles who introduced the term 'feeble-minded'—was urgently necessary, since they could not be cared for adequately in lunatic asylums or work-houses. Unlike the writer of the Park House brochure, they were not over-optimistic about the results of training: 'There is a large pro-portion of cases which, having achieved a certain improvement, are unable to get beyond this, and are indeed liable to retrogress.'

Possibly only two per cent could be trained to the point where they could be socially and financially self-supporting; but given a suitable environment, almost all could be improved to some extent. Their lives could be made less burdensome, and their usefulness increased.

One outstanding fact of this report is that the sub-committee concurred with Sir Charles Trevelyan's opinion that this was a field for state action. They recommended that, as for lunatic asylums, there should be a *per capita* grant of 4s. from the Consolidated Fund, and that the asylums should be financed out of local rates. In view of the well-known antipathy of the Charity Organisation Society to state action in most fields of social service, this recommendation carried extra weight.

The report pointed out that the Lunacy Acts were already wide enough in scope to allow local authorities to build idiot asylums; but that probably little or no action would be taken unless fresh legislation was introduced, since the justices had no incentive to undertake the extra expense involved.

The Idiots Act, 1886

A deputation headed by Lord Shaftesbury—who, though he disapproved of the Society's policy in other ways,[5] had supported Trevelyan on this issue from the early stages—took the report to the Local Government Board. It was eventually accepted in principle, but the results were disappointing. The Idiots Bill was so lukewarm in tone and so conservative in character that it achieved little. It passed both the Lords and the Commons without controversy, and received the Royal Assent on 25 June 1886—six days after Sir Charles Trevelyan's death.

The Act referred to 'an idiot or imbecile from birth or from an early age' and merely laid down conditions for admission, discharge, registration and inspection similar to those for lunatics. A medical certificate and a statement from the parent or guardian of the patient were necessary preliminaries to admission. The Lunacy Commissioners were responsible for visitation and inspection.

The Act also stated specifically that the terms 'idiot' and 'imbecile' did not include lunatics. Yet four years later, the Lunacy Act of 1890 completely overlooked this distinction, continuing to treat the terms 'idiot' and 'lunatic' as synonymous. It would appear that the Idiots Act made little public impact. Mrs Bosanquet's *Social Work in London—A History of the Charity Organisation Society*, which treats of its work in this connection at some length—does not even mention the Act.

Agitation for government action, 1886–1904

In the ensuing period, social issues connected with feeble-mindedness became hotly debated. Was the condition a product of heredity or environment? Could it be cured by suitable training? Could it be prevented in future generations by such means as sterilization, or segregation of feeble-minded girls of child-bearing age? Should the feeble minded be permanently segregated or could their return to the community be envisaged after a process of socialization?

The Charity Organisation Society continued to amass evidence. In collaboration with the British Association, it undertook the work of surveying the mental and physical condition of London children in elementary schools and Poor Law institutions. Evidence was also gained from the Metropolitan Association for Befriending Young Servants and the National Vigilance Society on the difficulties of feeble-minded girls and young women. General Moberley, a member of the Charity Organisation Society and vice-chairman of the London School Board, was instrumental in the operation of the Board's special schools for the physically and mentally defective from 1892.

Seven years later as a result of experimental special classes organized by the London County Council and other local authorities, came the Elementary Education (Defective and Epileptic Children) Act, 1899, which empowered all education authorities to set up special schools or classes for imbecile and feeble-minded children of school age, to board them out near a suitable school if necessary, or to provide transport for them. The school-leaving age for defectives attending these classes or schools was raised to sixteen, in order to give them an extra period of training. There was no compulsion on local authorities to make such provision. The Act was purely permissive.

The movement, which aimed at the full implementation of the Charity Organisation Society proposals, developed in 1896 into the National Association for the Care of the Feeble-minded.[6] The influence of this organization was largely due to the work of two women—Miss Mary Dendy and Mrs Hume Pinsent.[7]

Miss Dendy was a Manchester woman, a member of the School Board and the city Education Committee. Her experience in this connection led in 1898 to the setting-up of the Lancashire and Cheshire Society for the Permanent Care of the Feeble-Minded, which raised funds by public subscription, and founded the colony at Sandlebridge, Cheshire, now known as the Mary Dendy Homes. The land for this colony—twenty acres in all—was given by the David Lewis trustees, who were also responsible for founding the near-by David Lewis Colony for epileptics.

Mary Dendy believed that life-long segregation, or, in her phrase, 'permanent care', was the only answer. Her sketch of the work of the Sandlebridge Colony[8] begins firmly, 'These notes are based on the assumption that the children to be cared for are to be detained for the whole of their lives,' and she continues, 'It was determined from the beginning that only permanent care could be really efficacious in stemming the great evil of feebleness of the mind in our country. The idea at first met with much opposition . . . happily, it is now universally regarded as the proper method of dealing with the weak in intellect.'

When fully developed, the Sandlebridge Colony consisted of six residential houses, a day school, a hospital and a farm. It contained 170 boys and 116 girls aged between five and thirty; later two other houses, Warford Hall, which took 195 women, and Manor House, which took 200 men, were added. The children received habit training and were taught to do simple tasks. Much emphasis was laid on supervision, and on full occupation for all the patients.

Mrs Pinsent's background was a rather different one. She served on the Birmingham Special Schools sub-committee—these classes were instituted in Birmingham in 1894—and was surprised that so few children attended the classes. Visits to several schools in the area convinced her that headmasters and headmistresses often did not understand the purpose of the special class, or the type of child for whom it was intended. She gained permission to visit all fifty-six Birmingham schools herself, and personally selected 251 children for examination. The medical superintendent of a nearby asylum, when consulted, unhesitatingly certified 172 of these. Birmingham subsequently appointed a woman doctor, Dr Caroline O'Connor, as inspector; and within a few years, the number of children in special classes had risen from 100 to 600.

This was only the beginning. From considering Birmingham children of school age only, Mrs Pinsent began to consider the problem in a wider setting. She induced the Birmingham Education Committee to set up an after-care committee, which traced the children after school-leaving age, and tried to help them in the difficulties of social adaptation. She secured the institution of a girls' night shelter; but these measures were not enough. By 1903, she had formulated a scheme advocating a 'thorough and complete scheme of State intervention', which was published in the *Lancet*.[9]

Miss Dendy was the field-worker; she knew her children, and learned how to deal with their problems. Mrs Pinsent was the organizer. She saw a great need, and framed a limited, clear-cut objective. Finding that nothing stood in the way of its attainment save public apathy and ignorance, she marshalled her forces like a general, and organized her campaign. She wrote pamphlets and articles, circularized members of parliament and local authorities, addressed meetings and conferences. Much of the success of the movement was due to her gifts of organization.

At this point a new factor entered the situation—the views of what became known as the 'eugenic school'. To those who worked in the field of mental deficiency, the fast-growing science of genetics brought new and alarming evidence. The old, easy optimism—the belief that almost all defectives could be cured, given time and patience—had vanished. In its place grew a profound pessimism, a conviction that mental deficiency was hereditary, insusceptible to treatment and training, and a growing danger to the whole of society. Life-long segregation, and a public policy of sterilization of the mentally unfit, were seen as the only useful principles for action.

Considerable public alarm had been caused by three factors; the growth of a systematic study of eugenics, notably through the work of Sir Francis Galton;[10] the development of intelligence-testing; and, arising out of these two, the publication of family studies which purported to show that the effect of a morbid inheritance was almost inevitably social deterioration.

Galton, who was a half-cousin to Charles Darwin, and was associated with many of his evolutionary ideas, produced his important work *Hereditary Genius* in 1869, and *Natural Inheritance* twenty years later. He applied Mendel's Law to the human race, and claimed that it held good not only for physical characteristics, but also for mental ability. Just as two black-haired parents could expect to produce black-haired children, so parents of outstanding intelligence could expect to produce intelligent children. He claimed that ability of a particular kind could be transmitted—musicians sired musicians, and statesmen begat statesmen; but if this were true, then the converse was also true. The children of criminals had criminal tendencies, and the children of the feeble-minded would almost certainly be defective.

A man of outstanding ability and wide interests, Galton was to have a far-reaching influence not only in the eugenic field, but also in the now rapidly-developing fields of psychology and sociology. His was the first systematic attempt to apply statistical concepts to biological development. The danger of his method lay in the fact that it was only possible to study half the evidence. It was incontrovertible that the children of a feeble-minded mother often appeared feeble-minded, or that the children of criminals often drifted into crime; but there was no way then known of assessing the social factors involved of deciding how far childhood environment played a part in shaping these tendencies.

Galton founded the eugenic journal *Biometrika* in 1901. Three years later, his views were sufficiently acceptable in academic and medical circles to permit him to set up his eugenics laboratory at University College, London.[11]

Galton's early work on mental testing was taken up by an American, J. McKeen Cattell, who evolved systematic statistical tests of mental processes, particularly of perception and the association of ideas. Cattell published his first major study in 1896,[12] and exerted a considerable influence on the development of mental testing as Professor of Psychology in the University of Pennsylvania.

In 1903, this work was taken a stage further in France, when Binet published his *Étude Experimentale*. The famous Binet-Simon tests, which are still widely used in a revised form, were first published two years later. These tests enabled the 'mental age' of the subject to be fixed by establishing norms for each age-level.

The mental condition of a backward child might be expressed, for example, by the statement that when his chronological age was ten years and six months, his mental age was six years and three months.

The great advantage of the Binet-Simon method was that it introduced scientific method into a field where previously only a subjective judgement was made. It was now believed to fix a child's 'mental age' with some exactitude, and thus to make valid comparisons. It was also believed possible to separate acquired knowledge from innate intelligence. The danger of the method was that, in unskilled hands, it might be used to give an appearance of scientific fact where no true judgement was possible. The Binet-Simon scale necessarily defined 'intelligence' in a fairly limited way. It was perhaps not generally understood at the time that it was not an adequate guide to the whole personality, or to an individual's response to society.

The same appearance of scientific exactitude was introduced in the family studies which were published mainly in America, but had a wide-spread influence in England. These studies attempted to assess the influence of heredity on successive generations of large families of defective stock. One of the earliest was the study of the Juke family, published by Robert L. Dugdale in 1877.[13] This was a case which began with five mentally defective sisters, one of whom was said to be known as 'Margaret the mother of criminals'. Their descendants, at the time the study was made, numbered 540 persons, and these, together with 169 people connected with them by marriage or irregular union, made the basis of the study. Among them were 128 prostitutes, 142 habitual paupers on outdoor relief, 64 workhouse inmates, and 76 habitual criminals. A later study of the Jukes was undertaken in 1915 by Arthur H. Estabrook of the Eugenics Record Office in America, who concluded that 'over half the offspring either is mentally defective or has anti-social traits'.[14]

Another famous case was that of 'Martin Kallikak senior', published in 1912.[15] Kallikak had an illegitimate son by a presumably feeble-minded girl. This son, Martin Kallikak junior, had, in four generations, 480 descendants, of whom 143 were feeble-minded, 36 were illegitimate, 24 were alcoholics, and 33 were sexually immoral. Kallikak senior later married a normal girl, by whom he had 496 descendants. Of these, all except three were normal, and many reached high office in the state. The three failures were merely charted as being 'somewhat degenerate'.

Even Galton would scarcely have claimed that his propositions could be demonstrated with quite this clarity. Though the Kallikak case provided fuel for the protagonists of the 'eugenic idea', the evidence, at first sight overwhelming, was in fact of a very flimsy character. The feeble-mindedness of the mistress and the intelligence of the wife were taken for granted; but there was no proof, since both had died many years before concepts of mental grading had been evolved. The feeble-mindedness of the existing descendants could indeed be proved; but there was no way of proving that it was due to the Kallikak strain rather than to any of the subsequent marriage partners. If the descendants of the irregular union were socially and mentally inferior to those of the marriage, this might well be a result of the stigma of illegitimacy and lack of social opportunity; and it was at least possible that conduct which was merely described as 'somewhat degenerate' in a well-to-do relative of a high official might lead to pauperism or criminality in less fortunate circles. The Juke case is similarly open to criticism.

The results of these three kinds of research—in genetics, in intelligence-testing, and in family studies—were largely inconclusive. While medical research had a long and distinguished history, social research was in its infancy, and its methods, particularly when employed by those unaware of the inherent limitations, were of doubtful validity. Subsequent research was to show that mental deficiency was not a clear-cut entity with a single cause, but rather a description of a condition with a multiple aetiology.

Royal Commission on the care of the feeble-minded, 1904–8

At length, in response to the growing public pressure, a Royal Commission was appointed under the chairmanship of the Earl of Radnor. Its members included W. H. Dickinson, MP, chairman of the National Association for the Care of the Feeble-Minded; Mrs Hume Pinsent, who, in addition to her connection with the National Association, was now chairman of the Special Schools Sub-Committee of Birmingham Education Committee; and C. S. (later Sir Charles) Loch, secretary of the Charity Organisation Society. Other members included a barrister, two doctors, a Lunacy Commissioner, and the manager of an inebriate reformatory.

This group deliberated for four years, and received a quantity of evidence, much of it contradictory. Their final report steered a sane and sensible course between the Scylla of 'liberty-of-the-subject' agitation, and the Charybdis of eugenic theory.

The Commission came to the conclusion that heredity was an important factor in mental deficiency; that defectives were often highly prolific; and that other social problems, notably delinquency, alcoholism and illegitimacy, were aggravated by the fact that so many defectives were allowed complete freedom of action in the community. At the same time, they were unwilling to consider sterilization as a practicable policy, insisting that the main criterion in certification should be the protection and happiness of the defective rather than the 'purification of the race', and they stressed the possibilities of guardianship in selected cases as an alternative to permanent segregation.

Mental deficiency and other social factors

There was considerable evidence to show that mental deficiency was a key factor in crime, pauperism, illegitimacy and alcoholism. Mr Baldwin Fleming, General Inspector to the Local Government Board, stated that every board of guardians was familiar with the problem of the mentally defective girl who came to the workhouse, perhaps five or six times, to bear her illegitimate children. The children were nearly always defective. He instanced the following case as a typical one:

In C. workhouse, a girl, D.F., aged 25, had come into the
workhouse to be confined . . .. She had no idea what to do with
her child, which was a poor, undersized little object. . . . There
was no power to retain the mother against her wish, and it was
stated that she would probably leave the house as soon as the
child was strong enough to go out. What would be the almost
inevitable result? That in a few months . . . the mother would
again be pregnant.

On the question of delinquency, the Commission received the
evidence of Dr Kerr, school medical officer to London County
Council, who said he 'would like to take the fingerprints of every
special class child, and it would probably be found that in the
succeeding ten years, very many would be found under different
names in the hands of the police or in maternity hospitals'. He
believed that there was a great social danger in the malleability of
the average defective, who was imitative and suggestible, and could
therefore easily be led into crime, chronic alcoholism or sex offences
by unscrupulous acquaintances.

The medical officer at Pentonville stated that in one year, 1903–4,
389 juvenile offenders had passed through his hands, and that, on the
evidence of a literacy test, he considered at least 40 per cent of them
to be feeble-minded. (The literacy test was, of course, an even more
blunt tool than the Binet-Simon tests, particularly when compulsory
education had been in operation for so short a time.) Alcohol
aggravated the problem. Witnesses before the Commission considered
that 60 or 70 per cent of habitual inebriates were feeble-minded; and
alcohol increased their social irresponsibility, thereby increasing the
possibility of criminal or sexually immoral acts. The whole set of
problems formed a vicious circle. The Commission stated strongly
that 'people of this type *must not* be allowed to become habitual
delinquents of the worst type, and to propagate a feeble-minded
progeny which may become criminal like themselves'.

Existing modes of treatment

Many mental defectives came within the sphere of the Poor Law
authorities, as they were unable to find or to satisfy the conditions of
normal employment; but there was no authority for their compulsory
detention, and nowhere to send them. In the workhouses, they were
mixed with the normal inmates, to the detriment of both. There was

no suitable occupation for them, and the staff had neither time nor incentive to undertake systematic training. Some received outdoor relief; but they were usually in the care of their relatives, who might also be feeble-minded.

Many were to be found in lunatic asylums; for, as we have seen, the lunacy laws made no distinction between insanity and mental deficiency, and even regarded the two terms as synonymous; but this was no solution for the young defective, nor could the lunatic asylums provide suitable training and education.

By 1907, some 9,000 children had been accommodated in special classes and special schools instituted under the Elementary Education (Defective and Epileptic Children) Act of 1899; but well over half of these were in the London area, and there was little provision in the provinces. In most rural areas, there was no provision at all. The special school mechanism was, at best, only suitable for dealing with a proportion of cases for a limited period.

Many children were dismissed as being too defective to receive education. These were often locked up all day if their parents had a sense of responsibility to the neighbourhood, or were left to run the streets and get into trouble if they had not.

The more fortunate higher-grade cases went to special classes; but the Commission was by no means satisfied that they received the right kind of education in them. There was no special training for the teachers, and concentration in most schools was on reading and writing rather than on the acquisition of social skills and aptitudes.

Among the institutions which catered exclusively for defectives, the Commissioners found idiot asylums both of the educational and the custodial type. They considered the work of the Sandlebridge Colony, and Miss Dendy's view that the majority of feeble-minded children required in a suitable environment sustained care throughout the whole day, not merely in school hours.

Recommendations

When one considers the influences which were brought to bear on them, and the general climate of medical and social opinion at the time, the Commission's recommendations were remarkably moderate and far-sighted. They enunciated a series of general principles:

1. The need for protection. Mental defectives needed protection from the worst elements of society, and from their own instinctual

responses, because they were unfitted to 'take part in the struggle of life'.

2. Absence of social condemnation. 'The mental condition of these persons, and neither their poverty nor their crime, is the real ground of their claim for help from the State.'

3. Ascertainment. It was vitally necessary that all mental defectives should be ascertained, and brought into contact with the public services.

4. Administration. A central authority was necessary, to work in conjunction with powerful local bodies which would assume the responsibility for individual cases.

They therefore recommended the formation of a central Board of Control, which would consist of medical and legal members, and at least one woman. The Board would be responsible for a comprehensive service for the insane, the senile and epileptic as well as the idiot, imbecile or feeble-minded. Local authorities, county and county borough councils, should have a statutory committee for mental defectives.[16] This Committee would, in each area, take over the existing responsibility for mental defectives from the Asylums Visiting Committee and the Education Committee. It would be responsible for the ascertainment of defectives, for the provision and maintenance of residential accommodation, and for guardianship in the case of those remaining in the community.

It was suggested that the certification of mental defectives, as under the Idiots Act of 1886, should take place without the intervention of judicial authority. A medical certificate and the consent of a responsible relative were all that should be required.

Segregation was endorsed; but the suggestions concerning guardianship and supervision provided the opportunity for the development of community care in the future. The more drastic policy of sterilization was not envisaged as a practical possibility.

The effect of the report

Precisely because it steered a middle course, the report had a mixed reception. It did not go far enough to satisfy the eugenic school—and it went a great deal too far for the opponents of certification. There were other factors to be taken into consideration, too. The Liberal administration, under Asquith's leadership, was already engaged in its struggle with the House of Lords, and there was small hope, at that time, of getting a Bill of this nature through the Upper House. In the circumstances, there was much wisdom in the Government's decision to allow public opinion to crystallize before taking action.

There was no clear mandate from the country on social action. The Report of the Royal Commission on the Poor Laws, published in the following year, showed a strong division of feeling. There was the orthodox nineteenth-century view that poverty and social deterioration were the individual's fault, and that the intervention of the public services in his affairs should be kept to a minimum. This was the view of the majority of the Commission, whose report was drafted by C. S. Loch, then secretary of the Charity Organisation Society. The minority, whose report was drafted largely by Sidney Webb, were only four in number, but they commanded an influential following in the country as a whole. They believed that the social services should ensure an optimum condition of life for all citizens, and that social failure was a failure of society to provide adequate conditions of life for the individual. 'Interfere, interfere, interfere', urged Sidney Webb. This view was strongly supported by the growing Labour movement, particularly the Fabian wing. As far as mental deficiency was concerned, both believed that the presence of mental defectives in workhouses was wrong; but the majority wished to solve the problem by the provision of special institutions for defective paupers; the minority, by setting up a special mental deficiency authority which would have no reference to the patient's financial status.

The minority view was strongly critized by Sir Francis Galton in his presidential address to the Eugenics Education Society in 1909,[17] on the grounds that if all the feeble-minded were assured of reasonable conditions of life, their numbers would increase more than ever; but this probably did not represent the settled policy of the society.

The Eugenics Education Society (which was to change its name in 1926 to the Eugenics Society) was founded in 1907, largely as a result of the initiative of Mrs A. C. Gotto, a committee member of the Moral Education League. In the same year, Galton wrote to Karl Pearson, his successor at the eugenics laboratory: 'That Eugenics Education Society promises better than I could have hoped . . . They have got a particularly bright lady secretary who acts and works hard for the love of the thing. I have not yet ventured to join it, but as soon as I am sure that it is in safe hands, I shall do so.'[18]

By October 1908, Galton had not only joined the Society, but had become its president. In this capacity, he urged its members to form local associations in their own areas. He was largely concerned here with what he termed 'positive' eugenics—the encouragement of parenthood among 'worthy' couples, rather than with 'negative' eugenics—the prevention of parenthood among the 'unworthy'. He defined 'worth' in the eugenic sense as being a mixture of good physique, intellectual ability, and character—inferiority in any one of these qualities outweighing superiority in the other two.[19]

Galton died in 1909, but by that time the science of eugenics was firmly established, and the Society launched on its work. By 1910 Miss Dendy and Mrs Pinsent had become members, and there was a considerable degree of co-operation between the Society and the National Association for the Care of the Feeble-Minded.

The National Association's own campaign was already in operation. A joint committee in support of the Mental Deficiency Bill had been formed, headed by the Archbishops of Canterbury and York, and most of the bench of bishops, in addition to many doctors, clergy and titled people. The guiding hand was still Mrs Pinsent's. The joint committee circularized many organizations, asking that resolutions in favour of mental deficiency legislation might be sent to the Home Secretary and the local member of parliament. One of its pamphlets urged immediate action:

> BECAUSE at the date of the Report of the Royal Commission, there were 270,000 mentally defective people in England and Wales, of whom 149,000 are uncertified. There is for them no recognized and generally no possible means of control, although they are totally incapable of managing themselves or their affairs.
>
> BECAUSE 66,000 of the mentally defective are reported by the Commissioners* to be at the present time urgently in need of provision . . . .
>
> BECAUSE in consequence of the neglect to recognize and treat their condition, the mentally defective become criminals and are sent to prison; they become drunkards and fill the reformatories; they become paupers, and pass into the workhouses.
>
> BECAUSE they are frequently producing children, many of whom inherit their mental defect, and nearly all of whom become the paupers, criminals and unemployables of the next generation.

Another sheet was headed 'LIBERTY—Some examples of what is done in its name', and included brief case-histories as the following:

> H.R. A little feeble-minded girl. Turned into the streets by her

* i.e., the Lunacy Commissioners.

father. Found by the School Attendance Officer and placed in safe keeping. Was actually starving and filthy—verminous. Horribly disfigured by burns. Her feeble-minded brother (an adult) had put her on the fire and held her there.

C.A. A strong boy, small; high grade feeble-minded; subject to very violent attacks of temper in which he does not know what he is doing. His father murdered his mother. So far as the law goes, C.A. is 'at liberty' to leave his home at eighteen.

In 1910, the National Association for the Care of the Feeble-Minded and the Eugenics Education Society joined forces in the campaign. On double-headed stationery, their secretaries wrote to every candidate in the forthcoming general election asking: 'Would you undertake to support measures ... that tend to discourage parenthood on the part of the feeble-minded and other degenerate types?' Many of the answers received were equivocal (e.g. 'I will support any measure for the benefit of my constituents'); but some pledged whole-hearted support.[20] This helped to prepare the ground for the introduction of the Bill in the new parliament.

In September 1910, Mrs Pinsent read a paper on 'Social Responsibility and Heredity' to a Church Congress. It is interesting to see how far she had at that time absorbed the ideas of the eugenicists; for her case-histories, complete with genealogies, were modelled largely on the American family histories, such as the Kallikaks and the Jukes. There was the case of a normal man who married a mentally defective woman. Of the ten children of the marriage, three were dead, two too young for their mentality to be assessed (they were 'physically frail and verminous'); four were at a special school; and only one was normal. But Mrs Pinsent went further than the American theorists. She found out what the community was already trying to do for this family, how far personal failure in this case was a reflection of the community's failure to help. She came to the conclusion that the community had done all that could be expected, and more. The family was constantly being visited by no less than six officials—the sanitary inspector, the health visitor, the school attendance officer, the school nurse, the local officer of the NSPCC, and the relieving officer. And in spite of all that these people had done or were doing, the family was still neglected, dirty and verminous.

Today, with our rather more developed techniques of social casework, we might find other and subtler ways of helping such a

family than the frequent but fragmentary supervision of six unco-
ordinated officials; but in 1910, the issue seemed a clear one. State
action had failed. The whole thing was 'a tragic waste of time and
money' and permanent care of such people as the mother of this
family was the only answer.

So the two societies pursued their campaign, and their policies on
this issue to some extent merged. Before we turn to the battle for the
Mental Deficiency Act inside parliament, there is one more factor
which should be mentioned here. This was the publication in 1908 of
the first edition of Dr A. F. Tredgold's *Mental Deficiency*—a clinical
text-book which, revised in successive editions, has had an immense
influence as teaching-material on the development of this field.
Dr Tredgold was then consulting physician to the National Association for the Care of the Feeble-Minded, and had acted as medical
expert for the Royal Commission. His authoritative study did a great
deal to crystallize ideas on the subject.

Dr Tredgold believed that there were both 'intrinsic' (hereditary)
and 'extrinsic' (environmental) factors in the causation of mental
deficiency; but he added, 'It is agreed by all who have studied this
question that the most frequent cause of amentia is some ancestral
pathological condition—morbid heredity.' He thought that mental
deficiency was a clearly distinguishable condition: 'Between the
lowest normal and the highest ament, a great and impassable gulf is
fixed'.

Time and experience were to modify these views, and a consideration of the revisions which Tredgold made in his book in
subsequent editions provides a clear picture of the medical and
social advances in theory and practice which have taken place. Some
of these changes will be considered later; for the moment, it is only
necessary to note that the first edition, coming as it did at a time
when very little had been written on this subject on a sound academic
basis, formed a focal point for teaching and discussion, and had a
considerable impact on the reform movement.

The Mental Deficiency Act, 1913

The Report of the Royal Commission on Mental Deficiency was
presented in the Lords and Commons on 16 and 20 July 1908. It had
been awaited, in the Commons at least, with some impatience,
private members having twice drawn the Government's attention to
the lengthy nature of the Commission's deliberations and the

importance of publishing an authoritative statement at the earliest opportunity.

In 1909, the question of formulating legislation was raised on a number of occasions, but queries drew only evasive replies from the front bench. John Burns, at the Local Government Board, assured a questioner on 20 October that 'The recommendations of the Royal Commission . . . will not be lost sight of by me when any such legislation is proposed'. On 1 November the Prime Minister, Mr Asquith, was drawn into the twin admissions that there were 'considerable difficulties in the way of legislation' but that, at the same time, he 'hoped to make a practical effort next session in the direction of legislation'. On 13 June of the following year, when the session was drawing to its close, Mr Winston Churchill, deputizing for the president of the Local Government Board, announced that the Government was 'fully alive to the importance of this matter'.

Members, spurred on by their constituents, brought new evidence of the need for legislation. One knew of sixteen feeble-minded women in Liverpool, who had, between them, produced over 100 illegitimate children, 'thereby increasing pauperism, vice and crime'. Another had been told of a feeble-minded man who, in his occasional holidays from an idiot asylum, had begotten seven feeble-minded children.

Meanwhile, outside parliament, Mrs Pinsent and Miss Dendy were pursuing their campaign. Their influence on local authorities, on teachers, on doctors, and on taxpayers grew month by month.

Resolutions demanding legislative action began to come in from the local authorities. In February 1911, for instance, the Council of the City of Nottingham deplored the 'inadequacy of control of the adult feeble-minded, which . . . seriously reduces the mean average of the health, the intelligence, the morality and the physique of the race' and begged the Government to place in the hands of some responsible body the 'permanent control of these unfortunates'. In all, by the end of 1912, the Home Office alone had received no less than 800 resolutions from public bodies, including resolutions from 14 county councils, 44 borough councils, 110 education committees, and 280 boards of guardians. Some of these resolutions were no doubt mutually contradictory; but public opinion was roused; and it was becoming articulate.

In March 1912, Lord Alexander Thynne[21] stated in the Commons that 'the strides which public opinion has made on this subject in the last nine or ten months are very remarkable. Even the Right Hon.

Gentleman (the Home Secretary) will agree that the subject has ripened, and is now fit for legislation'. A few months later, the Home Secretary promised legislation 'very shortly'.

During 1912, two private members introduced Bills drafted by the Eugenics Society and the National Association for the Care of the Feeble-Minded. The Feeble-Minded Control Bill, which involved the assimilation of the new central powers with the work of the Lunacy Commissioners, was short-lived. The Mental Defect Bill envisaged a separate central authority for mental deficiency, and the repeal and radical redrafting of all lunacy legislation. This Bill ran into considerable opposition at its second reading from the liberty-of-the-subject school, who spoke with alarm of the grave possibilities inherent in 'capricious detention'.[22] It never emerged from the committee stage.

The introduction of these Bills may have been caused by impatience with the Government's delay; but it is possible that the Government was trailing its coat—trying to find out unofficially what was the temper of the House. This suspicion is heightened by the fact that it would not have been possible to make a parliamentary grant for administration on a private member's Bill, so that the Bills, even if passed, could not have attained their objective.[23]

In May 1912, Government action came at last. A Mental Defect Bill, Government-sponsored and supported by both parties, was introduced. It drew a strong objection from Mr Goldstone who, in a rather muddled speech, deprecated the setting up of 'some glorified Lunacy Commission which will dub the children lunatics . . . at a time when they might be brought into the fighting army of labour instead of being thrown into the scrap heaps of lunatic asylums'. The Bill was subjected to considerable comment and debate, but lapsed at the end of the session.

On 25 March 1913 the final Mental Deficiency Bill, incorporating the recommendations of the Royal Commission, and providing for the setting up of a central Board of Control which would also take over the work of the Lunacy Commissioners, was introduced by the Rt Hon. Reginald McKenna, then Home Secretary. It was immediately attacked by Josiah Wedgwood and Handel Booth.

Of Wedgwood, his obituary in *The Times*[24] said that 'There was a quixotic strain in him, and though he could be an admirable crusader for good causes, he was often led into wild knight errantry which bewildered his friends'. The obituary spoke also of his 'fierce individualism' and his 'not infrequent errors of judgement'.

This was a case in point. Wedgwood saw the issues involved as a clear battle between oppression and freedom, black and white. He was perhaps the last true Radical in English parliamentary history. He believed passionately in freedom at all costs, and was not disturbed by a gibe of Edwin Montague's, which he repeated against himself: 'You know, Jos., you can divide politicians into two classes—those who are statesmen, and those who are agitators. *I* am a statesman. *You* are an agitator.'[25] He saw the Mental Deficiency Bill as a measure designed to confine the free, to oppress the helpless; and characteristically, he poured all the zest and vehemence of a many-sided life into what he thought to be a battle against injustice. In retrospect, one might wish that such a champion might have had a better cause.

Here is Wedgwood's own story of what happened:

Whenever newspaper men have to fill up a personal column and remember me, they recount how *Athanasius contra mundum* fought the Mental Deficiency Bill through two all-night sittings, sustained on chocolate. I am the champion obstructionist, who left Sir Frederick Banbury and Handel Booth pale with envy.

The Bill had some merits, but it was one whereby prostitutes could be sent to feeble-minded houses to save mankind from infection. I do not know anything about prostitutes, a class now happily extinct, but I did know that this was a clear case of expediency v. justice. In 1912, I wrecked the Bill on Grand Committee and in the House . . . the Government reintroduced the Bill next year. When at last it got to report stage in the House, [26] I put down nearly two hundred amendments. I did fight it from 3.45 p.m. on Wednesday till 4.00 a.m. on Thursday, and from 11.00 p.m. on Thursday till 5.00 a.m. on Friday. Few took part except myself. It is quite true that on one occasion, a Tory M.P., Hohler, went out and brought me some sticks of chocolate from the bar; it is equally true that, while someone else was speaking, I dashed out to get a drink, and the Government rushed through a few lines of the Bill . . . but they got their Bill, and never dared to use it![27]

Wedgwood's attitude during this Homeric struggle was full of inconsistencies and misconceptions. He made it clear that he disliked the principle underlying the Bill, and preferred 'to put his trust in God rather than in the Home Secretary'. He thought the Government had 'followed up the suggestions of eugenic cranks' (a hit at the Galton school), and painted a picture of children being taken away in spite of paternal protests and maternal tears to be 'locked up for life'. In reply, Reginald McKenna was patient, almost courteous, and, as always, very sure of his ground. (His biographer notes that towards the end of his life, he re-read the speeches of twenty years before, and found nothing which he wished to alter.)[28] He pointed out that this was not the intention of the Bill; that certification could only take place with the parent's consent, or where the parent had clearly failed in his duty.

Wedgwood was not to be placated. He denounced the Bill as an 'illiberal, anti-democratic measure', and continued with a sneer against 'Miss Pinsent' who had 'wonderful ability, such as only ladies seem to possess these days'[29] and who had organized a nation-wide campaign in favour of the Bill. He quoted Charles Reade's *Hard Cash*[30] as evidence of the kind of abuse which might follow the passing of the Bill, and warned the House that, if it passed into law, the Bill would 'put into prison 100,000 people who are at present at liberty'.

Handel Booth, who followed him, was scarcely more logical. He considered it 'a pagan Bill, anti-Christian from its first line to its last'. He asked, 'What authority have you from God or Nature to interfere in this way?' and claimed that Francis Bacon's mother was a mental defective, which was proof of the non-hereditary nature of defect.

To the question of Divine authority another member retorted with 'Lead us not into temptation. . . . The temptation of these poor creatures is beyond description.' To the statement concerning Bacon, a medical member pointed out that Bacon's mother was an extremely able woman of great culture who died at the age of eighty-two after a short period of senile decay.

These were mere debating points; but replies to the charge that the Bill was illiberal and coercive came swiftly. Miss Mary Dendy wrote to *The Times* on 3 June 1813, describing the case of a feeble-minded child ill-treated by its parents. 'Where is the liberty for such a child as that? It is thraldom of the most horrible description.' Members rose in the House to bring repeated evidence of feeble-minded children taken from institutions by their parents when they were old enough to earn a small wage, and miserably ill-treated afterwards. There was no doubt that the general feeling of the House was in favour of a form of certification which would protect the feeble-minded against exploitation.

There was a great deal of discussion on the definition of mental deficiency. As we have seen, the terms 'mental defective', 'idiot', 'imbecile' and 'feeble-minded' had been used in a variety of contexts, often as synonyms. Many people were not clear about the distinction between mental deficiency and insanity—even Galton wrote in 1909 that 'one person in every 118 of our population is mentally defective, being either mad, idiotic, or feeble-minded'.[31] It was therefore necessary that, if effective legislation was to be introduced for these people, some clear statement as to who they were and how they were to be distinguished should be evolved. Definitions were formulated by the Royal College of Physicians and incorporated in the Mental Defect Bill of 1912. When that Bill was in the committee stage, no less than six days were spent on this question of a definition, and twenty-seven divisions were taken. In the committee stage of the final Bill, a further three days and six divisions were expended on the question. The resultant definitions were, as the Home Secretary warned, not watertight; but they were the best that could be devised in the circumstances.

The appointment of the Commissioners of the new Board of Control also provoked a certain amount of opposition. The Bill provided for fifteen Commissioners, of whom twelve were to be salaried. Four of these were to be doctors, four were to be barristers or solicitors of not less than five years' standing, and one was to be a woman. Of the three unpaid Commissioners also, one was to be a woman. McKenna proposed initially to appoint only eleven, of whom eight would be the former Lunacy Commissioners, four legal and four medical. He proposed a salary of £1,800 per annum for the chairman, and £1,200 rising to £1,500 for the others. Some members considered these figures too high, and deprecated the appointment of 'a horde of salaried officials'—this phrase being used by several in succession.

The debate continued through most of 28 and 29 July. There were lengthy and exhausting arguments, and repeated divisions in which the number of 'Noes'—the supporters of Wedgwood and Handel Booth—were gradually reduced to a mere handful. Their emotion was spent, their protest over. The final division on the third reading took place at 3.15 a.m. on the morning of 30 July. There were only three 'Noes' left. The Bill was passed, and a weary House was free to go home.

The Bill was then taken to the Lords where it received hasty consideration.[32] This was the acute period of the House of Lords controversy, and the Government was determined to force the Bill through in as short a time as possible. Lord Selborne[33] complained bitterly:

Everyone admits, whatever his opinion may be in the second Chamber controversy, that revision is one of the functions of a Second Chamber. In the conditions under which we have to work, revision is a farce . . . The days of this House as at present composed are nearly numbered. When the new House comes into existence, I devoutly hope that it will arrange its adjournments solely with a view to its duty of revision, and not to suit the convenience either of His Majesty's Government . . . or of the House of Commons.

But the Bill was rushed through before the end of the session. The only alternative was for it to lapse, and for the whole battle to be fought again in the next session. It completed its third reading in the Lords on 12 August, and received the Royal Assent on the 15th.

Definition of scope (section 1)

Four classes of persons who might be covered by the Act were defined: idiots, imbeciles, feeble-minded persons, and moral defectives. It was necessary for the condition to have existed 'from birth or from an early age' for the patient to come within the scope of the Act. '. . . from an early age' implied that the Act was not restricted to those suffering from congenital defect, but included cases where normal development had been arrested in childhood by illness or brain injury.

Idiots, imbeciles and the feeble-minded formed three grades of rising intelligence. Idiots formed the lowest grade. They were persons 'so deeply defective in mind as to be unable to guard against common physical dangers'. The inclusion of 'physical' in this context made it clear that higher-grade defectives could require protection from mental and moral dangers; but the idiot was as lacking in the powers of self-preservation as a baby taking his first steps.

Imbeciles were those who, while not suffering from a condition amounting to idiocy, were 'incapable of managing themselves or their affairs, or, in the case of children, of being taught to do so'.

Feeble-minded persons were defined in two ways. If adults, their condition was defined as one not amounting to 'imbecility', 'yet so pronounced that they require care, supervision and control for their own protection or the protection of others'. The criterion was thus a social one; but in the case of a child of school age, the position was quite different. Here, feeble-mindedness was defined as a condition not amounting to imbecility 'yet so pronounced that they by reason of such defectiveness appear to be permanently incapable of receiving proper benefit from the instruction in ordinary schools'. In other words, the standard was an educational and not a social one.

'Moral defectives' differed from the others in kind, not in degree. They were persons who from an early age displayed 'some permanent mental defect coupled with strong vicious or criminal propensities on which punishment had little or no effect'.

'*Subject to be dealt with*' (*section 2*)

The mere fact that a patient came within the foregoing definitions was not enough to bring him within the orbit of the public authorities. In certain circumstances, given a sympathetic and understanding guardian and a favourable environment, a defective might be capable of something approaching normal life. It was only when he was unable to be cared for in society in the normal way that he became 'subject to be dealt with'. He might be sent to an institution or placed under statutory guardianship only under the following circumstances:

1. If he was a low-grade defective (idiot or imbecile) and the parent or guardian petitioned the local authority.
2. If he was defective in any of the four grades, and under twenty-one, and the parent or guardian petitioned the local authority.
3. If he was defective in any grade and:
   (i) neglected, abandoned, cruelly treated, or without visible means of support:
   (ii) guilty of a criminal offence, or liable to be sent by court order to a certified industrial school;
   (iii) in prison, reformatory, industrial school, a lunatic asylum or an inebriate reformatory;
   (iv) an habitual drunkard within the meaning of the Inebriates Acts, 1879–1900.[34]
   (v) If incapable of receiving benefit from attendance at a special school; if his presence in such a school were detrimental to others; or if he attained the age of sixteen years after attendance at a special school, and the Board of Education certified that further care, either in an institution or under guardianship, was required.

Certification (*sections 3 and 4*)

The parent or guardian of an idiot or imbecile of any age, or of a defective of any grade but under the age of twenty-one, could place the patient in an institution or under statutory guardianship. Two medical certificates were necessary, one from a practitioner specially appointed by the local authority for this work. If the patient was not an idiot or an imbecile, a judicial order was also necessary.

Where the patient was neglected, abandoned, cruelly treated, or without visible means of support, the initiative lay with the magistrate: an officer of the local authority was responsible for bringing the case to his notice, and acting as his agent. Two medical certificates were required. Where the patient had come within the jurisdiction of the courts, he might be dealt with under a court order; and where he was already detained in one of the institutions specified under section 2, a Home Office order was necessary.

Effect and Duration of Orders (sections 5–12)

The patient was to be conveyed to an institution within fourteen days, or, if this was impossible, to a 'place of safety' within twenty-one. A *'place of safety'* was defined by section 71 of the Act as 'any workhouse or police station, any institution, any place of detention, and any hospital, surgery, or other suitable place, the occupier of which is willing to receive temporarily persons who may be taken to places of safety under this Act'.

If this patient was capable of living a protected life in the community, and a suitable guardian was available, he might be placed under a guardianship order. Whatever the actual age of the patient, this order conferred on the guardian powers and duties analogous to those possessed by a natural parent of a child under the age of fourteen years.

The original duration of an order either for institutional care or for guardianship, was one year. It might then be renewed for five years and successive periods of five years on a medical certificate. There was one exception: where the patient was under the age of twenty-one at the time of the original certification, he was to be examined on the attainment of that age by visitors specially appointed for each county under this Act. This enabled an independent lay judgment to be made at the time when the patient, if normal, would attain his majority.

Central Authority (sections 21–6)

A Board of Control was set up, consisting of not more than fifteen members, of whom twelve were salaried members. Four were to be legal Commissioners, and four medical. These eight Commissioners were in fact the existing Lunacy Commissioners, and under section 65 of the Act, all powers and duties of the Lunacy Commissioners were transferred to the Board. As far as mental deficiency was concerned, the Commissioners of the Board of Control were responsible for the 'supervision, protection and control' of all defectives; for the supervision of local authorities in the exercise of their powers under this Act; and for the approval and inspection of all institutions for defectives; for visitation, as follows: all institutions to be visited once a year by the Commissioners, a second visit to be made either by the Commissioners or their inspectors; and every defective under guardianship twice a year by the Commissioners or their inspectors.

The Board of Control was also to 'provide and maintain' special institutions for defectives of dangerous or violent propensities. The Commissioners had an overriding power of discharge except in the case of criminals or inebriates, for whose discharge the consent of the Home Secretary was necessary. They were to make annual reports on mental deficiency work to the Home Secretary.

Under Section 41, the Home Secretary was empowered to make regulations concerning a number of matters including the following: certification; the management of institutions; classification and treatment of patients; inspection and visitation; discharge and absence from an institution on licence; conditions of guardianship; and the study of improved methods of treating mental deficiency.

Local Authorities (*sections 27–33*)

The local authority unit, as for lunacy, was the county or county borough council. A special mental deficiency committee was to be set up in each area, composed largely of members of the council; but having also co-opted members with special knowledge and experience on this subject. Some of its members were to be women.

The committee was to provide for:

  (i) the ascertainment in the area of all persons subject to be dealt with;
 (ii) the provision and maintenance of suitable institutions;
(iii) the care, through officers appointed for the task, of mental defectives in the community, including the conveyance of

patients to and from institutions; the overall care of cases under guardianship orders; and the 'supervision' (this was not closely defined) of those cases where neither institutional care nor statutory guardianship appeared to be immediately necessary.

The local education committee was given special duties with regard to defectives of school age under section 31. They were made responsible for the ascertainment of such children, and for notifying the mental deficiency committee of those who appeared incapable of benefiting from instruction in special schools or classes. These duties were later linked with the Education Acts by means of the Elementary Education (Defective and Epileptic Children) Act of 1914 (see p. 209).

Effect of the Act

The Act made possible a rapid expansion and development in provision for defectives. Local authorities set up their mental deficiency committees; many of these committees financed the voluntary mental welfare associations which had sprung up in the past few years, rather than appointing officers of their own; and the Central Association for Mental Welfare, with Miss (later Dame) Evelyn Fox as secretary, came into being to encourage the implementation of the Act and to co-ordinate the work of these local bodies.

It will be noted that, in spite of the predominantly medical and educational influences which had gone to shape it, the Act dealt with mental deficiency in an adult primarily in social terms. It might involve a clinical condition, such as cretinism or mongolism; it might involve inability to profit from education; but the ultimate test was not physical abnormality or illiteracy, but social incapacity—an inability to guard against common dangers, a failure in self-sufficiency, a need of care and protection.

The definitions, though in some ways debatable in detail, were in principle a great achievement. It is seldom possible to come to grips with a problem until there is some measure of common agreement on terminology. The fact that it was now possible to talk about the subject with some degree of exactitude was of the greatest value in the development of both social and medical research.

One of the shortcomings of the Act from a modern view-point is the lack of a preventive element in its provisions. The patient did not become 'subject to be dealt with' until he was actually abandoned, an habitual drunkard, or already within the jurisdiction of the courts. The suspicion that he was in the care of an unfit or irresponsible guardian, that he was drinking too much, or keeping bad company, was not enough to secure his protection. This was an inevitable reflection of the agitation on the score of the liberty of the subject. The patient's right (or that of his parent or guardian) to freedom of action could not be infringed until he became a social casualty.

In spite of the strong agitation for the 'permanent segregation of the feeble-minded', the Act, by its careful division of the methods of protection into statutory guardianship, institutional care, and licence from the institution, made it possible for many defectives to continue living in the community while still receiving a degree of care and control.

One more feature of the Act deserves mention here: the list of matters on which the Home Secretary was empowered to make regulations. This is an example of a type of delegated legislation which has become increasingly common in the last sixty years. The Act did not attempt, like the Lunacy Act of 1890, to say the last word on every aspect of the subject. It laid down general principles, and left a great deal to be decided by administrative practice. The wisdom or unwisdom of delegated legislation may be debated on administrative and political grounds; but in dealing with this new and comparatively untried field of medical and social action, the decision to delegate ensured the maximum flexibility.

The Elementary Education (Defective and Epileptic Children) Act, 1914

While the Mental Deficiency Bill was completing its stages, another Bill, designed as its complement, had also been initiated. The president of the Board of Education, the Rt Hon. J. A. Pease, had stated as early as June 1913 that, of 48,000 backward children of school age, only one-third would come within the scope of the proposed mental deficiency authority. Well over 30,000 were thought to be above 'imbecile' and below merely 'dull and backward' level, and for these the special schools were the proper medium of treatment.

In March 1913 a Bill designed to deal with these children was introduced. There was already in existence the permissive Act of 1899, which enabled local authorities to set up special schools for handicapped children, and 176 out of 318 local education authorities had taken advantage of these powers. Now the right was to become a duty. The special school would serve two purposes: it would provide manual training and character training for the backward, but not ineducable, child; and it would serve as an observation centre for doubtful cases, so that those who were incapable of receiving education might be diagnosed and passed on to the mental deficiency authority. Some dissatisfaction was expressed against this Bill. Members felt that they had already assented to an expensive procedure for the welfare of mental defectives, and this new scheme seemed to some to involve overlapping and duplication of function. Reintroduced in the session of 1914, the Bill was passed after some discussion.

During the period 1914–39, parallel movements were taking place in mental deficiency work and in the care of the mentally ill. In both cases, there was a swing away from the concept of permanent detention, and a desire to find means of integrating patients more closely with the society which had previously been concerned only to reject them; but they were distinct movements, and there was comparatively little contact between them up to 1939, though the Board of Control exercised an over-riding supervision in both spheres. Even where the Board was concerned, there was one clear difference: developments in the treatment and care of the mentally ill were largely due to the initiative of statutory organizations and salaried workers; but mental deficiency work was from the outset a partnership between statutory and voluntary bodies in which often, the initiative came from the voluntary associations. The Board of Control supervised and approved. It seldom needed to initiate.

Why did the lay public, which on the whole remained untouched by the plight of the mentally ill, rally to the cause of the mentally defective? One reason is that the mental defective was generally thought of as harmless and simple, while the mentally ill person was dangerous; though he was no longer looked on as a source of supernatural power, as in the days of witchcraft beliefs, his actions were often 'unnatural', bizarre, and held a potentiality of violence. There was perhaps a certain emotional satisfaction for the philanthropic in protecting the weak and intellectually inferior, but the emotions aroused by the thought of mental illness were so painful that the whole subject tended to be blocked. The same phenomenon occurs in other branches of social work. Most social workers know that it is comparatively easy to obtain support for work in connection with children, who are generally attractive; it is much more difficult to get the public to care for the old, since old age is a future threat.

The Central Association for Mental Welfare

This body, known until 1923 as the Central Association for the Care of the Mentally Defective, was formed in October 1914. Its existence arose out of a public meeting called by the National Association for the Care of the Feeble-Minded, which had achieved its object in the passing of the 1913 Mental Deficiency Act, and was now ready to dissolve in favour of a broader-based association. The chairman of the new Central Association was Mr Leslie Scott, KC, MP; and the secretary was a young woman with an Oxford degree and a wide experience of social work, Miss Evelyn Fox. At that time Miss Fox was already showing the qualities which were later to make her the architect of the mental deficiency services. The first report of the Central Association notes, 'To her public zeal, her power of organization, her knowledge of the work . . . is due much of the achievement we are able to record in this report.'

The executive committee of the new association included representatives from the County Councils Association, the Association of Poor Law Unions, the Associations of Education Committees, the Prison Commissioners, the Charity Organisation Society, the NSPCC, and a number of religious bodies, and had a special sub-committee of eight members of parliament. A large number of public bodies and societies, in addition to individuals, became members of the Central Association.

The first report listed twenty-eight local voluntary associations which had been formed to carry out mental deficiency work, and pointed out that since many agencies, both statutory and voluntary, were concerned with defectives, there was a great need for co-ordination. Although the Central Association sometimes dealt with individual cases, it was from the first a co-ordinating and teaching body, strong enough to achieve its purposes. There was nothing like it in the field of mental illness.

Despite the outbreak of war in 1914, the work continued. Miss Fox, to quote her friend and biographer, Marjorie Welfare, 'travelled up and down the country interviewing officials, addressing meetings, holding conferences . . . sparing neither time nor trouble in her efforts to convert local authorities and social work agencies. . . . She knew how to fight, and when to fight, and she never made the mistake of going into battle unprepared'.[35] By 1918 there were forty-five local voluntary associations, many of which undertook the work of ascertainment for local authorities, and carried out casework. Local

H

authorities often felt that a voluntary worker gained the confidence of a family more easily than did a representative of Town Hall officialdom. The Central Association did valuable work in organizing training courses for teachers and social workers, and by 1918 was already advocating the setting up of occupation centres for mental defectives. In 1919 a conference of over one hundred representatives from statutory and voluntary organizations was held in London, and future annual conferences of a similar nature were planned.

Ascertainment and accommodation

On the appointed day under the Mental Deficiency Act (1 April 1914) there were 2,163 mentally defective patients receiving treatment in institutions built under the Idiots Act. By the end of that year, 796 more beds had been provided;[36] but though the energies of voluntary workers were undiminished, the work of organizing statutory committees, and of building and staffing hospitals, was seriously affected by the outbreak of war. With the many new problems brought before the local authorities by war conditions, mental deficiency became a small side-issue, and consideration was postponed in many cases until the end of the war.

There were in existence thirty-eight certified institutions, of which the largest were the five original 'hospitals for idiots': the Midland Counties Institution at Chesterfield, now known as Whittington Hall; the Western Counties Institution, Exeter, known as Starcross; the Royal Eastern Counties Institution, Colchester; the Royal Albert Institution, Lancaster; and Earlswood, in Surrey. Of the others, the Mary Dendy Homes at Sandlebridge were the best known. Small homes were run by various voluntary societies sponsored by the churches and by local welfare groups.

In addition, there were special workhouses designated under section 37 of the 1913 Mental Deficiency Act, where accommodation was set aside for groups of defectives. These accounted for 560 of the known defectives in the country. There were also certain small homes under private ownership.[37]

It was fairly clear, however, that the number of known defectives bore no real relation to the number of those actually requiring treatment; and the Board of Control directed its energies to urging the local authorities to proceed with the business of ascertainment. Some authorities were slow to do this; for the recognition of the existence of defectives in the area meant that provision must be made for them, and both buildings and staff made heavy demands on the rates. Development was also hampered by the administrative structure of the mental deficiency services. The Mental Deficiency Committee was attached, not to the Health Department, but to the Clerk of the Council's Department, which effectively cut off the treatment of defectives from the developing health services.

By 1920, 10,129 defectives had been ascertained. This was still only a proportion of the whole, and the Board thought that the real figure was about 3.55 per thousand of the population. The Board had recently sent out a circular to all local authorities. 'Eleven authorities', they complain in their report for 1920,

> have returned no answer at all to the circulars . . . others have sent answers from which we can only conclude that their search for defectives has been perfunctory. Others show misapprehension of the questions on the form circulated, thus rendering their return of little value. Some local authorities state that their ascertainment is 'complete', when the numbers returned are so small as to make it certain that many defectives must have been overlooked.

Other local authorities had taken their duties seriously, and had prepared schemes for the institutional treatment of defectives. The usual policy was to acquire a fairly small building—sometimes a country house, sometimes only a workhouse—and, using this as a nucleus, to add small villas as they were required and as building became possible again.

Despite the work of the Central Association in encouraging adequate provision, the development of institutional accommodation for defectives was very slow. By 1927, the total number of beds provided by local authorities was only 5,301, though the number of defectives, ascertained by that time was well over 60,000. 'It is difficult', commented the Board of Control,

> to convince members of Councils that the expense of maintaining the feeble-minded who cannot maintain themselves must eventually be borne by the community, and that it is a choice between maintenance under improper conditions in Poor Law institutions, in prisons, by out-door relief or unemployment benefit, or maintenance in institutions where they are under continuous training and care. . . . Exposed to temptations they have no power to resist, a misery to themselves and a source of

danger to their neighbours, these afflicted persons should be a first charge on any civilized community.[38]

More beds were urgently needed; but the Board was beginning to realize that there were many cases which could not, in the immediate future, be treated by hospitalization. Consequently, they turned to considering methods of community care. So strong was the influence of what might be called the Mary Dendy theory—the permanent segregation of all the feeble-minded—that community care was at first thought of as only a rather unsatisfactory expedient. During the nineteen-thirties, parallel with the development of a similar theory in the sphere of mental illness, came the gradual realization that community care was in many cases not only cheaper and more practicable, but better for the patient.

Both statutory and voluntary supervision were possible under section 30(*b*) of the 1913 Mental Deficiency Act, but the Board thought that both were insufficiently stressed by the Act. By 1927, eighteen local authorities had ignored the possibilities of supervision altogether, and seven more had less than five cases on their books. 'Some authorities have told us that they have not adopted supervision, as it is practically useless. At the same time, they have not sufficient institutional accommodation even to meet their most urgent needs. Under these circumstances, it seems to us wiser to use and to improve as far as possible the method of supervision.'

They recommended that local authorities should employ specially trained officers for the work of supervision and ascertainment. They suggested that supervision should be restricted to suitable cases, i.e. to those who could make a limited response to normal society under supervision; and that attendance at occupation centres and industrial centres should be encouraged.

Occupation centres were first mentioned by the Board of Control in 1922. At that time, there were twenty in existence, all run by voluntary associations, and catering in the day-time for trainable defectives who lived at home. By 1927 this number had risen to ninety-nine and over 1,250 defectives were attending regularly. The Board of Control stated that the occupation centres aimed at 'training low grade children and adults in good habits, self-control, and obedience, and at developing to the utmost their limited capacity to lead useful lives'. Those dealing with employable defectives were more properly known as industrial centres, and aimed at simple training which would make it possible for adult defectives to take up sheltered employment. Both, said the Board, were 'essentially for defectives living in good homes, and for those who can be taught to conform to ordinary social requirements.'

The Central Association was by this time providing special training courses in mental deficiency work for social workers, for medical officers, for teachers, and for occupation centre workers. Its advisers included Lord Dawson of Penn; Dr Tredgold, whose work in the clinical teaching of subjects connected with mental deficiency has already been mentioned; Sir Norwood East, the forensic psychiatrist and Dr Cyril Burt, the pioneer in the study of delinquency. A quarterly journal, at first rather unhappily titled *Studies in Mental Inefficiency* had been founded, and changed its name in 1925 to *Mental Welfare*.

The Mental Deficiency Act of 1927

Although the 1913 Act was on the whole working well, there were some respects in which it clearly needed amendment. While local authorities were responsible for the supervision and protection of defectives, they had no statutory responsibility to occupy or train them; and now that the experiment of occupation and industrial centres had been well proved, the time had come to ensure wider provision. Again, there was a need to stress the duty of supervision; for although the 1913 Act had made provision for the supervision of defectives, many authorities were still evading this responsibility.

The third point requiring amendment was brought home by the events of 1926, when there was a serious outbreak of *encephalitis lethargica*, or sleeping sickness. Where the patient had not yet reached maturity, he became in fact indistinguishable from a mental defective—intellectually backward, and often lacking in social capacity. Yet the 1913 Act specified that the condition must have existed 'from birth or from an early age', and was generally interpreted by doctors and magistrates to exclude cases of this nature.

A Bill to amend the Mental Deficiency Act of 1913 was introduced in the Commons in 1926; but the proposed definition of mental deficiency was very wide, and the Bill was wrecked by Col. Wedgwood, who was again wearing the 'Habeas Corpus look'. In 1927 a private member's Bill was introduced by Mr Crompton Wood, the member for Bridgwater, supported by Sir Leslie Scott.

Crompton Wood pointed out, in moving the second reading of the Bill,[39] that *encephalitis lethargica*, meningitis and frequent epileptic fits could all result in arrested development. Yet it was impossible at that time to deal with such cases under the Mental Deficiency Act unless they were very young, or unless a medical history of the first few years of life, proving arrested development at that time, was available. Clearly there had to be some age-limit. The Bill's supporters had tried to fix the age at which an adult reached maturity, and proposed the age of eighteen. He assured 'that well-known defender of the liberty of the subject, the Right Hon. and gallant member for Newcastle-under-Lyme' (Col. Wedgwood) that this proposal would not in any way interfere with the liberty of the subject.

Wedgwood, in reply, put in a strong, but unexpectedly moderate, plea for freer conditions.

> However excellent your institution may be, however carefully
> you may select the matrons and managers in charge, so long as
> you have a lock on the door, you cannot prevent suspicion of
> those minor cruelties, injustices and acts of arbitrary authority
> which may embitter the life of the inmates of these institutions.
> Once you have got rid of the lock, why then, your institutions,
> even without so much inspection, will improve, because freedom—
> publicity—is the cure for any inhumanity and injustice.

This last phrase is an excellent example of the development of an idea over more than a century. 'Publicity is the soul of justice', wrote Jeremy Bentham. Richard Paternoster used the quotation in the frontispiece to *The Madhouse System* in 1838. Charles Reade took it up in a garbled form in *Hard Cash* in 1863.[40] Now, in 1927, we find the same thought again expressed in a similar context; yet the implication is different; for Paternoster and Reade used the phrase to indicate that those believed to be insane should be able publicly to defend their sanity. Wedgwood was pleading that those who suffered from mental handicap should not be cut off from the community.

Despite Wedgwood's intervention, the general tone of the House was strongly in favour of the Bill, and it finally received the Royal Assent in December, 1927.

The Act amended the definition of mental deficiency by substituting for the expression 'from birth or from an early age' the following:

> For the purposes of this section, 'mental defectiveness' means a
> condition of arrested or incomplete development of mind
> existing before the age of eighteen years, whether arising from
> inherent causes or induced by disease or injury.

Section 2 of this Act amended the previous Act by stressing provision for the supervision of defectives. Section 7 added to the local authority's duty of supervision the duties of training and occupation.

The changes which the 1927 Act introduced altered the previous Act by only a few words, but the effect was to embody in the law a new idea; a widening of the definition of mental deficiency, but also a loosening of the statutory restraints. The emphasis was no longer on segregation at all costs. The system had become more flexible, and allowed for a variety of provision suited to the needs of the individual defective. He might go to an institution, or he might remain in the community; but in deciding his future, his own well-being and happiness would be the primary consideration.

Report of the Wood Committee, 1929

There was one other problem inherent in the administration of the mental deficiency services which could not be settled by Act of Parliament. This was the question of the division of powers in dealing with defective children. Some were cared for by Mental Deficiency Committees, some by Education Committees; and often there was confusion between the two. The Board of Control urged co-operation, and suggested that such children should receive a uniform kind of care and education.

As a result, a joint committee of the Board of Education and the Board of Control was set up in June 1924 on the initiative of Sir George Newman, then chief medical officer of the Board of Education. The chairman, A. H. Wood, was a member of Newman's own department. Other members, in addition to those representing their departments, included Professor Cyril Burt and Dr A. F. Tredgold; Dr Douglas Turner, a foundation member of the council of the Central Association for Mental Welfare, and medical superintendent of the Royal Eastern Counties Institution at Colchester; Miss Evelyn Fox; and Mrs Hume Pinsent, now a Commissioner of the Board of Control.

The committee's primary task was to answer two questions: 'How many defectives are there?' and 'What is the best way of dealing with mental defectives?' At first their terms of reference applied only to children, but early in 1925 they were extended to cover adult defectives also.

The existing services

The committee began its report with a survey of legislation: the Idiots Act of 1886, and its supersession by the Mental Deficiency Act of 1913; the Elementary Education (Defective and Epileptic Children) Act of 1899, which had empowered local authorities to set up special schools and classes; and the Act of the same title which, in 1914, transformed this power into a duty incumbent upon all authorities.

To this basic legislation had been added the Education Act of 1921. Sections 53–5 and 58 of this Act referred to defective children, and laid the following duties on the education authority:

The local education authority was to ascertain all defective children in the area, and had the right to enforce attendance at special schools and classes; though it was laid down as a general principle that the wishes of the parents should be consulted where possible.

These powers referred to all children between the ages of seven and sixteen, and meant that all the machinery of the educational system—the school medical service, the attendance officers, and so on—could be used to ascertain and deal with defectives.

The education authority was responsible for dividing the 'educable' from the 'ineducable' and for notifying the latter to the mental deficiency authority. Where there were no facilities for special education, or where a child was vicious or out of control, an 'educable' child might also be notified.

This was the outline of the scheme: the education authority provided for educable defectives between seven and sixteen, and the mental deficiency authority took care of the rest, by means of institutional care, guardianship, supervision, and in the last two cases, possibly by means of an occupation centre. On paper, it was an admirably simple scheme; but in fact, there were so many anomalies that the scheme was proving unworkable.

Anomalies in the existing services

The scheme might have worked reasonably well if only the mental deficiency authority had been attached to the health department, not the clerk of the council's department. This would have made possible a link with the school medical service, and thus brought the care of ineducable defectives into close administrative contact with the care of educable defectives. As it was, they were operating separately, and in fact three other types of authority were involved as well. These were the Poor Law authorities, the Lunacy authorities, and the Home Office.

Section 30 of the Mental Deficiency Act of 1913 stated, 'Nothing in this Act shall affect the powers and duties of the Poor Law authorities under the Acts relating to the relief of the poor, with respect to any defectives who may be dealt with under those Acts'. This meant that the Poor Law guardians had no duty to report mental defectives in their care to the mental deficiency authority; and that mental defectives dealt with under the Poor Law had none of the protection envisaged by the Mental Deficiency Act. They could not be sent out on licence, transferred to guardianship, or placed under voluntary supervision. The mental deficiency authority had no power to intervene until after they were discharged from the Poor Law institution; and, since they were not certified, they might be discharged by the guardians or withdrawn by relatives without the knowledge of the mental deficiency authority.

Local education authorities had no right of entry into Poor Law institutions, and though the Board of Control had such a right, and would use it when requested, this was not an adequate substitute for regular visitation on a local level. It was generally acknowledged that, with a very few exceptions, the guardians made no attempt at providing suitable training and educational programmes for defective inmates.

As far as the lunacy authorities were concerned, the position was almost as complicated. Although it was possible for mental defectives to be transferred from mental hospitals to mental deficiency institutions, the acute lack of beds in the latter made this impracticable in many cases. Mental hospitals were in the difficult position of having many patients for whom they could do little (since the framework and staffing of a mental hospital was not suitable for the training of defectives) while at the same time they wished to admit other patients for whom they had no beds.

The Home Office also had special powers in relation to mental defectives, since it was responsible for juvenile offenders. There was no compulsion on Home Office schools to notify the mental deficiency authority when a defective child was discharged; and the powers of the Home Office ceased when the child was eighteen or nineteen—an age at which it was sometimes exceedingly difficult to prove that a child was 'subject to be dealt with' though there might be good reason for thinking that care was urgently necessary. The mental deficiency authority had to wait, powerless, until one of the social disasters specified under the 1913 Mental Deficiency Act took place. Then, and only then, could they act.

It was thus clear that the mental deficiency authorities and the education authorities between them were dealing with only a percentage of the actual cases; and that the rest were scattered among authorities who had no real responsibility for their care. In fact, many defective children were receiving treatment not according to their condition, but according to the actual circumstances of social breakdown, which were largely irrelevant to the question of care.

The mentally defective child

In fact, even where the right authorities were able to deal with the child, the system was not working well. It depended primarily on the perception and understanding of two people, the class teacher and the school doctor. There were many class teachers who had no idea what the factors in mental deficiency were, and were quite unable to distinguish between a handicapped child and one emotionally disturbed. School doctors were primarily looking for physical disorders. Because of the large burden of work involved in regular medical inspections, their work was often hurried. Some thought in any case that it was useless to certify a child when there was no adequate provision in the area. (This, of course, was a vicious circle; for until the number of certified children was sufficiently high to warrant action by the mental deficiency committee, there would be no provision.) Both teacher and doctor often thought, not without reason, that there was a social stigma in certification, and avoided it wherever possible.

The position in 1929 was that 33,000 children between the ages of seven and sixteen were ascertained. This represented 6.0 per thousand of the school population. Sir George Newman had stated, shortly before appointing the Wood Committee, that he was convinced that the actual figure was in the region of 7.5 per thousand. In a special investigation sponsored by the Wood Committee, Dr E. O. Lewis was seconded from the Board of Control to carry out an investigation. He stated that a conservative estimate would be 8.0 per thousand of the school population.

There were probably 18,000 defectives still unascertained in the schools alone; and for those who had been ascertained, there were not enough special schools. Of the 33,000 children known to be defective, 14,850 attended day special schools, and 1,900 were in residential accommodation. The rest were still in the general educational framework—profiting little, and handicapping overworked teachers in the attempt to do their main task of dealing with the educable.

The adult defective

Many adult defectives were being dealt with, not by the mental deficiency authority, but by authorities whose main task was to deal with poverty, insanity, or delinquency. These were thought to account for about half the adult mental defectives ascertained at that time. Dr Lewis, in his survey, discovered that the actual position was much worse. In the six 'representative areas' he investigated, only 10 per cent of the defectives were in mental deficiency institutions; 25 per cent were in mental hospitals; 39 per cent were in Poor Law institutions. All the cases dealt with by the mental deficiency authority— by institutional treatment, by licence, guardianship, voluntary or statutory supervision amounted to only 40,000 out of a total of 175,000.

While the Board of Control and the Central Association for Mental Welfare were priding themselves on immensely improved services, these services were touching only a fraction of the total number needing help and treatment.

The Wood Committee thought that these were problems that could be solved by administrative means and under existing legislation. They recommended that all mental defectives in receipt of out-door relief should be transferred to the care of the mental deficiency authority; that certain Poor Law institutions should be used for the grouping together of defectives, and that these should then be transferred also; and that supervision, guardianship and licence should be developed to the full. At the same time, they stressed most strongly that 'the real criterion of deficiency is a social one'. The distinction between the patient in hospital and the patient under voluntary supervision had nothing to do with his scholastic ability. It depended entirely on whether he was capable of living a normal life under reasonably sheltered conditions without being exploited by other people, or himself causing difficulty in his environment. Those who were anti-social or in actual danger (such as alcoholics and those without sexual control) would still need institutional care; but the quiet, stable kind of defective, even with a comparatively low intelligence, might be discharged to the care of a suitable social worker.

Institutional care

In a memorable phrase, the Wood Committee laid down that the mental deficiency institution should be 'not a stagnant pool, but a flowing lake'. It should be equipped with a school, workshops, playing-fields and a small hospital block—the general outline being closer to that of a boarding-school than of a hospital; and the object should be to prepare patients for life in the community—not simply to confine them for life. The work of the 'school' would include much that elsewhere might be termed occupational therapy or even physiotherapy. Some patients would have to be taught the primary co-ordination of muscles—how to walk, how to climb stairs, and so on—while others could progress to simple handwork. Some might also be taught the normal primary school subjects, and older patients would learn simple processes in the workshops.

The Committee thought that the defective's failure to make a social response was often due to the fact that he could not work, and was thus dependent on charity. 'To deal with a defective simply as a pauper is to ostracize him: but let him render the community some service, however modest or humble, and he will acquire some measure of self-respect, and thus take the initial step towards socialization'.

It suggested also the extension of the 'half-way house' principle. A few authorities had already acquired hostels where suitable defectives could live under supervision while going out to work each day. The cost of maintenance was low, because the defectives could contribute towards their keep, or even pay the whole cost of it; and the patients had a greater degree of freedom and normality in living than was possible in the institution proper.

Main recommendations

The chief conclusions reached by the Wood Committee after its five years of deliberation were these:
1. The real criterion of mental deficiency should be social inefficiency, not educational subnormality.
2. The powers and duties of local mental deficiency authorities should be widened to deal with all mental defectives except those between five and fifteen who were capable of attending special schools run by the education authority.
3. The Board of Control should continue to be directly responsible for the management of institutions for those with 'incorrigible criminal tendencies.'[41]

4. Greater use should be made of all forms of community care—licensing from institutions, half-way houses, guardianship, statutory and voluntary supervision.
5. There should ultimately be a co-ordinated mental health service—one local authority in each area responsible for both mental patients and mental defectives. A specialist mental health officer should serve on the staff of the local health authority to co-ordinate and supervise this work.

The Local Government Act of 1929, which broke up the old Poor Law framework, made possible the transfer of certain Poor Law institutions to the mental deficiency authorities, and also provided for the transfer of responsibility for defectives receiving out-relief. The other recommendations—with the exception of the last, which was not to be implemented until the passing of the National Health Service Act seventeen years later—were a matter of departmental arrangement, and of reorientation of attitudes in dealing with mental defectives.

The growth of the community services for defectives which followed the circulation of this report was considerable. In 1929, the total number of persons cared for by mental deficiency authorities—including those in institutions—was 40,000. By 1934, the figures for community care alone were as follows:

Guardianship	. .	3,083
Statutory supervision	. .	33,377
Voluntary supervision	. .	22,544
		59,004

By this time, thirteen hospitals were sending patients out to daily work; nine hostels were in operation; and the number of occupation and industrial centres had risen to 191.[42]

Report of the Brock Committee, 1934

The Wood Committee, in its report, had made a courageous effort to deal with the question of mental deficiency as a genetic and social problem. This was still a highly controversial field where few facts were definitely established. The Wood Committee drew a distinction between primary amentia—due to germinal variation or defect—and secondary amentia—due to some accident or condition affecting a foetus or a live child. Primary amentia they described as 'the last stage of the inheritance of degeneracy of the subnormal group'. This subnormal group represented the lowest tenth of the population measured in social efficiency—the insane, the paupers, the epileptics, the criminals, the alcoholics, the prostitutes and the unemployables. They saw only two methods by which the existence of this sub-normal group could be eliminated—segregation and sterilization. It was essential that the 'lowest tenth' should be prevented from propagating its own kind.

Secondary amentia was a different matter. Here the inheritance was sound, and the causes of deterioration or destruction of brain tissue could be dealt with individually. Secondary amentia might be pre-natal—caused by an alcoholic or a syphilitic condition in the mother, for example. It might be natal—due to injuries from instruments or natural causes during the process of birth; or it might be post-natal. Cretinism was already recognized as a condition due to thyroid deficiency, and treatable by medical means. Similarly, treatments were being evolved for the hypo- and hyper-pituitary conditions. There was good hope that secondary amentia could gradually be eliminated by improvements in surgical and medical techniques.

Primary amentia remained the problem. Segregation was efficient, but very costly; and it made the mental deficiency institution a place of detention rather than a hospital. Sterilization was a highly controversial matter, involving religious and ethical principles as well as considerations of practicability.

At that time, twenty-two American States had sterilization laws, but only two had enforced them on any considerable scale. Even in these two states, it had not been found that the practice of sterilization noticeably reduced the numbers of mental defectives requiring institutional treatment. There were so many other factors besides that of heredity, which might render a defective incapable of normal living.

The practical argument against sterilization was that it would make doctors even more reluctant to certify a patient as a mental defective than they already were; and therefore that it might materially hinder the work of ascertainment. The medical argument was that both diagnosis and prognosis were extremely difficult, and that there would be great difficulty in making such an irrevocable decision in any particular case. From the psychological point of view, sterilization might have disastrous effects on the patient's personality, involving a deep and lasting loss of self-respect. From a religious stand-point, it involved depriving human beings of a fundamental human right— that of reproduction.

Yet, when all these arguments had been put forward, the fact remained that this group, the 'submerged tenth', was widely recognized; and that there seemed no other way of preventing it from growing and from being a permanent drag on the rest of the community.

In 1934 a departmental committee was set up under the chairmanship of L. G. (later Sir Laurence) Brock, Chairman of the Board of Control,[43] to investigate the question of legal sterilization. On behalf of the committee Dr Lionel Penrose and Dr Douglas Turner, two authorities on mental deficiency work, made an investigation through the agency of the local education authorities. They found that, of the children of mental defectives between the ages of seven and thirteen, 40.4 per cent were either mentally defective or seriously retarded. Of these, they considered that rather less than a third were definitely primary events.

The evidence that primary amentia existed on a wide scale was there; but it was not so wide-spread as to justify sterilization at all costs. The Brock Committee concluded that sterilization should be legalized; but that it should be on a voluntary basis only, and subject to stringent safeguards. However, the Government of the day was unwilling to introduce so controversial a measure, and no attempt was made, then or subsequently, to carry the recommendations into effect. Recent genetic research has modified the view of heredity on which the Brock Report was based, while the practical and ethical objections have not lost their force. Belief in the hopelessness of the condition of the 'submerged tenth' has been modified by social work practice in the intervening years.

9   Into the community

From a medical point of view, the Lunacy Act of 1890 was out of date before it was passed. It represented the legal view of mental illness—that here was a condition which made it necessary in certain circumstances to deprive a man of his personal liberty, and that every possible device must be used to limit these circumstances.

Asylums could only take certified patients; and patients could not be certified until the illness had reached a stage where it was obvious to a lay authority—the justice of the peace. This made it impossible for the asylums to deal with early diagnosis, and the treatment of most mild or acute cases. Their work thus became largely custodial.

The difficulties did not end there. Because certification was a necessary preliminary, many doctors tried to avoid sending patients to asylums except as a last resort, and sought other means of treatment;[1] and doctors who wished to specialize in psychiatry often avoided a sphere where most of the work was routine, and where there was little opportunity for improvement of professional techniques.

When new theories of the aetiology of mental illness developed, and new techniques for treatment were formulated, they at first by-passed the asylums completely. The treatment of neurosis developed in the consulting-rooms and the out-patient clinics of the nineteen-twenties and thirties. Later there were new neurosis units, of which the Maudsley was the prototype; but not until after 1930, when the Mental Treatment Act at last presented a means of dealing with mental patients under in-patient conditions without certification, was all this work brought into relation with the asylum service (see pp. 250–1).

The decline of asylum standards

The barrier of certification and the emphasis on custodialism which resulted from the 1890 Lunacy Act undoubtedly contributed to the decline in standards of care and treatment; but there were other factors involved also. One was the question of size. The original asylums were small institutions in which it was possible to preserve

226

some of the values of face-to-face relationships. Lincoln Asylum, built in 1820, had only fifty beds. Nottingham (1811) had eighty. Of the first nine asylums, built by 1827, the average size was 116 beds; but almost at once, it became clear that the number of beds needed had been seriously under-estimated in most areas, and the asylums grew rapidly in size. At Lancaster, the asylum was originally constructed in 1816 for 170 patients, and accommodated 600 by 1852. By 1870, the average size in England and Wales was 542 beds; by 1900, it was 961; and by 1930, it was 1,221 (see appendix 1, table 2).

These barrack-like institutions often had a very different atmosphere from the small homely asylums of earlier years. With more than ten times as many patients, they were forced to deal with people in the mass. Ten nurses dealing with a ward of a hundred patients do not generally achieve the same quality of personal relationship as one nurse with ten patients—they tend to form a social group of their own. Five doctors dealing with a thousand patients do not exert the same kind of individual influence that one doctor does in a community of two hundred. There was a loss of the sense of community, a quality of depersonalization, which often led to the isolation of the individual patient in a crowd rather than his integration in a friendly group.

Dr Granville, in the report of the *Lancet* commission, had noted this tendency in 1877. By that date, the number of patients in Hanwell had risen from the original 1,000 to nearly 2,000. 'The treatment,' he wrote, 'is humane, but it necessarily lacks individuality, and that special character which arises from dealing with a limited number of cases directly . . . it is only in a small asylum that this potent remedy, the sane will working quietly, patiently and directly, can be brought to bear on individual cases.'[2]

The medical superintendent was now bound to a heavy burden of paper-work which involved the repeated notification of details concerning every individual case to a central authority in London. Though other doctors might be employed on the asylum staff, the full responsibility for fulfilling the requirements of the law was his; but the requirements of the law were primarily concerned with ensuring that patients had been rightfully deprived of their personal liberty—not with what happened to them afterwards. In these circumstances, it is scarcely surprising that the gentle permissive influence which had characterized the best of the early asylums could no longer flourish.

The architecture of the asylums built in the late nineteenth century is indicative of the theory of mental illness which lay behind their building. Long corridors, large square wards and stout lockable doors made for easy surveillance. Patients worked on the farms and gardens, in the laundries and sewing-rooms; but their work was organized for the maintenance of the institution, not for their own benefit. They moved from place to place in groups, and they were 'counted in' and 'counted out' of the ward by nurses who often could not remember names or faces.

The impact of the first world war

War was to reduce standards of staffing and accommodation still further. The second Annual Report of the Board of Control (1915) stated that 42 per cent of asylum medical staff had volunteered, and been accepted, for military service. A special mention was made of Dr Crowther, newly-appointed medical superintendent of Netherne Hospital. On appointment, he asked that he might be allowed to defer taking up his duties until the end of the war; and the retiring superintendent, who had reached pensionable age, agreed to remain in office for that period. Dr Crowther enlisted for combatant service, became a despatch rider, and was killed by a shell at Armentières only a few weeks later. With varying degrees of tragedy, this story was repeated many times. The places of these trained and experienced men were taken by the physically unfit, or by retired medical practitioners with no previous experience of work in this specialist field. The loss to the patients was incalculable.

The Board of Control had no figures on the number of nursing staff who left for active service; but they believed that it was considerably higher than the figure quoted for medical staff. It was often impossible to replace mental nurses, even by untrained workers.

When war broke out, there were 140,466 'notified insane persons' distributed among ninety-seven county and borough asylums. London had ten asylums, of which eight had more than 2,000 beds. Lancashire had five, all of more than 2,000 beds. Asylums in small towns, on the other hand, often had only 300 or 400 beds. In all areas, there was a degree of overcrowding. By 1915, the position had worsened considerably, since nine of the larger asylums had been placed at the disposal of the War Office as military hospitals. As a result, the remaining mental hospitals became crowded with displaced patients. Standards of both care and treatment suffered, and the tuberculosis rates rose alarmingly.

One odd result of war conditions is that, during the war years, the number of 'notified insane persons' was considerably reduced. The figure for 1915 showed an increase of 2,411 on the previous year; but by the end of that year, the number had been reduced by 3,278. From that time, there was a marked reduction each year until about 1920—when the figures show a return to the pre-war increase rate of 2,000 to 3,000 a year.[3]

There were about 2,000 nervous and mental patients in military hospitals who would ultimately be certified; but even so, the variation in the annual incidence is sufficiently striking to require some explanation. War brings many kinds of mental stress: fear of death and disablement, grief at the death or disablement of others, bewilderment and rootlessness and loss of security. It would seem reasonable to expect that, if any variation took place, it would be in the form of an increase in mental illness. One explanation for the decrease is that war intensifies the sense of a communal purpose; that in war-time, everybody is busy, and has a task to fulfil. There is not much time for loneliness, and there are few opportunities for introspection. The stress of poverty is considerably reduced, too, for war usually brings material prosperity. Above all, there is an emotional focus—an enemy to hate, the weak to defend (note the amount of public sentiment poured out at this time on 'Little Belgium') and allies to support. Even grief and fear are not isolating factors, as they often are under normal conditions, for there is a consciousness that many others have the same griefs and the same fears. In short, many people suffered stress; but it was a bearable stress, because it was shared.

That is one explanation. It has received considerable support from the medical profession, notably from Professor F. A. E. Crew, later Professor of Social Medicine in the University of Edinburgh, on the grounds that those who are part of a close-knit social group seldom suffer from mental breakdown, and that the strong sense of group participation is a significant factor in the reduction of mental illness observable under war conditions.[4] But there is another explanation of a less encouraging nature.

War-time economy establishes an unusual series of priorities. The fitness and efficiency of the men in the Services is a top priority; next comes the well-being of productive workers. The mentally ill come a long way down the scale, for they play no part in the war effort; and their existence is, in fact, a handicap to the purpose in hand. The available beds are overcrowded, there are fewer doctors and nurses to give treatment, and the general emphasis is on giving treatment only where absolutely necessary. As a result, the decline in the number of those certified in the period 1914–18, may be due, at least in part, not to a decline in the amount of mental illness, but to a reluctance on the part of doctors to certify when adequate treatment was unlikely to follow certification.

Theory and practice after the war

When the war was over conditions in the mental hospitals, as they were now increasingly being called, began to improve again. Staff were demobilized, war hospitals closed down, and their premises returned. Members of the Board of Control also returned to normal duty; and in 1918 the Board drafted a report[5] for the Government Reconstruction Committee, making recommendations for the future.

The chief recommendation was that there should be treatment for limited periods without certification. Under the 1890 Act, it was possible for voluntary patients to be admitted to private, but not to public, asylums.[6] A Bill 'to facilitate the early treatment of mental disorder of recent origin' by means of voluntary admission had been introduced into the Commons by Cecil Harmsworth in 1915; but the time had proved unsuitable, and the Bill was withdrawn before the second reading.[7] Now that staffing and accommodation were improving, the proposal was renewed.

Together with this recommendation for the wider provision of voluntary treatment, the Board recommended that general hospitals should develop sections for the early diagnosis and treatment of mental illness, both for in- and out-patients. The gap between the treatment of mental and physical illness was imperceptibly narrowing, and it was felt that there should be provision, in the normal scope of the health services, for the many border-line cases.

Third, the Board of Control recommended that the more responsible posts in mental hospitals should be restricted to medical practitioners possessing the Diploma in Psychological Medicine, or Diploma in Mental Diseases as it was then sometimes termed. This diploma had been instituted in three universities—Edinburgh, Durham and London—in 1911, following a circular letter sent to all universities by the president of the Medico-Psychological Association in 1908–9. This was a parallel development to the institution of specialist post-graduate diplomas in other branches of medicine. By 1918, courses were also organized by the Royal College of Physicians, and by the universities of Leeds and Cambridge.

Fourth, the Board recommended the official encouragement of mental out-patient clinics, which they considered 'inseparably connected with the improvement of methods of dealing with incipient insanity'. These clinics had arisen in several centres—the report mentioned Sheffield, Manchester and Birmingham by name—and had excited considerable interest in the medical world.[8]

The fifth and last major recommendation was that the Board of Control should be empowered to make grants for the continuation of after-care work by voluntary societies.

Here we have the essence of the developments of the nineteen-thirties: the extension of voluntary treatment, the narrowing of the gap between mental and physical illness, the development of higher professional standards in psychiatry, out-patient clinics and after-care work; but although the need for these improvements was seen by the Board of Control, they could not be introduced suddenly on a national scale. The number of things that can be achieved by Act of Parliament alone is very small. The Board had to wait for the development of responsible public opinion—of groups which would press for legislative action as the National Association for the Care of the Feeble-Minded had pressed in an allied sphere.

By 1921, any plans for immediate improvement in mental hospital conditions had to be shelved. The Geddes Axe fell, severely curtailing expenditure in all government departments.

The Board reported 'great administrative difficulty. The stringency of the financial conditions prevailing throughout the country had compelled local authorities to check their expenditure in every possible direction'. Hardly any capital expenditure was authorized; and with post-war inflation, maintenance costs had risen considerably.

Thus on the financial side, the picture was a bleak one. The Board had excellent intentions, but its work was still suffering from the exigencies of the war years; and in a period when money for capital projects was hard to find, there was not a public mandate of sufficient force to demand that money be found.

Administrative change, 1919

One hopeful angury for the future was the setting-up of the Ministry of Health in 1919. The Local Government Board, which had inherited the powers of the Poor Law Board, and much of its attitude to social misfortune, was finally swept away. There was some significance in the fact that the new authority was entitled the Ministry of Health—public health was no longer to be conceived of as a junior partner to Poor Law administration, concerned only with the health of a section of the population.

The new Ministry took over all the functions of the Local Government Board, including the responsibility for many matters only indirectly connected with health policy, such as Poor Law, Housing and Local Government.

Within a year of its inception, the Ministry of Health took over powers in the control of lunacy and mental deficiency. By the Ministry of Health (Lunacy and Mental Deficiency, Transfer of Powers) Order,[9] it assumed those powers which were given to the Home Office under the Mental Deficiency Act of 1913. These included the general power to make regulations determining the activities of the Board of Control (section 25); the supervision and regulation of the activities of local authorities (section 30); the right to appoint the chairman of the Board of Control (section 22, iii) and the right to appoint and fix the salaries of the Board's secretary and inspectors (section 23, ii).

The Board of Control, though it imperceptibly lost its quasi-independent status after the acquisition of this new and powerful overseer, welcomed the change as 'an important step towards bringing the Board of Control into a proper and desirable relation with the central health authority'. The way was now open for the further assimilation of the treatment of mental illness with that of physical illness.

The Prestwich inquiry

One of the smaller powers affected by the Transfer of Powers Order of 1920 was that which enabled the Ministry to hold a public inquiry if the Board reported that a local authority was thought not to be carrying out its duties under the Lunacy and Mental Deficiency Acts. Within two years, this power was to be used by the Minister of Health in an inquiry at Prestwich Hospital, Manchester.

From 1922, there began the growth of a public interest in this field which can be compared more easily with the three 'waves of suspicion and excitement' of the nineteenth century,[10] than with any concurrent development. The agitation started with a book about Prestwich Hospital—*The Experiences of an Asylum Doctor*, written by Dr Montague Lomax, and published soon after the end of the war.

The picture which Dr Lomax drew was a grim one. He stated that the patients were poorly fed and poorly clad; that they were closely confined, though a number of them would have benefited from parole, with no detriment to the community; that the nurses were mostly unqualified, unsuited to the nature of their work, and that they had, in a number of specific cases, treated the patients with open cruelty. It was a picture of a drab institution life, unrelieved by hope or sympathy or understanding, where, as a result largely of ignorance and neglect, appalling cruelties were still possible.

The Minister of Health was then Alfred Mond; and when a spate of newspaper articles and indignant speeches followed the book's publication, he appointed a committee of the Ministry of Health 'to enquire into the administration of Public Mental Hospitals'. Being a departmental committee, it was responsible directly to the Minister, and not to parliament. It had the advantage of being a small committee, and therefore of being able to report more speedily. The members were Sir Cyril Cobb, MP;[11] Dr R. Percy Smith;[12] and Dr Bedford Pierce.[13] Their task was to inquire first, whether Dr Lomax had given a faithful representation of conditions at Prestwich; and second, whether his charges were applicable to other mental hospitals. The three members of the committee visited the hospital, and undertook a personal inquiry.

They pointed out in their report that Dr Lomax had served in Prestwich during the war, when conditions were far from typical. Moreover, he had no special qualification in psychiatry, and might therefore misconstrue certain measures of policy. They found no actual evidence of cruelty or flagrant abuse, and considered the part of the book relating to these charges to be unfounded.

At the same time, they agreed that conditions at Prestwich were not good. There was a great lack of staff, particularly trained staff; and a number of unsuitable untrained staff had had to be recruited, in order to keep the institution running at all. Lack of suitable staff led to a severe curtailment of the activities of the hospital. Thus it was seldom possible to allow patients out of the building, because there were no nurses who could be freed from other duties to accompany them. They agreed that the patients were poorly and uniformly clothed, and that their diet was monotonous and unappetizing.

How far did these considerations apply to other mental hospitals? The committee was greatly hampered in its work of discovery by the fact that, being only a departmental committee, it had no power to hear witnesses on oath, or to protect them against subsequent victimization. The Asylum Workers' Union, a body whose views on this subject should have been heard, refused to give evidence, or to allow its members to do so in an individual capacity, for this reason.[14] There seems little doubt now that the conclusions of the committee were tempered by the partial nature of the evidence available to them.

The committee accordingly had to confine their general findings to two major considerations: the construction of mental hospitals, and the recruitment of staff. They deprecated the erection of large barrack-like hospitals of the Prestwich type, and recommended that future mental hospitals should not have more than one thousand beds. They recommended construction on the villa-system, a number of small, separate units of accommodation being spread round the grounds.[15] This would make possible the designation of separate reception and convalescent wards, so that those patients who were most in contact with the community outside could be kept away from the 'asylum' atmosphere. They thought also that it was unwise to mix patients from differing social backgrounds—'some account should be taken of home conditions and the surroundings from which the patient has come'.

As far as the staffing situation was concerned, the committee found that in general there was a great lack of suitable nursing staff, both male and female. This was of course nothing new—for there had never been enough of the right kind of people to take up this exacting and widely misunderstood type of work; but the situation had been aggravated by the war. In 1922, the conversion from war to peace economy was not yet fully completed, and there was no real shortage of more congenial employment for those who sought it.

Examinations for nurses had been started on a national scale by the Royal Medico-Psychological Association in 1891.

In 1919, the Nurses' Registration Act made provisions for state registration, and for the setting up of the General Nursing Council. The GNC refused to recognize the existing RMPA examinations for mental nurses, stating that, as a matter of policy, it intended to run its own examinations and not to recognize the results of any other body. The Mental Nursing Certificate of the GNC was instituted in 1921. The theoretical standard required was higher than that of the RMPA examination.

By 1922, then, there were two separate forms of qualification for mental nurses; and there were many mental nurses with neither the will nor the apparent ability to take either. Prestwich was not alone in this respect.

The Maudsley Hospital

While the position in the asylums was a depressing one, and the work of the Board of Control and the more enlightened and devoted staff seemed to bring little progress, movements outside the normal administrative structure offered much hope for the future. Of these, perhaps the most far-reaching were the opening of the Maudsley Hospital to voluntary patients in 1923, and the growth of the Mental After-Care Association.

Dr Henry Maudsley, who was a son-in-law of John Conolly, had a brilliant career in psychiatry, and his personal influence was a major factor in the growth of this specialism in medicine.[16] Medical superintendent of the Manchester Royal Lunatic Hospital[17] at the age of twenty-three, he followed Dr Bucknill as editor of the *Journal of Mental Science*. In 1869 he became Professor of Medical Jurisprudence at University College Hospital, London, where Conolly himself had held a Chair for a time. In 1907 he decided on a generous and practical way of giving expression to his own ideas, and those of his colleagues, on mental treatment.[18] He offered £30,000 to the London County Council for a new mental hospital, on three conditions; it was to deal exclusively with early and acute cases; it was to have an out-patients' clinic; and it was to provide for teaching and research on the diagnosis and treatment of mental disorder.

The London County Council accepted this offer, and the new hospital was built at a total cost of over a quarter of a million pounds.[19] It was completed in 1915, in which year parliamentary sanction was secured to enable it to take patients without certification.[20] From 1915 until the end of the war it was used as a war hospital, and the Ministry of Pensions continued to use it for the treatment of shell-shock cases until 1923. In that year, the Maudlsey reverted to its original purpose,[21] and from then on took voluntary (civilian) cases only.

The classification and treatment of the neuroses, which owed much to the work of the psychoanalytic school, had become a matter of urgent public interest as a result of the war. Cases of 'shell-shock' —the second world war was to produce the term 'battle fatigue' for the same condition—had swamped the military hospitals. There was a gradual recognition that this was a form of mental illness, which, though not amounting to what was then termed insanity, was seriously disabling, but susceptible to treatment. The Maudsley had already pioneered in the treatment of war cases. From 1923, it was free to deal also with the neuroses of a peace-time economy, which though sometimes less dramatic in form, were no less seriously disabling.

In 1924 the Maudsley became a teaching school of the University of London—the first in the psychiatric field. In 1936 chairs in Psychiatry and in the Pathology of Mental Disease were instituted. The London County Council continued to bear the full cost of this undertaking until 1946, when, after an inter-departmental committee on medical schools had pointed out that the hospital occupied 'a special place in psychiatric work' and was serving a national purpose, the financial burden was taken over by the University of London.

The influence of the Maudsley as a centre of teaching and research has been incalculable. It received due recognition on the inception of the National Health Service in 1948 when, united with Bethlem, England's oldest mental hospital, it was designated as the only post-graduate teaching hospital exclusive to psychiatry. The medical school was then renamed the Institute of Psychiatry, and became one of the constituent institutes of the British Post-graduate Medical Federation.

The Mental After-Care Association

Though the major part in progress in the care of the mentally ill was played by statutory organizations, voluntary agencies had begun to play a part in this field also. The earliest of these was the Mental After-Care Association, founded in 1879. The impetus for the foundation of this society came from the chaplain of the Middlesex Asylum at Colney Hatch, who published two papers on social after-care in the *Journal of Mental Science*.[22] In these papers, he stressed the urgent necessity for some intermediate form of care for discharged mental patients. 'The prospect of permanent recovery,' he pointed out, 'greatly depends on the patient's circumstances on first resuming life's ordinary associations.' He pleaded for 'a brief interval of seasonable repose' for the patient facing the complexities and pitfalls of life in the community.

These papers aroused a widespread interest, and in June 1879 a meeting took place in Dr Bucknill's house[23] in Wimpole Street at which the chaplain, Mr Hawkins, and several leading alienists were present. Among them was Dr Hack Tuke (see pp. 49, 156). An association was formed, Dr Bucknill becoming the first president, and Mr Hawkins the secretary. In 1880 the Earl of Shaftesbury, chairman of the Lunacy Commissioners, accepted an offer of the presidency. He expressed his conviction that 'The After-Care Association was required to supply a real want. It was a seed plot from which in time good results would spring.'[24]

The work of the Association was on a comparatively small scale. As Madeline Rooff comments, 'The propaganda of this small society was very gentle, and its work in community care proceeded patiently and slowly in the early years of the twentieth century.'[25] The number of cases dealt with in 1887 was forty-one. In 1900, it had risen to 195, and in 1918 to 670. By this time, its finances were stretched to the limit. The work carried out was of two kinds, residential and personal. Residential after-care took the form of placing ex-patients for a short period in convalescent homes run by ex-matrons or senior nursing officers from the asylums, and paying a maintenance charge for them. Patients were sometimes also boarded out with individual families. Personal after-care was carried out by a number of 'voluntary associates', who undertook this work as a form of charitable enterprise. They found work and lodgings for friendless patients, or sometimes helped to adjust difficult family situations.

In 1919, MACA's work was recognized and considerably increased when the London County Council Asylums and Mental Deficiency Department authorized its sub-committees to make use of the Association in dealing with patients discharged on trial, and to make payments up to the full cost of maintenance.

By 1924 the Association was handling a fair amount of early care and after-care work in the London area[26]. Its pioneer work, in close connection with the statutory authorities, was repeatedly commended by the Board of Control in its annual reports, and was one of the factors considered by the Royal Commission of 1924–6 in its survey of the whole field of the care of mental patients.

The Royal Commission of 1924–6

On 25 July 1924 a Royal Commission on Lunacy and Mental Disorder was appointed. From the Board of Control's comments in their report for that year, it appears that the immediate cause of the appointment of the Commission was not its own desire to achieve legislation of a more enlightened type, but the 'uneasiness aroused in the public mind by a number of charges, somewhat recklessly made, to the effect that large numbers of sane persons were being detained as insane, that the whole system of lunacy administration was wrong, and that widespread cruelty existed in our public mental hospitals.'

The Commission's terms of reference, however, were wide enough to secure constructive as well as destructive evidence. They were to inquire into 'the existing law and administrative machinery in England and Wales in connection with the certification detention and care of persons who are, or who are alleged to be of unsound mind' and also into 'the extent to which provision is or should be made . . . for the treatment without certification of persons suffering from mental disorder'. They were not to deal with mental deficiency or with criminal lunacy.

The Royal Commission was appointed by the Home Secretary, the Rt Hon. Arthur Henderson. The majority of its members had legal qualifications—the chairman, Hugh Pattison (later Lord) Macmillan, was the Lord Advocate for Scotland. Other members included the future Lord Jowitt, then a KC, and member of parliament for West Hartlepool; Sir Ernest Hiley, a solicitor who had been Town Clerk successively of Leicester and Birmingham; F. D. (later Lord) Mackinnon, who was to resign early in the Commission's proceedings on his appointment as a High Court judge; the second Earl Russell, grandson of Lord John Russell, and elder brother of Bertrand Russell, who was a barrister; Sir Thomas Hutchinson, recently Lord Provost of Edinburgh; and Nathaniel Micklem, KC, who had retired from practice in the previous year.

There were two medical members—Sir Humphrey Rolleston and Sir David Drummond. Both possessed legal as well as medical qualifications. Sir Humphrey was at that time president of the Royal College of Physicians—a practising physician whose major interest lay in organic diseases and the physical decay associated with old age. Sir David was Professor of Medicine in the University of Durham, and an authority on diseases of the brain and the nervous system.

Two members of parliament were appointed—in addition to Jowitt, whose interest was primarily a legal one. They were Lord Eustace Percy, a younger son of the Duke of Northumberland, and Mr Harry Snell. Lord Eustace, whose major interests lay in the field of education and public administration, resigned late in 1924 on his appointment as president of the Board of Education. Thirty years later, he was to return to this subject as chairman of the Royal Commission on Mental Illness and Mental Deficiency appointed in 1954. Mr Snell was a Labour member with a background of co-operative and trade union interests, and became one of the first Labour peers in 1931.

The Commission set out to do two things; it received evidence on

the existing system from those who operated it—government departments, voluntary agencies, relieving officers, magistrates,
psychiatrists and others; then it turned to receive evidence on the
shortcomings of the existing system from the National Society for
Lunacy Reform and from individual members of the public. Here
there is some evidence of impatience among the Commission's
members. The National Society for Lunacy Reform brought forward
a number of ex-patients who wished to give evidence. After the
first day's hearing in public, the Commission decided that the atmosphere was one of 'recrimination and controversy', and directed that
future hearings of this kind should be held in camera. 'We do not
find,' they record, 'that the evidence received from this source made
any constructive contribution to the main purpose of our Inquiry'.[27]
Again, the Commission received over 360 letters from patients.
'Some of these,' they note, 'were unintelligible'. These letters were
presumably passed on to the Board of Control, but it is perhaps an
indication of the growing remoteness of twentieth-century administration that very little time could be spared for the investigation of
individual cases, and that almost all of the evidence came from
official and semi-official sources. In the past, agencies with an exclusively 'liberty-of-the-subject' interest had often been clamorous,
time-wasting and retrogressive. Nevertheless, this kind of agitation
was an outlet for a genuine public anxiety, and might have been
allowed a greater measure of publicity.

The existing system

The Commission found that there still existed a clear distinction
between the treatment of paupers and that of persons of means. In
this respect, 'pauper' had a special meaning, since it referred to any
patient maintained in a public asylum, even though the relatives
were in fact paying the whole cost of maintenance. Because they could
not afford private treatment, the old connection with the Poor Law
remained. Admission procedure was by the 'observation' order
(1890 Act, sections 20 and 21) and the summary reception order
(sections 13–19). The 'observation' order had an initial duration of
three days, but could be extended for a further fourteen. It involved
the removal of a patient by a police constable or a relieving officer to
a workhouse until suitable provision for treatment could be made.[28]
The summary reception order required that proceedings should be
taken by the relieving officer, and that there should be one medical

certificate and a magistrate's order. These procedures, which brought upon the family the double stigma of insanity and Poor Law, were often a source of much distress, and therefore a barrier to early treatment.

For a person of means, it was still possible to obtain a writ from a Judge in Lunacy *de lunatico inquirendo*. This procedure was still relatively costly, and its use was rare. The usual methods of certification were the urgency order and the order on petition. Under the 1890 Act, an urgency order (section ii) had a duration of only seven days, and was obtainable on the application of a relative and one medical certificate. An order on petition (sections 4–8) required a relative's application, a magistrate's order, and two medical certificates.

Private patients were still to be found in licensed houses, registered hospitals, single care (which classification might include treatment in a nursing home if the patient were the only mental patient in that particular home) and in amenity beds in the public mental hospitals. 'Pauper' patients were accommodated generally in the public mental hospitals, though a proportion—the Report did not state how many —were still in Poor Law institutions.

General considerations of policy

(*i*) *The interaction of mental and physical illness.* Perhaps the most valuable part of the Commission's work, from a long-term viewpoint, lay in its statements on the nature of mental illness. They are the product of expert knowledge and clear thinking—a fairly rare combination in mental health work at this time.

Mental illness was defined as 'the inability of the patient to maintain his social equilibrium'. This was 'essentially a public health problem, to be dealt with on modern public health lines'. It should be a community service, based on the treatment of patients in their own homes wherever possible, and with a strong preventive element.

The statement on the interaction of mental and physical illness has become a classic, and is here quoted in full:

It has become increasingly evident that there is no clear line of demarcation between mental and physical illness. The distinction as commonly drawn is based on a difference of symptoms. In ordinary parlance, a disease is described as mental if its symptoms manifest themselves predominantly in derangement of conduct, and as physical if its symptoms manifest themselves predominantly in derangement of bodily function. A mental illness may have physical concomitants; probably it always has, though they may be difficult of detection. A physical illness, on the other hand, may have, and probably always has, mental concomitants. And there are many cases in which it is a question whethei the physical or the mental symptoms predominate.

This was perhaps a common-place to psychiatrists; but for many people, even in the medical profession, it was thinking of a new kind. Insanity had always been treated as a subject bearing little relation to general medicine. This statement, backed by two of the greatest medical brains of the day, meant that a patient should no longer be regarded as a 'case' of peptic ulcer or dermatitis, schizophrenia or hysteria. He was a unique fusion of mind and body, and illness, whether mental or physical in symptomatology, was something which affected his whole nature.

To the psychiatrist, this was not new. Freud had demonstrated long before how many apparent physical ailments could be the product of 'hysteria' and something was known about the effect of mental processes on skin conditions and gastric disorders; but the authority of this statement, and the wide publicity accorded to it, make it a landmark in the development of the public attitude to mental illness.

(ii) Voluntary treatment. 'The keynote of the past', said the Commission, 'has been detention. The keynote of the future should be prevention and treatment'.

The 1890 Act represented one solution to the problem of how to deal with those whose behaviour conflicted with that of the society in which they lived. It was the solution of compulsion, hedged in with 'anxious provisions' and 'bristling with precautions against illegal detention'.

The other solution was voluntary treatment. It had been suggested many years before by some asylum doctors and by Shaftesbury and his associates. It had been granted a grudging and very limited approval in 1862 and 1890 by the provision that voluntary boarders could be accepted in private asylums. It had been pressed for strongly by the Board of Control in 1918. The Maudsley Hospital was the only public hospital where psychiatric in-patient treatment could be given without preliminary certification.[29] The experience of the Maudsley, at that time treating approximately 650 new cases a year, showed that

treatment of this kind could be of the greatest benefit to the patient
without being in any way a threat to the liberty of the subject. It was
especially valuable for the neurotic patient, who was capable of
expressing volition and of co-operating in treatment. To certify such
a patient was often to destroy the possibility of co-operation.

In other mental hospitals, the old dilemma remained. In order to
get treatment, the patient had to be certifiable; and in order to be
certifiable, he must have reached such a stage in his illness that he was
quite probably incurable. This was 'contrary to the accepted canons of
preventive medicine'. Elaborate machinery and legal formalities
were positively harmful. (It should be noted also that the possibility
of illegal detention was by this time very small indeed. Licensed
houses had greatly decreased in numbers, and those that remained
were systematically visited. Mental hospitals were so overcrowded
that it is difficult to imagine any medical superintendent keeping
patients under detention any longer than was necessary.)

The Commission thought that, in future, legal intervention should
be confined to three functions: protecting the patient against neglect
or ill-treatment; ensuring that his liberty was infringed only as long as
necessary in his own or the public interest; and ensuring that he
received proper treatment.

(*iii*) *Class distinctions*. 'The present legal status of the great bulk of
insane persons in this country,' noted the Commission, 'is that of
paupers'. The Commission recommended not only the abolition of
the old connection with the Poor Law, but also the abolition of all
legal distinctions between private and pauper patients—'the justification for which has largely disappeared under modern social
conditions'. This was a sweeping proposal.

(*iv*) *Community care*. The Commission felt that much of the good
work being done by mental hospitals was being nullified by the lack
of suitable help for the patient in the period immediately following
discharge. 'The transition from asylum life to the everyday world is a
stage of peculiar difficulty for the recovered patient. The home and
family life to which he returns may be unsuitable or unsympathetic;
employment may be hard to obtain, and friends may be unable or
unwilling to help'.

They mentioned the work of the Mental After-Care Association
'with admiration', but pointed out that its work was largely confined
to the London area, and that there was no organized after-care work

in the provinces. They considered that, as a matter of principle, public funds should be made available for this work.

Recommendations

From the consideration of general issues, the Commission turned to clear-cut recommendations. These are summarized below:

1. Status and composition of the Board of Control: The Board was to remain under the aegis of the Ministry of Health, but to preserve its quasi-independent status. To meet criticisms that the Board was 'inaccessible', since its members (fifteen Commissioners had been appointed under the Mental Deficiency Act of 1913) were always on visitation, a smaller Board was recommended. This would consist of four members—a lay chairman, a legal member, a medical member, and a woman. Visitation would be carried out by fifteen Assistant Commissioners, while the members of the Board would generally remain in London for administrative work.

2. Admission to mental hospitals: 'The lunacy code should be recast with a view to securing that the treatment of mental disorder should approximate as nearly to the treatments of physical ailments as is consistent with the special safeguards which are indispensable when the liberty of the subject is infringed'. Certification should be a last resort, not a preliminary to treatment; and where it was necessary, there should be no distinction in the method of certification used for private and 'pauper' patients. Voluntary patients should be able to enter mental hospitals without legal formality, and to discharge themselves on giving seventy-two hours' notice to the authorities.

3. After-care: Local authorities should be encouraged to establish out-patient clinics, to provide observation beds in general hospitals, and to finance after-care work. After-care should remain in the hands of voluntary social agencies, and should not be 'an integral part of the official machinery'.

4. Mental hospital administration: Mental hospitals in future should not exceed a thousand beds, and should be constructed on the villa system. Nurses should be graded according to capability— the best receiving double training in both mental and general nursing, the average nurse being trained in mental nursing, and those who could not reach the required standard of theoretical work forming a separate grade. Entertainment and employment for patients should be developed, and a special officer should be

I

appointed in each hospital to take charge of this work of social rehabilitation. Voluntary unofficial visitors should be encouraged to act as friends of the patients; and a closer touch should be maintained between mental hospitals and general practitioners.

Developments 1926–30

The Royal Commission's Report marked a complete denial of the principles of 1890, and a development from the earlier and more enlightened principles of 1845. The legal view of mental illness was no longer acceptable. The medical view was fully endorsed; and the social view was encouraged in the clauses relating to rehabilitation and after-care.

The function of a Royal Commission is to sift out existing ideas on the subject under consideration, and to make recommendations which are in accord with informed and progressive opinion. This the Royal Commission of 1924–6 did brilliantly. The Report was more than an analysis of the existing situation. It was also a stage in development.

In its Annual Report for 1927, the Board of Control made a plea for parliamentary action. Legislation had been postponed for a familiar reason—'pressure of parliamentary business'. 'It is re-grettable,' stated the Board, 'that the poorer classes should be denied facilities for treatment which are open to those more fortunately circumstanced'. Two contradictory movements were taking place: as the general standard of living rose, so the expectations of patients and their relatives rose and created pressure for improvements; at the same time, over-crowding tended to depress standards.

Inside the mental hospitals, changes were gradually taking place. In some hospitals, patients were allowed to wear their own clothes if they wished, instead of the drab and depressing garments usually provided. Small articles previously regarded as unnecessary for 'paupers' were now being supplied—nail-brushes, for example, and writing paper and envelopes. In many hospitals, the comparatively new invention of the cinema had been introduced, with beneficial effects. (Four years later, the Board was to deplore the coming of the talking film, on the grounds that silent films of good quality were becoming increasingly difficult to obtain, and that talking films were too complicated and too expensive to be used in mental hospitals. Fortunately, this was only a temporary difficulty.)

Occupational therapy was being introduced in some hospitals, on the Dutch pattern. At Santpoort and Maasoord hospitals in Holland, this activity was highly organized, and had proved of great benefit to patients.[30] The Board of Control stressed in 1927, and in subsequent reports, that patients must not be left to 'deteriorate in wearisome idleness'. Some hospital authorities were taking the view that a patient should only work if his employment was of value to the hospital. This was a wrong view. It was of the greatest importance in the patient's treatment and ultimate cure that he should be occupied and interested when not actually receiving treatment—in fact, occupation and interest were part of the treatment. It did not matter whether the work could be sold for profit, or whether it saved the hospital money. The Board stressed again and again the Royal Commission's recommendation that a 'special officer' should be appointed in each hospital to direct the patients' activities.[31]

Physical methods of treatment were rapidly developing. The Board was convinced that research could produce great advances in treatment, but was pessimistic about the financing of large-scale research projects while the purse-strings were held by local authorities.

Pre-care, after-care, and research: these three topics occur repeatedly in the Board's annual reports of the late twenties and the early thirties. 'The successful treatment of mental disorders on modern lines', stated the 1928 report, 'is prejudiced by the inability to make adequate provision for the patient except during the relatively acute phase'.

Out-patient clinic work was on the increase; but there was still no system of after-care outside the metropolis. In 1928 came the first recommendation from the Board that a mental hospital should have 'someone analogous to the almoner of a large voluntary hospital', whose task it would be to allay the patient's anxieties about home conditions during treatment, and to help him with employment and domestic difficulties after discharge.

This recommendation was evidently made with developments in the training of psychiatric social workers in mind. In 1926, an appeal had been made to the Commonwealth Fund of America by a number of interested individuals, notably Professor Cyril Burt and Mrs St Loe Strachey, who were aware of the work which the Fund had undertaken in training psychiatric social workers in the United States. In response, the Fund's trustees offered to train a small group of English social workers, and the first English psychiatric social workers were thus American-trained.

In 1929, the first English training course was begun in the Social

Science department of the London School of Economics. This venture, and the foundation of the London child guidance clinic, where students undertook practical work, were at first also financed by the Commonwealth Fund.[32]

In the administrative field also, there were changes about this time which would materially affect the future. These resulted from the passing of the Local Government Act, 1929, which finally implemented some of the recommendations of the Royal Commission on the Poor Laws of 1905–9. In a long-overdue reform, Boards of Guardians were abolished, and Public Assistance Committees of the county and county borough councils took their place. The words 'pauper' and 'Poor Law' were replaced by 'rate-aided person' and 'Public Assistance'. The Public Assistance Committee was to work in close collaboration with the health authorities, through the department of the local Medical Officer of Health.

Section 104 of the Local Government Act provided that the Minister might reduce a local authority's grant if certain services were not maintained to his satisfaction; and section 134 listed these services, including lunacy and mental deficiency services. Section 135 provided that, if any material additional expenditure should be imposed on local authorities, provision should be made for an increased contribution out of monies provided by Parliament.

One effect of this Act was thus to provide a groundwork for the development of community mental health services. The local authority, already responsible for in-patient treatment through its Asylum Committee and for mental deficiency work through its Mental Deficiency Committee, acquired a wider responsibility for the poor person suffering from mental illness. The Poor Law had nominally ceased to exist, and some of the stigma of pauperism had gone with it. In the Mental Treatment Act of the following year, parliament tackled the stigma of certification.

The Mental Treatment Bill of 1928–30

To some extent, these events overlap. The Mental Treatment Bill was initiated in the House of Lords in November 1928 by Earl Russell, then Parliamentary Secretary to the Ministry of Transport. If opposition to the Bill's abolition of legal safeguards was to come at all, it would come from the Lords, who had imposed those safeguards in 1890. The choice of Lord Russell as sponsor for the Bill is interesting. He explained in his speech that the introduction of the

Bill fell outside his normal parliamentary duties, but that he had a close personal acquaintance with the services for the mentally ill. He had been a member of the Royal Commission of 1924–6, and he had been chairman of the visiting committee of Hanwell Asylum for some years.

Lord Russell, a barrister himself, took up the legal issue at the outset:

> A doctor is not that sinister figure which in former times he was represented to be, anxious simply to confine a man in a dungeon for life . . . he is treating mental disorder in exactly the same way as he treats any other disease, with a sole view to its cure. When we use such phrases as 'the liberty of the subject'—and no one attaches more importance to real liberty of the subject than I do—let us reflect on what the circumstances are. If your daughter has a fever, is she not restrained in bed instead of being allowed to run out into the cold air to die of double pneumonia? You do not invite the justices to do that—you do it as a matter of course . . . when the patient has recovered, the patient is grateful for it.

As always, a speech on this subject sparked off opposition; and, as always, it was emotional opposition. On this occasion,[33] the mouthpiece was Viscount Brentford, who, with a lavish use of such terms as 'asylum' and 'insanity', strove to demonstrate that the dangers of 1859 were still present in 1929. Lord Russell's comment was, 'It rather breaks my heart, at this time of day, to hear this sort of statement'.

Yet, so far had public opinion moved, Lord Russell was forced to defend his position from the opposite angle—to defend the retention of a very small degree of legal intervention from those who wanted to sweep it away completely. The clause requiring a voluntary patient to give seventy-two hours' notice of discharge was criticized by those who felt that he should be free to walk out at any given moment. Lord Russell admitted that 'in a purely legal and technical sense' this three days' restraint on a patient who wished to leave might be considered detention; but in fact it was a mere breathing-space—an opportunity for the patient to change his mind, for the hospital to make the necessary arrangements for his discharge, and to ascertain that he was not in a certifiable condition which would make him a danger to himself or to others.

Lord Dawson of Penn, who was perhaps the most eminent physician of his day, made an interesting plea for the development of community services from a medical point of view:

The fact is that disease, if I may use the expression, breeds less and less true. It conforms less and less to type. In the days of acute infection . . . the force of the external agent was such that it reduced the sufferers almost down to a common type, with the result that the type of illness was relatively easy and uncomplicated to treat and manage. But in these days, when the external agents are less strong, the colour and pattern of disease is more likely to be determined in greater degree by a man's make-up, his family history, his environment, the strain he has been liable to meet. The result is that you get a more complex picture than in days gone by.

In the Commons, the Bill was introduced by the Rt Hon. Arthur Greenwood, then Minister of Health, on 23 December 1929. He made it clear that the Bill embodied only 'the less controversial proposals of the Report'. No attempt had been made to abolish the 1890 Act. The intention of this Bill was to by-pass it—to provide a framework of treatment which would make it unnecessary to use the older Act, except in extreme cases.

Greenwood quoted extensively from the Macmillan Report of 1926, laying particular stress on its recommendations with regard to preventive work and early treatment. He pointed out the passing of the Local Government Act had facilitated the changes proposed.

A full House listened to the Minister. The debate which followed his speech went on until 4 a.m. During this time the Board of Control came under considerable fire, and there were many speakers who thought that it would be an advantage if all its functions were to be transferred to the Minister direct. 'The mysterious and awful Board of Control,' Dr Ethel Bentham[34] called it. 'People do not know of its name, or how to get at it'. 'An unapproachable body,' supplemented Jack Jones, MP for Rhondda, perhaps better known as the author of *Rhondda Roundabout*. 'You can write them letters, you can send appeals, but you get the same old stereotyped reply every time'. Dr Bentham believed that there were still mistakes in certification, and that the public should not be lulled by the introduction of the 'voluntary' system into thinking that all was well. She instanced the case of a man who was found wandering, and was said to be suffering from mutism. He appeared silent and morose, refusing to answer any questions, or to give any account of himself. On an irrational impulse, Dr Bentham spoke to him in French—and discovered that he was a Frenchman who spoke no English.

There was little serious criticism, apart from that directed at the Board of Control, Captain D. W. Gunston[35] called the Report 'one of the most magnificent reports which has ever been written' and spoke with some wonder of the lack of opposition to the main clauses of the Bill. 'We know,' he added, 'that, as a general rule, one only has to mention the liberty of the subject, and lawyers flock to the House, a sort of Habeas Corpus look comes over their faces'. Possibly the 'Habeas Corpus look' was forestalled on this occasion by the fact that Lord Macmillan, Lord Jowitt and Lord Russell had already supported the Bill in the Lords.

Colonel Wedgwood, who had opposed the Mental Deficiency legislation of 1913 and 1927,[36] was absent from the first and second readings; but at the third reading,[37] he put down twenty questions, and spent some time recounting to the House the plot of G. K. Chesterton's novel *The Ball and the Cross*, in which more and more people are found to be insane until only a psychiatrist is left—and he reveals himself as the Devil. Eventually Col. Wedgwood suffered a rebuke from the patient Speaker: 'If the Rt Hon. and gallant gentleman would only read the Bill. . . .'

Mr W. J. Brown then took up the entertainment of the House by recounting the case of his sister, who had suffered from the delusion that she was being poisoned. A mental hospital wanted to practise forcible feeding. A Harley Street psychiatrist diagnosed dementia praecox, and said that the prognosis was hopeless. An elderly aunt of Mr Brown's then gave the patient several doses of Epsom salts, and she recovered in a few days.

The ramifications of this fascinating case might be discussed by psychiatrists for a very long time; but as far as the House was concerned, it was a mere debating point. Most of the discussion was serious and responsible, concerned with the detailed working of a new system which nearly all were agreed was desirable. Again the debate went on until the early hours of the morning. It was to be many years before the House again showed much interest in the mentally ill.[38] 'A very excellent Bill,' one member called it, 'and . . . a great charter for the poor of this country'. It received the Royal Assent on 10 July 1930.

The Mental Treatment Act 1930

The Mental Treatment Act did four things; it reorganized the Board of Control; it made provisions for voluntary treatment; it gave an official blessing to the establishment of psychiatric out-patient clinics and observation wards; and, in line with the Local Government Act of 1929, it abolished out-moded terminology and brought the official expressions used in connection with mental illness more into line with the modern approach to the subject.

The central authority (sections 11–15)

The reorganization of the Board of Control provided for the establishment of a chairman and not more than five members, who were to be styled Senior Commissioners, and all of whom were to be salaried officials. One was to be a legal Commissioner, two were to be medical Commissioners, and one was to be a woman. There was no requirement that the woman member should possess either legal or medical qualifications.[39] The Senior Commissioners were to be appointed by the Crown on the recommendation of the Minister of Health, or of the Lord Chancellor in the case of the legal Commissioner.

The Senior Commissioners were to constitute the Board of Control. Their main task was to handle administrative work in London, and to supervise the visitation carried out by the other Commissioners. The visiting, or junior, Commissioners were to be appointed by the Board with the approval of the Minister of Health, and were, from the date of the appointed day under this Act, to be exclusively full-time and salaried officials. Under the Mental Deficiency Act of 1913, unpaid Commissioners had been appointed; but the nature of the work was now so exacting that it was no longer a suitable sphere for voluntary public service.

The local authorities (sections 6–10 and 19)

County and county borough councils were authorized to make provision for the establishment of psychiatric out-patient clinics at general hospitals or mental hospitals, to make arrangements for after-care, and, with the consent of the Board of Control, to foster research[40] (section 6 (2)). Under section 19, patients liable to be detained in a workhouse under section 11 of the Lunacy Act 1890 could be sent instead to 'any . . . hospital or part of a hospital provided by the council of a county. . . .'[41]

Voluntary and temporary patients (sections 1–5)

The Act established three categories of patient—'voluntary', 'temporary' and 'certified'. The procedure for certified patients was already established under the Lunacy Act of 1890.

The procedure for voluntary patients was as follows: any person wishing of his own free will to undergo mental treatment (the Act used the phrase 'desirous of voluntarily submitting himself to treatment' which was perhaps unfortunate) could make a written application to the person in charge of any establishment approved by the Board of Control, and could be received as a patient without the necessity for a reception order.

In the case of a patient under sixteen, the volition was that of the parent or guardian, who could make a similar application, accompanied by a medical recommendation from a practitioner approved for this purpose by the Minister of Health or the local authority.

A voluntary patient might discharge himself at any time on seventy-two hours' notice. The essential nature of voluntary status involved the capacity of the patient to make a decision about his own treatment. If at any time he became incapable of such volition, he was to lose his voluntary status. It would then be necessary to discharge him from hospital, certify him, or treat him as a temporary patient.

Temporary patients (section 5) were defined as persons 'suffering from mental illness and likely to benefit by temporary treatment, but for the time being incapable of expressing (themselves) as willing or unwilling to receive such treatment'. The intention was to provide for a variety of recoverable cases where improvement might be expected in a short space of time. Recognition as a temporary patient involved a petition from a near relative, and two medical certificates made out within five days of each other, and not more than fourteen days before reception into hospital.

If the patient regained the power of volition, he would be obliged either to make application for treatment as a voluntary patient or to be discharged within twenty-eight days. The initial duration of a temporary order was six months; this might be extended for two further periods of three months each with the permission of the Board of Control, but could in no case exceed one year in all.

Change of terminology

The Local Government Act of 1929 had already swept away such terms as 'pauper' and 'Poor Law'. Now came the abolition of those outdated words which were still used officially in connection with mental illness. 'Asylum' was replaced by 'mental hospital' or simply 'hospital'; and 'lunatic'—except in certain specific legal contexts, such as 'criminal lunatic'—was replaced by a variety of phrases such as 'patient' or 'person of unsound mind' as the context might require. A 'pauper lunatic' was thus, by virtue of two Acts of Parliament, now a 'rate-aided person of unsound mind'.

Reactions to the Mental Treatment Act

In July, 1930—only a few days after the Act became law—the Board of Control held a two-day conference at the Central Hall, Westminster. It was attended by medical superintendents of county and county borough mental hospitals, by members of the visiting committees of such hospitals, by representatives of local health authorities, and by voluntary workers.

The general atmosphere was one of jubilation. The Act was hailed as being a long-overdue reform, and one which would in a short space of time revolutionize the treatment of the mentally ill. The work of the best authorities had been officially endorsed. The work of the less progressive authorities would now have to be brought up to standard.

An address was given by the Minister of Health, the Rt Hon. Arthur Greenwood, in which he said:

> If this Act means anything at all, it means that we have ceased to think of mental disease as something that is so indecent that it has to be kept in a separate category of its own . . . It has taken ten years and a Royal Commission to get where we are today, and it has not been easy . . . You asked for these powers: you have got them. I hope you will use them.

There was no lack of goodwill to carry out the Minister's behest; but some speakers were already becoming aware of the difficulties inherent in the Act. It was an opportunity—but it was not a panacea. The real problems remained to be worked out in terms of administrative and medical practice.

Dr Beaton, of the City Mental Hospital, Portsmouth, referred to a danger which was inherent in the creation of voluntary status; that the voluntary patients would form a kind of élite, receiving a better type of treatment and a greater proportion of available resources, than the certified patients. He stressed something which was already in danger of being overlooked—that voluntary and certified patients were not patients of differing social levels, persons of differing types of behaviour, or people suffering from different forms of illness. The sole difference between the two categories was that one had the power of volition, and wished to undergo treatment; the other either had not the power of volition, or resisted the suggestion of entering a mental hospital.

There was another problem also: that voluntary patients, being able to come and go almost at will, might consume a great deal of time and money without being cured or improved. They might enter hospital, and then refuse treatment. They might start on a course of treatment, and then leave without completing it.

A third problem, discussed by a number of speakers, was that of inducing patients to accept this new form of admission. The stigma of certification, of treatment as a 'pauper lunatic', was still very strong, and it would be many years before the old words and the old attitudes were finally eradicated.

The difficulties of getting voluntary patients into hospital; of seeing that they received full treatment where possible; of ensuring that certified patients did not suffer by comparison; all these were inherent in the Act; but to them was added another special difficulty, arising from the economic state of the country at that time. Between 1929 and 1931, the numbers of the unemployed more than doubled.[42]

As the numbers of the unemployed rose, unemployment benefit was repeatedly cut, and there were many people living lives of unwanted idleness near the starvation level. A hint of this social tragedy can be seen in a speech from Sir William Lobjoit: 'There are many people . . . who would like to make a home in a mental hospital as a voluntary boarder. It would be a relief from standing from day to day outside an Employment Bureau, to have a home in one of the comfortable well-staffed mental hospitals we know of. We shall therefore have to be on our guard against the malingerers'.

Possibly some speakers felt that Sir William's view of existing mental hospitals, like his view of the popular attitude to mental illness, was over-optimistic; but the fact remains that, during this period, some mental hospitals did have difficulty in distinguishing those who were in real need of mental treatment from those whose primary need was a bed and four square meals a day. The danger of confusing the poor and the mentally sick had arisen again, this time in a different context.

Sir William's reference to 'well-staffed' mental hospitals needs perhaps a word of explanation, since only two or three years previously there had been an acute staff shortage; but the very factor which had increased the number of would-be patients knocking at the doors of the mental hospitals had also increased the staff available. Other kinds of employment were hard to find; and there was, during these years of financial crisis, a considerable influx of new recruits, particularly men, into mental nursing. Many of them came from depressed areas—among them, small tradesmen, miners, and crafts-men. The hospitals usually required that they should be physically fit, and able either to take part in organized games or to play a musical instrument. Although some went back into other employment when the crisis years were passed, a surprising number remained to make excellent trained mental nurses. Already, in 1930, we were learning that it is almost impossible to staff mental hospitals in times of national prosperity; and only too easy in times of depression.

Temporary status was seen by most of the speakers at this con-ference as a kind of half-way house between voluntary status and certification. It was intended to involve no stigma; and it involved no judicial intervention. At the same time, it made provision for the treatment of non-volitional patients. The inherent difficulty here was in defining 'recovery of volition'. A patient might say, 'I want to go home' long before he was fit to make a settled judgment about his own future. He might demand his discharge one day, and be afraid to leave the hospital the next. There was no kind of precedent, medical, legal, or psychiatric for judging the existence of reasonable powers of volition on this point.

Out-patient clinics were more generally hailed as a settled and workable device. There seemed to be no difficulties here. 'All you need', declared one speaker jubilantly, 'is a chair and yourself and a patient'. Dr Good, of the Oxford County and City Mental Hospital, who was associated with an out-patient clinic started originally in 1916 to deal with shell-shock cases, thought that the general estab-lishment of such clinics would inevitably lead in time to an increase in the right sort of voluntary patients. Patients who fought shy of mental treatment in the first place would go to a general hospital 'because they are not afraid of being locked up there or specially labelled. . . . A patient will not come to me, perhaps, as Dr Good, the specialist of Littlemore, but he will come to me at the Radcliffe; and when I have treated him at the general hospital, he will then not care two straws whether he goes to see me at the Radcliffe or the mental hospital'.

He felt that another beneficial effect of the foundation of psy-chiatric clinics at general hospitals was that they generated among medical students a new and often intense interest in psychological medicine. From all aspects, the increasing links between general and mental hospitals were advantageous to both.

A further subject which received much attention at this conference was that of after-care, and the relation of social work in mental illness to that of the general social services. The published report of the conference contained an appendix describing the newly-inaugurated course for psychiatric social workers at the London School of Economics, and there is no doubt that this new development, financed by the Commonwealth Fund of America, was very much in the minds of those present. All agreed that social care was a necessary part of the patient's treatment and rehabilitation to conditions of normal living. Some contended, with Dr Lord, that after-care was 'a definite part of clinical psychiatry—no longer a purely human and benevolent activity'; others felt that the task of integrating the patient back into normal society was one for the general social worker, who was in close touch with the other statutory services. Miss (later Dame) Evelyn Fox, who was then secretary of the Central Association for Mental Welfare, made a clear-cut and valuable statement on the task of a social worker. She also emphasized that any person undertaking this work should be trained. Social work was more than sympathy and common-sense. It was a skill which could be communicated, a technique to be acquired. Where a social worker worked in conjunction with a psychiatrist, her task was to provide him with the social background of the case, and then to act as his instrument in adjusting domestic situations where necessary. In the after-care phase, when the patient no longer needed psychiatric treatment, the social worker continued this difficult and delicate task of social readjustment until the patient was capable of managing his own situations. The conference was a great success. It ventilated a few grievances, raised a few doubts, and aired a few prejudices; but it was at the same time a most valuable instrument of discussion and of the propagation of new ideas. This was not the first conference of this sort organized by the Board of Control; but the pattern was now set for many future fruitful meetings, in which all the parties concerned in operating mental health legislation might consider their joint problems.

Developments 1930–9

The Report of the Board of Control for 1930 showed great satisfaction with the achievements of the new Act. It stressed that most of its provisions were permissive, and that 'it might be described in the main as an enabling measure'. The conference which followed had been organized with the intention of encouraging the local authorities to use the Act to the fullest extent.

Accommodation for voluntary and temporary patients

Although the Act had resulted in an immediate and startling increase in the number of out-patient clinics, little progress had been made in the task of setting aside special accommodation for the new categories of patients. This was partly a matter of cost. Lay committees were ready enough to agree to setting up psychiatric out-patient clinics, which required little capital expenditure, and represented an obvious saving of hospitalization costs. A new unit for voluntary patients, on the other hand, was a heavy charge on capital funds; and it was by no means easy to prove that the ultimate result of building such a unit would be to save money, because the patients would get better more quickly.

Another reason for this slowness of development was that many psychiatrists, like Dr Beaton of Portsmouth, were not convinced as to the necessity for, or advisability of, special units. While they were agreed that beds should certainly be provided for voluntary patients, and that they should have the best treatment available, they felt that special accommodation would improve treatment for these patients at the expense of the certified patients. The stigma of certification would be increased; and there would be a tendency for the new units to be developed as 'show places' at the expense of the rest of the hospital.

Development of the use of voluntary procedure for admission was at first distinctly unequal. By the end of 1931, one area[43] could boast that 45 per cent of all admissions were voluntary; yet another, containing a total population of over four million people, had not admitted one voluntary patient by the summer of 1932.[44] In the subsequent years, however, voluntary admissions rose steadily. In 1932, the overall figure was 7 per cent of total admissions. By 1936, it was 26.9 per cent; and by 1938, it had risen to 35.2 per cent, while fifteen hospitals were admitting more than half their new patients in this way.

Conditions in mental hospitals

The re-constituted Board of Control was waging a vigorous battle for better conditions for all mental hospital patients. Annual reports in the nineteen-thirties show a capacity for independent assessment, lively comment, and occasionally stinging rebuke. A note on the necessity for the provision of mental hospital libraries runs: 'Because patients are allowed to read anything, it must not be assumed that they will be content with any rubbish produced by past piety or present ineptitude. . . . A generation accustomed to Edgar Wallace will not, even in dementia, take kindly to Victorian sentimentality, or the "life and remains" of eminent divines'.

They suggested that the Red Cross or the local county library might supply suitable books, and added that clubs and hotels could often be induced to donate magazines.

Women patients had a champion—probably Dame Ellen Pinsent, who was now the woman Senior Commissioner of the Board. 'Only advanced dementia', runs the 1932 report, 'would reconcile the average woman to the type of garment still worn in some hospitals'. Two years later came the comment, 'A good hair cut and shampoo have a real tonic value . . . the woman who is content to wear her hair untrimmed and a frock like a sack certainly is not normal'. This recognition of the therapeutic value of clothes and hairdressing facilities was new to many hospitals, where committees were apt to consider such things as unjustifiable luxuries.

Food was important, too—and not merely as a means of existence. Patients need to be reassured by familiar dishes ('a generation accustomed to fish and chips cannot be expected to eat steamed cod with anything but reluctance') and occasionally surprised by some special meal. This was not mere sentimentality on the Board's part. Many patients who came into mental hospitals in the period of economic depression were suffering from malnutrition; and more recent anthropological studies have shown that diet and the choice of food may be closely linked with mental health. Primitive communities have been found to deteriorate both mentally and physically when their own traditional dishes are replaced by the diet sheets of nutrition experts; and many a mental patient's re-socialization has begun under the influence of a good Christmas dinner.

In 1934, the Board of Control undertook a survey of entertainments and recreations provided in mental hospitals. They found that almost all hospitals had a programme of activities covering the whole year. There were frequent cinema shows, and sports such as cricket, football and hockey. A number of hospitals had organized dancing-classes. Most had regular dances for men and women patients, and were beginning to break down the rigid segregation of the sexes which had previously been the rule in mental hospital life. Segregation had been emphasized by the administrative pattern of mental hospitals, where the 'male side', headed by the chief male nurse, and staffed by male nurses, was separate from the 'female side', headed by the matron and staffed by female nurses.

The question of open and closed wards figures prominently in the Board of Control's reports at this time. The general practice was for almost all wards (the 'ward' comprising both day and night rooms for its patients) to be kept locked. Nursing and medical staff were accustomed to walk the hospital to the accompaniment of jangling bunches of keys, and for a nurse to lose his or her keys was the swiftest road to dismissal. Mental hospitals had long been dominated by the symbol of the locked door, though there had always been 'working out' and 'convalescent' wards which were not locked. Now the admission of voluntary patients indicated that more doors should be opened, and some patients at least should be free to come and go independently. The introduction of open wards at first aroused many tensions, particularly among the older nurses, some of whom found it difficult to adapt to the new situation; but it was found that, except where very disturbed patients were concerned, opening the doors was often a tranquillizing influence. The patient no longer felt that he was being 'locked away', and became more amenable as a result.

With the gradual introduction of the open door came the development of the parole system. Many patients could be given a limited degree of freedom, and be trusted to keep it. There developed a system of gradually extending parole as the patient's condition warranted it—'hospital parole', which meant that he could go anywhere in the building not specially out of bounds; 'ground parole', which enabled him to go as far as the outside gates of the hospital; and 'outside parole', which allowed him to go out alone, or with another patient, to visit relatives or to go into the nearest town at week-ends. Finally came 'week-end parole'—the patient being allowed home on trial for a short period before final discharge. The parole system did much to break down the barriers between the mental patient and the community outside. The Board stressed year after year the importance of this system, and looked for its extension in all mental hospitals.

Professional training

Training courses in psychiatry were now well organized. The Diploma in Psychological Medicine was offered by the universities of London and Manchester, and the conjoint boards of England and Ireland. This was the recognized post-graduate qualification for medical practitioners until 1971, and involved in most cases a two-year course, undertaken as a supplement to clinical work in a mental hospital. For a time, a short refresher course on a lower professional standard was organized at the Maudsley Hospital; and the University of London Extension Movement, in association with the Royal Medico-Psychological Association, arranged a yearly course of its own.

Training for both male and female nurses was still orgainzed by both the General Nursing Council and the RMPA. The GNC course took three years in an approved training school, or four years in an affiliated school. A State Registered Nurse could take the Mental Nursing Certificate in two or three years respectively. The RMPA course operated separately until 1957 and was less exacting as far as theoretical knowledge—in allied subjects such as anatomy and physiology—was concerned.

Several universities now ran basic training courses for social workers. These courses, first founded in the universities of London, Liverpool and Birmingham in the early years of this century, combined an academic course in social theory and social policy with practical work experience under supervision. By 1918 Miss Elizabeth Macadam, who had been responsible for the institution of the Liverpool course, had organized a national body—the Joint Universities Council for Social Studies—which made requirements with regard to professional qualifications. The universities recognized these qualifications by the award of certificates and diplomas. The first degree course for social workers was instituted in the University of Manchester in 1937. Many avenues of social work were open to these workers, and a number found their way into the mental health field, practising social case-work in mental hospitals and out-patients clinics.

The specialized course in psychiatric social work (see p. 245) was at this time available only at the London School of Economics. The course lasted one year, and was open only to mature and experienced social workers, usually of some academic standing.

The first trained occupational therapist to work in England was Mrs Glyn Owens, who trained in America and set up a training school for occupational therapists in conjunction with Dr Elizabeth Casson at Dorset House, Bristol, in 1930. The Association of

Occupational Therapists was founded in 1936, and a system of qualifying examinations was started in 1938.

New mental hospitals

Two mental hospitals of the present day express the concept of mental treatment which was developed in the nineteen-thirties—Bethlem and Runwell. Bethlem was a charitable foundation with a very long and chequered history which has been detailed earlier. After 1853, however, when the hospital was brought under the supervision of the Lunacy Commissioners, conditions improved considerably; and by 1930, Bethlem was again one of the foremost centres for the treatment of mental illness.

The hospital had already moved twice. The first Bethlem, in Bishopsgate, was left for a site in Moorfields in 1676. This second hospital was the 'Bedlam' of the eighteenth century. The third, at Southwark, was occupied in 1815. The fourth Bethlem is the present-day one, at Beckenham, in Kent. When the Southwark premises became overcrowded, and the limited space available too small for modern methods of treatment and occupation, the Court of Governors issued an appeal and £50,000 was subscribed for a new building. This, completed in 1930, consists of a number of buildings, set in a park of 200 acres of land. Four houses were built for the patients, each with between 40 and 100 beds; and a nurses' home, a block of flats for married male nurses, and extensive science and treatment laboratories were constructed.

Bethlem remained a charitable foundation until 1948, though the patients it has received in this century have differed considerably from the 'Bedlam beggars' of earlier times. As the county asylums absorbed the insane poor, Bethlem drew its patients increasingly from the professional and middle classes. Many of these were people in straitened financial circumstances; but when the move to Beckenham took place in 1930, a proportion of patients were paying the full cost of maintenance.

Runwell was a completely new hospital—the first to be planned since the first world war, designed to embody new ideas in mental treatment. Larger than Bethlem, it had at the time of opening in 1937 a patient-population of 1,010; but this total was broken down into small units, each largely self-contained. Runwell is the only English mental hospital to be built entirely on the villa-system. Small one- or two- storey blocks with flat roofs were scattered over a wide area of garden and parkland. Parole patients, who required relatively little supervision, were housed in units for twenty to twenty-five persons, where they might live something approaching a normal life, unhampered by the weight of institutionalism. Separate blocks were constructed for patients' clubs, where resocialization through group methods could be tried out; and a research wing was built and equipped for the examination of the biochemical and neurological bases of mental disorder.

In both Bethlem and Runwell, the main emphases in design and planning were the same; the breaking-up of the total patient population into smaller social groups; the provision of extensive grounds, to enable parole patients to have relative freedom of movement; the architectural design, unlike the Victorian barrack-pattern; the building and equipping of research laboratories. The appearance of these two hospitals differs from that of the late nineteenth-century mental hospitals as greatly as the 1930 Act differs from the Act of 1890—and for the same reasons. They are the only two of their kind to have been built between the two world wars. There has been no mental hospital building at all, apart from small satellite units, since 1945.

10   Towards a National Health Service

Development of the mental health services so far had been both divided and sporadic. The dichotomy between the services for the mentally ill and the mentally defective was complete. Some local authorities had developed services for one group, but had neglected the other. Some had neglected both. Where medical, nursing and social work staff were well qualified and enthusiastic, an excellent and efficient service had developed; but where the old ideas about mental deficiency and mental illness were still current, there was apathy and indifference. There was no effective central authority—for while the Board of Control was doing good work in bringing mental hospitals and mental deficiency institutions into line with modern social and psychiatric theory, those institutions no longer represented the whole range of available treatment. The community services— out-patient clinics, domiciliary visits by social workers, occupation centres, industrial centres, were of increasing importance; and though the Ministry of Health exercised a certain control over these activities of local health authorities, it was largely a financial control. The Ministry appears to have taken little positive action to encourage the development of more specialized services. The initiative lay with the energetic local authorities; the apathetic were allowed to rest in peace.

The Oxford Mental Health Services, 1937

Dame Ellen Pinsent was asked in 1937 if she would undertake a survey of the Oxford mental health services on behalf of the Oxford Delegacy for Social Studies. Dame Ellen was now a Senior Commissioner of the Board of Control, with a record of over thirty years' continuous association with the problems of mental disorder. Her report gives an interesting picture of the better type of provision available at that time.

Dame Ellen did not claim that the services she described were 'typical' of anything at all. Oxford, by reason of its traditions and its unusual population-structure, was very much of a special case; but she extended her survey over the counties of Oxfordshire and Berkshire, and was able to draw some illuminating comparisons with the city service.

The city of Oxford's mental health scheme was said to be the finest in England for diagnosis and early treatment. It was based on a belief in the paramount importance of maternity and infant welfare clinics, where abnormalities could be detected at the earliest possible stage. There were twelve such centres in the city. The city council was responsible for the salaries of doctors and nurses, and for the rent of two centres. All other expenses were met from funds voluntarily subscribed. All mental health problems, whether in the mother or the child, were referred to the mental health services as a matter of routine.

There was a child guidance clinic, run by a team consisting of a general practitioner, a psychiatrist, and a social welfare worker. An observation school for problem children had been opened in 1930, where the reaction of these children to work and play situations could be studied over an extended period. There were forty-eight children, all suffering from personality disorders. The IQs ranged from 70 to 95. Dame Ellen stressed that there was no organized after-care from this school, though the headmaster did a good deal of informal follow-up work on a personal basis. For retarded children, there were the usual 'special classes', operating in conjunction with the primary schools. Eight such classes dealt with 175 children. The special class children were not visited regularly by either a psychiatrist or an educational psychologist, and the child's progress was thus judged only by the teacher. Supervision of mental defectives in the city area was carried out by the Mental Welfare Association.

For adult patients, there were several types of provision—a county mental hospital, a registered hospital, an out-patient clinic, a colony for mental defectives, and, of course, the residuary services of Public Assistance. The county mental hospital, Littlemore, had 880 beds, no overcrowding, and no waiting-lists. The buildings were old, having been completed in 1846, but in good repair. The staffing position was good—a ratio of approximately one nurse to five patients. All sisters and male charge nurses possessed either the RMPA or the GNC qualification. The matron and several others were doubly trained—that is, they had the general nursing training leading to state registration as well as a mental nursing certificate. Nearly all the wards were open, and suitable patients were allowed out of the hospital on parole. The patients were occupied during the day, either on occupational therapy or on suitable light work in the hospital, and there were frequent entertainments, such as cinema shows and dances. The main difficulty was that the hospital was not free to concentrate on acute cases of mental illness, for which its services were best suited. There were many mild senile dements, and many mental defectives, for whom no other accommodation could be found.

The Warneford Hospital was a private non-profit-making hospital for 'the educated classes'. Treatment was provided in pleasant conditions at an average cost of £4 8s. 0d. per patient per week. Since the patients were self-maintained, they could not be employed on utility services—sweeping, cleaning, gardening, laundry work, and so on—as were the patients in Littlemore. Dame Ellen found that this was in fact a disadvantage, since occupation was an integral part of treatment, and it was difficult to find substitute occupations to fill the whole day. There was a certain amount of occupational therapy; but on the whole the patients were less occupied, less useful, and more inclined to brood about their own inadequacies than those in the county hospital.

Borocourt Colony for mental defectives had been opened in 1934.[1] There were 45 male and 157 female patients, all adults, and more accommodation was planned. All the patients were employed on utility services, and there were adequate recreational facilities. Most of the patients were allowed home from time to time on holiday leave; and there was a small holiday home at Caversham for the benefit of those unable to rejoin their families.

The out-patient clinic at the Radcliffe Infirmary had been opened in 1918. Patients came to it readily, because it was situated in a general hospital. The services of the medical staff who came from Littlemore, were given voluntarily, and the local authority lent a mental health visitor for social work. At the time of Dame Ellen's visit, there were 234 patients on the books.

The Public Assistance services presented a less happy picture. There were many mental defectives and mentally disordered persons in the two Oxford Public Assistance institutions, in addition to numbers of confused and incoherent old people. No psychiatrist visited them, and often the mental health authorities had no knowledge of them.

In fact, even in this, probably the most advanced service in the country, there were two overall criticisms to be made: failure to secure diagnosis by a properly qualified person—a psychiatrist or an educational psychologist, as the case might be; and failure to make referrals to the proper authority. The first was due to lack of knowledge on the part of the authorities concerned—they often had no understanding of the necessity for accurate diagnosis. The second was frequently due to the difficulty in deciding who was the 'proper authority'. The committees involved in mental health work at the local authority level included the Mental Health Committee, the Mental Deficiency Committee, the Asylum (Mental Hospital) Visiting Committee, the Public Assistance Committee, the Education Committee, and the Finance Committee. It is easy to understand why adequate referrals were often not made.

In the rural areas of Oxfordshire and Berkshire, the overall picture was far less encouraging. The county authorities were dealing with large areas containing a scattered and sparse population. The population of rural Oxfordshire was so small that a penny rate would raise only £2,500. There were no special classes, no facilities for observation work on behavioural problems, no out-patient clinics. The county sometimes sent cases to the out-patient clinic at the Radcliffe, but made no financial contribution to the running of this clinic. No duties were delegated to a local Mental Welfare Association, and ascertainment and supervision were carried out on a much smaller scale by the health visitor—who, however high her standards and conscientious her work, had no special training or interest in mental health.

There was one small occupation centre, and mental defectives were sometimes sent to Borocourt. There was not even a Mental Deficiency Committee.

Dame Ellen's general conclusion was that, though the gross cases of mental defect or disorder would receive institutional care in time, no attempt was being made to secure early diagnosis and treatment, and the community services were almost non-existent. In Berkshire, the position was very similar. Forty per cent of all known mental cases were in Public Assistance institutions.

The distinction in treatment was thus not between the rich and the poor, as it had been before 1930; but between the urban and the rural. The latter were the under-privileged class.

Dame Ellen's general conclusions from this brief survey were two-fold: first, that the local authorities were not making the best use of the services already available; and second, that they had no incentive to improve on them. The lack of interest in or understanding of mental health problems could reach all down the line—from the committees and the medical officer of health who ignored the whole subject except when it was thrust upon them, to the health visitor who was inclined to resist a mental health component in her work on the grounds that a particular patient was 'not bad enough to be put away'.

The implications of this study reached out far beyond the boundaries of Oxfordshire and Berkshire. These were the problems of many local authorities all over England. Dame Ellen suggested three methods for the improvement of local authority mental health services:

1. The appointment of a Medical Officer of Mental Health, either co-existent with or immediately subordinate to the Medical Officer of Health. If appointed to the subordinate position, he should have direct access to the relevant committees of the local authority.
2. A joint user agreement to be made for the use of psychiatric facilities where the areas of two or more local authorities formed an obvious geographical or administrative whole.
3. Each area so formed to employ at least one fully-trained psychiatrist for local authority work, principally for prevention and diagnosis.

Thirty-five years later, Dame Ellen's proposals seem limited and somewhat lacking in social inventiveness, but they were counsels of perfection to local authorities at the time.

The voluntary mental health services: The Feversham Report

In 1939 public interest switched from the work of local authorities to that of voluntary associations. These, as we have seen, had a long history in the field of community work, particularly in mental deficiency. They had grown up piece-meal, in response to special needs, as voluntary services often do; and the time had come when effective community work depended on co-ordination of effort.

This was the outstanding conclusion of the members of the Feversham Committee, which made its report to the Ministry of Health in 1939. The members of this committee all had a long personal association with the problems involved. They included the Earl of Feversham, who was the current President of the Child Guidance Council; Sir Henry Brackenbury, Vice-president of the British Medical Association, and also Vice-president of the Tavistock Clinic (see p. 272); Dame Katherine Furse, Director of the Women's Royal

Naval Services; Lord Horder, the King's Physician; the Earl of Listowel, later Postmaster General, and then a Labour member of the London County Council; and Mrs Montague Norman (later Lady Norman), who was associated with the work of the Central Association for Mental Welfare and the Child Guidance Council.

The report included a short account of the history of the mental health services, a review of existing conditions, and a series of recommendations for future action. The historical account is a little misleading, less because of its occasional inaccuracies of fact than because of the particular emphasis which the experience of the committee's members tended to give it. The emphasis on community development, particularly through voluntary agencies, tends to detract from a full appreciation of the part played by the statutory authorities in reform and development.

In 1939, four voluntary associations operated on a national scale in the mental health field. These were the Mental After-Care Association, founded in 1879, which helped patients discharged from mental hospitals (see pp. 236–7); the Central Association for Mental Welfare, founded as the National Association for the Care of the Feeble-Minded in 1896, and reconstituted in 1913 to organize the community care of mental defectives under the new Act through its local associations; the National Council for Mental Hygiene, founded in 1918, which concentrated on educational and preventive work, and maintained links with similar organizations in other countries; and the Child Guidance Council, founded in 1927. There were also many local clinics, some operating in conjunction with local authorities, which appeared to be unattached to any central society.

Four separate associations had thus been created in response to four distinct needs. In some areas their work overlapped, because the field of operation could not be neatly divided into four. In others, particularly in rural districts, there was no provision at all. Sometimes a single society was found to be carrying an overwhelming quantity of work for which its small staff and slender budget were wholly inadequate.

The first conclusion of the committee was obvious: whatever the cost in personal loyalty, the four associations should amalgamate, to form a national Mental Health Association.

In a review of legislation for the mentally ill, the Feversham Committee deprecated the effects of the 1890 Lunacy Act, and stressed the need for full-scale revision of existing legislation to meet the new developments in the treatment of psychoneurosis. The 1930

Act had done much to improve the situation, but its implications had not yet been fully recognized throughout the country. Out-patient clinics were generally ill-equipped, under-staffed, and had inadequately trained personnel. The committee considered that an adequate team in such a clinic would consist of a psychiatrist and a psychotherapist, both of whom should be on the staff of the local mental hospital, and employed on a sessional basis; a psychologist; a psychiatric social worker; and a secretary. It was clear that the theory of out-patient work had travelled a long way.

The increase in voluntary admissions was encouraging. Temporary status, on the other hand, was being used very little. There was some uncertainty as to the type of case which was eligible; and the awk-wardness and expense of procedure, together with the fact that the order had to be extended after six months if the patient had not recovered, meant that it was seldom employed.

In the mental deficiency services, shortages and inadequacies were everywhere to be seen. There was a great lack of occupation centres and special schools. There appeared to be no generally-accepted definition of what mental deficiency was, and the deciding factor in an individual case was too often the IQ which could be measured easily, rather than the degree of social adaptation, which could not.

The reason for this general failure of the mental health services was primarily the lack of public knowledge and interest in the work. Many local authorities, when asked if they carried out mental health education, replied that the subject was 'taboo', and that there was 'no demand' for such education. To the Feversham Committee, the fact that the subject was taboo was precisely the reason for starting educational work.

Some local authorities had pointed out that while general health education could be undertaken on a popular level by posters and slogans, such means were inappropriate for mental health propa-ganda. The Feversham Committee thought that more subtle ap-proaches might be used.

Educational work had been sponsored with some success by a few mental hospitals, where the staff had set themselves the task of integrating the hospital with the local community. Lectures and informal talks had been given to a variety of local groups—church organizations, youth clubs, and so on. A general letter to relatives, to be given to them on the patient's admission, could be framed to reassure them, and to give them some information about the hos-pital's work and the changing attitudes to mental illness. Some hospitals had instituted an occasional 'Open Day', when the general public could see the work for themselves. The dissemination of information could be a powerful force in overcoming the stigma which still remained.

On a different level, the work which the voluntary associations had undertaken with professional bodies, such as general practitioners and teachers, had a great value.

The Feversham Committee made many recommendations, ranging over a wide field. The most outstanding of these were as follows:

1. *Voluntary Societies*. Amalgamation of the four main central agencies—the Mental After-Care Association, the Central Association for Mental Welfare, the National Council for Mental Hygiene and the Child Guidance Council—to take place at the earliest practicable date.

2. *Educational Work*. The new national association to undertake the encouragement of educational work of all kinds, through local authority staff, mental hospital staff, and local voluntary associations.

3. *Mental Health Social Workers*. A minimum standard and a national qualification to be established, accompanied by a rise in status and salary-scale.

4. *Mental Hospital Services*. Out-patient clinics to be increased. Mental hospitals to work in close conjunction with the universities (for research purposes), the general hospitals (for border-line and 'observation' cases) and the local authorities (for community care).

5. *Mental Deficiency*. The criterion of 'social inefficiency' to be generally adopted. Special schools and occupation centres to be extended.

Many of the Feversham Committee's recommendations were in the nature of hopes for the future rather than concrete recommendations for immediate action. The amalgamation of three of the four voluntary associations was to take place under emergency conditions later in 1939; the integration of mental hospitals with medical schools and general hospitals was in some measure achieved by the National Health Service Act of 1946 (see p. 276), and the question of the training and status of mental health social workers has been taken up by the Mackintosh and Younghusband committee (see pp. 301–2). The great value of this report, apart from these factors, lay in its unhesitating emphasis on the community aspects of the mental health services.

The second world war

The outbreak of war in September 1939 made the full implementation of the report impracticable for the time being, and brought a crop of special problems. Inevitably, all the existing shortages were accentuated. As in the 1914–18 war, many doctors were called for service with the Forces. Some mental hospitals were taken over for emergency purposes—such as military or air-raid casualties, or to provide general hospital accommodation outside densely-populated areas—their patients being crowded into other hospitals, already full. Out-patient clinics collapsed for want of trained staff, or staff of any kind. Male nurses in the Territorial and Reserve Forces were called up. Some female nurses left to work in munitions. Those mental hospitals which continued their normal work faced all the problems of institutional life in war-time—acute shortages of clothing, food and heating—plus an unprecedented degree of overcrowding and understaffing. This meant the return of the locked door, of inactivity, of isolation.

At the same time, mental health work received a new and wider significance. The extension of the war to the civilian population meant that public morale was a major factor in victory or defeat.

There was a general fear in psychiatric circles in 1939 that the outbreak of war would be followed by widespread mental breakdown.[2] The whole community was in a state of extreme apprehension. Books such as Beverley Nichols's *Cry Havoc*, which forecast the end of civilization and an international holocaust if war were declared, had a wide circulation. Films such as 'The Gap', which depicted the effect of a major air-raid on an unprepared London in all its horror, were shown to large and fearful audiences. By the time of Munich, public apprehension was so great that the issue of gas-masks, the erection of air-raid shelters, the digging of trenches in public parks and back gardens, the general acceptance of the inevitable, actually relieved the tension.

The administrative and medical problems consequent on public panic—and it seemed that such panic could easily be triggered off by the outbreak of hostilities—could be enormous. In October 1938, a committee of psychiatrists from the London teaching hospitals was set up to consider the formation of a nation-wide mental health service to meet such a situation.

The committee came to the conclusion that the conditions of war would so lower the threshold to stress that three to four million acute psychiatric cases could be expected with six months of the outbreak of war. To deal with these cases, an elaborate scheme involving local treatment centres, mobile psychiatric teams and special neurosis hospitals were suggested.

It is doubtful whether sufficient resources could have been spared under war conditions, or whether any resources would have been adequate to meet the problems envisaged. By the summer of 1940, it was clear that the committee's estimate had happily been wide of the mark. The effect of heavy bombing was to raise civilian morale rather than lower it. The spirit of urban populations in England during the 'blitz' is something which has not yet been adequately explained; there was fear, but no panic; material destruction, but mental and spiritual survival.

Yet, if war did not produce the mass hysteria which had been feared, it certainly produced psychiatric problems of a varied nature. Among these were the problems consequent on evacuation. In Professor Titmuss's descriptive phrasing 'Every conceivable kind of psychological misfit, Conservative and Labour supporters, Roman Catholics and Presbyterians, lonely spinsters and loud-mouthed boisterous mothers, the rich and the poor, city-bred Jews and agricultural labourers, the lazy and the hard-working, the sensitive and the tough, were thrown into daily intimate contact'. The abrupt change of living conditions, the mixing of social and occupational classes, brought fewer dramatic problems than had been envisaged. There was no mass panic. Instead, undramatically, there was an increase in enuresis among children, and in psychosomatic disorders among adults.

To meet the new needs of war-time society, a Mental Health Emergency Committee had been set up by three of the four voluntary associations in 1939, following the recommendations of the Feversham Committee[3]. Three years later, this became the Provisional National Council for Mental Health. Its work in the provinces was based on the thirteen Civil Defence regions. It included supervision of evacuation problems, the rehabilitation of those unable to stand the strain of changed conditions, and a host of *ad hoc* activities which in retrospect are difficult to classify. By 1944, its workers were also dealing with the after-care of Service personnel discharged on psychiatric grounds. Each of the thirteen regions had an office, staffed by two or three workers, some of them psychiatric social workers, and others drawn from the societies which had amalgamated. The amount of work which could be done was strictly limited in scope by the small size of the organizations; but it was of great value in many individual cases, and formed a nucleus from which work in the provinces could later be developed.

The Tavistock Clinic

The work of the Tavistock Clinic, which began in 1920, attracted much public attention during the second world war, when its Director Dr J. R. Rees, became Director of the Army Psychiatric Services, and a number of his staff joined the army with him. The clinic, started by Dr Hugh Crichton-Miller as a somewhat *avantgarde* out-patient clinic, had developed between the wars into a highly psychodynamic centre specializing in child guidance and the use of multidisciplinary teams. Under the direction of Dr Rees in the 1930s, its slogan was 'no research without therapy, and no therapy without research', and a considerable volume of research and teaching of a distinctive kind was undertaken. As Dr H. V. Dicks notes in his history,[4] 'Tavi' was always somewhat isolated from the main stream of medicine and psychiatry on one hand, and from general developments in psychoanalysis on the other; but the independent and unorthodox nature of the clinic gave it a special position and made possible a powerful influence.

Among the people who worked with J. R. Rees in the army were Dr Ronald Hargreaves, later to be Chief of the Mental Health Section of the World Health Organisation and Professor of Psychiatry at Leeds; Dr John Bowlby, later best known as the author of *Child Care and the Growth of Love*; Dr T. F. Main, later Director of the Cassell Hospital; Dr Ferguson Rodger, later Professor of Psychiatry at Glasgow; and the psychologist W. R. Bion. From their collaboration was to come many of the ideas which shaped psychiatry and social psychology in the fifties and sixties.

In 1945, the clinic, which had been supported by voluntary subscriptions and public appeals, became part of the National Health Service. Its subsidiaries, including the Tavistock Institute of Human Relations, remained independent.

The Mental Health Services in 1946

An important study which was to have considerable effect on the development of the post-war mental health services was Dr C. P. Blacker's *Neurosis and the Mental Health Services*, published in 1946. This study was begun in 1942 on the suggestion of Dr Aubrey Lewis, Clinical Director of the Maudsley Hospital, in order to survey the country's psychiatric resources in war-time. It was continued under the sponsorship of the Ministry of Health in order to make proposals for a new psychiatric service; and though Dr Blacker's final recommendations were not official, they carried considerable weight in official circles.

The report was primarily concerned with community services—which at that time meant only out-patient clinics; but it gave some interesting pointers for the future. (Incidentally, the title is an interesting example of that cleavage between the treatment of neurosis and the treatment of psychosis which the new National Health Service was to end.)

General practitioners on the whole retained a deep-seated prejudice against psychiatry. Blacker comments:

> The neurosis survey has shown that there exists throughout much of the country prejudices against psychiatry . . . there is in the provinces a fairly widespread disinclination to utilize the psychiatric services which already exist . . . the main cause is a failure on the part of many general practitioners to appreciate the character of these services, an unawareness of the nature and prevalence of neuroses, and a widespread mistrust of psychiatry, largely focused on analytic procedures, which are considered a decadent and modern fad.

Blacker recommended that there should be closer links between general and mental hospitals, and that there should be better prospects for clinicians in mental hospitals. At that time, the only prospect of advancement was to the post of medical superintendent. This often meant that in a large hospital, a good clinician would be lost to clinical work and would have to apply himself to the unfamiliar and possibly uncongenial task of administration.

The total psychiatric services recommended by this survey were as follows: an increase of 75–100 per cent in out-patient clinics in the next five years; three or four mental hospitals of a maximum of 1,000 beds to one million people—the existing provision was roughly 3,000 beds to one million population, but these were largely in big hospitals with a thousand or more patients; at least one psychiatric social worker to each mental hospital—there were then 27 for 101 hospitals; a doubling of the existing institutional provision (46,000) for mental defectives; and a hundred beds per million population outside mental hospitals—that is, in teaching units or in general hospitals in large towns.

Existing provision when the Health Service came into operation was very much below the optimum framed by Dr Blacker.

The National Health Service

While the war was in progress, and even when its outcome seemed at times doubtful, plans for social reconstruction were being actively discussed. Among these was the plan for a national health service, including the mental health services.

The Beveridge Report on Social Insurance and the Allied Services, published in 1942, had made it clear that, if want in its grosser forms was to be abolished in England, three 'basic assumptions' must be made: the provision of children's allowances, a policy of full employment, and a national health service. From this basis came the series of interlocking pieces of legislation which in 1946–8 were to create the Welfare State.

A national health service was not only socially desirable, but also administratively inevitable. The piece-meal provision of the pre-war years, the complex of voluntary hospitals, municipal hospitals and Public Assistance hospitals, had been hammered into a single service by the necessities of war. An emergency medical service, divided into twelve regions, each with a senior hospital officer, had already created a nation-wide hospital service on war footing. As early as 1940, a Medical Planning Commission consisting of representatives of the British Medical Association and the two Royal Colleges had been set up 'to study war-time developments, and their effects on the country's medical services, both present and future'.

The Beveridge proposals gave an added impetus to these movements, and put the whole question on a wider basis. Beveridge stressed that the development of a social insurance scheme which would provide adequate benefits in time of sickness was contingent on a reduction in the frequency and duration of sickness. A national health service 'should provide full preventive and curative treatment of every kind to every citizen without exceptions, without renumeration limit, and without an economic barrier at any point to delay recourse to it'.

In 1943, discussions between the Ministry of Health and the

interested parties—in particular, the British Medical Association, representatives of the voluntary hospitals, and representatives of the local authorities—began. In April of that year, the Minister of Health stated in parliament that the new scheme for a national health service would not include the mental health services;[5] but this decision was a short-lived one. The mental health services were included in the scheme set out by the White Paper of 1944, which quoted from the Report of the Macmillan Commission of 1924–6 in stressing that there was an interaction between mind and body, and that it was unreal to develop services for one without reference to the other.

A report, *The Future Organization of the Psychiatric Services* was published in June 1945. This was a result of deliberations between representatives of the Royal Medico-Psychological Association, the Psychological Medicine Section of the BMA and the Royal College of Physicians. The report stressed that 'the argument for treating psychiatry in all essential respects like other branches of medicine' was 'strong and conclusive . . . there is everything to be said for making the administrative structure of psychiatry exactly the same in principle and even in major detail as that of other branches of the health services'.

The advantages of this policy were manifest. It would give the psychiatric services parity of esteem with other branches of medicine. It would end the artificial divorce between the treatment of the mind and the treatment of the body which had become impossible to maintain with the development of psychosomatic medicine. It would increase the available resources, end the cleavage between the treatment of psychoses (mainly carried out in county mental hospitals) and the neuroses (mainly carried out in large voluntary hospitals associated with the teaching of psychiatry, in out-patient clinics, or in private practice) and reduce the stigma which still attached to the mental patient.

The disadvantages were largely administrative. In the new Health Service, the local authorities were to be given wide powers in community care; but the hospitals were to be removed from the care of the local authorities, and placed under joint boards,[6] while general practitioners were to be dealt with by a third branch of the service, the Executive Councils. The patient would thus pass from the care of one branch to the other, and back again. He might begin by being under the care of his family doctor; go into a mental hospital for a time; be discharged to the care of the local authority mental health service; and finally return to the care of his family doctor again. Like

K

many patients since 1930, he might return to the mental hospital for short periods of treatment from time to time. In all this, continuity of care could be lost, because the service was to operate in three sections which had little connection with one another.

Many people in the mental health field were aware of this difficulty. The problem was not entirely confined to the psychiatric services, since it affected two other fields where continuity of care before, during and after hospitalization was of special importance—the tuberculosis services and the maternity services. The proposal that these three services should remain in the hands of the local authorities was widely canvassed; but this could only be done through the perpetuation of the idea that these services existed in isolation, apart from the general stream of medicine and public health work. The dilemma was absolute. In the circumstances, the decision to proceed with full integration, even at the cost of administrative trichotomy, was a wise one. It was widely endorsed by the medical profession in the columns of the *Lancet* and the *British Medical Journal*.

The National Health Service Act: provisions relating to mental health

The main body of the Act contained few specific references to mental illness. The mental health services were to form part of the comprehensive health service for England and Wales. (The former county mental hospitals, like other hospitals, were to come under the authority of the new Regional Hospital Boards.[7]) Local authorities were charged with the 'prevention, care and after-care of illness and mental defectiveness'[8]—'illness'—including both mental and physical illness.

The Minister of Health now became the central authority for mental health.[9] The Board of Control continued as an independent body, and retained its quasi-judicial interest in the liberty of the subject. Its Commissioners and inspectors were still empowered to visit mental hospitals and mental deficiency institutions, to review individual cases, and to receive statutory documents relating to admission and discharge; but the Minister assumed responsibility for the administration of hospitals and institutions, the licensing of private homes and hospitals for the mentally disordered, and the control of local authority work.

The Central Health Services Council, which was to be the main advisory body, was to include among its forty-one members two medical practitioners and two laymen with knowledge and experience of the mental health services.[10] There was also to be a Standing Mental Health Advisory Committee, which might advise both the Minister and the Central Council.[11]

Local authorities acquired wide powers under section 28 of the Act in 'prevention, care and after-care'. The local Health Committee now took over she statutory duties previously carried out by the Public Assistance Committee and the Mental Deficiency Committee. Their full duties in relation to mental health were:

(a) The initial care and removal to hospital of persons dealt with under the Lunacy and Mental Treatment Acts.

(b) The ascertainment and (where necessary) removal to institutions of mental defectives, and the supervision, guardianship training and occupation of those in the community, under the Mental Deficiency Acts.

(c) The prevention, care and after-care of all types of patients, so far as this was not otherwise provided for.[12]

While the duties under the first two heads were statutory duties, the last section, covered in section 28 of the Act, was permissive. The actual phrase used shows some ambiguity: 'Local authorities may, and to such extent as the Minister may direct, shall . . . make provision. . . .'

There was thus a hint of possible future mandatory action, but a wide scope was in fact given to local authorities in their implementation of section (c).

The result was inevitably a great variation in practice. Some authorities rose to the challenge, notably in the large towns, and initiated a new mental health scheme which provided comprehensive care. Others were content to carry on with the statutory duties, without attempting to do more than was mandatory upon them. Some set themselves to work to find means of co-operation and co-ordination with the hospital services, to ensure continuity of care. Others remained in comparative isolation.

In the mental hospitals, too, considerable changes took place as a result of the Act. The responsible authority was now the Regional Hospital Board, whose area centred on the university medical school.[13] This brought the practice and the teaching of psychiatry closer together, and enabled the mental hospitals, which generally existed in geographical and professional isolation, to form closer contacts with the teaching facilities of the region. The only hospital group at first designated purely as a post-graduate teaching hospital for the psychiatric services was the Bethlem and Maudsley Group.[14]

Regional Hospital Boards were charged with the duty of setting up Hospital Management Committees, each of which would administer a small group of hospitals. No central direction was given as to whether mental hospitals should be grouped separately, or whether a single mental hospital might be included in general groups with hospitals of other types. Again there was a variation in practice: in one or two regions, notably Leeds and Birmingham, the latter policy was followed where geographical consideration made it advisable, though some mental hospitals were so large that they required a hospital management committee of their own. A typical group might contain a general hospital, a tuberculosis hospital, a maternity hospital, a mental hospital and a convalescent hospital—thus providing for all the varied needs of an area. This created some problems, since the traditional administration of a mental hospital was substantially different from that of other types of hospital. In other regions, this difference of administration was considered so important that mental hospitals, even though some miles apart, were grouped together under Hospital Management Committees of their own. The dilemma at local level was precisely that which had been faced at the centre: was it better to safeguard the special needs of the mental patient at the risk of separating off the mental health services from other branches of the Health Service, or to press ahead with full integration at the sacrifice of those special needs? Regional Boards varied in their answer to this question.

As far as the psychiatric services were concerned, it can be seen that the National Health Service Act provided for a firm central framework, but for considerable administrative flexibility at local level. In the early experimental stages of the new service, this was all to the good. Although there were plenty of problems to be worked out in practice—and some of them were never completely solved—the basic structure allowed room for experiment and initiative. In doing so, it had inevitably to leave room for a certain amount of apathy, for false starts and doubtful decisions. This was the reverse side of the coin.

Nearly two years of questioning and preparation lay between the passing of the Act and the appointed day. On 5 July, 1948, as Sir James Stirling Ross says in a rare poetic moment, 'The whole gigantic scheme wheeled into line. It was like the slow opening of the immense hydraulic doors of the vaults of a great bank.'[15] Controversies had held up development, and recrimination was not yet finally stilled;

but the scheme, ready or not, had to go forward, in order to synchronize with other major schemes of social change which formed the basis of the new Welfare State.

The National Health Service Act meant many things to many people: to general practitioners, a period of serious overwork; to former voluntary hospitals, frustration, and chafing under unfamiliar controls; to local authorities, new responsibilities and opportunities in an expanding field: to members of Regional Hospital Boards and Hospital Management Committees, new powers: to medical specialists, new possibilities of knowledge and professional advancement; but the most important single factor was its effect on the patient. By dissociating medical care and treatment from the ability to pay for it, by making free treatment available as of right and not as of charity, the Act brought freedom from fear for many who had never been able to afford adequate medical treatment.

Part Three

1946–1971

11   The three revolutions

Between the Appointed Day of the National Health Service Act and the passing of the Mental Health Act is a period of a little over eleven years. As far as the mental health services are concerned, the two pieces of legislation are complementary. The period between them thus had an unusually transitional character.

The first major change after 1948 was the entry of statutory authorities into the field of community work, and the consequent shift in the role of voluntary organizations. Local authority mental health departments began to shoulder the burden of care in the community. Community services for the mentally handicapped date back to the 1913 Act, which provided for supervision and guardianship, and occupation centres have a history of nearly forty years, but services for the mentally ill were originally conceived of in a more rigid way. Out-patient clinics were the first attempt to break away from the concept of the institution as the only means of treatment apart from charity or the Poor Law. After 1948, local authority care, day and night hospitals, sheltered workshops and other experimental forms of care did much to break down the old distinction between being totally well (at home) and totally sick (in hospital). Britain began to attempt the provision of a flexible range of services to meet the varying needs of individuals.

Liaison problems

The greatest barrier to development was the artificial division between local authority, general practitioner and hospital services introduced by the National Health Service Act. The alternative—the exclusion of the mental health services from the general pattern of health provision in order to keep continuity of care—would have meant a great loss of status and of opportunities for progress; but the new administrative pattern meant that a great deal of energy had to be expended on liaison problems between the three branches of the service at local level.

These problems were acute. They were exacerbated by the fact that local authority boundaries and the boundaries of hospital catchment areas bore no relation to one another. In Lancashire, for example, there were within the Regional Hospital Board area seventeen county boroughs, each operating its own mental health service, and seventeen divisions of the County Council. One local authority might have patients in eight or nine different hospitals. One hospital might have patients from thirteen or fourteen different local authority areas. Liaison was tenuous, and difficult to maintain. It was often impossible for all the workers concerned with a single patient to get to know one another personally; sometimes the issue of confidentiality was raised between workers of different professional backgrounds. Mutual mistrust between general practitioners and psychiatrists, between the medical profession and social workers, and between social workers of different backgrounds and training, meant that written referrals were not always adequate, and sometimes did not exist at all.

The Messer Committee, in a report published in 1952,[1] pointed out that there were always severe administrative problems in large-scale organizations. The National Health Service had become the third largest concern in the country, employing over half a million people. Centralization involved one set of problems; devolution on a geographical or functional basis would have involved another. 'The greater the delegation to the periphery, the greater the problem of maintaining internal cohesion.' Either way, there were no easy answers.

The committee saw the problems of trichotomy as inevitable, but stressed that they had produced a serious situation in administrative practice. Co-ordination existed only at national level, in the Ministry of Health. Below that level, the three branches functioned separately; and even within each branch, there was no uniform or unitary structure. The hospital service contained both Regional Hospital Boards and independent Boards of Governors of teaching hospitals; the local authority service was complicated by local government boundaries, which separated county boroughs administratively from the surrounding county areas; and in the general practitioner services, local professional committees operated separately from Executive Councils. Over all was the problem of 'numbers and geography'. The Regional Hospital Board areas, based on university medical schools, bore no relation to local authority areas. One Regional Hospital Board area might contain a dozen or more local authorities and Executive Councils, whose areas also did not coincide with each other's. A reverse situation existed in the London area, where one local health authority (the LCC) covered an area split between four Regional Hospital Boards, containing in all twenty-five Hospital Management Committees and twenty-six independent Boards of Governors. Rarely was it possible to work out a simple relationship between a Hospital Management Committee, an Executive Council, and a local health authority. 'The geographical pattern', concluded the report, 'is so complicated that any one authority must find it difficult to be conscious of its opposite number.'

The report listed mental health, tuberculosis, maternity and child welfare and geriatric services as those in which it was most necessary to find ways of overcoming the disadvantages of tripartite structure. In all these services, there could be no clear-cut distinction between care and after-care, and continuity of service was all-important. In the mental health services in particular 'systematic provision for co-operation' was 'imperative'.

Local authorities needed the expert psychiatric advice which only mental hospital staff could give them. Psychiatrists needed detailed information about their patients' home circumstances which could generally only be obtained from the local authority.[2] Both needed to combine on the task of following up discharged patients, and on the question of finding beds for new admissions. (This last question had become a point of friction in many regions; the local authorities were responsible for submitting cases for admission to mental hospitals and mental deficiency hospitals, but those hospitals necessarily determined priority of admission for themselves. In some areas, bed bureaux had been set up at regional level, to which local authority mental health workers could apply; but in others, the worker often had to contact several hospitals in succession; and between the worker's determination to find a bed for his patient and the hospital's determination to avoid further over-crowding, the situation often developed into a personal battle of wits.)

Existing methods to improve co-operation at local level included inter-locking membership between the different statutory authorities, the exchange of papers between authorities, *ad hoc* meetings at officer or committee level to exchange information or reach decisions, and *ad hoc* co-operation between individuals. Interlocking membership was provided for by the National Health Service Act, which had laid down that Regional Hospital Boards should include nominees of the university, the medical profession and the local health authorities in its area;[3] that Hospital Management Committees should include nominees from the local health authorities and the Executive Council;[4] that Boards of Governors of teaching hospitals should include nominees from the local health authorities and the Regional Hospital Board;[5] and that Executive Councils should have eight of their twenty-five members appointed by the local health authority.[6]

Ad hoc meetings and co-operation were perhaps the most valuable means of healing the existing divisions. 'If there were always close co-operation between officers, few difficulties would arise . . . (but) one must look for other means which will work where personalities are conflicting or where officers . . . overlook the effect of their actions upon others.' The report concluded that joint health consultative committees should be set up for 'local health service areas'. These areas should be based on a county borough or other large town, and the extent of the area should be determined by geographical and administrative considerations, by local agreement between the parties concerned. One or two Hospital Management Committees might thus find it convenient to meet members of the county borough health authority, the county health authority for the surrounding area, and the Executive Council or Councils which covered the same population.

Local authority services

In fact, very few local authorities were able to use the device of the joint health consultative committee with any marked degree of success. As the Messer Committee had pointed out, the problems of 'numbers and geography' were intractable as far as existing local authority boundaries were concerned.

The plan of centring an area service on a county borough was workable for other branches of the Health Service, since the hospitals for the area were probably within the county borough boundaries; but mental hospitals and mental deficiency institutions were seldom so placed. They were generally built in rural areas, away from centres of population. This was partly because country land is comparatively cheap, and mental hospitals require more land than general hospitals. A general hospital is built upwards, and does not need extensive grounds, while a mental hospital, with a largely ambulant population, was generally constructed to give the patients access to walks and gardens. Public prejudice also played a part in siting—townspeople often objected to the thought of having the mentally ill in their midst, and so built their mental hospitals in completely isolated areas, or near villages which were too small to raise a loud objection.

The normal process of hospitalization was reversed where mental hospitals were concerned; instead of the rural area going to the town for hospitalization, the urban population went out into the country.

The problem of collaboration was acute in county areas, because of their size, and the scattered nature of population. There might be several mental hospitals within the county boundaries; but many of their patients came from the county boroughs, which operated separate mental health services. It was often equally acute in large towns for the reverse reason. The hospitals which served the town might be some miles outside its boundaries. The most satisfactory situation existed in medium-sized county boroughs of comparatively recent growth. A mental hospital was often sited within the current boundaries, and had a catchment area which roughly coincided with them. It is no accident that the local authority mental health services which became well-known after 1948 for efficiency of administration and co-operation with the other branches of the Health Service were in centres of this kind—Nottingham, Oldham, Portsmouth, York and Bristol. Here personal contacts and case conferences made it possible to obtain a high degree of continuity of care.

The powers and duties of local authorities are set out in the previous chapter. Development in the fifties was distinctly uneven, partly because of the difficulties outlined above; partly because of the unequal distribution of social workers, who tended, like most professional people, to prefer to work in large towns, where opportunities for promotion and the development of professional skills are greater; and partly because some Medical Officers of Health did not regard mental health work as a priority.

In a few areas, the initiative in development of after-care services came from the hospitals, the local authorities continuing to carry out only the statutory duties under the Lunacy and Mental Deficiency Acts. Graylingwell Hospital, near Chichester, carried out with the consent of the South-west Metropolitan Regional Hospital Board a pilot scheme for psychiatric community service in Worthing and the surrounding area. This involved domiciliary visiting by psychiatrists, out-patient clinics, and a day hospital, all designed as part of an integrated scheme with the aim of keeping patients out of hospital and in the community wherever possible. The Worthing experiment was initiated in 1957, and in 1958 a similar service was developed by the same hospital in the Chichester area. The Medical Director's report on these two schemes stated:

In this way, the work of the out-patient treatment services and the work of the hospital will dovetail harmoniously, and be providing a psychiatric service meeting the needs of all types of patients . . . as this set-up is essentially a psychiatric service, it would be best for it to be administered and staffed by the parent hospital.[7]

The North Wales Hospital at Denbigh, which had a well-staffed psychiatric social work department, operated a similar hospital-based scheme; but in most areas, section 28 of the National Health Service Act was interpreted as placing a clear responsibility on the local authority. For a time, hospital-based and local authority-based schemes were allowed to operate side by side. It was not until the passing of the Mental Health Act of 1959 that the responsibility was placed squarely on the local authorities.

The voluntary services

Following the recommendations of the Feversham Report of 1939, three of the four main voluntary associations—the Child Guidance Council, the National Council for Mental Hygiene and the Central Association for Mental Welfare, formed a Provisional National Council for Mental Health in 1942. This body, organized on the basis of the thirteen Civil Defence regions, ran small but useful social work services for mentally ill members of the Forces and their families, and for other special categories of war-time need. In 1946 the work was reorganized on a peace-time basis, and the National Association for Mental Health was formed.

Since that time, NAMH has worked in partnership with the statutory authorities, organizing professional conferences and short training courses, conducting public enlightenment campaigns and providing advice and consultation for Government. The Association's annual conference, attended by 2,000 or more delegates—psychiatrists, mental health social workers, committee members, university teachers and others—became a major occasion for those connected with the mental health services.

In 1954 NAMH opened a northern branch in Leeds. Since then the development of its educational work and of its local associations has been notable. Local associations have run extensive public enlightenment campaigns, helped in staff recruitment for hospitals, provided services for patients in hospitals, prodded local authorities, and more latterly provided hostels and other services through their own organizations.

The parliamentary debate of 19 February 1954

At the beginning of 1954, there had been no major revision and consolidation of the law relating to mental illness and mental deficiency for sixty-four years. The Lunacy Act of 1890, though to some extent by-passed by the 1930 Mental Treatment Act and the Mental Deficiency Acts 1913–27, was still in force. It was over a quarter of a century since the Macmillan Committee had recommended sweeping changes in the relation between services for physical health and those for mental health, but the majority of these recommendations had not been implemented. The few workers in the community services struggled against the handicaps of too little training and too many cases—often with little understanding from committee members. Mental hospitals and mental deficiency hospitals continued to operate a fairly humane but partially closed system, reaching out where they could for public support and finding little. After the initial upheaval of 1948, the whole system settled down again for over five years; then in the winter of 1953/4, it flared into life.

Afterwards, commentators were to talk of the 'three revolutions'—pharmacological, administrative and legal—which dated from that same winter. The curtain-raiser was a parliamentary debate—the first on mental health for twenty-four years—which held up a mirror to the existing services, and let Britain see how great was the need for change.

The debate was initiated on a Private Member's Bill by Kenneth Robinson, then Labour member of parliament for St Pancras North and chairman of the Mental Health Committee of the North-Western Metropolitan Regional Hospital Board.[8] The terms of the motion set the tone for the debate:

> That this House, while recognising the advances made in recent years in the treatment of mental patients, expresses its concern at the serious overcrowding of mental hospitals and mental deficiency hospitals, and at the acute shortage of nursing and junior medical staff in the Mental Health Service; and calls upon H.M. Government and the hospital authorities to make adequate provision for the modernisation and development of this essential service.

Mr Robinson directed attention to four main shortages: shortage of beds, shortage of suitable buildings, shortage of staff, and shortage of money.

There was serious overcrowding in many mental hospitals. Sometimes beds were placed in the corridors, or crammed up in the wards no more than nine inches apart—and still there were not enough beds. A small number of short-stay beds had a rapid turnover of patients; in the rest chronic patients lived out their institutional lives over many years. Despite advances in treatment, there was no evidence that the rate of chronicity was dropping. With an ageing population, it was likely to increase.

On the mental deficiency side, the position was even worse. The ascertained waiting list for the country as a whole was 9,000, of whom nearly half were children.

> I want the House to reflect on what the existence of one of these low-grade defectives means in a family . . . somebody in the family, usually the mother who is perhaps harassed with several other young children, has got to be constantly cleaning up after this child, keeping a constant eye on it to see that it does not injure itself or set fire to the house or do some damage . . . this means an intolerable strain. . . . This situation causes untold misery, and every one of these defectives in a family means that the lives of two, three or half a dozen other people must be affected adversely.

Not only was there an overall shortage of accommodation, but most of the accommodation which existed was unsuitable, since the hospitals had been designed to meet concepts of treatment now long outmoded: 'The Victorians could not build other than solidly, and there the buildings stand, grim, almost indestructible, and they constitute the majority of our mental hospital accommodation.'

Regional Hospital Boards faced a dilemma of considerable dimensions: should they spend their limited resources on trying to patch up these 'really hopeless buildings'? Most of them had tried to develop small modern units for short-stay patients; but the chronic and long-stay patients remained in the 'institutional atmosphere of . . . Victorian barracks'.

Shortage of money was at the root of many difficulties. The Medical Research Council had spent nearly eight million pounds on research in the past eight years, but only one per cent of this sum had been spent on research into mental illness and mental deficiency, despite the fact that patients in these categories filled 42 per cent of all hospital beds in the National Health Service.[9] Out of the total of forty million pounds spent on capital expenditure in the first five years of the Health Service, only 16 per cent had been spent on mental and mental deficiency hospitals. The Minister had (as a somewhat belated gesture) set aside a million pounds for them in the coming year,[10] '. . . but he knows, and we all know, that this is a drop in the ocean. We want many, many millions, and we want them urgently.'

The Government spokesman, Miss (later Dame) Patricia Hornsby-Smith, agreed that existing buildings were 'an appalling legacy' and pointed out that replacing them was 'not a question of a few million pounds . . . (but) a question of thousands of millions over many years.'

The prospect was a sobering one. Comparatively few people had any knowledge at that time of the great changes which were about to alter the scope of the entire field.

The three revolutions

In the early nineteen-fifties, three new movements started: new kinds of drugs, first developed in France, were used in the treatment of mental illness; mental hospitals began the 'open-door' movement which was in time to reduce their numbers and to bring their work closer to those of the community services; and the Government of the day appointed a Royal Commission on the Law Relating to Mental Illness and Mental Deficiency, thus starting a movement for the reform of the law which was to culminate in the Mental Health Act of 1959.

From the point of view of therapy or of public policy, the coincidence of these three movements was fortunate, since each reinforced the other. From the point of view of social analysis, it was less so, since it made it impossible to trace cause and effect with any confidence. The three strands of development crossed and re-crossed, becoming so interwoven that it will probably never be possible to determine what influence each had.

Tooth and Brooke were later to call 1954–9 'the key years . . . the years of therapeutic flux' (see pp. 322–3) and it is necessary to look at each of the three movements contributing to change before attempting an assessment of its extent.

The pharmacological revolution

The chlorpromazine group of drugs, popularly called tranquillizers, were first developed in 1952. Chlorpromazine (Largactil) enabled patients under stress, even stress of extreme kinds, to relax and to become indifferent to their surroundings, although remaining fully conscious. It could thus be used to relieve the more disturbing symptoms of mental illness, while leaving the patient accessible to other forms of therapy.

The use of the new drugs quickly spread, and by the summer of 1955 they were being widely prescribed. Within the hospitals, they created a totally different atmosphere. There was no longer any justification for 'refractory' wards, for wired-in airing courts, for strong-arm tactics on the part of staff. The more distressing sights of mental hospital life—and even if they were less common than the general public imagined, they did exist—disappeared within a matter of months.

The hospital atmosphere changed, and this undoubtedly facilitated both the concurrent open-door movement and the movement to bring psychiatric nurses into closer contact with general nursing. At the same time, it meant that some patients could go home sooner: once a condition was stabilized, there might be no need for further hospitalization provided that the patient had home support, and his doctor could be sure that he would continue to take his pills. It also meant that some patients did not need to come into hospital at all, because their symptoms could be controlled and the illness treated while they remained at home. Imperceptibly the emphasis began to shift from talk of 'after-care' to talk of 'alternative care'.

In the early days, the new drugs were prescribed very freely, and there was a buoyant optimism among psychiatrists. Only gradually was it realized that the psychotropic drugs alleviated, but did not cure. While they often made the patient much more accessible to psychotherapy and enabled him to live a more normal life during treatment, they generally left the causes untouched; and while some form of mental illness, such as reactive depression, tended to be self-remitting, others were not.

By 1961, a mood of doubt was setting in. Professor Morris Carstairs noted in the *Practitioner* that 'Few would claim that our current "wonder drugs" exercise more than a palliative influence on psychiatric disorders. The big change has been rather one of public opinion.'[11] And Dr Jacobsen commented 'We try to treat diseases of which we know next to nothing with drugs of which we know next to nothing.'[12]

In the United States, Brill and Patton contributed a thoughtful study of the effects and limits of chemotherapy:

Coincident with the general availability of tranquillizing drugs in about 1954 and 1955, mental hospitals experienced an abrupt unprecedented cessation of growth of population. Growth has not been resumed, and decreases of 1 to 2 per cent a year are widely reported. . . . The effects on population and on symptom control have proved to be stable enough although there is an increased tendency for intermittent rehospitalization. . . .

Recent advances have been revolutionary, but it is possible to exaggerate what has taken place, to become over confident and to neglect the serious difficulties which still lie ahead in hospital psychiatry. Chronicity has not been abolished, although its conditions have been vastly ameliorated. . . .

With the recent gains has come a period of increasingly sharp review of the existing order, with reactivation of old issues as well as creation of new ones. There are questions about hospital location, organization and size, pressures for the integration of intramural with extramural psychiatry, and for creation of a spectrum of psychiatric services to fill the gap between full mental care and simple individual out-patient treatment . . . however, this profusion of new ideas and new agents creates an urgent problem in evaluation, and psychiatric evaluation is notoriously slow and difficult. In this direction lie dangers as well as opportunities.[13]

The administrative revolution

In September 1953—pre-dating the development of the new psychotropic drugs by a few weeks—the Third Expert Committee on Mental Health of the World Health Organisation produced a report which offered a new model for the development of the Mental Health Services.[14] The 'classical' system, they stated, was one in which the mental hospital dominated the service, operating virtually a closed system, and controlling any services in the surrounding community. This was contrasted with the 'modern' system, in which a variety of services—in-patient, out-patient, day care, domiciliary care, hostels and so on—operated as 'tools' in the hands of the community, and the hospital became only one tool at the disposal of the medico-social team. This concept of a community mental health service was still far from reality in the England of that time, but it formed part of the thinking of the Royal Commission, and developments in different parts of the service were to make it a policy issue within a decade.

The open door policy. Partly in response to a changing climate of opinion, partly in response to the opportunities created by the new psychotropic drugs, mental hospitals began increasingly to open their doors. Few, if any, had ever been completely closed. The modern emphasis on recent enlightenment in this respect does less than justice to the mental hospitals of the past, which for many years— even back in the second half of the nineteenth century—had had their working parties, their outings, their Open Days, their parole systems, their open wards. 'Lunatic escapes' was a headline which owed more to the misconceptions of the popular press than to the reality of mental hospital life. What isolated the hospitals was often less the attitudes of the staff or the behaviour of the patients than the fears and prejudices of the general public.

But the new 'open door policy' went further than these limited and traditionally sanctioned forms of participation. The average length of stay of short-stay patients began to drop dramatically, while admissions rose—particularly readmissions, which gave rise to the widespread comment that the open door was really only a revolving door. But it was generally accepted that a series of short periods in hospital offered a better mode of treatment for most patients than continuous hospitalization. Wards which had previously been kept locked were unlocked, and soon hospitals were boasting that they had no locked wards at all. Unsightly airing courts were dismantled. A party of American psychiatrists, visiting Britain in 1958 under the auspices of the Milbank Memorial Fund, were astonished at the degree to which the British relied on voluntary status and on the patient's co-operation rather than on restraint and compulsion. One member of the team stated: 'Those of us who have had a good "take" from the British vaccine underwent a revolutionary upheaval and emerged with a whole new set of concepts about our patients, about our institutions, about our professional roles, and we see almost every detail of our work from a radically different point of view.'[15]

Others gave detailed accounts of how they had opened up their own hospitals on the British model, with successful results.[16]

Industrial therapy. New movements began to give expression to the idea that the hospital was a part of society—or, as some said, a microcosm of society—rather than an alienated social system. One method was that of industrial therapy, where patients could work— sometimes side by side with industrial workers from homes in the neighbourhood—at tasks for which they were paid a normal, if rather low, industrial wage. The difficulty was to find work which was not sufficiently remunerative to raise trade union objections, but which still paid sufficiently well to make it worth doing. Prisons were later to encounter the same difficulties in taking outside contracts. However, many fairly dull and routine tasks were found—assembling electric plugs, fitting together umbrella spokes, making Christmas paper hats, painting soap novelties, and so on—which were capable of being broken down into very simple processes. This movement coincided with the period in which mental hospitals were selling their farms, long a source of fresh produce and patient-employment, on the grounds of expense. The new industrial activities were certainly closer to the kinds of activities open to urban patients in their own home neighbourhoods than was farm life, and Wing, Bennett and Denham found the system highly beneficial to long-stay schizophrenic patients.[17] However it came under much criticism from trained occupational therapists on the grounds that OT was designed with the patient's needs in view, to increase muscular co-ordination and self-confidence. In IT on the other hand, it was the quality of the work which counted. The patient set a simple piece of repetition work was often expected to carry out the same task over and over for low piece-work rates, with little hope of progression to more complex tasks. The controversy has continued, but after a time OT and IT were seen not as alternatives to one another in their entirety, but as two complementary methods which might be considered in the case of an individual patient.[18]

The 'shift system'. This involved the double use of patient facilities and accommodation. As day hospital care became popular in the mid-fifties, some hospitals were able to match a group of day-patients with a group of night patients, the first living at home and coming into the hospital by day for treatment and activity, while the second lived in the hospital and went out daily to work. In the same way, it was possible to have weekly patients who went home to their families at weekends, and weekend patients who came to the hospital only from Friday night to Monday morning. The administrative neatness of such schemes, with their tempting offer of two patients for the price of one bed, made them perhaps a little suspect, but the principle of breaking up the mental hospital system and developing flexible systems of patient care was one of the great advances of this period.[19]

The therapeutic community system. This system of patient care started with war cases at a military hospital in Mill Hill during the second world war. It substituted human relations, and particularly group relations, for the more orthodox methods of psychiatry.

As outlined by Dr T. F. Main in 1946, the system was an attempt to get beyond the traditional stereotypes of mental hospital life, and to rediscover the realities of human contact:

> The anarchical rights of the doctor in the traditional hospital society have to be exchanged for the more sincere role of a member in a real community, responsible not only to himself and his superiors but to the community as a whole. . . . He no longer owns 'his' patients. Patients are no longer his captive children obedient in nursery-like activities, but have sincere adult roles to play, and are free to reach for responsibilities and opinions concerning the community of which they are a part.[20]

In the hands of Dr Maxwell Jones, first at Belmont and then at Dingleton, it became an ideology in which the whole life of the hospital community was structured for therapeutic potential. Formal role—doctor, nurse, patient—was abandoned, and the four 'themes of treatment' were rigorously applied:

> The sorts of attitude which contribute to a therapeutic culture would be essentially an emphasis on active rehabilitation as against 'custodialism' and segregation; 'democratisation' in contrast to the old hierarchies and formalities of status differentiation; 'permissiveness' rather than the customarily limited ideas of what may be said and done; and 'communalism' as opposed to an emphasis upon the original and specialised therapeutic role of the doctor.[21]

The basic method of the therapeutic community was the group meeting. In addition to the daily community meeting, including both patients and staff of a hospital or unit, there would be smaller meetings on a ward or activity basis. These were 'selected and grouped on the basis of a number of attributes, clinical type, age, sex, intelligence, motivation etc., as being suitable to interact together under the guidance of their doctor or therapist, in a small group treatment process.'[22]

Through group meetings, tensions would be ventilated, communication would be established, defences would be broken down, and problems could be worked through.

For some patients—and staff—the system proved an astonishing liberation. For others, probably only a minority, the 'Unit culture' was as demanding and as encapsulating as that of any traditional mental hospital. Rapoport's careful and balanced assessment of the system's successes and failures at Belmont tends to suggest that it worked best with young male patients of working-class origin, for whom it was originally devised.[23]

The main theoretical input was from social psychology, notably from the work of Bion,[24] and Foulkes.[25] However, the system raised sociological and organizational issues of some complexity. These often deterred those who started experiments on similar lines in other hospitals.[26] A particular problem was the adoption of what, in organization theory, is known as the 'no-conflict assumption':[27] the assumption that any problems uncovered could be 'talked out' or 'worked through' to a state of common satisfaction and group harmony. There were many occasions on which the conflicts appeared to be both bitter and irreducible.

Subsequent experiments, notably those of Dr Denis Martin at Claybury Hospital[28] and Dr David Clark at Fulbourn[29] developed on somewhat different lines. Probably the greatest achievements of the therapeutic community movement have been not in the few units which for a time adopted intensely psychodynamic systems but in the many which have been led to liberalize fairly autocratic systems. It may be that no psychiatrist ever completely succeeded in role-abandonment (how could he, when he was being paid to treat his patients, and the authorities held him responsible for their care?), but most psychiatrists came to rely less on formal role and more on skill and the formation of a set of personal relationships. Probably no group ever solved the problems of all its members—but many patients discovered, in groups, a form of social support which helped them. Probably no hospital ever became completely permissive; but many were led to examine their rules and regulations, and to substitute a flexible and relaxed system for a rigid and unimaginative one. Despite a certain theoretical naiveté, the therapeutic community system made a considerable contribution to the liberalization of mental hospitals.

Out-patient clinics. After great hopes had been placed on them in the early 1930s, out-patient clinics achieved only a limited provision for some years. The model clinic, with its team of psychiatrist, psychologist, psychiatric social worker, nurse and secretary, developed in a very few places, mainly in the London area. According to Blacker's survey published in 1946, provision at the end of the second world war was very patchy, and much of it of a dismal quality.[30]

Under the National Health Service, conditions began slowly to improve. Premises were upgraded, and the volume of work greatly increased. While clinical psychologists and PSWs remained in very short supply, most had a social worker attached, and regular secretarial help was secured. By 1957, the directory of adult psychiatric out-patient facilities in England and Wales published by the National Association for Mental Health listed over 800 clinics, and it was the practice for most consultant psychiatrists to spend at least two or three sessions a week on out-patient work. With the introduction of the psychotropic drugs, clinic work was greatly increased, since many patients who would formerly have required hospitalization could be dealt with on an out-patient basis.

Day hospitals. If out-patient clinics were the panacea of the thirties, day hospitals were equally the panacea of the fifties. They are said to have started in the USSR. Certainly the first in England was the Marlborough Day Centre, opened by Dr Joshua Bierer in Hampstead in 1948.[31]

Farndale's *The Day Hospital Movement in Great Britain*[32] sets out the whole story; the excitement at the discovery of a new mode of treatment; the claims that it was 'cheaper and better for the patient'; the development of facilities attached to mental hospitals, attached to general hospitals, or physically separate. (But not, however, administratively separate. A day hospital had to be run by the Hospital Service. If a local authority provided exactly the same facilities, in official parlance it could only offer a day centre.) Many day hospitals offered a full range of hospital facilities, including meals, patient activities, education, OT and psychiatric consultation.

Gradually, the limitations of the new method were discovered and accepted. It looked much cheaper than it actually was (psychiatrists calculating costs often used the facilities of the parent hospital, but did not include a charge for them). It worked well in densely populated urban areas, where transport problems and costs were minimal, but was unsuitable for more scattered areas. It tended to require a high ratio of social work staffing. It was suitable for some patients, but not for others. While patients with a good supportive home background could often make the daily transition from home to hospital without difficulty, and could benefit from keeping in touch with their families, those with difficult home environments found their problems exacerbated. Some day hospitals, started with high hopes, have since closed down. Others have continued, and found a place in a developing system.

Hostels. The Mental Health Act specifically mentioned the provision of hostels, and a number of local authorities and hospitals began to experiment in this field. There was a good deal of confusion— partly because there was no central guidance and partly because different authorities saw hostels as being the panacea for their own particular problems. In 1960–61, the National Association for Mental Health called two conferences, one in Leeds and one in London, to debate what was being done. It was clear from the papers presented at these conferences that some speakers were thinking primarily of permanent homes for the subnormal (hostels of this kind had been started as early as the eighteen-nineties and developed under the 1913 Mental Deficiency Act) while others were thinking of 'half-way houses' for mentally ill patients who had been in hospital and were not quite ready to return to their own homes. Some wanted to mix patients of different types, while others laid emphasis on the importance of selection. Some thought this a local authority responsibility, and some that the hospitals should be responsible for patients until they were fit to go home. Some thought in terms of permanent care, and some spoke of the dangers of 'silting up' and clearly wanted a population that would move on. Many must have agreed with Dr Rose of Brockhall Hospital, who commented, 'I have carefully read again those parts of the Royal Commission's Report that deal with hostel care, and I have come to the conclusion that they did not give quite as much thought to the working out of practical details as they might have done.'[33] It might be said that the working out of practical details is not a task for a Royal Commission, and that there was wisdom in allowing diverse ideas to develop; but a number of authorities became somewhat disillusioned with hostels when their first hopes of rapid turnover or limited costs were dashed. Good hostels did not turn out to be a cheap form of care.

Therapeutic social clubs enjoyed a vogue in the fifties. Hospitals developed their own patients' social clubs, and began to experiment in letting them run their own affairs. Local authorities similarly began to run clubs for ex-hospital patients. In 1948, Dr Joshua Bierer had convened a conference on the subject and a subsequent publication outlined some of the early experiments.[34] Dr Bierer's own clubs at the Institute of Social Psychiatry and the Stepping Stones Club at Bow acquired a reputation as notable experiments, but the movement was comparatively short-lived. At best, the therapeutic social club was a hybrid. Eventually, its function was filled by more intensive kinds of group therapy[35] on one hand and by clubs not confined to psychiatric patients on the other. Hospital clubs have become less easy to run as the pace of discharge has quickened, and the standard of potential sociability among patients has consequently dropped.

Psychiatric units in general hospitals. In the 1950s, a few general hospitals were experimenting with the development of psychiatric wards or wings, or even the inclusion of selected psychiatric patients on general medical wards. Though this movement was comparatively small before the Mental Health Act took the legal provisions out of psychiatric care by abolishing the concept of designated beds and allowing informal admission, it was to have considerable consequences. The prophet of the fifties was Professor Thomas McKeown of the University of Birmingham, who proposed a radically new concept of hospital care.

McKeown argued that most of our hospital services were unplanned. Hospitals were on the wrong sites, often convenient neither for patient access nor for staff recruitment. They were often the wrong size, in the wrong specialisms, and large numbers of patients were in the wrong place—patients who needed minimum care blocking beds intended and staffed for acute care. The answer to this was the concept of a 'balanced hospital community' where a common staff, on a common site, could classify and locate patients according to the patients' needs. Such a hospital could have simpler, and hence better, relationships with local authority and practitioner services. Planning could be based on demographic and epidemiological analysis of the whole population. This indicated that the real needs of patients were not in the traditional clinical specialisms but in three main groups: problems of childhood, associated with birth and growth; problems of early adult life, often associated with the wear and tear of a working life; and problems of middle and later life, associated with the degenerative process. In a rationally planned system, these would be dealt with within a single hospital complex.[36]

Social workers in the community. Back in 1946, Dr Blacker had been very despondent about the prospect of training enough qualified social workers to run adequate services in the community. The Mackintosh Committee[37] on 'the supply and demand, training and qualifications of social workers in the Mental Health Service' published a report in June 1951 on psychiatric social workers, and took an equally dismal view of the situation.

Between 1928 and 1950, 523 students in all had qualified as psychiatric social workers. Of these, 331 were currently working in the United Kingdom, and the wastage rate was known to be very high. Sixty-five were working in mental hospitals, and only eight in local authority mental health departments. The other 258 were divided between out-patient clinics and child guidance. This very skewed distribution reflected patterns of training and professional expectations.

The Mackintosh Committee estimated that, on the basis of existing facilities, only 65-70 psychiatric social workers could be trained annually. Blacker had estimated that over a thousand were needed at once.

By 1956, the number of psychiatric social workers in local authority mental health departments had risen from eight to thirty-two; but many local authorities had, for all practical purposes, abandoned the attempt to attract these qualified workers into their employment. They had looked elsewhere for their social workers, and other methods of training had to be considered.

When the new mental health departments of local authorities were set up in 1948, they recruited two very different kinds of workers: relieving officers of the Public Assistance service which had now been superseded by the National Assistance Act 1948, and mental welfare workers from the voluntary associations which had previously been responsible by delegation for the bulk of mental deficiency work in the community.

Until 1948, the relieving officer was the person 'duly authorized' under the 1890 Lunacy Act to take proceedings in the case of certification. When the National Assistance Act and the National Health Service Act came into force, some of these men transferred to the employment of the National Assistance Board, whilst others retained their status as 'duly authorized officers' and entered the mental health departments. In most county areas, a form of joint appointment was used, the duly authorized officer also being responsible for welfare services under Part III of the National Assistance Act. Most of the duly authorized officers had an excellent background of work in an administrative setting, but little social work experience, since the previous context of their work had been one in which principles and practice were somewhat rigidly laid down by higher authority.

Under the Mental Deficiency Acts 1913–27, many mental deficiency authorities had delegated their duties to voluntary mental welfare associations, paying the salaries of the associations' workers. Most of these workers were women, many of whom had twenty or thirty years' experience. Their position in 1948 was the reverse of that of the duly authorized officers: they had considerable social work experience—the phrase 'qualified by experience' has a real meaning in social work, where there is much that cannot be learned theoretically, but only by face-to-face contact—but generally little knowledge of the administrative complexities of local authority work.

Both groups were able, in favourable circumstances, to learn much from the other. In May 1954 the professional associations concerned amalgamated, forming the Society of Mental Welfare Officers.

To the older workers transferred in 1948, and to the few psychiatric social workers in the field, younger entrants were added. Some were graduates in Social Science, who had a wide basic knowledge of the social services in general, though they had little case-work experience, or specialized knowledge of mental health work. Some were qualified mental nurses who transferred from mental hospitals, preferring the more varied settings offered by community care. Some were local authority clerical workers who discovered a personal bent for this kind of work, and transferred from office duties.

A survey undertaken in Lancashire in 1953–4[38] showed that mental health workers in the county area and the seventeen county boroughs came from diverse backgrounds. The total number was 109; of these 36 were previously relieving officers, 4 were previously employed by a mental welfare association, 12 (excluding psychiatric social workers) had a degree or a diploma from a university, 14 were trained nurses, and 22 were ex-clerical staff. Only three—employed in Manchester, Liverpool and Oldham—were psychiatric social workers; and eighteen had other types of background which were not classifiable.

Outside Liverpool, Manchester, Salford and Oldham, which had highly-organized services, most county boroughs in Lancashire had only two or three mental health workers. Lancashire county had thirty-nine for seventeen health divisions—an average of just over two to each.

In 1959 the mental health services of local authorities, and social work generally, received considerable stimulus and support from the publication of the Younghusband Report.[39] Miss (later Dame) Eileen Younghusband had long urged upon Government the importance of restructuring the social work services, and had written two previous reports on this subject under the auspices of the Carnegie United Kingdom Trust.[40] The terms of reference of the Working Party which reported in 1959, and of which she was chairman, were limited to the local authority services, and to only two areas, health and welfare. Nevertheless, the opportunity for development was there, and Miss Younghusband and her colleagues seized it. They recommended that in future two grades of social worker should be trained and employed:

1. 'Professionally trained and experienced case-workers to undertake casework in problems of special difficulty.' In mental health work, this grade would consist of psychiatric social workers, who would 'have psychiatric consultation and themselves provide casework consultation for mental welfare officers.'

2. Officers with a general training in social work and a new qualification known as the National Certificate in Social Work. Training for this certificate would involve two years' full-time study or the equivalent, and would take place in colleges of further education. In addition, 'welfare assistants' would be employed and given in-service training to help them to deal with 'straightforward or obvious needs'.

This three-tier structure, it was hoped, would provide for a realistic level of service despite the bottlenecks which affected training facilities. It was recommended that a National Council for Social Work Training should be set up, and that a national staff college should be founded to give impetus to training. In the local authorities, better working conditions were imperative. It was recommended that salary levels and salary-structure should be reviewed; that more senior posts should be established, and that clerical help and transport should be provided on a much more generous scale.

In 1959, these recommendations did much for morale. In time, they were to revitalize the health and welfare work of local authorities.

In all the varied movements of the administrative revolution, common themes can be discerned: the move from traditional patterns to new and flexible ones; from stereotypes to fresh and illuminating discoveries; from clinical models to social ones. From this time on, the accumulating knowledge of the social sciences, particularly of sociology, began to permeate a sphere which had been inexorably and exclusively medical for over a century—ever since, as Professor G. R. Hargreaves put it, medicine 'lost the social view' in the 1850s, on the passing of the Medical Qualification Act.

The legislative revolution

The Royal Commission on Mental Illness and Mental Deficiency sat from 1954 to 1957 against a background of change which must have bewildered many of its members, experienced as they were. Many of them had a long acquaintance with the mental health field, but this was not necessarily helpful when established assumptions were being challenged and frames of reference re-drawn.

The chairman was Lord Percy who, as Lord Eustace Percy, had served for a short time on the Macmillan Commission of 1924–6. On the medical side, there were such distinguished names as that of Sir Russell Brain,[41] the neurologist, and Dr T. P. Rees, well-known for his development of the open-door policy at Warlingham Park Hospital. Lady Adrian, daughter of Dame Ellen Pinsent, acted as spokesman for the voluntary services. Mrs Bessie Braddock, MP, was Labour's champion of the urban poor. Other members included two eminent jurists, a consultant psychiatrist from a mental deficiency hospital, and the president of the Confederation of Health Service Employees.

The full terms of reference of the Commission were as follows:

> To inquire, as regards England and Wales, into the existing law and administrative machinery governing the certification, detention, care (other than hospital care or treatment under the National Health Service Acts 1946–52), absence on trial or licence, discharge and supervision of persons who are or alleged to be suffering from mental illness or mental defect, other than Broadmoor patients; to consider, as regards England and Wales, the extent to which it is now, or should be made, statutorily possible for such persons to be treated as voluntary patients, without certification; and to make recommendations.

Though the discussions later recorded in the Minutes of Evidence were to range over a wide field, the Commission was thus limited to legal and administrative issues, with a clear directive to the effect that they were to consider ways of reducing the existing formalities of admission and discharge, and ways of extending community care. They were concerned only with what the law could do, not with the wider problems.

After more than three years' work, the Royal Commission drew up a report[42] of a little over three hundred pages which summarized the main problems and the main trends of public opinion, and provided a blue-print for a comprehensive mental health service. The written style is a little laborious, and the Report lacks the clarity, the sudden vivid and memorable phrases, which characterized its predecessor of 1926; but this may be due to a change in the subject-matter. Issues which appeared simple and clear-cut in 1926 were seen to be many-sided in 1957; and mental health is now too complex a subject, with too great a weight of material, for vivid, simple writing.

12   The Mental Health Act 1959

The main recommendations of the Royal Commission's Report were based to a considerable extent on a memorandum submitted and oral evidence given by the chairman of the Board of Control, Mr Frederick Armer, who was a permanent official of the Ministry of Health, and the Senior Medical Commissioner to the Board, Dr the Hon. W. S. Maclay. This joint evidence represented the most highly-informed and official view of the shape which future legislation should take. Mr Armer and Dr Maclay proposed the abolition of special legal formalities connected with mental illness and mental deficiency, including the abolition of the Board of Control itself and the introduction of completely informal admission procedures; the absorption of the mental health services in the general adminstrative pattern of the Health Services; and the extension of local authority powers and duties. These proposals were to form the backbone of the Report and of the subsequent legislation. Though there were alterations in detail, the general outline was so fully accepted by the Royal Commission (there were no minority reports) and by the Government that it would be tedious to repeat at the Report and Bill stages what finally became law. We shall therefore proceed to a brief consideration of the Commons debates on the Mental Health Bill, and then to the terms of the Act as it reached the Statute Book.

The Mental Health Bill in the Commons
The Bill was published, and had its first reading, in December 1958. The second reading was introduced in the Commons by the Minister of Health, Mr Derek Walker-Smith, on 26 January 1959. He pointed out that the Bill was a long one—it contained 146 clauses and eight separate schedules—but that it replaced in comparatively simple form a mass of legislation, repealing fifteen whole Acts, and thirty-seven Acts in part. He referred to *The Times*, which had called the existing laws on mental health 'a jungle':

> They are certainly complex, difficult, and in many respects out of date. Consequently, in replacing the mosaic—to use a politer term

—of the law and procedure produced by our fathers and forefathers, with a single contemporary design, we are making a
clean sweep. But this holocaust of the laws made by our
predecessors does not carry any condemnation of their actions.
They, particularly in the nineteenth and early twentieth century,
laboured for progress in their day as we do in ours. . . .

The existing laws had been good in their day; but advances in
medical and social skills, a new change in public attitudes 'as rapid as
it is welcome' had rendered them out of date. In the new Bill, two
principles had been followed: the provision of as much treatment as
possible on a voluntary and informal basis; and a new system of safeguards where compulsion must continue to be used, which would
attempt to draw anew the line between the liberty of the subject and
the protection of society.

The Minister outlined the provisions of the Bill, touching particularly on points at which it diverged from the recommendations of the
Royal Commission. To the three categories of patients—mentally ill,
psychopathic, severely subnormal—a fourth, subnormal, had been
added.[1] A definition of psychopathy had been attempted, involving
three factors: a persistent disorder of personality, 'abnormally aggressive or seriously irresponsible conduct', and susceptibility to medical
treatment.

'One of the main principles we are seeking to pursue,' said the
Minister, 'is the re-orientation of the mental health services away from
institutional care towards care in the community.' The mental health
services of local authorities, judging from expenditure, were expanding rapidly. In 1954–5, their cost was a little over £22 million. In
1957–8, it was over £3½ million; and in 1958–9, it was estimated that
it would increase again by half a million pounds, to over £4 million.

The Royal Commission had recommended that there should be a
specific grant for capital development by local authorities. The
Minister admitted that this had not been possible, and also that the
grant to the mental health services was now part of the general grant.
This was whether members liked it or not, a *fait accompli*. 'We cannot
debate the issue of the general grant all over again in the course of this
Bill.'

Although he felt that the principles of the Bill were right, he wished
to keep an open mind as to details:

When we come to Committee, we shall come with no obstinate
pride of authorship. We shall listen to suggestions, animated by

L

the desire to make this as good a Bill as our corporate wisdom can achieve. . . . On the Statute Book, it will mark a notable chapter in the history of social progress, and reflect credit on the Parliament which enacts it.

Sir Hugh Lucas-Tooth was concerned about the split between hospital care and local authority care. The boundary problem, in its present form, seemed insoluble; but gradually the large old hospitals were to be broken up, and he felt that the most acceptable solution was to site small hospitals, where possible, to fit in with local authority areas.

Several members continued the discussion about local authority services. Mr Christopher Mayhew sounded a cautious note: 'What matters is not passing the Bill, but what comes after it.' The record of the local authorities 'with certain spectacular exceptions' had not been encouraging to date. He endorsed the suggestion of Mr Kenneth Robinson that local authorities should be required to put forward their plans for development over the next two years. This Bill, though it described the powers of local authorities in more detail, in fact added nothing to the powers they already possessed under section 28 of the National Health Service Act. They could do a great deal; they were actually required to do very little.

Mr Mayhew urged the House to think carefully about the matter of care in the community. A great deal of lip-service was paid to the idea of getting patients out into the community again, but this was not a simple matter. There was a good deal of public prejudice to be overcome; and quite apart from prejudice, there were deeper problems: 'We shall not get anywhere unless we realize frankly that, by the very nature of their handicap, mentally ill and mentally deficient people are, and always will be, particularly hard to integrate into the community.'

Mrs Braddock also urged that the implementation of local authority powers should be made mandatory:

In scattered areas and country areas, local authorities which are not so progressive or compact as city councils or local borough councils simply will not bother to put the services into operation unless there is some form of compulsion and extended financial assistance from the Government. The Royal Commission made great play of that point.

Other subjects of considerable discussion in this debate were the questions of research, of the care and treatment of the psychopath, and of the position of medical superintendents in mental hospitals.

There was general agreement that research was of the utmost importance. Mr Mayhew thought that the Medical Research Council was spending 'a fabulously small amount' on research into mental illness, and pointed out that success in the research field, particularly in research into the treatment of the more serious mental illnesses, could have a 'magical' effect on the whole field. Mr Austen Albu and Mr Richard Fort wanted more research into the social causes and effects of mental illness—particularly follow-up studies, since, to quote Mr Fort, 'we have been woefully inadequately informed about how many people are improved by one form of treatment or another'.

There was some disquiet about the provisions of the Bill concerning the psychopath. 'The fact is,' said Dr Summerskill, 'that we have done little research into the problems of the psychopath.' Dr A. D. D. Broughton was not happy about the proposal that psychopaths should be treated in general or in mental hospitals: 'I have found that they can be a very disturbing influence, tiresome to the staff, and harmful to the other patients.'

Dr Reginald Bennett had had experience of treating psychopaths, and was prepared to say without hesitation that they were almost entirely unsuitable for hospital treatment:

No hospital can stand more than one or two psychopaths in the whole hospital, let alone in one ward. The place becomes a bear garden. They put the other chaps up to tricks, and they are frightfully clever in finding out bright ideas for perhaps the duller members of the community or the more disturbed ones. The hospitals are going to refuse these chaps. . . . I do not think that we can really compel any hospital to admit more than it chooses to say is its maximum allowance of these appalling people.

If the proposals of the Bill were to have any effect, special institutions would be necessary to deal with them.

The question of the position of the medical superintendent was raised by Dr Broughton. The Bill referred throughout to the 'responsible medical officer' in a mental hospital. Was this to mean the medical superintendent, or the doctor who had immediate clinical charge of the patients? Mr Kenneth Robinson thought that 'the medical superintendent has been abolished as far as his legal status goes', and asked for clarification; but no clarification was forthcoming.[2]

The most striking fact about this debate to an outside observer is the very high level of information and discussion which it shows. There is a marked contrast with the mental health debate of February 1954, when many members showed a great lack of even basic knowledge, muddling mental illness with mental subnormality, and admission rates with beddage. In 1959, the House showed itself alert, interested, and exceedingly well-informed. Perhaps this is as good an index as any other of the change in public opinion which had taken place in the intervening years.

A good deal of solid work was put into the Bill at the Committee stage. Ideas were tested, opinions were sought, and when the Bill returned to the Commons on 5 May, a number of amendments had been made—though, as the Minister of Health had forecast at the second reading, these were concerned with legal and administrative details, rather than with major matters of principle. There was general agreement as to principle—to an extent which is surprising when we recall the stormy controversies which this subject had evoked in parliament in earlier generations.

It had been pointed out that, although the Bill provided for the safeguard of the rights of patients compulsorily detained by means of the new Mental Health Review Tribunals, it did not provide that patients should be informed of these rights. Many patients, and their relatives, are bewildered people who do not read Acts of Parliament, and who might have no means of knowing how and when to apply to a tribunal—or even of the tribunal's existence. An amendment provided that patients and their relatives should be supplied with 'such written statements of their rights and powers under this Act as may be so prescribed.'

The criterion for severe subnormality was extended. It had referred to patients 'incapable of living an independent life'; but since this was a criterion which could sensibly only apply to adults, a phrase to cover severely subnormal children was added: 'or will be so incapable when of an age to do so.'

A further amendment laid the duty of making application for admission to hospital or guardianship on the mental welfare officer in cases where such action was necessary. The Society of Mental Welfare Officers had pointed out that some patients might be overlooked if this was not done, and the Minister of Health agreed that the mental welfare officer should have the discretion. He or she was not to be simply 'a rubber-stamp'.

At the third reading, on 6 May, it was announced that other points made by members had been met. A circular had been sent from the Ministry of Health on 4 May to all local authorities, drawing attention to the Royal Commission's recommendation that there should be a re-orientation of the mental health services away from institutional care and towards community care. They were asked to make a review of their mental health services, and to make plans for development. In fulfilment of the resolution of 26 January the Minister had agreed to use his powers under section 28 of the National Health Service Act to make the provision of mental health care mandatory on local authorities.

The Medical Research Council had also taken note of the views expressed in the debate, and had set up two committees for further mental health research—one on the epidemiology of mental disorder, and another on clinical psychiatry.

The Bill passed its third reading, again without a division, and then went to the House of Lords.

The Mental Health Bill in the Lords

The debate on the second reading of the Bill in the House of Lords[3] provides interesting comparisons with the past. The 1890 Act, as we have seen, was the culmination of the work of three Lord Chancellors —Selborne, Herschell and Halsbury. It was born of legal determination, and debated in the Lords by a group which still had a good deal of political power, but which knew little of the real issues at stake.

The 1959 Bill came up to the Lords from the Commons. It was introduced by the Lord Chancellor (Lord Kilmuir); but his powerful legal talents were devoted, not to legalistic definition, but to support of a Bill designed to minimize the legal elements in mental treatment. He described the Bill as 'the first fundamental revision of the English mental health laws since 1845, when the two Bills introduced by Lord Ashley,[4] later the seventh and famous Earl of Shaftesbury, created the system on which all the latest additions of the last hundred years have been based.' No specific mention was made of the Act of 1890.

In 1889 and 1890, the lawyers dominated the debate. In 1959, the Lords could provide a series of experts, some hereditary peers and some life peers, to speak with knowledge and first-hand experience of varying aspects of mental health work—a psychiatrist (Lord Taylor); a social scientist (Lady Wootton); the chairman of the National Association for Mental Health (Lord Feversham); the chairman of the National Society for Mentally Handicapped Children (Lord

Pakenham); and Lord Grenfell, who, in a moving speech, told the House of his own experiences as the parent of a mongol child.

After the third reading, the Lords sent the Bill back to the Commons, with a series of amendments. Many of these were concerned with exact legal definition rather than with the spirit and intention of the Act, but three proposed changes in practice. The substitution of 'remuneration' for 'fees' in the section dealing with the payment of members of Mental Health Review Tribunals was proposed, to enable the chairman or other members to be paid a permanent salary if necessary; a clause was introduced, laying on Regional Hospital Boards the duty of notifying local authorities of the availability of beds for urgent cases—this was very necessary if the hospitals were no longer to be obliged to take certain kinds of patients; and the rights of the patient in his dealings with the Mental Health Review Tribunal were clarified and extended.

It is noticeable that the part played by the Lords in discussion and amendment of the Bill was a constructive and valuable one. Though the Upper House had lost much political power since 1890, it demonstrated, at least in this sphere, that it had still much to contribute to the national life.

The Lords' amendments were accepted by the Commons in a debate on 24 July 1959. The Bill received the Royal Assent on 29 July.

The Mental Health Act, 1959

The Act repeals all previous lunacy, mental treatment and mental deficiency legislation, and provides a single code for all types of mental disorder.

Definitions

'*Mental disorder*' is defined as 'mental illness, arrested or incomplete development of mind, psychopathic disorder, and any other disorder or disability of mind.'

'*Mental illness*' is not further defined.

'*Arrested or incomplete development of mind*' is defined under the headings 'severe subnormality' and 'subnormality'. 'Severe subnormality' is of such a nature or degree that the patient is incapable of leading an independent life, or of guarding against serious exploitation. 'Subnormality' is a condition which does not amount to severe subnormality as defined above, but which is 'susceptible to medical treatment or other special care and training of the patient.' Both must include subnormality of intelligence.

'*Psychopathic disorder*' is defined as 'a persistent disorder or disability of mind (whether or not including subnormality of intelligence) which results in abnormally aggressive or seriously irresponsible conduct . . . and requires or is susceptible to medical treatment.'

All these definitions are given in section 4 of the Act, which also contains a clause to the effect that persons are not to be regarded as suffering from a form of mental disorder 'by reason only of promiscuity or other immoral conduct.'

A *hospital* is defined as a hospital within the National Health Service, any special hospital (the former 'State Institutions' for dangerous or violent patients) and any accommodation provided by a local authority for hospital and specialist services (section 147).

A *mental nursing home* is defined as any other place for the reception of one or more patients suffering from mental disorder (section 14).

'*Medical treatment*' includes nursing care and treatment, and any kind of care and training taking place under medical supervision (section 147).

'*Local health authority*' means the council of a county or county borough, or a joint board set up for health purposes by two or more such bodies (section 147 and National Health Service Act 1946, section 19).

'*Responsible medical officer*' means the senior doctor in charge of the patients' case.[5]

Administration

(*i*) *Central.* The Minister of Health was already, by the terms of the National Health Service Act, responsible for the mental health services; but the Board of Control, which had been set up in 1913 and had inherited the work of the Lunacy Commissioners, was still in existence as a quasi-independent body. The Mental Health Act dissolved the Board of Control (section 2), existing officers of the Board being transferred to the Ministry of Health. The Board's functions of inspection and review of individual cases of compulsory detention were transferred to local bodies (see below). The Minister has no overriding power of discharge of individual patients, but may refer any case to a Mental Health Review Tribunal (section 57).

(*ii*) *Local*. Local authority mental health services provided under section 28 of the National Health Service Act were to continue, and the Mental Health Act gives a statement of their powers at some length, including the provision of residential accommodation, the provision of centres for training and occupation, the appointment of mental welfare officers, the exercise of the functions of guardianship, and 'the provision of any ancillary or supplementary services' for the mentally disordered (section 6). This section simply defines in greater detail what some authorities were already doing under section 28.

Section 12 gives the local authority the power to compel children, but not adults, to attend occupation and training centres.

Mental welfare officers were given powers of entry and inspection (section 22). They may apply to a magistrate for a warrant to search for and remove a person believed to be suffering from mental disorder (section 135). It is the duty of the mental welfare officer to make application for admission to hospital or guardianship where such action is 'necessary and proper' (section 54).

Local health authorities are designated as registration authorities for mental nursing homes (section 14). The Minister of Health may make regulations for the conduct of such homes (section 16) and may exempt the registered hospitals from local authority inspection (section 17).

Although the local health authority has the primary responsibility for mentally disordered persons through its mental health service, other local authority bodies may assume responsibility for them in suitable circumstances. Arrangements may be made for them to be housed in Part III accommodation under the National Assistance Act, 1948, which is amended for the purpose. This would bring them under the care of the welfare authority; and the children authority constituted under the Children Act, 1948, may assume responsibility for mentally disordered children (sections 8 and 9).

Mental Health Review Tribunals. These new bodies took over the 'watchdog' functions of the Board of Control. They are to review individual cases of compulsory detention at the request of patients or relatives (section 3 and section 122) or at the request of the Minister (section 57). One Tribunal is constituted for each Regional Hospital Board Area (section 3). The constitution of Tribunals is set out in the first schedule to the Act. They consist of an unspecified number of persons:

(i) Legal members, appointed by the Lord Chancellor.

(ii) Medical members, appointed by the Lord Chancellor in consultation with the Minister of Health.

(iii) Members 'having such experience in administration, such knowledge of the social services, or such other qualifications or experience as the Lord Chancellor considers suitable', also appointed by the Lord Chancellor in consultation with the Minister of Health. The chairman must be a legal member. A Tribunal sitting on any particular occasion need not call on all its members, but members present must include one or more from each of the three categories set out above, appointed by the chairman. If the chairman himself is not present, the acting chairman must be a legal member (schedule I).

Detailed rules for the regulation of Tribunal proceedings are laid down, subject to the discretion of the Lord Chancellor (section 124). Tribunals have the power to discharge patients from compulsory detention or from guardianship (section 123). Application for a hearing by a Tribunal must be made by or in respect of a patient 'by notice in writing addressed to the tribunal for the area in which the hospital or nursing home is situated' (section 122) at specific times laid down in the Act.

Admission to hospital

(*i*) *Informal admission.* Hospitals are no longer obliged to take patients; but it is the duty of the Regional Hospital Board to give notice to the local health authority of where beds are available for urgent admissions (section 132).

Patients may be admitted to any hospital or mental nursing home without formalities of any kind, and without liability to detention (section 5). This clause, which is phrased negatively ('Nothing in this Act shall be construed as preventing . . .') replaces the previous arrangements for voluntary treatment set down in the Mental Treatment Act of 1930. Since the patient's volition is no longer required, this section can be taken to cover a large section of mental hospital patients who have no power of volition, provided that they do not positively object to treatment.

Children over the age of sixteen may be admitted for informal treatment without the consent of their parents and guardians, but only if they are capable of expressing their own wishes (section 5).

'*Any hospital*'. The separate designation of mental hospitals was ended. The provision of beds for mentally disordered patients became an administrative and clinical matter, and no longer a legal one.

(*ii*) *Compulsory admission*. There are three kinds of compulsory admission: admission for observation, admission for treatment, and emergency admission. These apply, like the rest of the Act, to all kinds of patients suffering from mental disorder.

An observation order is of twenty-eight days' duration. It must be made on the written recommendations of two medical practitioners who state that the patient either (*a*) is suffering from mental disorder of a nature or a degree which warrants his detention under observation for a limited period or (*b*) that he ought to be detained in the interests of his own health and safety, or with a view to the protection of other persons (section 25).

A treatment order (section 26) is similarly to be signed by two general practitioners, one of whom may be on the staff of the hospital into which the patient is received,[6] and the other of whom must be appointed for the purpose by a local health authority (section 28). The duration of a treatment order is for periods of one year, one year, one year, and then two years at a time (section 43). The grounds for recommendation of admission by treatment are three-fold—the conditions are not alternative, like those for admission by observation, but must all be fulfilled:

(*a*) The patient must be suffering from mental illness or severe subnormality; or from subnormality or psychopathic disorder if he is under the age of twenty-one.

(*b*) He must suffer from this disorder to an extent which, in the minds of the recommending doctors, warrants detention in hospital for medical treatment under this section; *and* his detention must be necessary in the interests of his own health and safety, or for the protection of other persons.

An emergency order (section 29) lasts only for three days. The application must be made by a mental welfare officer or a relative of the patient, and backed by one medical recommendation. No grounds for this recommendation are laid down, but the patient must be discharged after three days unless a further medical recommendation has been given, satisfying the conditions of section 28 (i.e. for a treatment order).

These clauses are a development from existing practice, the main change being the abolition of a magistrate's order in admission for treatment.

Care and treatment in hospital

The Minister may provide pocket money for patients who would otherwise be 'without resources to meet personal expenses' (section 133).

Patients are not to be ill-treated or wilfully neglected by the managers or staff of hospitals or mental nursing homes (sections 126).

Mentally ill and severely subnormal women are protected against unlawful sexual intercourse (section 127).

No restrictions are placed on the correspondence of patients informally admitted (section 134). The correspondence of patients liable to compulsory detention may be supervised by the 'responsible medical officer' in three ways: he may keep a letter written by a patient from the post if it is offensive or defamatory, or if it is likely to prejudice the interests of the patient; or if the addressee in a particular case has requested that letters should not be forwarded. Letters addressed to certain people, including the Minister of Health, any member of parliament, and a member of a Mental Health Review Tribunal at a time when the patient's case is due for review, must be forwarded in all cases, and are not within the discretion of the 'responsible medical officer' (section 36). Letters written to a patient are also subject to supervision: the 'responsible medical officer' may withhold a letter if he feels that its delivery might interfere with the patient's treatment, or cause him unnecessary distress (section 36).

Visitation. Any medical practitioner appointed by the patient or a relative may visit and examine the patient in private, for the purpose of advising whether an application should be made to a Mental Health Review Tribunal; or of advising the nearest relative on the question of the patient's suitability for discharge by the exercise of his special rights (see below under 'Discharge'). The Regional Hospital Board or the registration authority may send visitors, medical or lay, to have private interviews with patients in mental nursing homes (section 37).

Leave of absence. The 'responsible medical officer' may grant any patient leave of absence for up to six months, making any conditions which he considers necessary for the patient's custody and welfare, 'in the interests of the patient or for the protection of other persons.'

If a patient liable to be detained is absent without leave, he may be taken into custody and returned to the hospital within a specified period by any mental welfare officer, any constable, any member of the hospital's staff, or any other person authorized in writing by the managers of the hospital or the local health authority. The specified period is six months in the case of a psychopathic or subnormal patient between the ages of twenty-one and twenty-five who is liable to detention on a treatment or guardianship order; and twenty-eight days in all other cases (section 40).

Discharge

A patient is discharged when the order requiring his detention lapses; or by the 'responsible medical officer' or the managers of the hospital or mental nursing home (section 47) or by a Mental Health Review Tribunal after application and hearing (section 123); or, if, in the case of a subnormal or psychopathic patient, he was detained on a treatment order before he was twenty-one, and has now reached the age of twenty-five; or any patient on a treatment order can be discharged at seventy-two hours' notice by his nearest relative, provided that the 'responsible medical officer' does not certify that he would be 'likely to act in a manner dangerous to other persons or himself' (section 48). 'Nearest relative' is defined in some detail in section 49.

Guardianship

The concept of guardianship which had its origin in the Mental Deficiency Acts could now be applied to all types of patients suffering from mental disorder. An application for guardianship may be made on the grounds that:

(*a*) the patient is suffering from mental illness or severe subnormality; or that he is under the age of twenty-one, and suffering from psychopathic disorder or subnormality;

(*b*) that the disorder is of such a nature or degree as to warrant a guardianship order;

(c) that the guardianship order is necessary in the interests of the patient, or for the protection of other persons.

The guardian appointed may be an individual (possibly the individual making the application) or a local health authority (section 33). A guardianship order is of the same duration, and, subject to relevant modification, of the same type and conditions as a treatment order.

Patients concerned in criminal proceedings

This part of the Act gives Courts of Assize, Quarter Sessions, and magistrates' courts power to order admission to a specified hospital or guardianship for patients of all ages suffering from mental disorder of any kind (section 60). The recommendation of two medical practitioners is required, and one of these must be a psychiatrist approved by a local health authority (section 62). Courts of Assize and Quarter Sessions may place special restrictions on the discharge of such patients (section 65). Power to grant leave of absence, to transfer the patient to another hospital, or to cancel any restrictions placed on his discharge, is reserved to the Home Secretary (sections 65 and 66). Limitations are placed on the appeal of such patients to Mental Health Review Tribunals (section 63). The normal right of the nearest relative to discharge does not apply to them (section 63).

Prisoners detained 'during Her Majesty's pleasure' may be detained in hospital by warrant from the Home Secretary (section 71).

Prisoners already in custody or serving a sentence of imprisonment may be transferred to hospital or to guardianship by warrant from the Home Secretary (sections 72 and 73).

An order for a prisoner to be detained in hospital ceases to have effect at the time when his sentence of imprisonment would have expired; and a prisoner who recovers from his mental illness before the expiry of his sentence may be returned to prison to serve the remainder (sections 78 and 76).

The provisions of this part of the Act also apply to children and young persons in connection with Borstals or approved schools.

Management of patients' property and affairs

This part of the Act confirms the existing system for safeguarding a patient's financial interests through the offices of the Court of Protection. It codifies and extends the law relating to the management of property for or on behalf of a person suffering from mental disorder (sections 100–19).

Members of parliament

A section which gave rise to some comment in the press was that relating to members of the House of Commons. This lays down special procedures for ascertaining the mental condition of a member of the House of Commons through notification to the Speaker; and provides that, if the member is compulsorily detained by reason of mental disorder for more than six months, his seat in the House shall become vacant. This does not extend to members of the House of Lords (section 137).

So the 'three revolutions of the fifties' were accomplished. There had been more change in ten years than in the preceding century. Though there were problems enough—in 1960, one university Social Studies department set a question which read 'The Mental Health Act is a springboard, not a sofa. Discuss'—it looked as though the blue-print had been drawn up for development on the principles of the WHO Report, in the sixties and long after. But there was still more change to come.

13   Community care?

By the early sixties, it had become the tradition for the Minister of Health to make the inaugural speech at the Annual Conference of the National Association for Mental Health, and to use the occasion for a review of developments or an announcement concerning Ministry policy. In 1961, most of the two thousand delegates who gathered to listen to the Right Hon. Enoch Powell probably expected a review. They found themselves listening to a startling new policy announcement.[1] After reference to the forthcoming Hospital Plan for England and Wales Mr Powell said:

> I have intimated to the hospital authorities who will be producing the constituent elements of the national hospital plan that in fifteen years' time there may well be needed not more than half as many places in hospitals for mental illness as there are today. Expressed in numerical terms, this would represent a redundancy of no fewer than 75,000 hospital beds. Even so, if I err, I would rather err on the side of under-estimating the provision which ought to be required . . . if we are to have the courage of our ambitions, we ought to pitch the estimate lower still, as low as we dare, perhaps lower.

He hoped that most of the patients receiving hospital treatment in fifteen years' time would not be in 'great isolated institutions or clumps of institutions' but in wards or wings of general hospitals. The mental hospital was to go.

Now look and see what are the implications of these bold words. They imply nothing less than the elimination of by far the greater part of this country's mental hospitals as they stand today. This is a colossal undertaking, not so much in the physical provision which it involves as in the sheer inertia of mind and matter which it requires to be overcome. There they stand, isolated, majestic, imperious, brooded over by the gigantic water-tower and chimney combined, rising unmistakable and daunting out of the countryside—the asylums which our forefathers built with such immense solidity. Do not for a moment underestimate their power of resistance to our assault. Let me describe some of the defences which we have to storm.

Later, Mr Powell made references to 'erring on the side of ruthlessness', to 'doomed institutions' and to setting 'the torch to the funeral pyre'.

The Ministry circular

Three weeks later, a Ministry circular (HM (61) 25), gave a more detailed view of the new policy. As a result of a statistical analysis undertaken by the General Register Office, a sixteen-year projection had been undertaken on the beddage figures for mentally ill patients. This indicated 'a large and progressive decline' in the number of beds needed, and although all the variables could not be controlled or even taken into account, it seemed likely that the need for beds would drop from over 150,000 beds to about 80,000 in sixteen years. In the new service of the future, there would be four kinds of accommodation: acute units for short-stay patients, usually in general hospitals; medium-stay units for medium-stay patients; units for long-stay patients, many of whom, it was thought, could be cared for in hostels or long-stay annexes of general hospitals; and units providing 'adequate security arrangements for patients whose condition makes this necessary', possibly on a regional basis. Regional Hospital Boards were asked, as a matter of urgency, to review their mental hospital accommodation and to make plans for redundancy,

> . . . to ensure that no more money than is necessary is spent on the upgrading or reconditioning of mental hospitals which in ten to fifteen years are not going to be required for some different purpose . . . for the large, isolated and unsatisfactory buildings, closure will nearly always be the right answer.

The Tooth-Brooke projections

The third and most interesting account of the new policy came a few days after the circular, in an article in the *Lancet*.[2] The authors were respectively Principal Medical Officer of the Ministry of Health and a statistician from the General Register Office, and they gave a technical report on the statistical projection. Dr Tooth and Miss Brooke had taken the figures for resident populations in psychiatric beds from

1954 to 1959, and had found a drop of over 8,000. They felt that this 'small but steady reduction' was due to three factors: an extension of out-patient treatment; more active in-patient treatment; and the rehabilitation of long-stay patients. All these factors were likely to have increased effect in the future. There were trends which 'might have the reverse effect'—the rising population of old people, which meant that more were at risk to conditions involving unmodifiable cerebral deterioration; the fact that more liberal discharge policies had affected first those who were comparatively easy to discharge and might come up against a hard core of organically deteriorated patients; the uncertainty of public tolerance or of an economic climate which made it possible for such people to be financially self-supporting.

On the basis of the assessment of these and other factors, bed-requirements for a standard million population were calculated in some detail, to produce the figures quoted in the circular. The Tooth-Brooke paper ended: 'It seems unlikely that trends of this magnitude based on national figures are no more than temporary phenomena; though many factors may modify the rate of change, the direction seems well established.'

This was in effect a much more modest claim than that made by either the Minister or the circular.

Reactions to the new policy

Even on the day of Mr Powell's first announcement, reactions at the NAMH Conference were both violent and mixed. Dr Stanley Smith, among others, spoke with enthusiasm of 'the pharmaceutical age' and concluded his speech: 'Let us be frank: we believe that the days of the large purely mental hospital are over. Let us welcome the change, not bury our heads.'

Dr D. H. Clark, on the other hand

. . . hoped the comments made at the Conference would go back to the Minister. That the mental hospitals were finished and had nothing further to contribute had been said before over the past 20 years. He would like to remind everyone of the revolution which had taken place in British psychiatry during the past decade which had originated in the mental hospitals, and that it was the hospitals which had led the world by their work in getting patients back into the community. He was particularly worried about two implications arising from the speech: did it mean there was to be no further upgrading in mental hospitals?

Was a running down process intended? That must not happen.
Squalid conditions still endured in many psychiatric hospitals.

Mrs Bessie Braddock, MP, was particularly disturbed that the new
policy had been introduced without consultation in the mental health
field:

This was not the proper place for much comment, but she could
promise there would be a lot in Another Place. Although she had
been constantly in touch on questions of integration, and the
health service generally, she had not known that a new policy of
pulling down all the old mental hospitals . . . had been
established.

On the second day of the Conference, one of the principal speakers
was Professor Richard Titmuss of the London School of Economics
who cast considerable doubt on the Government's ability to provide
or intention of providing an adequate community service:

If English social history is any guide, confusion has often been
the mother of complacency. . . . What some hope will exist is
suddenly thought by many to exist. All kinds of wild and
unlovely weeds are changed, by statutory magic and comforting
appellation, into the most attractive and domesticated flowers. . . .

So the 'everlasting cottage-garden trailer, "Community Care" '
joined 'that exotic hot-house climbing rose, "The Welfare State" with
its lovely hues of tender pink and blushing red, rampant all over the
place, often preventing people from "standing on their own feet".'
Community care was in fact limited to 'a few brave ventures scattered
up and down the country from Worthing to Nottingham'. The pace
of discharge from hospitals had been accelerated, but the community
services were not available to meet the patients' needs when they
came out. At the existing rate of progress in training psychiatric
social workers, it would be 2014 AD before there was even one per
local authority. It was probable that the amount of money spent per
head on the mentally ill in the community had actually decreased in
the past decade; and we certainly spent less money on the mentally ill
in the community than we did on fowl pest.

Professor Titmuss ended by asking for three acts of policy as an
assurance that the Government 'really meant business': a specific
earmarked grant to local authorities for mental health services in the
following financial year; central government grants for the training of

all social work students; and a Royal Commission on the training of doctors. There was no official reply, and only the third of these proposals, the setting up of the Todd Commission,[3] of which Professor Titmuss was to be a member, actually took place.

Opinion in the mental health field as a whole was similarly mixed. Dr A. A. Baker produced a paper on 'Pulling Down the Old Mental Hospital' within three weeks of the official announcement, in which he forecast that mental hospitals would continue to empty and that long-stay populations would gradually disappear.[4] This started a lengthy correspondence in the medical journals, one group of doctors contending that Mr Powell's reading of the situation was correct, and that the progressive policy was the running down of the mental hospital, while the other held that the impact of pharmacotherapy was very limited and that the community services were unlikely to expand to meet the demands thrust upon them. On the whole the first group was optimistic, politically right-wing, and inclined to the organic school of psychiatry, which most easily assimilated with the ethos of general medicine. The second tended to be pessimistic, politically left-wing, and with a stronger interest in psychotherapy and the contribution of the social sciences.

A number of commentators were critical of the nature of the statistical projections on which the new policy was based. Rehin and Martin described the statistical work as 'the arbitrary application of a not very sophisticated numerical formula.'[5] Jones and Sidebotham questioned the decision to base a fifteen-year prediction on a five-year trend which contradicted all previous trends.[6] Dr Alan Norton made a simple mathematical point when he questioned whether the decline, if it took place, would be linear: a curve would produce a different answer and a slower rate of change.[7] Professor Morris Carstairs pointed out that the mental hospitals of Paris had not shown corresponding changes, even though the new ranges of psychotropic drugs had been developed in France.[8]

During this chorus of discussion, the Ministry continued to plan for the new policy. In 1962, the Hospital Plan for the next fifteen years was published, followed by the publication of *Health and Welfare: the Development of Community Care* in 1963.

The hospital plan

This document introduced the concept of the District General Hospital—a new large hospital which would cover all medical specialisms and so lead to the phasing out of specialist hospitals, such as those for the mentally ill and the chronic sick. In the following fifteen years, mental hospital beds were to be reduced by half, as proposed in the Tooth-Brooke plan. At the same time, beds for geriatric patients were to be reduced so that there was no possibility of transferring numbers of psycho-geriatric patients to another part of the service. It was clear that in future the Hospital Service was to be a service for acute patients, geared to an 'admission-treatment-discharge' model, and not to the long-term care of the sick.

The community care plan

The companion document on community care, published a year later, had been eagerly awaited. It consisted of 48 pages of general text on the desirability of community care for the chronic sick, for maternity cases and for psychiatric and geriatric patients, some glossy photographs, and 321 pages of detailed local authority returns on their future plans. Those who looked for a rationale of community care and a positive lead from central Government were disappointed.

Hospital censuses

Meanwhile, some research workers had turned to the study of patient populations as a way of establishing what the actual needs of psychiatric patients were. Again, the factors were not easy to assess or to quantify. Cooper and Early[11] estimated that 47·1 per cent of their patients were not in need of hospital facilities, and that 29·3 per cent were already in the employment of an outside employer. This survey was undertaken from a hospital with a particularly active and well-known industrial therapy unit. Hassall and Hellon,[12] working from Moorhaven Hospital, near Plymouth, which also has a good industrial therapy unit, found that 'Cooper and Early's optimism for the present accommodation of patients is not shared . . . little reason for optimism exists.' They had concluded, on analysis, that 80·3 per cent of male patients and 71·0 per cent of female patients were unfit for discharge, even to supervised hostel care. It was evident from such small surveys that the accuracy of the Ministry's final percentage figure was somewhat illusory. Judgements on what particular patients could be discharged to community care depended partly on how active the hospital's rehabilitation policy was, partly on how satisfactory the neighbouring community care services were, and partly on the point of view of the writer. The largest of these censuses was probably that produced for the Leeds Regional Hospital Board in 1963.[13] This covered the whole mental hospital population of the region—nearly 10,000 patients in all—and included a detailed statistical forecast of trends in the region up to 1975. The authors concluded, after considering population trends in the region and the community care plans of the local authorities in the area that the psychiatric hospital population might fall slightly by 1975, but that it was very unlikely to fall by the 50 per cent envisaged by the Ministry of Health. They noted:

> It is, of course, always possible to discharge patients and empty beds by administrative decision; but it seems clear from the survey that, in the absence of some favourable and major change in the situation, this could only be done at the cost of much hardship to patients and their families.

Hoenig and Hamilton, on the other hand, working in the Burnley area, came to the conclusion that the service offered in a 'predominantly extramural type of care' was adequate and that the effects were 'acceptable to the vast majority of clients.'[14]

The literature of protest

When the new Powell policy was first introduced, it drew much of its support, as might be expected, from the political Right. It was soon to receive unexpected support from the Left. In 1962 came the publication of Dr Erving Goffman's *Asylums*[15] which was to make a strong appeal to university radicals, particularly in Sociology departments. If Mr Powell longed to set fire to the chimneys and the water-towers, there were many on the other side of the political fence who were longing to storm the Bastille.

Goffman was one of the leaders in a new school of phenomenological studies which had developed in the States in the second half of the fifties. An academic derivative of existentialism, phenomenology involves the study of interpersonal relations without reference to outside concepts of a traditional or structured kind. Goffman introduced a new concept, that of the 'total institution', cut off from the wider society, ruthless and authoritarian in imposing its will on its inmates. Evidence from a year spent as a remedial gymnast in a psychiatric hospital in Washington was thrown together with a variety of literary sources to produce a vivid picture of the institution as tyrant, processing its inmates into cogs in an impersonal and self-serving machine. Goffman's contention that institutions of apparently different functions such as mental hospitals, prisons, schools, religious communities, old people's homes and others shared this capacity for dehumanizing made his findings of wide interest. Basic to Goffman's argument was the belief that human beings ought to have separate spheres of activity for work, leisure and domestic life, and that institutional living was detrimental to human personality because it collapsed all three circles into one, with consequent impoverishment of social opportunities. In particular, he argued, human beings ought to live their domestic lives in families. The institution was blamed for the 'suppression of actual or potential households.'[16]

Goffman was, as he makes clear, delineating an ideal type—an institution of the most authoritarian, encapsulated and remote kind. There were many who misunderstood both the method and the target, and took his description to apply to the average mental hospital on both sides of the Atlantic.

In England, the publication of *Asylums* led to a flood of empirical work on the evils of institutions. Peter Townsend's *The Last Refuge*,[17] an exhaustive and detailed study of old people's homes, included in its original hard-back edition a chapter on 'Effects of Institutions on Individuals' in which much of the evidence was drawn from studies of mental hospitals and all was of an adverse kind. The therapeutic community system did not even earn a mention. Russell Barton's *Institutional Neurosis*,[18] took a very similar line, and made a considerable impact with the contention that many long-stay patients in mental hospitals had two illnesses: the one which had caused their admission, and the one which the hospital had given them. Barton's delineation of this new clinical entity was treated with some caution by his colleagues in psychiatry, some of whom pointed out that the symptoms of 'institutional neurosis' were very similar to those of advanced schizophrenia, and that over two-thirds of long-stay patients in mental hospitals were in fact diagnosed as schizophrenics. Nevertheless, the book made an important point vividly, and was much used in nurse training.

Terence and Pauline Morris's *Pentonville* (1962) and Ann Cartwright's *Human Relations and Hospital Care* (1964) also used concepts derived from Goffman's analysis, though somewhat more selectively, and Pauline Morris was to adopt the same conceptual framework in analysing the work of hospitals for the mentally handicapped for *Put Away* (1969); but before then, the publication of *Sans Everything*

—*a case to answer* in 1967[19] brought a new dimension to the anti-institutional movement, since it contained detailed and specific charges against individual members of staff nursing geriatric and psychogeriatric patients, including the evidence of sworn statements. When Hack Tuke wrote that 'Waves of suspicion and excitement ... occasionally pass over the public mind in regard to the custody of the insane',[20] it was not that he regretted the exposure of scandals; his regret was that the movements were so short-lived, and so ill-informed that they often hit the wrong targets. The agitation of the late nineteen-sixties was in many ways reminiscent of the days of Dillwyn's Committee, the Weldon case and the crossing-sweeper judgement (see chapter 7), but with these differences: information was widely disseminated through the popular press; it was disseminated at a time when the public had an unusually explicit taste for details of violence, sexual aberration and refinements of cruelty (admittedly there was a market for such material in Victorian England, but it is difficult to imagine a Victorian audience sitting through *Marat/Sade* or *A Clockwork Orange*); and the movement acquired overtones of extreme moral indignation. The addition of left-wing polemic to popular sensationalism made it extremely difficult to get at the truth.

There were short outbursts of local and specific criticism in all parts of England and Wales—so widespread that many hospital authorities must have wondered where the axe would fall next. In 1968, 1969 and 1970, hardly a week passed without newspaper reports of cruelty and ill-treatment at one hospital or another. The pattern was a fairly common one: nurses, usually male nurses, would be accused by ex-staff or by patients' relatives. An inquiry would be set up—in a minor case, through a sub-committee of the Hospital Management Committee, in a more serious one, through the Regional Hospital Board. In the case of the *Sans Everything* allegations and in three subsequent cases, the allegations were held to be so serious that a special tribunal was appointed by the Secretary of State, and an official report was subsequently published.[21] Whatever the level of the inquiry, an attempt was made to establish the facts of the case, to assess the reliability of accusers and witnesses, and if possible to assign responsibility. In some cases, including some of the seven inquiries set up as a result of *Sans Everything*,[22] papers would be forwarded to the Director of Public Prosecutions, and legal action would follow. The inquiries involved much patient sifting of evidence, but often the trails were cold, witnesses refused to repeat allegations, and the strictly legal nature of the proceedings in the major inquiries made it difficult to collect evidence. In a few cases, staff were dismissed and subsequently sent to prison. In a few cases, the charges were emphatically disproved; but in the majority, the only possible verdict was 'not proven'.

It could be argued, on one hand, that the patients were basically normal people denied the opportunity to live a normal life, and the staff at best insensitive and at worst sadistic; or, on the other, that the staff were average employees doing a particularly difficult job without the training and support the work demanded. In *Sans Everything*, Professor Brian Abel-Smith had outlined a case for a 'Hospital Ombudsman' who would be appointed to deal with such cases, and this appointment was eventually to be approved by the Conservative Government in February 1972 as the 'Health Service Commissioner'. The Hospital Advisory Service, set up in 1968 under the direction of Dr A. A. Baker, has not been intended to fill this 'watchdog' function; but teams of advisers have made short intensive visits to hospitals, advising Hospital Management Committees and Regional Hospital Boards of serious deficiencies and suggesting improvements.

The agitation against mental hospitals and hospitals for the mentally handicapped probably reached its height in the early summer of 1970, when the then Secretary of State for the Social Services, Mr R. H. S. Crossman, made a series of visits to hospitals to see conditions for himself. Whatever responsibility attached to individual nurses for their actions, it had become very clear that understaffing, overcrowding and poor material provision created such a low quality of life that the assignment of blame was almost irrelevant. Everything was in short supply—money, space, staff, training, plant and equipment. The 'chintz and cream paint' policy of the fifties had made superficial improvements, but they did not go deep enough to remedy the problems.

In a sense, the problems were self-expanding; for a decade of criticism and reproach, from 1961 on, hampered recruitment and destroyed morale. Mrs Robb had been careful, in the introduction to *Sans Everything* to make it plain that the allegations related to only a small minority of hospitals, but as the movement gathered force, it brought the attack on all hospitals indiscriminately.

Social work and social workers

While sociologists were helping to pull down the institutions, their colleagues in social work training were increasingly drawn into the provision of workers for the community services.

Professor Titmuss had criticized the Government for doing so little to produce the social workers who were necessary to staff the extended services. It was already clear in 1961 that specialist workers, i.e. psychiatric social workers, were unlikely to be forthcoming in large numbers. An outstanding feature of the Younghusband Report had been the contention that workers in different branches of local authority health and welfare work (and, indeed, in many other kinds of social work) have a common task and require a common training. From the early sixties, university courses in social work became increasingly generic in character. Students preparing for careers in Child Care, Probation, Medical Social Work or Psychiatric Social Work were increasingly trained together, though their field-work placements were related to their ultimate career.

The Health Visitors and Social Workers Training Act of 1962 implemented many of the Younghusband proposals. It set up two councils, the Health Visitors Training Council and the Council for Training in Social Work,* with a common chairmanship and a common secretariat. The National Institute for Social Work Training, founded in 1963, fulfilled many of the functions of a staff college.

Courses for the Certificate in Social Work were set up in institutions for Further Education (Colleges of Commerce and technical colleges, many being later merged in Polytechnics) under the direction of the Council for Social Work Training. For the first time, workers were being trained specifically for local authority work. By 1969 CSW courses were training 435 students a year in 23 courses, and in addition some students were obtaining degrees under the Council for National Academic Awards scheme. During the period 1963–71, non-university and university courses ran side by side, without official contact, though there was a good deal of informal exchange and co-operation on a local basis.

In 1968 the Seebohm Committee reported on Local Authority and Allied Personal Social Services.[23] Its terms of reference were 'to review the organisation and responsibilities of the local authority personal social services in England and Wales, and to consider what changes are desirable to secure an effective family service.' The main recommendations related to the setting up of local authority Social Services Departments and the appointment of Directors of Social Services. This created a new managerial framework for the local authority

* The CTSW was responsible only for non-university courses.

social services, and replaced a number of fragmented specialisms with a confident generalism.

The section on social services for the mentally ill and mentally handicapped made some fairly strong strictures on the lack of provision:

> . . . despite the national commitment to 'community care', and official plans to run down the number of mental hospital beds (local authority expenditure) still represents a small fraction of total health service expenditure for the mentally disordered. Although some local authorities have been remarkably successful in developing mental health services, there is a serious lack of staff, premises, money or public concern in other areas. The widespread belief that we have 'community care' of the mentally disordered is, for many parts of the country, still a sad illusion and judging by published plans will remain so for years ahead.[24]

The Committee touched on the 'iceberg' problem—'needs that are not even expressed in demand for services'. They stressed the fact that many mental health needs were unmet, and that they tended to be unevenly distributed—decaying city centres could 'carry a fearful burden of social pathology.'

The committee's main concern was with whether the mental health services of local authorities should go into the new Social Services Departments with other social work services, or be left to the Health Departments as mainly clinical in character. The decision was not an easy one, particularly in view of the fact that some Medical Officers of Health had built up very good services since the responsibilities were first placed on them in 1948. They concluded that mental health work ought to be included in the Social Services Departments for two main reasons: first, because mental disorder tended to trigger off a variety of social problems and social disabilities in families, and social workers should be able to take responsibility for the whole family. Second, because:

> not to include these services in the social service department would mean further segregation of the mentally disordered when in fact the community is becoming ready for their further integration . . . to separate social work for the mentally disordered from the rest of the local authority social services would perpetuate just those difficulties and failures that led to the establishment of our committee in the first place.[25]

The Seebohm proposals were in the main put into effect by the Social

Services Act, 1970,[26] which came into effect on 1 April 1971. Meanwhile, the main branches of what was now coming to be thought of as the profession of social work had gone through the throes of founding a professional association. The Association of Psychiatric Social Workers held its farewell dinner in the Tower of London restaurant on 29 November 1969. Among the guests were three of the original four psychiatric social workers trained in the United States in 1928–9. The Association of Mental Welfare Officers was also dissolved at this time.

The British Association of Social Workers held its first Annual General Meeting a year later.

Psychiatry and the District General Hospital

Reference has already been made to the early experiments in siting psychiatric wards or wings in general hospitals, and to the proposals of the Hospital Plan, 1962, for the development of District General Hospitals. During the sixties, there was a strong movement within psychiatry which advocated very much closer links with general medicine. The arguments took several different forms, and had varying degrees of emphasis. In summary, these were as follows:

1. Psychiatric patients admittedly need a different kind of architecture and use of space from general patients, being ambulant; they also need a different regime, a different style of patient care and a differently-trained staff from patients on general wards; but all these special features could be provided and preserved in small units within the District General Hospital complex.

2. Challenges as to whether all the differences listed in (1) were really necessary.

3. A revival of the argument of the Macmillan Commission (1926) that the interaction of mind and body were so complex that the treatment of one necessarily involved the treatment of the other. Therefore psychiatry needed a basis in physical medicine, and physical medicine could only benefit from the proximity of psychiatry.

4. A more extreme argument that psychological methods of treatment were either ineffective or dangerous, and that the sound treatment of the mentally ill involved methods very close to the treatment of the physically ill. Dr William Sargent made a very strong plea on these lines to the National Association for Mental Health Conference in 1961:

> most types of patients now being admitted to mental

hospitals can be investigated and treated perfectly well in general
hospitals, if only facilities and beds are made available for them.
We even do quite a number of leucotomies every year in this
unit, and the advent of the new, tranquillising drugs has
enabled us to treat a much larger number of really acute
schizophrenic patients. . . . What is so important for the
psychiatric patient . . . (is) closer contacts with general medicine,
and general hospitals should help to foster a demand for entirely
new standards of treatment for the mentally ill, more similar to
those provided for and thought essential for the physically ill . . .[27]

5. The most extreme form of argument is that which takes a frame of
reference for the future hospital services which excludes the needs of
the mentally ill entirely, unless they happen to be physically sick at
the same time. McKeown, Garratt and Lowe got near to this in 1958,
when they reported on the findings of a survey of psychiatric patients
in the Birmingham Region. They concluded that 75 per cent of
psychiatric patients required 'only limited hospital services consisting
of supervision because of their mental state' and only 13 per cent
required 'the full facilities of a modern hospital' including 'skilled
nursing'.[28] In this view, the general medical model is so dominant that
models appropriate to other branches of medicine are not seen to
have objective reality.

In the training field, there were other developments which
strengthened the tie between psychiatry and general medicine. The
Royal Medico-Psychological Association, which had conducted
examinations leading to the qualification of Registered Mental
Nurse, handed over responsibility to the General Nursing Council in
1957, and a new GNC syllabus was developed.[29] The RMPA then
embarked on its own change of identity, and after a lengthy process of
policy discussion and legal delays, became the Royal College of
Psychiatrists on 16 June 1971.[30] Its first task was to consider the
drafting of a syllabus for the new Membership examination of the
College, which was to replace the Diploma in Psychological Medicine
as a postgraduate medical qualification, and to bring the training of
psychiatrists into closer similarity with other post-graduate medical
specialisms. The first Maudsley Lecture to be given under the auspices
of the new college was entitled, significantly 'Morale in Clinical
Medicine.' For the second time in its history, psychiatry was 'losing
the social view'; but perhaps the Seebohm reorganization had made
that inevitable.

Anti-psychiatry

A strong reaction at one pole of the psychiatric continuum has produced an equally strong reaction at the other. The psychological
school, which began by seeking explanations of bizarre behaviour
within the individual's experience, has developed groups which have
moved from individual psychoanalysis into the field of interpersonal
relations, and in some cases beyond, into phenomenology. To
Goffman, therapeutic community methods or the methods of psychoanalysis were even more of a threat to the patient than ECT or brain
surgery—more insidious, because less crude, and capable of 'looping'
back on the patient's defences in order to defeat him.

Goffman himself was not really very interested in mental hospitals
as such, and went on after *Asylums* to explore other problems in
social psychology, but phenomenology reached psychiatry through
the work of R. D. Laing and his colleagues at the Tavistock Clinic.[31]
Laing published *The Divided Self* in 1960 and *Sanity, Madness and the
Family* (with A. Esterson) in 1964. Both books expound his contention
that some forms of mental illness—particularly schizophrenia—are
not disease entities but are simply the names given by society to the
reactions of normal human beings to abnormal circumstances.

> . . . something like one per cent of the population can be
> expected to be diagnosed as 'schizophrenic' if they live long
> enough. Psychiatrists have struggled for years to discover what
> those people who are so diagnosed have or have not in common
> with each other. The results are so far inconclusive.
>
> No generally agreed objective clinical criteria for the diagnosis
> of 'schizophrenia' have been discovered.
>
> No consistency in pre-psychotic personality, course, duration,
> outcome has been discovered . . .
>
> There are no pathological anatomic findings post mortem. There
> are no organic structural changes noted in the course of the
> 'illness'. There are no physiological-pathological changes that
> can be correlated. . . .[32]

The answer to behaviour described as 'schizophrenic' is found in the
family situation, and frequently in the manipulation or oppression of
children by parents. (This may account in part for the popularity of
'anti-psychiatry' among students and other groups of young people.)
Dr David Cooper followed a similar line of argument in *Psychiatry*

and Anti-Psychiatry (1967) and *The Death of the Family* (1971), both of which are heavily influenced by phenomenological concepts.

Reorganization of the health services

Finally, while the balance of care has shifted within the mental health field, the social services have undergone a major reorganization, and psychiatrists still debate the nature of their subject, the health services as a whole have been actively debating a reorganization of their own. Dissatisfaction with the tripartite structure of the National Health Service had been expressed since its inception. By the early sixties it had become clear that, though it could not be blamed for all or indeed most of the deficiencies of the service, it was outliving its usefulness. The Porritt Committee,[33] appointed by a group of medical organizations, recommended in 1963 the setting up of Area Health Boards which would bring together the hospital, local authority and general practitioner services on a new and integrated basis. The proposal was new, and perhaps prejudiced by its authors' strong advocacy of medical representation; however, the idea took root, and developed through two Green Papers[34,35] to find fruition in the Consultative Document issued by the Department of Health and Social Security in 1971.

The proposal is still for Area Health Boards, though with some important modifications from the earlier plans. The emphasis on community participation which was so marked in the Crossman Paper (1970) has been largely replaced by an emphasis on managerial efficiency.[36] A regional structure is to be retained, and teaching hospitals will continue to exist and keep their endowments.

For both psychiatrists and psychiatric nurses, the impact of the managerial revolution has already been experienced through the new staffing structures introduced by the Cogwheel[37] and Salmon[38] Reports. The gradual implementation of these schemes is having the desired effect of shifting professional organization from a hospital base to an area base. The structure is a tight one, dictated primarily by the needs and traditions of general medicine and general nursing.

Policy in the seventies

Under the Conservative Government which came to power in 1970, the policy trends of the sixties have been confirmed and accentuated. To summarize, these are:

(i) the integration of psychiatry with general medicine
(ii) the reduction of hospital beds
(iii) the development of day patient and out-patient facilities
(iv) the shift to the local authority of the responsibility for residential and social care.

Two policy documents—a White Paper entitled *Better Services for the Mentally Handicapped* and a circular entitled *Hospital Services for the Mentally Ill* have spelled out these proposals in detail in 1971. Both propose radical changes in the existing services.

Better Services for the Mentally Handicapped[39] follows some years of debate as to the best form of care. Until 1967 hospitals for the mentally handicapped remained relatively untouched by the controversies which affected hospitals for the mentally ill. They took a steady 60,000 patients, the physician superintendents often retaining a remarkable degree of power and authority. Perhaps because the therapeutic community system could not be extended to the patients, it did not reach the staff either. While provision was made in the 1963 Community Care Plan for extended community care, it was generally considered impracticable to run down the hospital beds because of the considerable waiting lists and the increase of life-expectancy among the subnormal themselves.

There was little public interest in these quiet backwaters. Professional interest centred on the work of the few pioneers, such as Professor Tizard at the Institute of Psychiatry and Dr Albert Kushlick in the Wessex Regional Hospital Board area. Professor Tizard argued that the existing divisions between hospital and community services prevented staff from making the best use of either, and proposed an integrated service in which the resources of both hospital and community could be more fully used for both groups of patients. Tizard was probably ahead of his time in his disregard for administrative boundaries—including those which Seebohm and the Consultative Document were still to create when he wrote;[40] both he and Kushlick[41] looked at subnormality from an epidemiological standpoint, calculating what a reasonable provision would be for a standard population.

Hospitals for the mentally handicapped were abruptly pulled into the news in 1967, when allegations of staff cruelty and misconduct at the Ely Hospital, Cardiff and Farleigh Hospital, Somerset, were published, and the Department of Health and Social Security set up committees of inquiry. In both cases, some allegations were proved, and prosecutions followed. The inquiries revealed such gaps in the administration, and such a lack of suitable administrative machinery that it was clear that a new policy had to be developed.

In 1969 came the publication of Pauline Morris's *Put Away* which contained a detailed and not unsympathetic account of the problems of a sample of hospitals, and a concrete proposal for reorganization. Dr Morris argued that hospitals for the mentally handicapped were only partly medical in function. They required a 'training' arm which would utilize the skills of education and the social sciences as fully as the medical arm utilized those of medicine and nursing. She foresaw that the reorganization involved would lead to professional conflict, but she thought that it might be creative conflict, leading to growth.

The White Paper of 1971 did not adopt these recommendations. It drew the line between 'medical' and 'social' firmly outside the hospital door, leaving social and educational care to the local authorities. There is a new concept of the role of the hospitals: instead of providing long-term residential care for a population of about 60,000, they will be expected to provide active treatment facilities for little more than half that number, and with a higher proportion of children.[42] Day care is to be expanded—from the 1969 figures of 500 places for adults and 200 for children to 4,900 and 2,900 respectively. A much closer relationship is proposed between the treatment of subnormality in children and paediatrics,[43] and the assumption is made throughout that the subnormal should wherever possible be treated through the medical services available for the general population rather than being treated as a special group.

Psychiatrists are expected to develop much more active preventive and early treatment services, including genetic counselling, diagnosis and assessment services. These may be based in a number of different administrative settings, including District General Hospitals and clinics.

Local authorities will take over the responsibility for residential care, the number of places expanding from a total of 6,750 in 1969 to 42,700. Most of these places are expected to be in residential homes— 'homes, not hostels'—but it is suggested that local authorities should develop other forms of care, such as boarding out, group homes, or flats with social work support.

An expansion in education and training provision is also proposed. Local education authorities took over the responsibility for the education of all mentally handicapped children of school age in April 1971, which meant that the hospital schools came under their jurisdiction for the first time. It is planned that school provision, in the hospital schools and community schools combined, will be increased by about 30 per cent and that both kinds of schools will take a dual intake—i.e. that hospital schools may take children living in their own homes or in residential accommodation under the local authority, while schools in the community may take children living for the time being in hospital. Training places for adults are expected to increase by over 40,000, and again will be able to take a dual intake, whether hospital or local authority based.

The intention is that the mentally handicapped will no longer be treated in a segregated group, but will be pulled increasingly into the general provision of social, educational and medical services for the whole community. This involves a major shift from hospital to community care. But though the number of patients dealt with by the hospital services will be smaller, it is anticipated that the standards of provision will be higher and the services correspondingly more expensive. Of the £40 million available from central government funds for development in 1971–5, about £30 million is expected to go to the hospitals, which leaves comparatively little for the considerable expansion expected from the local authorities.

On the mental illness side a very similar plan, but involving a much more drastic reduction in hospital facilities, is proposed. *Hospital Services for the Mentally Ill*[44] proposes the complete abolition of the mental hospital system. Within fifteen or twenty years, it is planned, all provision will be in District General Hospitals, which will provide 'a department for the mentally ill, including day patient and outpatient services.' This will be very much smaller than existing provision. It will be recalled that, at the time of the 1961 controversy, Mr Enoch Powell's proposal was to reduce beds for mental illness from 3·4 to 1·8 per thousand population. By 1971, beds had been run down to about 2·0 per thousand.[45] The new proposal is for psychiatric teams, each of which 'should be responsible for a defined geographical area of about 60,000 population within the district served by the hospital and . . . based on a 30-bed ward' (para. 11). This gives a ratio of 0·5 beds per thousand population.

It is stated that this new and smaller service is dependent on the backing of 'a well-developed geriatric department', but no figures are given for geriatric beds.

It is clear from the document that the 30-bed ward which is to take all the hospital cases for a population of 60,000 should be quite unlike a general hospital ward. It may include severely disturbed

M

patients—though they must be 'managed discreetly without distressing other patients' (para. 21). It should include a 'considerable variety' of regular daily work for most patients, though this is conceived of on fairly orthodox concepts of sex roles: the women are to practise domestic skills, such as shopping, cooking, dressmaking and needlework, while the men are occupied with carpentry and 'do-it-yourself'. The service will be complemented by day care, out-patient care and if necessary emergency services, including domiciliary psychiatric consultations. There is to be close consultation with the local authority Social Services Department, the Department of Employment and the family doctor.

Hospital Services for the Mentally Ill does not involve planning as precise as that of the White Paper on the Mentally Handicapped. An appendix 'Guidelines for Mental Illness and Related Provision' gives figures which are difficult to relate to existing provision because of the form in which they are expressed, but which seem in almost all cases to be significantly lower than those at present obtaining (see Appendix 3).

'Psychiatry', said Sir Keith Joseph in announcing the new policy, 'is to join the rest of medicine'. He believed that

the treatment of psychosis, neurosis and schizophrenia have been entirely changed by the drug revolution. People go into hospital with mental disorders and they are cured, and that is why we want to bring this branch of medicine into the scope of the 230 district general hospitals that are planned for England and Wales.[46]

14   The price of integration

The theme of this book has been the gradual emergence of the mental health services out of the general provision, mostly punitive, for the social misfits of the eighteenth century; the building up of a specialist and highly distinctive tradition in the nineteenth century; and the destruction of that tradition in the twentieth.

Paradoxes abound. Lord Shaftesbury fought a bitter battle to keep the asylums free of the Poor Law, arguing that a Poor Law-dominated service would have lower standards and poorer quality staff; today we are integrating the psychiatric services with the general medical and social provision of the day, in the interests of higher standards and better staffing. Asylums were necessary in the nineteenth century because the causes of distress 'lay hidden', and needed to be brought into the light of day. The 'conspirational school', as Siegler and Osmund term the followers of Erving Goffman, use precisely the same argument in reverse: the asylums must be emptied because they are hiding—and even causing—distress. A mere forty or so years ago, social workers were brought in as the handmaidens of the medical profession; today, a strong and largely male-dominated social work profession bids fair to take over the bulk of the work.[1]

The key to understanding these paradoxes is perhaps this: there are some fields—race relations springs to mind—in which the issue of 'separation versus integration' can be argued in the abstract. Some people believe in apartheid. Others believe that it is socially and morally wrong, and will adduce a battery of arguments from philosophy, ethics and related fields to prove their case; but in issues of social policy, separation and integration cannot be argued in moral terms, but only in terms of effectiveness. The question is not 'Is it right?' but 'Does it work?'; and the answer depends not on a value position, but on an informed assessment of a given situation at a given point in time. Separation is not inherently better than integration: Lord Shaftesbury's solutions do not bind his successors. Even today, while we are integrating in many directions, we are specializing in others—the setting up of special services for dyslexic children is a recent example.[2]

Separation, at its best, can bring into the spotlight of professional and public concern a group of people needing service and previously overlooked. It can encourage specialization, and the development of advanced techniques, and co-ordinate services or skills previously fragmented. The other side of the coin is that it can cut off the group served from advances in general social or medical provision. It can lead to the kind of occupational in-breeding in which the appeal is always to a narrow tradition, and there is no stimulus from developments in other fields; and it can lead to a service so unadaptable to change that we try to break it up, arguing that a period of flux, unsettling as it is, is better than stagnation.

The first kind of situation we are apt to call 'specialization'; the second 'segregation'. Integration is similarly two-sided. At its best, it involves bringing fresh life to an unsatisfactory service by bringing it into relationship with services with higher standards, freeing it from arbitrary and outworn restrictions. At its worst, it means a kind of take-over bid in which the interests of the smaller or less powerful group are completely submerged. The integration of psychiatry into the work of District General Hospitals could mean that the human understanding of psychiatry will spread into medicine and surgery, and that there will be a new appreciation of the importance of mind-body relationships throughout District General Hospitals; or it could simply mean that the methods and assumptions of general medicine will be applied to psychiatric patients, whether they are appropriate or not. Dr David Hamburg, working in the United States in the late nineteen-fifties, studied a psychiatric unit in a general hospital and came to the conclusion that

> when a psychiatric unit is established in a general hospital, there is a strong tendency to adopt methods of policy-making that are very similar to those used previously in the hospital. In fact, the first step is often to accept most of the policies used throughout the hospital as a matter of routine.[3]

Examples of this kind of 'integration' are not difficult to find in the history of the mental health services over the past twenty-five years. Many hospital matrons, impatient of the unfamiliar values and professional standards of psychiatric nurses, have gradually replaced them in psychiatric units under their control with SRNs, whose professional norms are more congenial. Some local authorities strongly resented a Ministry injunction in 1948 that they should set up separate mental health sub-committees. More than one got over the difficulty by holding the sub-committee five minutes before the main meeting, and with the same membership. What happened in practice was that a mental welfare officer spent those five minutes reading out the names of patients who had been taken into hospital or discharged from hospital while the members struggled out of their coats and hung up their hats. For the rest, mental health was 'integrated'. Again, one Regional Hospital Board received an inquiry from the Ministry asking why none of the members of the Board had experience of the mental health services. The answer was that special representation was no longer necessary because mental health had been 'integrated'.

The question is not merely one of replacing separation (bad) with integration (good). It is whether separation represented specialization or segregation; and whether integration will represent partnership or take-over.

There are forces in our society which are likely to encourage take-over rather than partnership. The chief of these are the interests of the professions, the use of mechanical managerial techniques, and the state of public opinion.

First, the professions: out of the ideas and experiments of the last twenty years have emerged three strong professional groups: the doctors, the nurses and the social workers. The effect of current policy could be to make the first two the rulers of a health 'empire', while the social workers become the rulers of a welfare 'empire'.

In all three cases, there are strong professional pressures towards generalism and away from specialism. In training terms, it is clearly more convenient to have a general intake and to allow specialism later as an optional frill, than to take specialized intakes. It allows the students to opt for different kinds of work after they have developed a general understanding of the field, and saves tutors from having to work out complex routes from one kind of training to another. Similarly, generalism benefits the student by widening his area of choice, both initially in the courses he can take and ultimately in posts he can apply for. We can therefore expect a growing resistance to the idea that psychiatric patients should be treated only by doctors, nurses and social workers with a special kind of training and experience, and an increasing tendency to use the generalist in all three cases. The effect of the Cogwheel and Salmon schemes is to shift professional organization from a hospital base to an area base; but the structure is based on the imperatives of general medicine and general nursing.

Second, managerial techniques. The Consultative Document on the Health Service has made it plain that 'management' considerations are to be uppermost in the plans for the future. It may well be that the interests of managerial efficiency will pull psychiatric medicine into an ever tighter structure dominated by general medicine. Economic techniques, such as cost-benefit analysis, are likely to be used increasingly to assess the resources to be directed to particular sectors; while management by objectives or some similar system may well be invoked to determine the aims of service. Such techniques tend to favour those sections of medicine where aims are clear-cut, treatment is standardized and end-results easily quantifiable. It is notable that the proponents of these systems usually draw their examples from such areas—peptic ulcers and tonsillectomies are often quoted. Correspondingly, less than justice may be done to areas like psychiatry and geriatrics, where aims are often multiple and possibly conflicting, treatment is highly individualized, and end-results defy quantification.[4]

Third, public opinion: in a notable American report, *Action for Mental Health*, Dr Jack R. Ewart posed the question of why advance in the mental health services was so slow, and why 'while each reform appears to have gained sufficient ground to give its supporters some sense of progress, each has been rather quickly followed by backsliding, loss of professional momentum, and public indifference.'[5]

The Commission came to the conclusion that Americans were 'alarm-minded and action-oriented'. When confronted with a deplorable condition, they wanted to 'do something about it':

> Our first inclination in practice appears to be to expose, in
> muckraking fashion, the alarming condition, enumerate the
> victims, name the 'villain'. But such an attack begs the question
> of what can be done. Consequently, our second inclination is to
> appoint a commission to study the problem.[6]

British reactions appear to be very similar. One explanation for this phenomenon is that human beings, at least in western society, are highly ambivalent about mental illness and mental handicap. Reason says that these conditions occur in any society, and that the people who suffer from them must be treated with kindness and compassion. It is very easy to get popular assent to a general proposition such as 'We ought to provide good psychiatric services' or even 'We ought to spend much more on psychiatric services'—until an attempt is made to implement this through rates and taxes. Most people will agree that the mentally ill and the mentally handicapped should be given as much freedom as possible, and should live as part of a normal community—until a proposal is made to build a local authority hostel next door to them, or to let children of rather odd behaviour or appearance travel to school on the same bus as their own children.

Attitudes to mental disorder are highly complex and potentially very volatile. Most of us are capable of being rational and kindly on the surface, but a law of inverse distance seems to apply; the closer the subject gets to our own interests, the less enlightened we become. Perhaps any of us, given sufficient provocation, is capable of re-enacting the whole history of the mental health services in personal attitudes—right back to the days of the witch-hunts.

If this is so, we have an explanation for why the reform movements are so often 'alarm-minded and action-oriented'. Intellectuals can get out of an uncomfortable double bind ('either I act against my instincts or against my conscience') by means of a simple projection mechanism—it is all somebody else's fault; but if this is so, reason is an exceedingly slender chain on which to hang our hopes for future progress.

This is a crucial point in development. It is only by careful and analytical monitoring over the next decade or two that we can determine whether integration, in the long run, has meant partnership or take-over, whether it has operated to the benefit or to the detriment of patients. This is a vital area for social research. In particular, we need to know whether the run-down of the services we had—mainly in the shape of hospital beds—is in fact being compensated for by an extension in the services we would like—small group homes, acute medical services of a high standard, and skilled counselling in human relations. What follows is an interim assessment based on available statistics from 1960 to 1970.

Services in the sixties[7]

The first important factor is that, within ten years, the stock of beds for mental illness has been reduced by 30,000 or more than one-fifth, and this has taken place at a time when the population at risk has increased by over four million. The net effect of these two movements has been to reduce the ratio of beds to population from 3·0 per thousand to a little over 2·1. On this basis, it seems likely that the Tooth-Brooke forecast of a decline of 1·8 per thousand by 1975 will easily be fulfilled; what the statistics do not show is whether this has happened as a result of a reduction in demand or a reduction in supply. Has the number of beds contracted because the patients did not come forward, or because the doctors did not send them into hospital in circumstances where they previously would have done so? Was this better or worse for the patients?

Admissions to mental hospitals rose until 1968, but now seem to have levelled off. First admissions ran for some years at rather more than half of the total of admissions, but the latest figures show a considerable drop—to about 37 per cent of all admissions. Again, this is difficult to interpret. Does it mean that there are now less new cases in need of treatment? Or that they are being diagnosed in some other way—as physically ill, or as being in need of social care—and thus appearing in some other set of statistics? Or are the needs of patients who have previously had treatment now sufficiently pressing to take priority?

These issues illustrate the urgent need for research which will trace individual cases through the service, and indicate what the total pattern of treatment is. Crude statistics tell us little about the real significance of the events recorded in the life either of the patient or of the hospital.

Following the review of patients' legal status required by the Mental Health Act, 1959, the proportion of mentally ill patients with informal status has remained above 92 per cent of all patients, and in 1970 stood at 93·2 per cent. The volume of work of Mental Health Review Tribunals has been considerably less than was at first antici- pated, and except for 1963, when it reached 1,157 cases, has stood at less than a thousand cases a year. The proportion of discharges directed has varied from 10 to 18 per cent, and appears to be rising. This could indicate that the patients now coming forward for hearings are more often suitable for discharge, that the community services are more able to cope with patients after discharge, or that the tribunals are now tending to favour discharge in a higher proportion of cases.

Hospital provision for the mentally handicapped was, as previously noted, almost static. There were 61,164 mentally handicapped patients in hospital in 1961, and 59,918 in 1970.

General indications are that the non-residential services are beginning to expand, though this expansion is rather slow and very difficult to quantify. Official data are collected in forms which do not allow of comparison with each other, or with hospital data. However, there were 37,000 more new out-patient registrations in 1970 than in 1961, and by the end of the sixties, new out-patients were being added to clinics at the rate of about 180,000 to 190,000 a year. We do not know how many out-patients there were in all, how many times they attended on average, or what proportions had routine check-ups as opposed to active treatment. Latest figures indicate some falling off in the numbers attending, but it is difficult to say whether this is a temporary variation or a long-term trend.

Local authority statistics show a considerable increase between 1962 and 1970 in the number of persons 'receiving mental health services provided by local authorities'. Presumably this refers to patients 'on the books', but the accuracy of the figure is doubtful since local authorities vary a good deal in their recording practices, and again one has no information about the content or value of the contact.

Hostel care has increased—from the very low figure of 968 places for the whole of England and Wales in 1962 to 2,755 by the end of 1970.

Figures for the employment of mental health social workers by local authorities show a steady increase. In 1962, there were only 1,247. The jump to a total of 1,872 in 1968, of whom 213 had a university qualification and 297 a CSW qualification, indicates an expansion of the work before it was overtaken by the reorganization proposed by the Social Services Act 1970. Detailed figures for 1969 and 1970 are not very reliable since many departments were already reorganizing on generic lines.

The evidence we have suggests that the mental health services responded to the policy changes proposed in the Mental Health Act and the Community Care Plan, and that the more progressive authorities at least made a start in making good the loss of hospital beds by expanded provision in out-patient and community care; but as yet we know very little about the quality of this care—how thinly it is spread, who gets it, whether it is given by single agencies or by a number of agencies, whether they co-operate or act in ignorance of each other's contributions. We do have evidence of considerable inequalities between regions and between local authorities.

Regional variations

Mr Alan Maynard of the University of York has analyzed hospital staffing figures,[8] and found that the proportion of psychiatric consultants per hundred mentally ill patients varied in 1969 from 0·44 in the South Western Region to 1·05 in the Oxford Region. For nurses, trained and untrained, the lowest figure was 27·6 (East Anglian Region) and the highest 39·3 (Oxford Region); and for social workers, the lowest was 0·25 (East Anglian Region) and the highest 0·76 (Oxford Region). Mr Maynard deals with the hypothesis that regions which are poorly staffed on one criterion might compensate with above average staffing elsewhere, but a correlation matrix shows this to be unlikely. He concludes '. . . there are substantial inequalities, and there is no evidence to show that regions that are badly endowed in one sphere are compensated by better endowments in other spheres.'

The exercise was repeated for hospitals for the mentally handicapped, and indicates a similar pattern. The South Western Region again had the lowest figure for consultants: 0·11 per hundred patients, while East Anglia this time produced the highest: 0·49. The figures for nurses varied from 23·16 (South Eastern Region) to 41·51 (Liverpool Region) and that for social workers from nil in the Liverpool Region to 0·39 in the Oxford Region. Again, there was no evidence of compensation.

Some of these differences may, of course, relate to labour supply. It is probably easier to recruit nurses and ward orderlies in Liverpool than East Anglia because of the availability of Irish labour; and it may be easier to recruit social workers for Oxford than for Liverpool because social workers tend to flock to the south; but if Liverpool can recruit nurses for the mentally handicapped, why should they have one of the lowest figures for nurses for the mentally ill? And if social workers tend to flock to London, why does the North West Metropolitan Regional Hospital Board have nearly three times the proportion of its neighbour, the South West Metropolitan Regional Hospital Board?

Whether the cause is labour supply, explicit policy, or, in the case of some of the authorities with low figures, the reflection of low expectations for a low prestige service, the differences are very great— often of the order of 100 to 300 per cent between the highest and the lowest. If this is so for the Hospital Service, where there is a fair degree of central direction, we must expect even greater inequalities on the local authority side.[9]

MIND, the National Association for Mental Health appeal, produced two papers in 1971 on local authority community care facilities. MIND Report no. 4, on provision for the mentally ill, concluded that 'the facts reveal such grave deficiencies that the public has every reason to be greatly concerned.' Report no. 5, on the mentally handicapped, quoted the 1971 White Paper on the mentally handicapped:

It is right to acknowledge the progress made by the local authorities in the last ten years in developing good quality services for the mentally handicapped in the community. But in national terms, these are still grossly deficient in quantity . . . the developments recommended by the Royal Commission fourteen years ago are far from being accomplished.

In each case, the National Association had sent a questionnaire to Directors of Social Service in July 1971. This was only three months after they took office,* and understandably some of the results were rather sketchy; but by steady persistence, a good response rate was achieved, and the act of persistence must have engraved the mental health movement on the mind of many a new Director at a crucial and impressionable stage in his career.

NAMH took the unusual step of publishing in these reports the names of the local authorities with the highest and lowest provision under a number of heads—for the mentally handicapped, staffing, sheltered workshops, residential accommodation, training centres and social clubs; for the mentally ill, staffing, hostels, day centres, and social clubs. The detail, like that in Mr Maynard's report, may only be of historical interest if the reports achieve their purpose: to make the authorities with the least provision aware of what is being provided elsewhere, and to urge them into action.

A number of commentators have drawn attention to the fact that the switch from hospital to community care involves a substantial shift from central government to local authority financing, and that this increases the difficulty of monitoring and reform. Local councillors are much more subject to local pressures than members of parliament, and less publicly accountable for their decisions. They are unlikely to be generous to a cause which still does not command much popular enthusiam; and the single national cause very easily fragments into dozens of local affrays. Since local authorities receive a block grant from central Government, there is no way of ensuring that a particular proportion of funds is channelled to this cause or that.

The need for public vigilance is very great; but it will need to be an informed vigilance—not merely 'alarm-minded and action-oriented'.

Which model?

For over two hundred years, the mental health services operated on a
* The Social Services Act came into force on 1 April.

single model: the model of an asylum or mental hospital service, centralized, specialized and self-contained. In time, it became a segregated and second-class system; and perhaps the asylums were always the architectural embodiment of a rejection mechanism. People whom society scorned and ill-treated sought 'asylum' because there was no place for them outside.

Now we are more enlightened—or at least, we hope that we are more enlightened; and the old model has been scrapped. In its place we are offered five different possibilities:

(i) *the WHO model.* The proposals sketched out by the World Health Organisation's Expert Committee on Mental Health in 1953 saw the alternative as a flexible and varied service in which a number of different agencies—day hospitals, out-patient clinics, domiciliary social work, and so on would work side by side with mental hospitals and psychiatric wards of general hospitals. From the patient's point of view, the scheme was an excellent one—it gave a number of possibilities for treatment, and might even have allowed him some choice. It failed to commend itself in practice because it offered little guidance to the very complex planning problems involved—how much day care? How many hospital beds? How many beds equals one social worker?—and it left out of account the very strong professional interests which were to develop in the sixties.

(ii) *the medical model* in which hospital services are seen as of prime importance, social work services being merely 'ancillary to medicine'. Psychiatry is seen primarily as a clinical specialism, to be fitted into the traditions and routine of general medicine and general nursing. District General Hospitals will provide highly efficient services in good modern buildings, well-placed for transport routes and access to city centres. This is currently the most popular model for most of the medical and nursing professions, and for a variety of health organizations from the Office of Health Economics to the Royal Society of Health.

(iii) *the Seebohm model* in which mental illness and mental handicap are seen primarily as social problems demanding skills in social diagnosis and human relations. While there are few supporters in psychiatry for the viewpoint put forward by Dr Szasz, there are many in social work:

Mental illness is a myth. Psychiatrists are not concerned with mental illnesses and their treatments. In actual practice, they deal with personal, social and ethical problems in living . . .

(psychiatry) provides professional assent to a popular rationalisation, namely that problems in human living experienced in terms of bodily feeling or signs . . . are significantly similar to diseases of the body . . . powerful institutional pressures lend massive weight to the tradition of keeping psychiatric problems within the conceptual fold of medicine.[10]

The advances made by social work as a profession in the post-Seebohm era have been so striking that it is no longer impossible that this should in future become the dominant viewpoint. In this case, psychiatric medicine, organized for short-stay patients in 30-bed wards of general hospitals, would almost have become a 'profession ancillary to social work'.

(iv) *the 'conspirational' model*, to use Siegler and Osmund's term, in which mental illness and mental handicap are, so to speak, in the eye of the beholder, and their definition an act of political outrage. This point of view is frequently adopted by sociologists, since it provides a particular application of three very popular branches of their subject —labelling theory, the general theory of deviancy, and conflict theory. Goffman used these insights to considerable effect in *Asylums*. More recently, Townsend has applied them to subnormality, arguing that the mentally handicapped are defined by society, not by their own limitations of capacity, and that '*any* physical segregation, even of people of extreme handicap, may be improper'.[11] It should perhaps be noted that, while the application of these theories to the current British services seems somewhat inappropriate to most observers, there are other societies where the analysis fits only too well.[12]

(v) *the 'no-model' model*. By its nature, this is the most difficult to describe; but it is possible to hold a view of society and medicine in which there is no place at all for mental illness and mental handicap. Laing gets near it by projecting the problem out on to other people— if a girl shows symptoms of schizophrenia, it is not because she has schizophrenia, but because of the behaviour of her parents or teachers. Goffman and Townsend get near it by assuming that fundamentally there is no problem—only a conspiracy and that the so-called patient is being scape-goated by society.

It is possible to provide alternative explanations for almost any symptoms of mental illness or mental handicap—the patient can be seen as wicked, politically disaffected, physically ill or drunk. With different conceptual models, the whole problem can quite easily be fragmented; and many people have a motive for fragmentation in that they have a built-in resistance to the whole subject, and would be happy to be told that it did not exist. 'Don't look at it, and perhaps it will go away' might express a popular reaction.

At present, it is not at all clear which of these five models will ultimately find acceptance. Current plans for development offer us a mixture of the medical model and the Seebohm model, with perhaps an unresolved battle for supremacy. The 'conspirational' model, for most of us, is only a sinister possibility, though one which we ought not to ignore. The real danger is that, by default, we shall slip into the 'no-model' model, and a group of very damaged and unhappy people will not get the help they need.

The themes which have dominated the mental health services in the sixties and early seventies have been those which have dominated other areas of the national life—government control and local authority autonomy, authority and protest, professional teamwork and professional conflict. Because the services are a response to the society they serve, and from which they derive their sanctions, the care of the mentally ill and the mentally handicapped will continue to reflect the values of that society—good, bad or merely muddled.

Appendix 1
Statistics of mental illness and mental handicap

The main sources of statistical information about the mental health services are the *Annual Reports of the Lunacy Commissioners* (1845–1913); the *Annual Reports of the Board of Control* (1914–59); the *Annual Reports of the Ministry of Health* (1948–67) and of its successor, the *Department of Health and Social Security* (1968 to date); the *General Register Office Supplements on Mental Health* (1952–3, 1954–6, 1957–8, 1959 and 1960) and *Studies in Medical and Population Subjects, no. 16 and no. 18*; and the Department of Health and Social Security *Statistical Report Series nos. 3–13* inclusive.

The procedures for the collection and analysis of statistical material changed radically as a consequence of the recommendations of the Royal Commission on the Law Relating to Mental Illness and Mental Deficiency (1954–7). In its report, the Commission drew attention to the complexity of existing procedures. 'Board of Control statistics' related to patients in hospitals and homes covered by the Lunacy and Mental Treatment Acts and the Mental Deficiency Acts, but gave no information on other forms of treatment.[1] Ministry of Health statistics, contained in Part I of the Annual Reports of the Ministry, were collected on a different basis. They included out-patients and some in-patients not covered by the relevant Acts of Parliament (e.g., those in 'de-designated' beds or in teaching hospitals), but excluded certain categories of care, such as the special hospitals. The GRO, under a scheme started in 1949, collected very full and detailed statistics, including information otherwise unobtainable about diagnosis and length of stay, but only for very limited categories of patients. The three sets of statistics were in many respects not comparable, and the Royal Commission, in its calculations, had to work on approximate figures and leave many gaps. They recommended a review of procedures and the institution of a single system for 'whatever special mental health statistics are considered necessary, either from the administrative or the medical point of view.' These should be collected for all mentally disordered patients, irrespective of the designation of the hospitals to which they were admitted or the use of particular admission procedures.[2]

Under the provisions of the Mental Health Act, 1959, which closely followed the recommendations of the Commission, the Board of Control was abolished. The Ministry of Health and the General Register Office discussed the collection of statistics, and concluded in 1960 that two sets were necessary: the Ministry figures were needed for 'general planning and administrative purposes', while the GRO figures were 'designed primarily to contribute to medical knowledge and to help medical research workers.'[3] However, this decision was rescinded three years later, when it was agreed that 'in practice, the mental health statistics collected by (the GRO) have proved of considerable value for planning purposes, and since the existence of the two schemes resulted in some duplication, it was decided in 1963 to amalgamate them and bring the statistical work under the control of the Ministry of Health as the main user.'[4] From 1963, therefore, the Ministry's Statistics and Research Division became responsible, and its work is published either in the Annual Reports or in the special publications of the Statistical Report Series.

The recommendations of the Royal Commission, as embodied in the Mental Health Act, affected the statistical material available in another and more fundamental way. The special designation of mental hospitals and mental deficiency hospitals was abolished; the terminology was changed, 'mental disorder' now covering the previous categories of mental illness and mental deficiency, with four sub-categories: mental illness, psychopathic disorder, subnormality, and severe subnormality; admission procedures were changed, with a strong emphasis on informal admission; and a considerable expansion in community care was envisaged. Not only were the categories for the collection of statistics altered, but the whole shape of the mental health services changed, so that it is virtually impossible to make comparisons of the work before and after 1959. (It should be noted that earlier Acts, notably the Lunacy Act of 1890, the Mental Deficiency Act of 1913, the Mental Treatment Act of 1930 and the National Health Service Act of 1946, had a somewhat similar effect in changing the shape of the services—mental health statistics can only usefully be studied in comparatively short runs between major pieces of legislation).

While these changes were in progress, statistics were necessarily somewhat patchy. The Annual Report of the Ministry of Health for 1960 gave only very brief tables. In the following year, more figures were available, but only for a limited period—1 November to 30 April. Full statistics in the new form were given from 1962, but in the first few years of operation these were often subject to subsequent revision. We have at present only a run of five or six years' figures from which to deduce current trends.

In the late fifties and early sixties, the re-planning of the mental health services generated a variety of statistical material. Outstanding among the forecasts published is the work of Tooth and Brooke (1961), which formed the basis of the Ministry policy, expressed in Circular HM(61) 25, of running down beds for mental illness in England and Wales from about 3·4 per thousand population to about 1·8 per thousand population in 1975. The same policy underlay the calculations in the *Hospital Plan* (1962) and *Health and Welfare: the Development of Community Care* (1963). The quantitative forecasts involved were described as 'of the most rudimentary kind' by Rehin and Martin (1963) and contested by Gore, Jones, Taylor and Ward (1964).

Miss Brooke's cohort study of *Patients first admitted to Mental Hospitals in 1954 and 1955* provided a valuable study of patterns of utilization in the mental health services in terms of age, sex, diagnosis and area of origin of patients, but was limited to a two-year follow-up period. This was the first serious attempt in an official inquiry to obtain records of what happened to patients as individuals. More recently, the *Statistical Report Series* has provided detailed information on the activities of psychiatric hospitals by region (nos. 3 and 6); a useful pilot study of the work of day hospitals (no. 7); and the first results of the on-going Mental Health Enquiry (in-patient statistics for 1964, 1965 and 1966, published in no. 4, and for 1967, published in no. 5). All these publications refer to particular points in time, and do not give comparisons over time.

There is thus a good deal of material available, but it has a number of limitations. First, apart from the Brooke cohort study, it is a record of events and not of persons. It records admission, discharge, registration on the books of a local authority or an out-patient clinic, but not what sequence of events individual patients go through. Second, the means of care are now so diversified that it is almost impossible to get a picture of the work of the mental health services as a whole—statistics for hospitals, local authority work and out-patient work are collected in different forms, and cannot be consolidated for analysis. Third, the Royal Commission made a strong recommendation that the mental health services should be regarded as 'an integral part of the national health and welfare services',[5] and that 'no-one should be excluded from benefiting from any of the general

social services simply because his need arises from mental disorder.'[6]
This means that mental health statistics now give only a very partial
picture, and do not reflect the totality of care and treatment.

Tables 1–15

Sources: Annual Reports of the Ministry of Health and the Department of
Health and Social Security unless otherwise stated. Figures for 1961 and
subsequent years have been checked by the Statistical and Research Division
of the Department of Health and Social Security, and in some cases recen
statistical revisions have been incorporated.

Table 1   Total number of known persons of unsound mind, 1859–1909

1 Jan.	Known persons of unsound mind (thousands)	Rate of Increase	Estimated total pop. of England and Wales (millions)	Known persons of unsound mind per thousand in total population
1859	31·4	—	19·6	1·60
1864	38·7	+7·3	20·0	1·88
1869	46·7	+8·0	21·5	2·17
1874	54·3	+7·6	23·0	2·36
1879	61·6	+7·3	25·2	2·44
1884	69·9	+8·3	25·2	2·77
1889	75·6	+5·7	28·4	2·66
1894	83·0	+7·4	29·8	2·79
1899	95·6	+12·6	31·6	3·03
1904	117·2	+21·6	33·6	3·49
1909	128·2	+11·0	35·0	3·66

Source: 54th Report of the Lunacy Commissioners, 1900, Appendix A.
Figures for total population estimated from decennial Census returns.

'Known persons of unsound mind' includes both 'lunatics' and
'idiots', and all patients whether in public asylums, private hospitals,
private nursing homes or single care; but not those in workhouses, or
prisons, for whom no figures appear to have been kept. The rising
percentage probably indicates not a rise in the proportion of insane
persons, but an increasing awareness of what was at least in part a
submerged social problem; the diligence of the Lunacy Commissioners in identifying and listing patients in small private nursing
homes and single care; and the increasing provision in public

asylums. In particular, the steep rise shown in the figures for 1899 and 1904 is related to new accommodation built after the 1890 Act, when fewer patients were sent to workhouses.

Table 2   The size of mental hospitals (county asylums) 1827–1930

1 Jan.	No. of county county borough and city asylums	Total patients in public asylums	Average number of patients per asylum
1827	9	1,046	116
1850	24	7,140	297
1860	41	15,845	386
1870	50	27,109	542
1880	61	40,088	657
1890	66	52,937	802
1900	77	74,004	961
1910	91	97,580	1,072
1920	94	93,648 (104,298)	996 (1,109)
1930	98	119,659	1,221

Source: Annual Reports of the Lunacy Commissioners before 1913, Board of Control after 1913.

Figures in parentheses for 1920 are those for the total number of beds available as distinct from the total number of beds occupied. Many beds had then recently been freed from use as emergency beds for war cases, and the normal flow of civilian cases had not yet been resumed.

No figures are available for 1940, as no reports were issued during the war period.

Figures for the period since the inception of the National Health Service would be misleading, since a number of psychiatric patients are now accommodated in wards or units attached to general hospitals.

The statistics for the average number of patients per asylum indicate strikingly the rise in the size of asylums which was partly responsible for the loss of human relationships in asylum administration, and the common policy in this respect, which was to add to the size of existing asylums rather than building new ones, from motives of economy.

Table 3   Mental illness: resident population of mental hospitals and other institutions, 1904–54

1 Jan.	In-patients (thousands)	Total population England and Wales (millions)	In-patients per thousand population
1914	138·1	36·6	3·77
1919	116·7	37·7	3·09
1924	130·3	38·4	3·39
1929	141·1	39·6	3·56
1934	150·3	40·5	3·71
1939	—	—	—
1944	—	—	—
1949	144·7	43·3	3·34
1954	151·4	44·0	3·44

Source: Annual Reports of the Board of Control.

Figures include patients in state institutions, mental nursing homes and general hospitals, as well as mental hospitals. Figures for total population estimated from census returns.

The total percentage of persons receiving in-patient treatment was higher in 1914 than it has ever been since. This is due to the sharp drop in accommodation and treatment facilities resulting from two world wars, the transfer of mental defectives to mental deficiency hospitals as accommodation became available; and to the increasing provision of out-patient treatment through clinics and (latterly) local authority care.

Table 4   Mental illness: resident population: patients in hospital beds as at 31 December 1959–70

	In-patients (thousands)	Total population England and Wales (millions)	In-patients per thousand population
1959	133·2	45·4	2·9
1960	—	—	—
1961	135·4	45·8	3·0
1962	133·8	46·7	2·9
1963	127·6	47·0	2·7
1964	126·5	47·3	2·7
1965	123·6	47·7	2·6
1966	121·6	48·0	2·5
1967	118·9	48·3	2·5
1968	116·4	48·6	2·4
1969	105·6	48·9	2·2
1970	103·3	49·2	2·1

Figures for 1959 refer to 'hospitals vested in the Minister of Health—mental hospitals' and exclude about 3,000 patients separately listed as in teaching hospitals, Broadmoor, registered hospitals, licensed houses, and under single care. Figures from 1961 include all patients under psychiatric care in the National Health Service—i.e., they include patients in teaching hospitals; from this date, patients in the other categories listed above are no longer included in returns.

No figures are available for 1960.

Table 5   Mental illness: direct admissions to hospital care 1955–70

Year	Admissions
1955	78,586
1956	83,994
1957	88,943
1958	91,558
1959	95,344
1960	—
1961	138,716
1962	146,458
1963	160,405
1964	155,017
1965	155,554
1966	160,523
1967	165,095
1968	170,527
1969	162,313
1970	162,864

No figures given for 1960. The figure for 1961 (69,358 for the period 1 November 1960 to 30 April 1961) has been doubled here for the purposes of comparison.

Figures up to and including 1959 are for admission to designated beds in mental hospitals and units. The Royal Commission stated in 1957 (*Report*, p. 308) that patients receiving treatment outside the purview of the Lunacy and Mental Treatment Acts constituted 'a considerable proportion of the total receiving in-patient psychiatric treatment every year.'

In 1958 a revised figure of 94,083 was issued to include informal patients. See Registrar General's Statistical Review for the year 1959: *Supplement on Mental Health*, p. 2 table M1(a).

Table 6   Mental illness: first admissions to hospital care 1964–70

	First admissions	All admissions	% First admissions
1964	76,628	155,017	49·4
1965	81,369	155,554	52·3
1966	83,699	160,523	52·1
1967	87,308	165,095	52·9
1968	90,699	170,527	53·2
1969	86,337	162,313	53·2
1970	60,704	162,864	37·3

Separate figures for first admissions, i.e. 'patients who have not previously received in-patient treatment in a psychiatric hospital or a psychiatric unit' were first given in 1964.

Table 7   Mental illness: patients under in-patient care with informal status 1961–70

	% Informal admissions during year	% Residents having informal status December 31st
1961	79·0	92·2
1962	79·3	92·4
1963	79·2	92·9
1964	79·4	92·6
1965	80·0	93·1
1966	80·5	92·8
1967	82·1	93·3
1968	82·3	93·4
1969	82·6	93·4
1970	82·5	93·2

Figures for 1961 refer to the half-year 1 November 1960 to 30 April 1961.

Table 8   Mental health review tribunals: outcome of hearings 1961–79

	Application determined	Discharge directed	% Discharge directed
1961	710	86	12·1
1962	692	71	10·3
1963	1157	161	13·9
1964	960	122	12·7
1965	933	122	13·1
1966	913	122	13·4
1967	942	132	14·0
1968	826	117	14·2
1969	948	168	17·7
1970	732	132	18·0

Figures for 1961 refer to the period 1 November 1960 to 30 April 1961 (six months only).

The grouping of 'discharge directed' figures for 1964, 1965 and 1966 appears to be fortuitous.

Table 9   Mental illness: out-patients 1961–70

	Annual no. of clinic sessions (000)	New out-patients (000)	Total attendance (000)
1961	115	145	1078
1962	125	159	1189
1963	133	166	1227
1964	138	168	1240
1965	140	175	1250
1966	142	180	1261
1967	137	191	1312
1968	138	193	1329
1969	134	186	1270
1970	141	182	1305

Figures refer to adult patients and mental illness only. They exclude child psychiatry, subnormality and severe subnormality, and the chronic sick under psychiatric supervision. Figures for all groups in 1970 were as follows:

	Annual no. of clinic sessions (000)	New out-patients (000)	Total attendances (000)
Mental illness (adult)	141	182	1305
Child psychiatry	62	32	214
Subnormal severely subnormal	3	3	9
Chronic sick under psyciatric provision	—	—	3

Table 10   Mental defectives under statutory forms of care 1947–57

31 Dec.	Patients in institutions	Under guardianship or notified	Under statutory supervision	Total
1947	54,229	5,373	43,719	103,321
1948	54,887	5,724	44,787	105,398
1949	56,506	4,558	47,158	108,222
1950	56,726	4,095	48,295	109,116
1951	57,661	3,850	50,049	111,560
1952	59,006	3,690	56,140	118,836
1953	60,065	3,446	55,452	118,963
1954	60,868	3,303	57,734	121,905
1955	61,439	3,135	59,594	124,168
1956	60,927	3,084	60,467	124,478
1957	60,919	2,939	60,388	124,246

Source: Annual Reports of the Ministry of Health.

'Patients in institutions' includes those in hospitals vested in the Minister of Health, Rampton and Moss Side Institutions, certified institutions and approved homes, and patients on licence. The figures show an increase in institutional care and in statutory supervision, and a considerable decrease in guardianship and notification. The latter is probably due to a greater use of voluntary supervision, for which no figures are available. The increase in total numbers ascertained, though marked, similarly does not take account of those cases where no statutory action was taken.

Table 11   Subnormality and severe subnormality, resident population: patients in hospital beds as at 31 December 1959–70

	Subnormal	Severely subnormal	Total
1959			63,893
1960	—	—	—
1961	14,103	47,061	61,164
1962	13,804	47,667	61,471
1963	16,339	48,283	64,622
1964	14,165	45,643	59,808
1965	14,029	46,299	60,328
1966	13,938	46,586	60,524
1967	13,791	46,921	60,712
1968	13,522	46,978	60,500
1969	14,100	46,703	60,803
1970	13,732	46,186	59,918

Figures for 1959 refer to patients received under the Mental Deficiency Acts 1913–38 and patients outside the provisions of the Mental Deficiency Acts. The distinction between subnormal and severely subnormal dates from the 1959 Mental Health Act.

No figures are given for 1960.

Table 12   Persons receiving mental health services provided by local health authorities as at 31 December 1962–70

	Mentally ill or psychopathic	Subnormal or severely subnormal	Total
1962	51,032	83,984	135,016
1963	55,734	85,628	141,362
1964	64,884	87,743	152,627
1965	71,379	90,384	161,763
1966	80,818	93,486	174,304
1967	87,279	97,476	184,755
1968	94,158	99,820	193,978
1969	82,321	96,024	178,345
1970	85,682	97,732	183,414

These figures were provided for the first time in the 1963 Report, when statistics for the two years 1962 and 1963 were quoted.

Includes persons in local authority residential care (see Table 13).

Table 13   Mentally disordered persons receiving residential care from local health authorities as at 31 December 1962–70

	Mentally ill or psychopathic	Subnormal or severely subnormal	Total
1962	968	1,435	2,403
1963	1,200	1,957	3,157
1964	1,568	2,707	4,275
1965	2,044	3,526	5,570
1966	2,572	4,254	6,826
1967	2,846	4,818	7,664
1968	3,366	5,645	9,011
1969	2,426	6,122	8,548
1970	2,755	6,950	9,705

Table 14   Social workers in mental health employed by local health authorities as at 31 December 1962–70

	PSW	CSW	Other	Total
1962				1,247
1963	105	—	1,255	1,360
1964	109	55	1,234	1,398
1965	139	135	1,297	1,571
1966	156	160	1,365	1,681
1967	179	231	1,384	1,794
1968	213	297	1,362	1,872
1969	208	267	1,285	1,760
1970	197	365	1,246	1,808

Part-time staff are included as whole-time equivalents. Welfare assistants are not included.

'PSW' means a member of staff with a Psychiatric Social Work training or the equivalent, i.e. a university Applied Social Studies course. 'CSW' means a training for the Certificate in Social Work or the equivalent.

A breakdown by training was first given in the Annual Report for 1964.

Table 15   Average cost of maintaining in-patients in hospital In-patient cost per week (£) 1959/60 to 1969/70

	Mental illness	Mental subnormality	Chronic	Acute
	£ s. d.	£ s. d.	£ s. d.	£ s. d.
1959/60	7 12 8	7 0 0	10 18 7	25 16 7
1960/61	8 7 5	7 9 6	11 14 3	27 16 11
1961/62	9 2 10	8 2 0	12 17 4	30 1 3
1962/63	9 15 5	8 12 8	13 14 9	31 8 5
1963/64	10 9 5	9 1 8	14 9 5	33 6 4
1964/65	11 5 11	9 17 6	15 9 5	35 14 5
1965/66	12 12 3	10 17 8	17 6 5	39 11 9
1966/67	13 11 1	11 11 7	18 6 2	43 2 8
1967/68	14 7 5	12 5 7	19 1 2	45 11 1
1968/69	16·06	13·51	20·74	49·39
1969/70	17·63	14·96	22·50	54·45

The financial year operates from 5 April.

Figures refer to all Health Service hospitals administered by Regional Hospital Boards and Hospital Management Committees i.e., excluding Teaching Hospitals. The average in-patient cost per week for a London Teaching Hospital bed in 1967/8 was £67.2.10.

Appendix 2
Changes proposed in services for the mentally handicapped 1971

Source: Department of Health and Social Security, *Better Services for the Mentally Handicapped*, Cmnd. 4683, 1971.

Type of accommodation	Number of places, 1969	Number proposed	increase/ decrease
Hospital			
in-patients (adults)	52,100	27,000	−25,100
in-patient (children)	7,400	6,400	−1,000
day patient (adults)	500	4,900	+ 4,400
day patient (children)	200	2,900	+2,700
Community care			
residential homes (adults)	4,300	29,400	+25,100
residential homes (children)	1,800	4,900	+3,100
fostering etc. (adults)	550	7,400	+6,850
fostering etc. (children)	100	1,000	+900

Appendix 3

Guidelines for mental illness and related provision 1971

Source: Department of Health and Social Security, *Hospital Services for the Mentally Ill*, December 1971, page 12.

1. Mentally ill adults	in-patients	0·5 beds per 1,000 population.
2. Mentally ill adults	day patients	0·65 places per 1,000 population.
3. Mentally ill adults	out-patients	A minimum of 6 clinic sessions per week per 100,000 population.
4. Mentally ill or seriously maladjusted children	in-patients	20/25 beds per million population.
5. Mentally ill or seriously maladjusted adolescents	in-patients	20/25 beds per million population.
6. Psycho-geriatric assessment	in-patients	10/20 beds per 250,000 population.
7. Longer-stay psycho-geriatric patients		Under review.

Notes

Chapter 1   Eighteenth-century custom

[1] B. Hart, *Psychology of Insanity*, p. 5; see also M. Murray, *The Witch Cult in Western Europe*, p. 86.
[2] 'Lollers' .. vagabonds.
[3] F. Eden, *State of the Poor*, pp. 146–7.
[4] M. Summers, *History of Witchcraft and Demonology*, p. 35.
[5] D. H. Tuke, *Hist. of Insane*, Chapter 1, *passim*.
[6] A. Chaplin, *Medicine in the Reign of George III*, pp. 18–19.
[7] *A Statement by the Society of Apothecaries*, 1844, p. 20. (Evidence of Sir David Barry and Mr. R. D. Grainger before Select Committee, 1834.)
[8] op. cit., p. 35.
[9] Trephining was the forerunner of the modern surgical operation of pre-frontal leucotomy. See W. R. Brain and E. B. Strauss, *Recent Advances in Neuro-Psychiatry*, 5th edition, p. 126.
[10] Archbishop Herring. See Introduction to 1821 edition.
[11] *Northanger Abbey* was published in 1818, and *Pride and Prejudice* in 1813. Both were written some years before publication.
[12] S. Butler, *The Analogy of Religion*, 1736.
[13] Argument of the Frontispiece, *Anatomy of Melancholy*.
[14] *Hume's Essays and Treatises on Several Subjects*, Edinburgh, 1804, vol. 2, p. 319.
[15] B. Willey, *The Eighteenth-Century Background*, p. 123.
[16] Hermann Andrew Pistorius.
[17] Pistorius, *Notes and Additions to Dr Hartley's Observations on Man*, 3rd edition, p. 8.
[18] *Life and Letters of the 3rd Earl of Shaftesbury*, 1900 edition, p. 226.
[19] *Life and Letters of the 3rd Earl of Shaftesbury*, p. 96.
[20] Halsbury's *Laws of England* states (2nd edition, vol. 9, p. 718): 'The writ may issue at the instance of any person who is wrongfully kept in confinement under the pretence of insanity or unsoundness of mind, to compel the person having the custody of the person alleged to be insane to produce him in court so that the legality of the detention may be inquired into.' This was also the law in the eighteenth century.
[21] Conditions in private madhouses are discussed in Chapter 2 in relation to the events of 1763.
[22] See Tuke, op. cit., p. 45 *et seq.*; Zilboorg and Henrey, *Hist. of Medical Psychology*, p. 564, and O'Donoghue, *Story of Bethlehem Hospital*, *passim*.
[23] 22 Geo. III c. 77.

²⁴ Pictures of the Bedlamite badge and horn may be seen in the Print Room at the British Museum.
²⁵ J. Aubrey, *Natural History of Wiltshire* (written 1656–91), p. 93.
²⁶ 'Loving Mad Tom', *Giles Earle's Song Book*, 1615, and broadsheets.
²⁷ In the Print Room at the British Museum, and also at the Victoria and Albert Museum.
²⁸ 'Great Cibber' was Colley Cibber, the actor. D. H. Tuke (*Hist. of Insane*, p. 71) states that a vitriolic reply made to *The Dunciad* by Cibber hastened Pope's death; but as the poem was published in 1728, and Pope died in 1744, this seems far-fetched.
²⁹ Tuke, op. cit., p. 73.
³⁰ O'Donoghue, *Story of Bethlehem Hospital*, p. 237
³¹ The House Governor, a paid official.
³² Tuke, op. cit., p. 75.
³³ See Chapter 4.
³⁴ O'Donoghue, op. cit., pp. 261–4.
³⁵ O'Donoghue, op. cit., p. 264.
³⁶ 1815 *Report on Madhouses*, p. 110.
³⁷ See p. 78.
³⁸ O'Donoghue, op. cit., p. 273 and illustration, among many other references.
³⁹ *Report of Select Committee on Criminal and Pauper Lunatics*, 1807, Appendix 1.
⁴⁰ Tuke, op. cit., p. 173.
⁴¹ After the passing of Gilbert's Act, 1782, and the introduction of the Speenhamland system.
⁴² Eden, *State of the Poor*, pp. 318–19.
⁴³ S. and B. Webb, *English Poor Law History*, vol. I—The Old Poor Law, p. 155.
⁴⁴ Rigby, *Further Facts Relating to the Care of the Poor . . . in the City of Norwich*, 1812, p. 43 and illustration.
⁴⁵ Kirkman Gray, *History of English Philanthropy*, p. 25.
⁴⁶ S. and B. Webb, op. cit., pp. 304–8.
⁴⁷ *Bristol Corporation of the Poor. Selected Records*, 1696–1834, ed. E. E. Butcher, 1932.
⁴⁸ S. and B. Webb, op. cit., p. 86.
⁴⁹ *Howard on Prisons*, p. 71.
⁵⁰ R. *v.* Arnold, 1723. *English and Empire Digest*, vol. XIV, p. 56, para. 223.

Chapter 2   The growth of public concern

¹ 39 Eliz. c. 4.
² 17 Geo. II c. 5, section 1.
³ 12 Anne (2)c. 23, sometimes cited as 13 Annec. 26.
⁴ Protection for the property of the small category of Chancery Lunatics was more effective.
⁵ *English Reports*, vol. 97, p. 741.
⁶ op. cit., vol. 97, pp. 875–6.

[7] Quoted by Jesse, *Memoirs of the Life and Reign of George III*, vol. III p. 45.

[8] op. cit., p. 91.

[9] *Diaries of Robert Fulke Greville*, Equerry to the King, pp. 118–19.

[10] Jesse, op. cit., p. 265.

[11] *Dictionary of National Biography* (*DNB*).

[12] Jesse, op. cit., vol. III, p. 257.

[13] *HCJ*, 4 December 1788.

[14] *DNB*.

[15] Fulke Greville, op. cit., pp. 159–60.

[16] *HCJ*, 13 January 1789. The context makes it clear that the 'Great Person' was the Queen, who naturally wished to protect the King against attempts to secure a Regency.

[17] op. cit., p. 156.

[18] The remainder of this account of the illness of George III is taken from vol. III of Jesse's *Memoirs of the Life and Reign of George III*, unless otherwise stated.

Chapter 3 Subscription hospitals and county asylums

[1] See J. H. Jesse, *Celebrated Etonians*, vol. I, pp. 18–25. 'Battius, faber fortunae suae . . . medicus perspicax.'

[2] Published as *Dr Battie on Madness*.

[3] Published as *Dr Monro's Reply to Dr Battie*.

[4] *Raffald's Manchester Directory*, and contemporary maps.

[5] Account Book of the Manchester Royal Infirmary.

[6] See pp. 29–30.

[7] Since its removal to Cheadle in 1850, the hospital has been restricted entirely to private patients.

[8] This was a small subscription asylum erected at Newcastle-on-Tyne. See S. Middlebrook, *Newcastle-on-Tyne: Its Growth and Achievements*, p. 161. The treatment was apparently not of a high standard, and the administration left much to be desired. Considerable reforms took place at this asylum in 1824.

[9] J. Ferriar, *Medical Histories and Reflections*, vol. III, pp. 83–112.

[10] *Account of the Rise and Present Establishment of the Lunatic Hospital in Manchester*, 1771, p. 17.

[11] Ferriar, op. cit., p. 111.

[12] B. Kirkman Gray (*Hist. of Eng. Philosophy*, pub. 1905) states (p. 140) that the influence of the Manchester Lunatic Hospital was 'probably . . . negligible'. This appears to have been the general view until the publication of Brockbank's *Short History of Cheadle Royal* in 1934.

[13] See H. C. Hunt, *A Retired Habitation*, and S. Tuke, *Description of the Retreat*, passim; D. H. Tuke, *Hist. of Insane*, pp. 115–116.

[14] G. Higgins, *Letter to Earl Fitzwilliam*, 1814, p. 4. 'A general belief was prevalent in the county that great abuses did exist in the York Asylum . . . attempts had previously been made to reform it . . . they always failed.' See also *Edinburgh Review* for March, 1817.

[15] D. H. Tuke (*Hist. of Insane*, p. 112), gives the date as 1791. See Hunt, *A Retired Habitation*, p. 5 and note.

[16] See Appendix to Higgins' *Letter to Earl Fitzwilliam* for list of Governors.

[17] The 'Quarterly Meeting' is a local executive body of the Society of Friends.

[18] *DNB*.

[19] Thomas Wilkinson, friend of Wordsworth. Hunt, op. cit., p. 52.

[20] The artist H. S. Tuke, son of D. H. Tuke.

[21] *DNB*. Samuel Tuke, 1784–1857.

[22] *DNB*. Daniel Hack Tuke, 1827–95.

[23] Provided by Tuke, Son & Co.

[24] *Report of Select Committee on Madhouses*, 1815, p. 160.

[25] ibid. Cp. the activities of Catherine Cappe at the York Asylum. See pp. 74-5.

[26] Hunt, op. cit., pp. 49–50.

[27] D. C. Somervell, *English Thought in the Nineteenth Century*, p. 1.

[28] E. Halévy, *A History of the English People in the Nineteenth Century*, Vol. I—England in 1815, p. 433.

[29] S. Finer, *Life and Times of Sir Edwin Chadwick*, p. 14.

[30] *Suggestions of Sir George Onesiphorus Paul, Bart., to the Secretary of State*, 1806. Published as an appendix to the 1807 *Report on Criminal and Pauper Lunatics*.

[21] W. L. Clay, *Memoir of the Rev. John Clay, B.D.*, p. 63.

[32] *DNB*.

[33] 1746–1820.

[34] The Act of 1744.

[35] S. and B. Webb, *English Poor Law History* vol. I—The Old Poor Law, p. 304.

[36] The date is given in Wilson's *Biographical Index to the House of Commons* (article on Wynn) 23 January 1807. *HCJ* has no reference to the first appointment of this committee.

[37] Charles Watkin Williams-Wynn, 1775–1850. Brother of Sir Watkin Williams-Wynn. See *DNB*.

[38] His presence was mentioned in debate by Sir James Graham. Hansard, 6 June 1845.

[39] *DNB*.

[40] 1807 *Report*, Appendix I. The total figure of 1765 included ten in Wales.

[41] 48 Geo. III c. 96.

[42] A. Aspinall, *Politics and the Press*, 1780–1850, p. 163.

[43] 23 June 1808. See Holland's *Memoirs*, vol. I, p. 22 for an estimate of Portland's political affiliations.

[44] Section 17. This limit was removed in 1815 (section 7 of amending Act).

[45] *Nottingham Evening Post*, 10 October 1811.

[46] Sir G. O. Paul, *Doubts Concerning the Expediency . . . of immediately proceeding to provide a Lunatic Asylum for the County of Gloucester*, p. 14.

N

[47] 1815 *Report*, p. 152.
[48] The new importance attached to the medical certificate at this stage is a reflection of the rise in professional standards in the medical world. The Company of Barber-Surgeons had split in 1750, the Surgeons forming their own company. In 1800, they were granted a Crown Charter, and the College of Surgeons was established. The apothecaries —who were in effect the forerunners of the general practitioners of today—regularized their position in 1815, an Act of that year defining their status and qualifications.
[49] Hunt, *A Retired Habitation*, p. 27. Certificate of a patient admitted to the Retreat.
[50] 1815 *Report*, p. 317. Certificate delivered to the Select Committee by Mr Finch, of Laverstock. Broadway was a local druggist without qualifications.

Chapter 4 The reform movement 1815-27

[1] Higgins, *Letter to Earl Fitzwilliam*. The incidents at York Asylum are discussed in detail later in this chapter.
[2] See illustration in O'Donoghue, *Story of Bethlehem Hospital*, facing p. 320.
[3] *DNB*.
[4] *Diaries of the Rt Hon. George Rose*, vol. II, p. 517.
[5] E. Baines, *History of the County of York*, 1823, p. 55.
[6] Higgins, op. cit. (This volume contains, in addition to the original letter, a collection of letters and reports relevant to the reform of York Asylum.) Appendix, p. 19.
[7] Thurnam, *Statistics of Insanity*, Appendix 1, p. 3.
[8] See Higgins, op. cit., pp. 3–9 and Appendix.
[9] op. cit., pp. 16–17.
[10] *York Herald*, 9 December 1813.
[11] Higgins, op. cit., p. 12, and (lists of Governors before and after 10 December respectively) Appendix, pp. 16 and 18.
[12] op. cit., p. 12.
[13] Baines, op. cit., p. 55.
[14] Higgins, op. cit., p. 13.
[15] op. cit.
[16] *York Herald*, 21 March 1814. The evidence given by Higgins before the 1815 Committee was slightly more detailed than the newspaper version, and is quoted here.
[17] Letter from S. W. Nicol, a Governor, in Higgins' *Letter to Earl Fitzwilliam*.
[18] Letters in *York Herald*, 12 and 19 December 1814.
[19] 1815 *Report*, p. 28 Rose in questioning Best spoke of 'The Asylum of which you were physician.'
[20] Higgins, op. cit., Appendix, pp. 37–44.
[21] Higgins, op. cit., Appendix to the letter to the Committee, p. 14.

22 Father of Edward Gibbon Wakefield and a notable Quaker philan-thropist. 'Mr Wakefield's circumstances were by no means prosperous: he was, however, an active, zealous advocate for any thing likely, in his opinion, to be useful to mankind . . .'—Francis Place, quoted in R. Garnett's *Edward Gibbon Wakefield*, 1898 edition, pp. 6–7.

23 pp. 102–9. Patients at Bethlem had, on admission, to be certified as 'strong enough to undergo a course of treatment'. See also Appendix to the 1815 *Report*.

24 Though Monro was forced into an admission which he subsequently retracted.

25 See W. L. Clay, *Memoirs of the Rev. John Clay, B.D.*, p. 76.

26 Secretary to the Metropolitan Commissioners.

27 Edward Wakefield set up as a land agent from offices at 42 Pall Mall, after an unsuccessful farming venture, in 1814.

28 Under 14 Geo. III c. 9 (1774).

29 W. Ll. Parry-Jones, *The Trade in Lunacy*, 1972.

30 Halliday, *General View of Lunatics*, 1828, p. 12: 'The Bill . . . was uniformly rejected by the Lords, and after that it got into Chancery, and there it has slept for the past nine years.' (A reference to the obstructive tactics of Lord Eldon.)

31 O'Donoghue, *Story of Bethlehem Hospital*, p. 324. 'He was turned out of the hospital at the age of fifty-two without a pension.'

32 *DNB*.

33 *Gent. Mag.*, 1844, vol. 22, p. 322.

34 *The Observations of Dr Monro*, read before the Governors at Bethlem, 30 April 1816.

35 Halliday, op. cit., p. 17.

36 Halliday's list. In fact, Nottingham, Stafford and Gloucester were at this stage joint county and subscription asylums. Lincoln was entirely a subscription hospital.

37 Figures of total cost and accommodation are taken from Halliday, op. cit., p. 25. Wages and prices fluctuated considerably during the period 1810–23, due to the economic effects of the Napoleonic Wars, and the figures are therefore not strictly comparable. For wage-fluctuations in the building trade at this period, see A. L. Bowley, *Wages in the Nineteenth Century*, pp. 82–4.

38 1808 Act, section 16.

39 Address to the Magistrates of the County of Lancaster. James Gerard, MD, *et al.*, 1810.

40 Opened in 1792. See T. H. Bickerton, *A Medical History of Liverpool*, pp. 28–30.

41 Gerard *et al.*, op. cit.

42 They are still (1972) contiguous.

43 *Report of the Society for the Improvement of Prison Discipline*, 1823, p. 100.

44 Report of Metropolitan Commissioners in Lunacy, recorded in Visitors' Book of the Cornwall Asylum, 1842.

45 Halliday, op. cit., p. 23.

46 Battelle, *Rapport sur les établissements alienés d'Angleterre*, 1851, p. 22.

[47] 1815 *Report*, p. 158.

[48] This was after the reform of conditions at Bethlem.

[49] This declaration, signed by Potts, is incorporated in the minute book.

[50] 48 Geo. III c. 96, section 23.

[51] 1st Minute Book, Cornwall Asylum.

[52] Cash-book of the Lancaster Asylum, 1828, where the figures for each quarter of the foregoing year are given as 176–180–181–198. Halliday op. cit., p. 25) gave the figure for the same year as 300, but was evidently mistaken.

[53] See pp. 79–80.

[54] Report of the Metropolitan Commissioners in Lunacy, recorded in the Visitors' Book of the Stafford Asylum, 1842.

[55] *Knight on Insanity*, p. 95.

[56] ibid. There is a chapter on the management and occupation of patients.

[57] Halliday, op. cit., pp. 19–23: a survey of conditions in the various county asylums.

[58] *Knight on Insanity*, p. 91.

[59] 1st Visitors' Book of the Cornwall Asylum.

[60] A. Aspinall, *Politics and the Press*, 1780–1850, pp. 23 and 31.

[61] Aspinall, op. cit., p. 10.

[62] Aspinall, op. cit., p. 247.

[63] *The Times* lost its subsidy from the Tory party in 1799 as a result of an alleged libel in a report of parliamentary proceedings, and was thereafter relatively independent.

[64] Aspinall, op. cit., p. 271.

[65] Thomas Wakley, 1795–1852. See *DNB* and *Gent. Mag.* obit. (1862, vol. II, p. 364).

[66] P. Pinel, *Traité Medico-Philosophique*, quoted in translation by Zilboorg and Henrey, *Hist. of Medical Psychology*, p. 334.

[67] Thomas Thompson, MP for Midhurst, 1807–18, was a merchant from Hull, a friend of Wilberforce, and a member of the Clapham Sect. See *DNB* article on his son, General Thomas Perronet Thompson (1783–1869) and Halévy, *Hist. of the English People in the Nineteenth Century*, vol. I—England in 1815, p. 436.

[68] See Statutory Reports of the Metropolitan Commissioners in Lunacy, 1830 (unpublished, handwritten. PRO, London).

[69] Burrows, *Commentaries on the Causes of Insanity*, p. 1.

[70] Probably a reference to Herbart's *Text-book of Psychology*, published in 1816, in which the writer contended that psychology was a separate study allied to philosophy rather than to medicine. Herbart was Kant's successor in the Chair of Philosophy at Konigsberg.

[71] A reference to Mesmerism, then in vogue on the Continent.

[72] Burrows, op. cit., p. 7.

[73] This corresponds to the French use of 'moral', and may have originated with Pinel.

[74] Halliday was MD FRS and LRCP. He held the post of domestic physician to the Duke of Clarence, later William IV. See *DNB*.

[75] Halliday, op. cit., p. 74.

Chapter 5   The Metropolitan Commissioners

1 *Gent. Mag.* obit., May, 1864, which states that Gordon was known as 'the Dorsetshire Joseph Hume.'

2 D. H. Tuke, *Hist. of Insane*, p. 203.

3 Anthony Ashley Cooper, Lord Ashley, later 7th Earl of Shaftesbury. See Hodder's *Life*, Hammond's *Lord Shaftesbury*, *DNB*, etc. 1801–85.

4 Hansard, 19 February 1828.

5 *The Times*, 20 February 1828—a fuller account than that given in Hansard or the Report.

6 This clause was inserted by the House of Lords.

7 Monro returned to private practice in 1816, following his dismissal from Bethlem.

8 The Phillips case was recounted in full to the House in the debates preceding the Lunatics Act of 1845. See Hansard for 11 July 1845. Duncombe (1796–1861) was well known as a champion of lost causes and a discoverer of abuses of the law. He had succeeded Wakley as MP for Finsbury.

9 *Report of Metropolitan Commissioners in Lunacy*, 1844, Appendix D. No figure was given for the Surrey Asylum, which was still in the course of erection.

10 R. Gardiner Hill, *The Non-Restraint System of Treatment of Lunacy, etc.*, 1857, p. 184.

11 Tuke, op. cit., p. 204.

12 *Report of Metropolitan Commissioners*, 1844, pp. 137–8.

13 Gardiner Hill, op. cit., *passim.*

14 Thane, *Medical Biographies.* (The lectures of Sir George Thane, Professor of Anatomy at University College Hospital, London. A student's notes in manuscript, UCH Library).

15 Gardiner Hill, op. cit., p. 17.

16 Quoted by Tuke, op. cit., p. 207.

17 *On the Treatment of Insanity*, 1856, pp. 276–7.

18 Published in 1838. Caleb Crowther was then the senior physician to the West Riding Asylum at Wakefield.

19 *Rules of the Surrey Asylum.* Published with Visiting Justices' Reports for 1844–6.

20 *Reports of Visiting Justices of Surrey Asylum*, 1844–6. This asylum was subsequently transferred to the Middlesex County Council, and is now Springfield Hospital, near Tooting, London.

21 *Report of Poor Law Commissioners* (hereafter referred to as *PLC Reports*)—1834, vol. I, p. 128.

22 op. cit., p. 148.

23 Tuke, op. cit., p. 173.

24 *PLC Report*, 1845, pp. 186–7. The Lunacy Commissioners in the previous year gave a much higher figure—9339. See tables at end of their Report of 1844.

25 *PLC Report*, 1834, vol. I, p. 97.

26 S. and B. Webb, *English Poor Law Policy*, pp. 61–2.

27 The Madhouse Act of 1828.

28 *Official Circulars of Poor Law Commissioners*, vol. III, p. 49, 14 July, 1842.

[29] *Report of Metropolitan Commissioners in Lunacy*, 1844, p. 10.
[30] *Report of Select Committee on the Poor Law Amendment Act*, 1838, vol. I, pp. 10–11.
[31] Mr Fazakerly, formerly a member of the 1827 Committee on Pauper Lunatics.
[32] S. Finer, *Life and Times of Sir Edwin Chadwick*, pp. 133, 194, 205, *et seq.*
[33] op. cit., p. 239.
[34] Figures for both workhouses and county asylums taken from *11th Annual PLC Report*, 1845, pp. 186–9.
[35] Boyd, *Report as to Lunatics Chargeable to the Parish of St. Marylebone*, 1844.
[36] Printed directions of PLC, 5 February 1842. Quoted in *Report of Metropolitan Commissioners in Lunacy*, 1844, pp. 95–6.
[37] O'Donoghue, *Story of Bethlehem Hospital*, p. 357.

Chapter 6 Ashley and the achievement of reform

[1] Section 2. Presumably because midwifery or surgery might demand their urgent attention at any time, thus distracting them from their duties under the Act.
[2] 1844 *Report*, pp. 29–30.
[3] op. cit., pp. 11–12.
[4] op. cit., pp. 29–30.
[5] Near Oxford, formerly the Radcliffe Asylum.
[6] See 'Refutation of the Assertions made by the Writer of the Article in the *Quarterly Review* for October, 1844'—by the chairman of the Warneford Asylum, 1944.
[7] 1844 *Report*, p. 33.
[8] op. cit., p. 33.
[9] op. cit., p. 44.
[10] op. cit., p. 53.
[11] op. cit., p. 71—quoting from S. Tuke's introduction to Jacobi's *Treatise on Hospitals for the Insane*.
[12] op. cit., p. 223.
[13] op. cit., p. 226.
[14] op. cit., p. 99.
[15] Hansard, 16 July 1842.
[16] *Epistle to Mr Ewart, MP, by a Rev. Gentleman lately a patient in the Middlesex Asylum*, 1841—Hume Tracts.
[17] Quoted by Hodder, *Life of Shaftesbury*, vol. II, p. 61.
[18] *Westminster Review*, March 1845.
[19] An article in the *Edinburgh Review* for April 1803, took the opposite view. It appears in fact that the work of Pinel and that of the Tukes existed independently of each other for some years. See D. H. Tuke, *Hist. of the Insane*, pp. 133–4, and H. C. Hunt, *A Retired Habitation*, p. 11.

Chapter 7 The triumph of legalism

[1] Select Committee of 1859, p. 214.

² Hansard, 3 July 1845. Thomas Slingsby Duncombe was a nephew of the first Baron Feversham.

³ (Sir) John Charles Bucknill, (1817–97). Medical superintendent of the Devon Asylum 1844–62. Lord Chancellor's Medical Visitor, 1862–76. Editor of the *Journal of Mental Science* until 1862, when Dr Henry Maudsley became editor.

⁴ *Asylum Journal,* Second edition No. 1, November 1853.

⁵ *J. Ment. Sci.,* March 1959; an open letter to S. T. Kekewich, MP. Kekewich was chairman of the visiting committee at the Devon County Asylum, where Dr Bucknill was medical superintendent.

⁶ D. H. Tuke, *Hist. of Insane,* p. 190.

⁷ There were also over 100 private licensed houses at this time.

⁸ Section 45 of the Poor Law Amendment Act, 1834, provided that *dangerous* mental patients should not be detained in workhouses. There was no machinery to ensure that quieter patients were also sent to the asylum.

⁹ Such an order was already necessary in pauper cases.

¹⁰ And incorporated in the Acts of 1889 and 1890.

¹¹ Twenty-ninth Report of Commissioners in Lunacy, 1837. See J. Watson Grice, *National and Local Finance,* p. 57. S. Webb, (*Grants in Aid,* p. 43) gives the date erroneously as 1859.

¹² Reade's biographer, Malcolm Erwin, writes that Reade 'habitually forgot to date his letters' (*Charles Reade—A Biography,* p. 145). The vagueness about dates may have been unconscious.

¹³ R. Paternoster, *The Madhouse System,* p. 55 also quotes an instance of this kind.

¹⁴ A. Swinburne, *A Note on Charlotte Brontë,* 1894.

¹⁵ op. cit., vol. II, pp. 218–19. Dr Granville's italics.

¹⁶ See *The Times* Law Reports, 1884, especially 14 March—2 April.

¹⁷ Dr Lyltelton Forbes Winslow was the son of the founder and editor of the *Journal of Psychological Medicine.*

¹⁸ This appears to be the Alleged Lunatics Friend Society under a changed name. No records have been traced.

¹⁹ *The Times* Law Report, 1 December 1884. Judgement was given for £500 to Mrs Weldon.

²⁰ *Standard,* 19 March 1884. Baron Huddleston was the last of the old Barons of the Exchequer. The title dated back to the days before professional judges. See *The Times,* Obituary, 6 December 1890.

²¹ *J. Ment. Sci.,* October 1884.

²² *DNB.*

²³ J. B. Atlay, *The Victorian Chancellors,* vol. II, p. 420.

²⁴ Hodder, *Life of Shaftesbury,* vol. III, p. 513.

²⁵ *Memoirs Personal and Political.* Roundell Palmer, 1st Earl of Selborne.

²⁶ *The Times,* 11 July 1884. Winslow *v.* Semple.

²⁷ Hansard, 5 May 1884.

²⁸ Lord Chancellor February–August 1886.

²⁹ In fact the protection given was largely illusory. Vexatious actions continued to be fought and won until new provisions were introduced in the Mental Treatment Act of 1930.

[30] Hansard, 2 March 1888.

[31] Hansard, 30 July 1889.

[32] Hansard, 3 March 1890.

[33] Hansard, 20 March 1890.

[34] One of a special panel appointed in each area with authority under this Act; but any justice of the peace could act in the case of a pauper patient (see 'Summary Reception Order').

[35] 'committee.' The accent is on the last syllable. This refers to one person, not to a group.

[36] The 'rota visit'. The normal practice was for the committee to meet at the asylum, and for some wards to be visited on each occasion of meeting.

Chapter 8   Mental defectives

[1] J. C. Flügel, *A Hundred Years of Psychology*, 1933, p. 109.

[2] Now Earlswood Hospital.

[3] Now the Royal Albert Hospital.

[4] D. H. Tuke, *Hist. of Insane*, p. 310.

[5] E. Hodder, *Life of Shaftesbury*, vol. III, p. 235. 'It acted, in his opinion, with too great severity, and arrogated to itself the function of being able to do everything.'

[6] For the development of earlier local voluntary agencies, see M. Rooff, *Voluntary Societies and Social Policy*, pp. 103–4.

[7] 1886–1949. Dame Ellen Pinsent, 1937.

[8] C. P. Lapage, *Feeble-mindedness in Children of School Age*, with an appendix by Mary Dendy, 1920.

[9] *Lancet*, 21 February 1903.

[10] 1822–1911.

[11] On Galton's death in 1911, he bequeathed £45,000 to University College, London, for the foundation of the first Chair in Eugenics. His colleague and friend, Karl Pearson, became first Galton Professor of Eugenics in the same year.

[12] Cattell, 'Address before the American Psychological Association', *Psychological Review*, vol. III, 2.

[13] *The Jukes: A Study in Crime, Pauperism, Disease and Heredity.*

[14] *The Jukes in 1915*, p. 77.

[15] H. Goddard, *The Kallikak Family*, 1912. 'Kallikak' was a pseudonym made up of 'kalos' and 'kakos', signifying the noble and ignoble parts of the family.

[16] The Radnor Commission seems to have been thinking of all the categories of people covered by the Board of Control as 'mental defectives'. The terminology was limited by the 1913 Act but was not at all clear in 1908.

[17] First Report of Eugenics Education Society, 1909.

[18] Quoted in K. Pearson, *Life of Galton*, vol. III, p. 339.

[19] First Report of Eugenics Education Society, 1909.

[20] Material in the library of the Eugenics Society.

²¹ Third son of the 4th Marquess of Bath. MP for Bath, 1910–18. Killed in action, 1918.

²² Hansard, 10 June 1912.

²³ J. and S. Wormald, *A Guide to the Mental Deficiency Act*, p. 4.

²⁴ 28 July 1943.

²⁵ J. Wedgwood, *Memoirs of a Fighting Life*, 1940, p. 71.

²⁶ 20 May 1913.

²⁷ Wedgwood, op. cit., p. 84.

²⁸ Stephen McKenna, *Reginald McKenna, 1863–1943*, 1948.

²⁹ This was the period of Suffragette agitation.

³⁰ See pp. 161–3.

³¹ Galton, *The Problem of the Feeble-Minded*, 1909. An abstract of the Report of the Royal Commission of 1904–8, with commentaries.

³² Lord Haldane's opening speech on the occasion of the second reading (7 August 1913) is an excellent summary of the whole Bill and the Government's intention.

³³ The second Earl.

³⁴ The Habitual Drunkards Act of 1879 (42 and 43 Vict. c. 19) defined an habitual drunkard as 'a person who, not being amenable to any jurisdiction in lunacy, is notwithstanding, by reason of habitual intemperate drinking of intoxicating liquor, at times dangerous to himself or herself or to others, or incapable of managing himself or herself and his or her affairs' (section 3(*b*)).

³⁵ Marjorie U. Welfare, 'Dame Evelyn Fox', reprinted from *Social Service*, Spring 1955.

³⁶ Annual Report of the Board of Control, 1914.

³⁷ Annual Report of the Board of Control, 1914.

³⁸ Annual Report of the Board of Control, 1927.

³⁹ Hansard, 18 March 1927.

⁴⁰ 'Justice is the daughter of liberty.'

⁴¹ Moss Side and Rampton institutions for defectives of this type had been founded after the first world war. There was also Broadmoor, founded in 1864, and at this time under the jurisdiction of the Home Office.

⁴² Annual Report of the Board of Control, 1934.

⁴³ 1879–1949. Formerly Assistant Secretary to the Ministry of Health.

Chapter 9   Into the community

¹ Dr Walk comments: 'The registered hospitals and licensed houses had no difficulty in receiving recoverable cases and could take voluntary patients.'

² op. cit., vol I, pp. 81, 254.

³ Annual Report of the Board of Control, 1915–20. See Appendix 1. A similar situation arose in the second world war. See p. 270.

⁴ Report of Annual Conference of the National Association of Mental Health, 1955.

⁵ Annual Report of the Board of Control, 1918.

⁶ With the exception of the Maudsley Hospital. See p. 235.

[7] Hansard, 20 April and 17 May 1915.

[8] Some asylums had a small number of out-patients from the eighteen-eighties. This development was not as new as the Board of Control's Report suggested.

[9] SR and O, 1920. No. 809.

[10] See D. H. Tuke's description in *Hist. of Insane*, p. 190.

[11] MP for W. Fulham. A barrister and formerly chairman of the LCC.

[12] Consulting Physician for Mental Disorders, St Thomas's Hospital.

[13] Lecturer in Mental Disorders, University of Leeds. A former medical superintendent of the Retreat.

[14] The AWU did give evidence before the Royal Commission two years later.

[15] Some hospitals had built villa-units in the 1880s and after; but the committee's recommendation referred to the construction of the entire hospital.

[16] 1835–1918. *Who's Who*, 1917 and *Annual Register*, 1918. Surprisingly, no account of his life is given in *DNB*.

[17] Founded in 1763 as a branch of the Infirmary at Manchester; now Cheadle Royal Hospital.

[18] A movement for a 'psychiatric clinic' of this nature had been discussed among psychiatrists for some twenty years before this date. See Dr A. Walk, 'Mental Hospitals', in *The Evolution of Hospitals in Britain*, 1958.

[19] Dr Maudsley subsequently increased his donation by £10,000.

[20] Under the LCC (parks, etc.), Act of 1915.

[21] K. J. Johnson, 'Bethlem and the Maudsley', *Bethlem and Maudsley Gazette*.

[22] Rev. H. Hawkins, *A Plea for Convalescent Homes in connection with Asylums for the Insane Poor*, 1871 and *After Care*, 1879.

[23] 39, Wimpole Street. For Dr Bucknill, see p. 155.

[24] Presidential address, 1883, quoted in MACA leaflet.

[25] M. Rooff, *Voluntary Societies and Social Policy*, p. 95.

[26] A branch was formed in Birmingham in 1912, but there was otherwise little activity in the provinces. 1,176 cases were dealt with in the London area in this year.

[27] This evidence was published among the minutes of the Royal Commission.

[28] This might in some cases be a special ward or block reserved for these patients.

[29] There were also a few beds of this kind in the City of London Hospital.

[30] Many war hospitals had developed OT, but the more highly organized Dutch system gave an added impetus to the movement.

[31] There were no trained occupational therapists in England until 1930. See pp. 259–60.

[32] For an account of the origins and development of psychiatric social work in England, see M. Ashdown and S. C. Brown, *Social Service and Mental Health*, *passim*.

[33] The second reading of the Bill, 28 November 1929.

34 Labour MP for East Islington. Member of the Metropolitan Asylums Board.

35 Conservative MP for Thornbury, Glos. and Parliamentary Private Secretary to the Minister of Health (Kingsley Wood) 1926–9.

36 See pp. 201 and 216.

37 Hansard, 11 April 1930.

38 The next full-dress debate on mental health took place on 19 February 1954.

39 Of the four women Senior Commissioners serving 1913–39, three (Miss Dendy, Mrs Pinsent and Miss Darwin) were lay and one (Dr Wilson) medical.

40 These clauses gave the local authorities wide scope for action. Very few seem to have taken full advantage of them.

41 Thus bringing mental treatment legislation into line with the intentions of the Local Government Act, 1929 (19 Geo. V c. 17).

42 Ministry of Labour; Abstract of Labour Statistics. Percentage of insured persons unemployed; 1929–10·2; 1930–17·4; 1931–20·8.

43 Un-named in the Board of Control's Annual Report, 1931.

44 The Lancashire Mental Hospitals Board area. As a result of this comment by the Board of Control, 5 per cent of all beds in the area were made available for voluntary patients in the next year.

Chapter 10   Towards a National Health Service

1 The name is an acronym of Berkshire, Oxfordshire, Reading and Oxford.

2 See R. Titmuss, *Problems of Social Policy*, p. 20, note.

3 The Mental After-Care Association remained a separate organization.

4 H. V. Dicks, *Fifty Years of the Tavistock Clinic*, 1970.

5 Hansard, 15 April 1943.

6 The National Health Service Act substituted Regional Hospital Boards for the original proposal of joint boards for local authority areas.

7 Section 2 and schedule III.

8 Section 28.

9 Section 1.

10 Section 2 and schedule i(i) *e*.

11 Constituted under section 2 (iii).

12 National Health Service Act 1946: Provisions relating to the Mental Health Services. Published by the Ministry of Health and the Board of Control, 1948.

13 An interesting feature is the speed with which RHB areas were determined. A detailed draft of proposed areas was sent to interested bodies on 15 November 1946, and the Determination of Regional Hospital Areas Order was laid before parliament on 18 December, only four and a half weeks later. There was thus very little time for local consultation.

14 A 'teaching hospital' is a hospital operating in close conjunction with a university medical faculty, and has a Board of Governors which is not responsible to the Regional Hospital Board. Other hospitals also have teaching facilities.

[15] J. S. Ross, *The National Health Service*, p. 128.

Chapter 11   The three revolutions

[1] Central Health Services Council: *Report on Co-operation between Local Authority, Hospital and Practitioner Services*. S.O. No. 32–419, 1952.

[2] A few mental hospitals had their own social workers, who undertook domiciliary visiting.

[3] National Health Service Act, 1946, schedule 3, part I.

[4] op. cit., schedule 3, part II.

[5] op. cit., schedule 3, part III.

[6] op. cit., schedule 5, part I.

[7] J. Carse, *The Worthing Experiment*, published at Graylingwell Hospital, 1958, p. 32.

[8] Minister of Health (1964–8). The debate is reported in *Hansard*, 19 February 1954.

[9] The duration of stay in mental hospitals and mental deficiency hospitals was much longer than in general hospitals—hence 42 per cent of all patients represented only 3 per cent of all annual admissions. Even so, the figure for expenditure on research was disproportionately low.

[10] To be known later as the 'mental million'.

[11] G. M. Carstairs, 'Advances in Psychological Medicine', *Practitioner*, Symposium on Advances in Treatment, 1961, vol. 187, pp. 495–504. See also M. Shepherd, N. Goodman and D. C. Watt, 'The Application of Hospital Statistics in the Evaluation of Pharmacotherapy in a Psychiatric Population', *Comprehensive Psychiatry*, 2, 1, (February 1961).

[12] Quoted in University of Cambridge Preliminary Report on Postgraduate Medical School Symposium on Depression, 1960, p. 18.

[13] H. Brill (Deputy Commissioner of Mental Hygiene, New York State) and R. E. Patton (Director of Statistical Services, New York State Department of Mental Hygiene), 'The Impact of Modern Chemotherapy on Hospital Organization, Psychiatric Care and Public Health Policies: its scope and its limits,' 1961.

[14] WHO Technical Report Series No. 73, 1953.

[15] Dr R. C. Hunt in *Steps in the Development of Integrated Psychiatric Services* (Milbank Memorial Fund), p. 18.

[16] 'I had a particularly difficult problem, I think, because of the extreme size of my hospital . . . over 10,000 patients . . . one of my first statements to my staff when I got back was that I would aim for a 30 per cent open ward program in two years. Yet after two years, this very large public mental hospital now has 7,172 patients living on open wards; that is 71·5 per cent of the patients. An additional 604 patients or 6 per cent have ground privileges. . . .' Dr F. J. O'Neill, op. cit.

[17] J. K. Wing, D. H. Bennett and J. Denham, *The Industrial Rehabilitation of Long-stay Schizophrenic Patients*.

[18] For a full discussion of these problems, see *The Place of Work in the Treatment of Mental Disorder*, Report of Annual Conference of the National Association of Mental Health, 1959.

[19] See J. Bierer, 'A Review of Modern Trends in Psychiatry and their Consequences for the Psychiatric Services', in *Proceedings of the Thirteenth International Hospital Congress*, Paris, 1963, pp. 161–3.

[20] T. F. Main, 'The Hospital as a Therapeutic Community', *Bulletin of the Menninger Clinic*, X (1946) 66–70.

[21] Maxwell Jones, *Social Psychiatry in Practice*, p. 87. (For expositions, see *Social Psychiatry, Social Psychiatry in the Community, in Hospitals and in Prisons*, and *Beyond the Therapeutic Community*, by the same author).

[22] ibid.

[23] R. Rapoport, *Community as Doctor*.

[24] See W. R. Bion, 'Experience in Groups', *Human Relations*, Vols 1–4, 1947–51.

[25] See S. H. Foulkes and E. S. Antony, *Group Psychotherapy*; and S. H. Foulkes, 'Group Analysis', *Lancet*, 2 March 1946.

[26] See K. Jones and R. Sidebotham, *Mental Hospitals at Work*, pp. 35–41, 75–6, and 91–4 for contemporary accounts of experimentation in three psychiatric hospitals in 1958–9.

[27] See S. Verba, *Small Groups and Political Behaviour; a Study of Leadership*, p. 222; and B. B. Zeitlyn, 'The Therapeutic Community—Fact or Fantasy?' *Br. J. Psychiat.* 113, 1083–6, 1967.

[28] D. V. Martin, *Adventure in Psychiatry*.

[29] D. H. Clark, *Administrative Therapy*.

[30] C. P. Blacker, *Neurosis and the Mental Health Services*.

[31] J. Bierer, *The Day Hospital*.

[32] W. A. J. Farndale, op. cit.

[33] *Hostels and the Mental Health Act*, National Association for Mental Health, 1961.

[34] J. Bierer, *Therapeutic Social Clubs*.

[35] See S. H. Foulkes and E. J. Anthony, op. cit.

[36] For a full expression of this view, see T. McKeown, *Medicine in Modern Society*.

[37] Ministry of Health: *Report of the Committee on Social Workers in the Mental Health Services*.

[38] K. Jones, 'Problems of Mental After-Care in Lancashire,' *Sociological Review*, July 1954.

[39] Ministry of Health: *Report of the Working Party on Social Workers in the Local Authority Health and Welfare Services*.

[40] *The Employment and Training of Social Workers*, and *Social Work in Britain*.

[41] Later Lord Brain.

[42] HMSO, Cmnd. 169, 1957.

Chapter 12   The Mental Health Act 1959

[1] Under the Royal Commission's fairly stringent definition of 'severely subnormal', only a small proportion of patients in subnormality hospitals would have been covered by the Act.

o

[2] Hospitals had been freed from the obligation to appoint a medical superintendent in 1959, but the rights of those in appointment were safeguarded.

[3] Hansard, 4 June 1959.

[4] Hansard reads 'George Ashley'—probably a transcriber's error.

[5] The regulations governing the special position of medical superintendents in mental hospitals were rescinded by Circular HM(60) 66.

[6] But not in the case of a private patient, or of admission to a mental nursing home, i.e. the hospital doctor can only give such a recommendation where his own financial interest is not involved.

Chapter 13   Community care?

[1] For full text, see the Report of the Annual Conference of the National Association for Mental Health, 1961, pp. 4–10.

[2] G. C. Tooth and E. M. Brooke, 'Needs and Beds: Trends in the Mental Hospital Population and their effect on Future Planning'. *Lancet*, 1 April 1961, pp. 710–13.

[3] Royal Commission on Medical Education, 1965–8.

[4] *Lancet*, 25 March 1961, pp. 656–7.

[5] G. F. Rehin and F. Martin, *Psychiatric Services in 1975*, p. 20.

[6] K. Jones and R. Sidebotham, *Mental Hospitals at Work*, pp. 11–21.

[7] Letter to the *Lancet*, 22 April 1961.

[8] G. M. Carstairs, 'Advances in Psychological Medicine', *Practitioner*, October 1961, vol. 187, pp. 495–504.

[9] Ministry of Health, *A Hospital Plan for England and Wales*.

[10] Ministry of Health, *Health and Welfare: the Development of Community Care*.

[11] A. B. Cooper and D. F. Early, 'Evolution in the Mental Hospital: Reviewing a Hospital Population', *British Medical Journal*, 3 June 1961, pp. 1600–3.

[12] C. Hassall and C. F. Hellon, 'Survey of a Long-stay Population in a Psychiatric Hospital', *Br. J. Psychiat.*, vol. 110, 1964, pp. 183–5.

[13] C. P. Gore, K. Jones, W. Taylor, B. Ward, 'Needs and Beds: a Regional Census of Psychiatric Hospital Patients', *Lancet*, 29 August 1964, pp. 457–60.

[14] J. Hoenig and M. W. Hamilton, *The De-segregation of the Mentally Ill*.

[15] Now available as a Pelican.

[16] For a critique, see M. Siegler and H. Osmund, 'Goffman's Model of Mental Illness', *Br. J. Psychiat.*, vol. 199, 1971, pp. 419–24.

[17] P. Townsend, op. cit. 1962

[18] R. Barton, op. cit., 1959. Some of Goffman's material had been circulating in the States since the mid-fifties.

[19] ed. Barbara Robb.

[20] D. H. Tuke, *Hist. of Insane*, p. 190.

[21] Ministry of Health: *Findings and Recommendations following Enquiries into Allegations concerning the Care of Elderly Patients in Certain Hospitals*, 1968.

DHSS: *Report of Committee of Inquiry into Allegations of Ill-Treatment of Patients and other Irregularities at the Ely Hospital, Cardiff,* 1969.
Report of the Farleigh Committee of Inquiry, 1971.
Report of the Committee of Inquiry into Whittingham Hospital, 1972.

22 See *Findings and Recommendations following Enquiries into Allegations Concerning the Care of Elderly Patients in Certain Hospitals,* op. cit.

23 Home Office, etc: *Report of the Committee on Local Authority and Allied Personal Social Services* (Chairman, Mr Frederic Seebohm).

24 op. cit., para. 339.

25 op. cit., para. 354.

26 18 and 19 Eliz. II c. 42.

27 NAMH Conference Report, 1961, pp. 47–48.

28 T. McKeown et al., 'Institutional Care of the Mentally Ill', *Lancet,* 29 March 1958, pp. 682–684.

29 See A. Walk, 'History of Mental Nursing', *J. Ment. Sci.* (1961), 107, 1.

30 Supplement to the *Br. J. Psychiat.,* October 1971.

31 For a critique, see M. Siegler, H. Osmund and H. Mann, 'Laing's Models of Madness', *Br. J. Psychiat.* (1969), 115, pp. 947–58.

32 Laing and Esterson, *Sanity, Madness and the Family.* The reference here is from the Pelican edition, 1970, p. 17.

33 Medical Services Review Committee, 'Review of the Medical Services in Great Britain.'

34 Ministry of Health, *The Administrative Structure of the Medical and Related Services in England and Wales,* 1968.

35 DHSS, *The Future Structure of the National Health Service,* 1970.

36 See R. G. S. Brown, 'The Consultative Document on the Future of the Health Service', in *A Year Book of Social Policy in Britain,* 1971, ed. Jones.

37 Ministry of Health, *The Organisation of Medical Work in Hospitals,* 1967.

38 Ministry of Health, *Report of the Committee on Senior Nurse Staffing Structure.*

39 DHSS 1971.

40 See J. Tizard and J. Grad, *The Mentally Handicapped and their Families,*1961; J. Tizard, *Community Services for the Mentally Handicapped,* 1964.

41 See A. Kushlick, 'Community Care for the Subnormal—a plan for evaluation', *Proc. Roy. Soc. Med.,* 58, pp. 374–80, 1965; and 'A Comprehensive Service for the Mentally Subnormal', in Freeman and Farndale (ed.), *New Aspects of the Mental Health Services,* 1967.

42 For a statistical summary, see Appendix 2.

43 The British Paediatric Association set up a Working Party on Mental Handicap. The Report (1971, so far unpublished) sets out in considerable detail how liaison can be achieved and joint services developed.

44 This paper was circulated within the Health Service as an adjunct to Circular 61/71 of December 1971. It does not appear on the list of Government publications.

[45] The latest national figures available at the time of writing are those for 1970 which indicated a continuing drop in provision for an increasing population at risk, and gave a figure of 2·1 per thousand population. See Appendix 1, Table IV.

[46] Hansard 879, 280–281, 7 December 1971. Written answer to question by Dr Stuttaford.

Chapter 14   The price of integration

[1] The British Association of Social Workers has over 10,000 members. The overwhelming majority of the Directors of Social Services appointed to local authorities in 1970/1 were men.

[2] See *Children with Specific Reading Disabilities*: Report of the Advisory Committee on Handicapped Children, HMSO, February 1972.

[3] D. A. Hamburg, 'Therapeutic Aspects of Communication and Administrative Policy in the Psychiatric Section of a General Hospital', in Greenblatt, Levinson and Williams (ed.), *The Patient and the Mental Hospital*, 1957.

[4] See K. Jones and R. Sidebotham, *Mental Hospitals at Work*, part III, passim.

[5] Joint Commission on Mental Illness and Health (US Department of Health, Education and Welfare), Final Report, 1961, p. xxix.

[6] ibid.

[7] Figures in this section are based on official DHSS returns. They were first quoted in a paper for *Trends in British Society since* 1900, ed. A. H. Halsey, Macmillan, 1972, which forms the basis of Appendix 1.

[8] A. Maynard, 'A Study of Some Aspects of Psychiatric care in England and Wales', *Social Science and Medicine*, Pergamon Press, 1972. The figures refer to staffing in 1969.

[9] Mr Maynard gives only one figure for local authority care, relating to expenditure on training centres. This indicates a difference of 496 per cent between the lowest (Hastings) and the highest (Bootle).

[10] T. Szasz, *The Myth of Mental Illness: foundation of a theory of personal conduct*, pp. 296–7.

[11] P. Townsend, in foreword to P. Morris, *Put Away: a sociological study of institutions for the mentally retarded*, Routledge & Kegan Paul, 1969.

[12] According to *Time*, 7 February 1972, the World Federation of Mental Health, the American Psychiatric Association and the Canadian Psychiatric Association have all tabled protests against the Soviet use of psychiatric treatment for political prisoners. See also, inter al., V. Tarsis, *Ward Seven* (1963) and R. Medvedev, *A Question of Madness* (1971).

Appendix 1   Statistics of mental illness and mental handicap

[1] The Lunacy Commission (1845–1913) and its successor, the Board of Control (1914–59) were responsible for the collection of data on the lines indicated; but by the mid 1950s, the work of the Board had so far been assimilated into the Ministry of Health that the distinction was largely nominal.

[2] *Report of the Royal Commission on the Law Relating to Mental Illness and Mental Deficiency*, Appendix IV, pp. 307–313.

[3] *Annual Report of the Ministry of Health*, 1960, Part I, p. 18.

[4] *Annual Report of the Ministry of Health*, 1963, p. 40.

[5] op., cit, p. 45.

[6] op., cit. p. 245.

Bibliography

Public General Statutes

39 Eliz. c. 4	Vagrancy Act, 1597
43 Eliz. c. 2	Poor Law Act, 1601
12 Anne (2) c. 23 (sometimes cited as 13 Anne c. 26)	Vagrancy Act, 1714
17 Geo. II c. 5	Vagrancy Act, 1744
14 Geo. III c. 9	Act for Regulating Private Madhouses, 1774
48 Geo. III c. 96	County Asylums Act, 1808 ('Wynn's Act') subsequently amended by: 51 Geo. III c. 79 (1811) 55 Geo. III c. 46 (1815) 59 Geo. III c. 127 (1819).
9 Geo. IV c. 40	County Asylums Act, 1828.
9 Geo. IV c. 41	Madhouse Act, 1828.
2 and 3 Will. IV c. 107	Lunatics Act, 1832.
4 and 5 Will. IV c. 76	Poor Law Amendment Act, 1834.
5 and 6 Vict. c. 87	Lunatic Asylums Act, 1842.
8 and 9 Vict. c. 100	Lunatics Act, 1845.
8 and 9 Vict. c. 126	Lunatic Asylums and Pauper Lunatics Act, 1845
16 and 17 Vict. c. 70	Lunacy Regulation Act, 1853.
16 and 17 Vict. c. 96	Lunatics Care and Treatment Amendment Act, 1853.
16 and 17 Vict. c. 97	Lunatic Asylums Amendment Act, 1853.
25 and 26 Vict. c. 111	Lunatics Law Amendment Act, 1862.
49 and 50 Vict. c. 41	Idiots Act, 1886.
52 and 53 Vict. c. 41	Lunatics Law Amendment Act, 1889.
53 Vict. c. 5	Lunacy (Consolidation) Act, 1890.
54 and 55 Vict. c. 65	Lunacy Act, 1891.
62 and 63 Vict. c. 32	Elementary Education (Defective and Epileptic Children) Act, 1899.
3 and 4 Geo. V c. 28	Mental Deficiency Act, 1913.
4 and 5 Geo. V c. 45	Elementary Education (Defective and Epileptic Children) Act, 1914.
17 and 18 Geo. V c. 33	Mental Deficiency Act, 1927.
19 Geo. V c. 17	Local Government Act, 1929.
20 and 21 Geo. V c. 23	Mental Treatment Act, 1930.
9 and 10 Geo. VI c. 81	National Health Service Act, 1946.
7 and 8 Eliz. II c. 72	Mental Health Act, 1959.

18 and 19 Eliz. II c. 42   Social Services Act, 1970.

Rejected Bills
Lunacy Acts Amendment Bill, 1887.
Lunacy Bill, 1887.
Feeble-Minded Control Bill, 1912.
Mental Defect Bill, 1912.
Mental Treatment Bill, 1915.

Official Papers (published by HMSO)

Board of Control
Annual Reports, 1914–59.
Colonies for Mental Defectives, 1931.
Pre-frontal Leucotomy in 1,000 cases, 1947.
Report of Conference on the Mental Treatment Act, 1930.
Study of Hypoglycaemic Shock Treatment in Schizophrenia, 1936.
*Suggestions and Instructions for the arrangement . . . of Mental
    Hospitals*, 1940.

Board of Education and Board of Control
Report of Joint Committee on Mental Deficiency, 1929 (Wood Report).

Central Health Services Council
*Report on Co-operation between Hospital, Local Authority and Practitioner
    Services*, 1952 (Messer Report).

Central Statistical Office
Annual Abstract of Statistics.
Social Trends No. 1, 1970; No. 2, 1971.

Department of Health and Social Security
Annual Reports, 1968 to date.
Better Services for the Mentally Handicapped, HMSO, Cmnd. 4683, 1971.
'Consultative Document on the Future of the National Health Service'—
    see unpublished papers.
The Future Structure of the Health Service (Green Paper), HMSO, 1970.
'Hospital Services for the Mentally Ill'—see unpublished papers.
*Report of Committee of Inquiry into Allegations of Ill-Treatment of
    Patients and Other Irregularities at the Ely Hospital, Cardiff*, HMSO,
    Cmnd. 3795, 1969.
Report of the Farleigh Hospital Committee of Inquiry, HMSO, Cmnd.
    4557, 1971.
Report of the Committee of Inquiry into Whittingham Hospital, HMSO,
    Cmnd. 4861, 1972.
Statistical Report Series No. 3: *The Activities of Psychiatric Hospitals:
    A Regional Comparison* (*Mental Hospitals and Units*, 1964), published
    1968.

Statistical Report Series No. 4: *Psychiatric Hospitals and Units in England and Wales: in-patient statistics from the Mental Health Enquiry for the years 1964, 1965 and 1966*, published 1969.

Statistical Report Series No. 5: *Psychiatric Hospitals and Units in England and Wales: in-patient statistics from the Mental Health Enquiry, 1967*, published 1969.

Statistical Report Series No. 6: *Facilities and Services of Psychiatric Hospitals in England and Wales, 1966*, published 1969.

Statistical Report Series No. 7: *Pilot Survey of Patients Attending Day Hospitals, 1967*, published 1969.

Statistical Report Series No. 8: *A Psychiatric Case Register*, published 1969.

Statistical Report Series No. 9: *Facilities and Services of Psychiatric Hospitals in England and Wales, 1967*, published 1969.

Statistical Report Series No. 10: *Facilities and Services of Psychiatric Hospitals in England and Wales, 1969*, published 1970.

Statistical Report Series No. 11: *Psychiatric Hospitals and Units in England and Wales: in-patient statistics for 1968.*

Statistical Report Series No. 12: *Psychiatric Hospitals in England and Wales: in-patient statistics for 1969.*

Statistical Report Series No. 13: Nottingham Case-Register. *Findings 1962–9.*

General Register Office

Studies on Medical and Population Subjects No. 16: *Area of Residence of Mental Hospital Patients. Admissions to Mental Hospitals in England and Wales in 1957 according to Area of Residence, Diagnosis, Sex and Age*, published 1962.

Studies on Medical and Population Subjects No. 18: *A Cohort Study of Patients first admitted to Mental Hospitals in 1954 and 1955*, by E. M. Brooke, published 1963.

Registrar-General's Statistical Review: *Supplements on Mental Health*, 1952–3, 1954–6, 1957–8, 1959 and 1960.

Hansard's Parliamentary Debates, 1804 to date.

Home Office, Department of Education and Science, Ministry of Hou..ing and Local Government, Ministry of Health.

Report of the Committee on Local Authority and Allied Personal Social Services, HMSO, Cmnd. 3703, 1968 (Seebohm Report).

House of Commons Journal.

House of Commons Select Committees, Reports.
— *on Criminal and Pauper Lunatics*, 1807.
— on *Lunatics*, 1859–60.
— *Madhouses*, 1763 (also published in HCJ).
— on *Madhouses*, 1815 (3 reports published May-July and subsequently reprinted in one volume).

— *Madhouses*, 1816 (3 reports published April-June and subsequently bound as one volume).
— on the *Operation of the Lunacy Law*, 1877–8.
— on *Pauper Lunatics in the County of Middlesex*, and on *Lunatic Asylums*, 1827.
— on the *Poor Law Amendment Act of 1834*, 1836, 3 vols.

House of Lords Journal.

Lunacy Commissioners Annual Reports, 1845–1912.

Metropolitan Commissioners in Lunacy.
Report to the Lord Chancellor, 1844.
Statutory Reports, 1830—see unpublished papers.

Ministry of Health
The Administrative Structure of the Medical and Related Services in England and Wales, HMSO, 1968 (Green Paper).
Annual Reports, part I, 1948–67.
Departmental Committees, Reports of
— on the *Administration of Public Mental Hospitals*, 1922.
— on *Senior Nursing Staff Structure*, HMSO, 1966 (Salmon Report).
— on *Social Workers in the Mental Health Services*, HMSO, Cmnd. 8260, 1951 (Mackintosh Report).
— on *Sterilisation*, 1934 (Brock Report).
— on the *Voluntary Mental Health Services*, 1939 (Feversham Report).
Findings and Recommendations Following Enquiries into Allegations concerning the Care of Elderly Patients in certain Hospitals, HMSO, Cmnd. 3687, 1968.
Health and Welfare: the Development of Community Care, HMSO, Cmnd. 1973, 1963, and subsequent revisions.
Hospital Plan for England and Wales, HMSO, Cmnd. 1604, 1962.
Joint Working Party: *Report on Medical Staffing Structure in the Hospital Service*, 1961 (Platt Report).
Joint Working Party: *Report on the Organisation of Medical Work in Hospitals*, HMSO, 1967 (Cogwheel Report).
Report on Public Health and Medical Subjects, no. 116. *A Census of Patients in Psychiatric Beds, 1963*, published 1967.
Working Party, *Report on Social Workers in the Local Authority Health and Welfare Services*, HMSO, 1959 (Younghusband Report).

Ministry of Health and Board of Control
The National Health Service Act 1946: Provisions Relating to the Mental Health Services, 1948.

Inter-departmental Committee (Ministry of Health, Ministry of Labour, Ministry of Pensions etc.)
Social Insurance and the Allied Services, 1942 (Beveridge Report).

Parliamentary History of England from the earliest period to the year 1803, 1806–19, 34 vols.

Poor Law Commission
Report of His Majesty's Commissioners for Inquiries into the Administration and Practical Operation of the Poor Law, 1834.
1st Annual Report of the Poor Law Commissioners, 1835.
11th Annual Report of the Poor Law Commissioners, 1845.
Official Circulars, 1835–54, 2 vols.

Royal Commissions, Reports
— on the *Care of the Feeble-minded*, 1908 (Radnor Report).
— on the *Laws relating to Mental Illness and Mental Deficiency*, Cmnd. 169, 1957.
— on *Lunacy and Mental Disorder*, 1926 (Macmillan Report).
— on *Medical Education*, 1968 (Todd Report).
— on the *Poor Laws*, 1909.

Woodfall's Parliamentary Debates, 1794–1803, 33 vols.

World Health Organisation:
Report of Third Expert Committee on Mental Health, Technical Report Series No. 73, September 1953.

Unpublished papers
Brill, H. and Patton, R. E., *The Impact of Modern Chemotherapy on Hospital Organisation, Psychiatric Care and Public Policies*. No date, about 1961.
Cornwall Asylum, records (at St Lawrence's Hospital, Bodmin).
Department of Health and Social Security, *Consultative Document on the Future of the National Health Service*, 1971; *Hospital Services for the Mentally Ill*, 1971.
Eugenics Education Society; minutes of Council 1907–12 (at the Eugenics Society).
Eugenics Education Society, Manchester Branch, minutes 1912 (at the Eugenics Society).
Eugenics Society and the National Association for the Care of the Feeble-Minded, records (at the Eugenics Society).
Lancaster Asylum, records (at County Record Office, Preston).
Manchester Royal Infirmary and Royal Lunatic Hospital, records (at Manchester Royal Infirmary).
Metropolitan Commissioners in Lunacy, *Statutory Reports*, 1830 (in Public Record Office, London).
Nottingham Asylum, records (at Saxondale Hospital).
Pinsent, private papers of Dame Ellen Pinsent, in the possession of the late Lady Adrian.
The Retreat, records and case-papers, in the possession of the Physician Superintendent and Trustees.
Stafford Asylum, records (at St George's Hospital, Stafford).
Thane, the Lectures of Sir George Thane, Professor of Anatomy in the University of London, 1877–1919. Notes taken by Dr H. A. Harris, no date (in University College Hospital Library, London.)

Journals

Asylum Journal, Journal of Mental Science, now *British Journal of Psychiatry*
Biometrika
British Journal of Preventive and Social Medicine
British Medical Journal
Comprehensive Psychiatry
Hospital and Social Services Journal
Human Relations
International Journal of Social Psychiatry
Lancet
London Kalendar (1814, 1815 and 1816)
Mental Health
Mental Hygiene (USA)
Information Psychiatrique (France)
Practitioner

Books and Articles

Adams, M. (ed.), *The Mentally Subnormal: the Social Casework Approach*, Heinemann, 1960.

AEGIS (Association for the Elderly in Government Institutions), see Robb.

Ainsworth, W. Harrison, *Jack Sheppard: a romance* (illustrated by Cruickshank), 1879.

Alleged Lunatics Friend Society, *Annual Report*, 1851.

An Account of Workhouses, see Workhouses.

Apte, R. Z., *Halfway Houses*, Bell, 1968.

Ashdown, M. and Brown, S. Clement, *Social Service and Mental Health*, Routledge & Kegan Paul, 1953.

Aspinall, A., *Politics and the Press, 1780–1850*, Home & Van Thal, 1949.

Association for Psychiatric Social Workers, *Training for Social Work*, no date, probably early 1950s.

Asylum for Idiots, Park House, Highgate, *Brochure*, 1847.

Atlay, J. B., *The Victorian Chancellors*, Smith, Elder, 1906–8.

Aubrey, J., *Natural History of Wiltshire*, David & Charles, 1969.

Baines, E., *History, Directory and Gazetteer of the County of York*, Leeds Mercury Office, 1823.

Baker, A. A., 'Pulling down the Old Mental Hospital', *Lancet*, 25 March 1961, pp. 656–7.

Baldwin, J. A., *The Mental Hospital in the Psychiatric Service*, Oxford UP, 1971.

Barr, A. W., *Mental Defectives: their History, Treatment and Training*, Rebman, 1904.

Barton, W. Russell, *Institutional Neurosis*, Wright, Bristol, 1959.

Battelle, M., *Rapport au Conseil Général des Hospices de Paris sur les établissements aliénés d'Angleterre, et sur ceux de Bicêtre et de la Salpêtrière*, Paris, 1845.

Battie, Dr, *Battie on Madness*, London, 1758.

Bentham, J., *Letters on the Management of the Poor*, Dublin, 1796, (including the 'Panopticon').

— *Works of Jeremy Bentham*, ed. Bowring, 1843, 11 vols.

Bethlem, *Bethlem Hospital: Brochure prepared for the official opening of the new buildings*, July 1930.

— *Charters of the Royal Hospitals of Bridewell and Bethlem*, 1807.

— *Sketches in Bedlam*, by a Constant Observer, 1823.

Bickerton, T. H., *A Medical History of Liverpool from the earliest days to the year 1920*, Murray, 1936.

Bickmore, A., *Industries for the Feeble Minded*, Bartholomew Press, 1913.

Bierer, J., *The Day Hospital*, H. K. Lewis, 1951.

— *Therapeutic Social Clubs*, H. K. Lewis, no date, probably early 1950s.

— 'A Review of Modern Trends in Psychiatry and their Consequences for the Psychiatric Services', *Proc. Thirteenth International Hospital Congress*, Paris, 1963.

Bion, W. R., 'Experiences in Groups', *Human Relations*, vols. 1–4, 1947–51. Published with other papers by Tavistock Publications, 1961.

Blacker, C. P., *Neurosis and the Mental Health Services*, Oxford UP, 1946.

Bosanquet, H., *Social Work in London—A History of the Charity Organisation Society*, Murray, 1914.

Bowley, A. L., *Wages in the United Kingdom in the Nineteenth Century*, Cambridge UP, 1900.

Boyd, R., *Report on Lunatics Chargeable to the Parish of St Marylebone*, 1844.

Brain, W. R. and Strauss, E. B., *Recent Advances in Neurology and Neuropsychiatry*, J. and A. Churchill, 5th ed, 1945.

Brill, H., *The Impact of Psychotropic Drugs on the Structure, Function and Future of Psychiatric Services in Hospitals*, Elsevier Publishing Co. Amsterdam; reprinted from *Neuro-psychopharmacology*, no date, probably about 1961.

Bristol Corporation of the Poor, *Selected Records, 1696–1834*, ed. E. E. Butcher, Bristol Record Society Publications, 1932.

Brockbank, E. M., *A Short History of Cheadle Royal from its Foundation in 1766*, Sherratt & Hughes, Manchester, 1934.

Brooke, E. M., *Cohort Study:* see General Register Office.

— *Trends in the Mental Hospital Population:* see Tooth.

Brown, G. W. and Wing, J., 'A Comprehensive Clinical and Social Survey of Three Mental Hospitals', *Sociological Review Monograph* No. 5, July 1962.

Brown, R. G. S., 'The Consultative Document on the Future of the Health Service', in *A Year Book of Social Policy*, ed. Jones, Routledge & Kegan Paul, 1971.

Browne, T., *What Asylums were, are and ought to be*, Black, Edinburgh, 1837.

Buckham, *Insanity considered in its Medico-legal Relations*, Philadelphia, 1883.

Burrows, G. M., *Commentaries on the Causes of Insanity*, Underwood, 1828.

Burton, Robert, *The Anatomy of Melancholy*, 1621; 1821 ed., 2 vols.

Butler, Samuel, *The Analogy of Religion*, 1736.

Cambridge, University of, *Report on Postgraduate Medical School Symposium on Depression*, 1960.

Cappe, Catherine, *Thoughts on the Desirableness and Utility of Ladies Visiting the Female Wards of Hospitals and Lunatic Asylums*, 1816.

Carse, J., *The Worthing Experiment*, Graylingwell Hospital, 1958.

Carstairs, G. M., 'Advances in Psychological Medicine', *The Practitioner, Symposium on Advances in Treatment*, no. 1, 1961, vol. 187, 495–504.

Cartwright, A., *Human Relations and Hospital Care*, Routledge & Kegan Paul, 1964.

Cattell, J. McKeen, 'Address before the American Psychological Association', *Psychological Review*, 3, 2.

Central Association for the Care of the Mentally Defective, *Annual Reports*, 1915–23

Central Association for Mental Welfare, *Annual Reports*, 1924–44.

Chaplin, A., *Medicine in England during the reign of George III*, Royal College of Physicians, Fitzpatrick Lecture, 1919.

Charity Organisation Society, *Report of Sub-Committee on the Education and Care of Idiots, Imbeciles and Harmless Lunatics*, Charity Organisation Series, 1877.

Charlesworth, E. P., *Considerations on the Moral Management of Insane Persons*, 1828.

Cheyne, G., *The English Malady, or, A Treatise of Nervous Disorders of All Kinds*, 1733.

Clark, David H., *Administrative Psychiatry*, Tavistock 1964.

Clark, D. Stafford, *Psychiatry Today*, Penguin Books, 1952.

Clark, Sir J., *Memoir of Dr Conolly*, Murray, 1869.

Clouston, T., 'Training Course in Psychiatry', *J. Ment. Sci.*, April 1911.

Collins, W., *The Woman in White*, 1st edn. 1869; Collins Classics, 1952.

Conolly, J., *An Inquiry Concerning the Indications of Insanity*, 1830.

— *On the Treatment of Insanity*, London, 1856.

Cooper, A. B. and Early, D. F., 'Evolution in the Mental Hospital: Reviewing a Hospital Population', *Br. Med. J.*, 3 June 1961

Cooper, Beryl P., *Minds Matter: A New Approach to Mental Health*, Bow Group, Conservative Political Centre, 1958.

Cooper, D., *Psychiatry and Anti-psychiatry*, Tavistock Publications, 1967.

— *The Death of the Family*, Allen Lane, the Penguin Press, 1971.

Crowther, Bryan (Surgeon to Bethlem and Bridewell), *Practical Remarks on Insanity*, 1811.

Crowther, Caleb (Senior Physician to the West Riding Asylum), *Observations on the Management of the Insane*, 1838.

Curran, D. and Guttman, E., *Psychological Medicine*, Livingstone, Edinburgh, 3rd ed., 1949.

David, Henry C., (ed.), *International Trends in Mental Health*, McGraw-Hill, 1964.

Davis, O. C. and Wilshire, F. A., *Mentality and the Criminal Law*, Simpkin Marshall, 1935.

Dendy, Mary, see Lapage, C. P.

Dicks, H. V., *Fifty Years of the Tavistock Clinic*, Routledge & Kegan Paul, 1970.

Dreikurs, R., 'Group Psychotherapy and the Third Revolution in Psychiatry', *Int. J. Soc. Psychiat.*, 1, 3.

Dreikurs, R. and Corsini, N., 'Twenty years of Group Psychotherapy', *Am. J. Psych.*, Feb. 1954.

Dugdale, R. L., *The Jukes: A Study in Crime, Disease and Heredity*, 1877; 4th ed., Putnam, 1910.

East, Sir W. Norwood, *An Introduction to Forensic Psychiatry in the Criminal Courts*, J. & A. Churchill, 1927.

Eden, Sir Frederick, *The State of the Poor, or, A History of the Labouring Classes in England, etc.*, 1797 3 vols.

Ellis, Sir William C., *A Letter to Thomas Thompson, Esq., containing Considerations on the Necessity of Proper Places being provided by the Legislature for the Reception of all Insane Persons*, Hull, 1815.

— *A Treatise on the Nature, Causes, Symptoms and Treatment of Insanity*, 1838.

Epistle to Mr Ewart, MP, see Hanwell.

Estabrook, A. H., *The Jukes in 1915*, Carnegie Institute of Washington, 1916.

Eugenics Education Society, *Annual Reports*, 1908–26.

Eugenics Society, *Annual Reports*, 1926–54.

Farndale, W. A. J., *The Day Hospital Movement in Great Britain*, Pergamon, 1961.

Farndale, W. A. J. (ed.), *Trends in the National Health Service*, Pergamon, 1964, see also Freeman.

Ferriar, J., *Medical Histories and Reflections*, Warrington, 1792.

Finer, S. E., *Life and Times of Sir Edwin Chadwick*, Methuen, 1952.

Flügel, J. C., *A Hundred Years of Psychology, 1833–1933*, Duckworth, 1933.

Foss, E., *The Judges of England from the Time of the Conquest*, 1848–70. 9 vols.

Foulkes, S. H., 'Group Analysis', *Lancet*, 2 March 1946.

Foulkes, S. H. and Anthony, E. J., *Group Psychotherapy: the Psychoanalytic Approach*, Pelican Books, 1957.

Freeman, H. (ed.), *Psychiatric Hospital Care*, Ballière, Tindall, 1964.

— and Farndale, W. A. J. (ed.), *New Aspects of the Mental Health Services*, Pergamon, 1967.

—and Farndale, W. A. J. (ed.), *Trends in the Mental Health Services*, Pergamon, 1963.

Galton, Sir Francis, *Hereditary Genius*, 1869.

— 'Local Associations for Promoting Eugenics', *Nature*, 22 October 1908.

— *Natural Inheritance*, 1889.

— *The Problem of the Feeble-Minded*, 1909.

Gardiner Hill, R., see Hill.

Garratt, F. N., Lowe, C. R. and McKeown, T., 'The Institutional Care of the Mentally Ill', *Lancet*, 29 March 1958, pp. 682–4.

— Investigation of the Medical and Social Needs of Patients in Mental Hospitals', *Br. J. Prev. Soc. Med.*, vol. 11, no. 4, October 1957; vol. 12, no. 1, January 1958.

Gerard, James, and others, *An Address to the Magistrates of the County of Lancaster on the Situation Proposed for the Intended County Lunatic*

Asylum, Liverpool, 1810.

Goddard, H., *The Kallikak Family*, 1912.

Goddard, H. A. et al., *The Work of the Mental Nurse*, Manchester UP, 1955.

Goffman, E., *Asylums: essays on the social situation of mental patients and other inmates*, Doubleday, New York, 1962.

Goldsmith, M., *Franz Anton Mesmer: The History of an Idea*, Baker, 1934.

Gore, C. P., Jones, K., Taylor, W. and Ward, B., 'Needs and Beds: A Regional Census of Psychiatric Patients', *Lancet*, 24 August 1964, pp. 457–60.

Granville, J. Mortimer, *The Care and Cure of the Insane*, London, 1877.

Grenville, Robert, *The Grenville Papers*, ed. W. J. Smith, Murray, 1952, 2 vols.

Gray, B. Kirkman, *A History of English Philanthropy from the Dissolution of the Monasteries to the Taking of the First Census*, 1905.

Greenblatt, M., Levinson, D. J. and Williams, R. H., *The Patient and the Mental Hospital*, Free Press, Chicago, 1957.

Greville, R. Fulke, *The Diaries of Robert Fulke Greville*, ed. F. McKno Bladen, Bodley Head, 1930.

Grice, J. Watson, *National and Local Finance*, 1910.

Halévy, E., *A History of the English People in the Nineteenth Century, Vol. 1, England in 1815*. 2nd English ed., Benn, 1949.

Halliday, Sir Andrew, *A General View of the Present State of Lunatics and Lunatic Asylums in Great Britain and Ireland, and in some otherKingdoms, 1828*.

Halsbury, Earl, *Laws of England*, Butterworth, 1907–17, 31 vols.

Halsey, A. H. (ed), *Trends in British Society since 1900*, Macmillan, 1972.

Hassall, C. and Hellon, C. P., 'Survey of a Long stay Population in a Psychiatric Hospital', *Br. J. Psychiat.*, vol. 110, 1964.

Hammond, J. L and Barbara, *Lord Shaftesbury*, 4th ed., Penguin Books, 1936.

Hanwell, *An Epistle addressed to Mr Ewart, MP, on his withdrawing his Notice of Motion for an Enquiry into the Total Abolition of all Restraint on the Pauper Lunatics at Hanwell*. By a Rev. Gentleman not under Restraint. Hanwell, 1841. Hume Tracts, University College Library, London.

Hargreaves, G. R., *Psychiatry and the Public Health*. Heath Clark Lectures, University of London, Oxford UP, 1958.

Hart, B., *The Psychology of Insanity*, Cambridge Manuals of Science and Literature, vol. 45, Cambridge UP, 1912.

Hartley, D., *Observations on Man*, 6th ed., 1734.

Haslam, J., *Observations on Madness and Melancholy*, 1809.
— *Considerations on the Moral Management of Insane Persons*, 1817.

Hawkins, Rev. H., 'A Plea for Convalescent Homes in connection with Asylums for the Insane Poor', (1871); 'After Care' (1879); *J. Ment. Sci.*

Herbart, F., *Lehrbuch zur Psychologie*, 1816. Translation in International Education Series, New York, 1891.

Higgins, Godfrey, *A Letter to the Right Honourable Earl Fitzwilliam respecting the Investigation which has lately taken place into the Abuses at the York Lunatic Asylum, together with various Letters, Reports etc.*, Doncaster, 1814.

Hill, R. Gardiner, *The Non Restraint System of Treatment in Lunacy*, Simpkin Marshall, 1857.

Hodder, E., *Life of Shaftesbury*, Cassell, 1887, 3 vols.

Hoenig, J. and Hamilton, M. H., *The De-segregation of the Mentally ill*, Routledge & Kegan Paul, 1969

Holland, Lord, *Memoirs of the Whig Party during my time*, Longmans, 1852–4, 2 vols.

Howard, John, *State of the Prisons in England and Wales, with Preliminary Observations and an Account of some Foreign Prisons*, 1st ed., 2 parts bound in one vol., Eyre, Warrington, 1777–80.

Hoyle, J. S. and Hawkesworth, T. S., *The Mental Health Officer's Guide*, Elsworth Bros., 1956 ed.

Hume, D., 'An Inquiry Concerning the Principles of Morals', in vol. 2 of *Essays and Treatises on Several Subjects*, Edinburgh, 1804.

Hunt, H. C., *A Retired Habitation. A History of the Retreat, York*, H. K. Lewis, 1932.

Hunt, R. C., see Milbank Memorial Fund.

Institute of Public Administration, *The Health Services: some of their Practical Problems*, Allen & Unwin, 1951.

Itard, J. M. G., *L'Education du Sauvage d'Aveyron*, 1801.

International Hospital Federation, *Proceedings of Thirteenth Hospital Congress*, Paris, 1963.

Jesse, J. Heneage, *Memoirs of the Life and Reign of George III*, 1867, 3 vols.

Joint Committee on Mental Illness and Health (USA), *Action for Mental Health*, Basic Books, New York, 1961.

Jones, Kathleen, *The Adult Population of Epileptic Colonies*, Special Studies in Epilepsy, No. 3, British Epilepsy Association, 1965.

—— *Community and Mental Health*. Proceedings of 16th Annual Meeting of the World Federation for Mental Health, Amsterdam, July 1963. Reprinted in H. C. David (ed.), op. cit.

—— *The Compassionate Society*, SPCK, 1966.

—— 'The Development of Institutional Care', *in New Thinking about Institutional Care*, Association of Social Workers, 1967.

—— *Mental Disorder and the Family*, Barnett House Occasional Papers, Oxford, 1964.

—— 'The Mental Health Services', *in* A. H. Halsey (ed.), *Trends in British Social Policy since 1900*, Macmillan, 1972.

—— *Mental Hospitals at Work* (with R. Sidebotham), Routledge & Kegan Paul, 1962.

—— *Psychiatric Social Work Comes of Age*, Presidential Address to APSW, 1967.

—— 'Problems of Mental After Care in Lancashire', *Sociological Review*, July 1954.

—— 'Revolution and Reform in the Mental Health Services', *Medical Care*, vol. i, no. 3, July–Sept. 1963.

— 'The Role and Function of the Mental Hospital', in Freeman and Farndale (ed.), *Trends in the Mental Health Services*.
— see also Gore.

Jones, L. Clark, *Clubs of the Georgian Rakes*, Columbia UP, 1942.

Jones, Maxwell, *Beyond the Therapeutic Community*, Yale UP, 1968
— *Social Psychiatry*, Tavistock, 1952.
— *Social Psychiatry in the Community, in Hospitals and in Prisons*, Charles Thomas, Springfield, Illinois, 1962.
— *Social Psychiatry in Practice*, Pelican Books, 1968.

Jones, W. Ll. Parry, *The Trade in Lunacy*, Routledge & Kegan Paul, 1972.

Keir, S., *The Royal Albert Institution*, Lancaster. Printed at the Institution, 1937.

Kirkbride, T., *On the Construction of Hospitals for the Insane*, 2nd ed., Philadelphia, 1880.

Kirkman Gray, see Gray.

Knight, Paul Slade, *Observations on the Causes, Symptoms and Treatment of Derangement of the Mind (Knight on Insanity)*, 1827.

Laing, R. D., *The Divided Self*, Tavistock, 1960.

Laing, R. D. and Esterson, A., *Sanity, Madness and the Family*, Tavistock, 1964.

Lapage, C. P., *Feeble-Mindedness in Children of School Age* (with an appendix on the colony at Sandlebridge by Mary Dendy), Manchester UP, 1920.

Leadbitter, A., *Heredity and the Social Problem Group*, Arnold, 1933.

Lomax, M., *Experiences of an Asylum Doctor*, 1921.

Macalpine, I. and Hunter, R., *George III and the Mad-Business*, Allen Lane, the Penguin Press, 1969.

McKenna, S., *Reginald McKenna, 1863–1943*, Eyre & Spottiswoode, 1948.

McKeown, T., *Medicine in Modern Society*, Allen & Unwin, 1965.
— see also *Garrett*.

Mackenzie, I., *Social Activities of the English Friends in the first half of the Nineteenth Century*, New York, 1935.

Main, T. F., 'The Hospital as a Therapeutic Community', *Bulletin of the Menninger Clinic*, X, 1946, 66–70.

Manchester Lunatic Hospital, *An Account of the Rise and Present Establishment of the Lunatic Hospital in Manchester*, J. Harrop, Manchester 1971.
— a fuller edition, 1778.

Manchester Royal Infirmary, *Rules for the Government of the Infirmary, Lunatic Hospital and Public Baths in Manchester*, 1791.

Martin, D. V., *Adventure in Psychiatry*, Bruno Cassirer, 1962.

Martin, F. M., see Rehin.

Mathews (ed.), *The Mental Health Services*, Shaw & Sons, 1948 and subsequent editions.

Mayer-Gross, W., Slater, E. and Roth, M., *Clinical Psychiatry*, Cassell, 1954.

Mead, Margaret (ed.), *Cultural Patterns and Technical Change*, UNESCO, 1955.

Medical Officer, A, 'Change in Mental Hospitals—A Therapeutic Community', *Manchester Guardian*, 28 and 29 January 1959.

Medical Services Review Committee, *Review of the Medical Services in Great Britain*. Social Assay, 1963 (Porritt Report).

Mental After Care Asociation, *Annual Reports*.

Middlebrook, S., *Newcastle-on-Tyne, its growth and achievements*, Newcastle, no date.

Milbank Memorial Fund, *Steps in the Development of Integrated Psychiatric Services*, New York, 1960.

MIND, see National Association for Mental Health.

Mitford, J., *The Crimes and Horrors of Kelly House; The Crimes and Horrors of Warburton's Private Madhouses*. Both undated, probably 1828–30. Hume Tracts, University College Hospital Library, London.

Moncrieff, J., *Mental Subnormality in London: a survey of Community Care*, PEP, undated, about 1968.

Monro, J., *Dr Monro's reply to Dr Battie*, 1758.

Monro, T., *Observations of Dr Thomas Monro upon the Evidence taken before the Commission of the Hon. House of Commons for regulating Madhouses*, Bridewell, 1816.

Morris, Cherry (ed.), *Social Casework in Great Britain*, Faber, 1950.

Morris, Pauline, *Put Away: a sociological study of institutions for the mentally retarded*, Routledge & Kegan Paul, 1969.

Murray, Margaret, *The Witch-Cult in Western Europe*, Oxford UP, 1921.

National Association for Mental Health, *Annual Reports*, 1946 to date.
— *Directory of Out-patient Facilities in England and Wales*, 1957.
— *Hostels and the Mental Health Act*, 1961.
— MIND Reports (1968–72), no. 1 *Farleigh Hospital;* no. 2 *Young Minds at risk—Psychiatric Treatment Facilities for Adolescents;* no. 3 *Stress at Work;* no. 4 *Community Care Provisions for the Mentally Ill;* no. 5 *Community Care Provisions for Mentally Handicapped Men and Women.*
— *Reports of Annual Conferences*, 1950 to date.

National Council for Civil Liberties, *50,000 Outside the Law*, London, undated.

Neild, James, *An Account of the Various Prisons of England and Wales, together with an Account of the Rise, Progress and Present State of the Society for the Discharge and Relief of Persons imprisoned for Small Debts*, . . 1802.

Nicholls, *Recollections and Reflections . . . as concerned with Public Affairs during the Reign of George III*, 2nd ed., 1822, 2 vols.

O'Connor, N. and Tizard, J., *The Social Problem of Mental Deficiency*, Oxford UP, 1956.

O'Donoghue, *The Story of Bethlehem Hospital from its Foundation in 1247*, 1913.

Osmund, see Siegler.

Paternoster, R., *The Madhouse System*, 1841.

Paul, Sir George Onesiphorus, 'Suggestions of Sir George Oneisphorus Paul, Bart., to Earl Spencer', 1806, published as Appendix IV of the *Report of the Select Committee of 1807 on Criminal and Pauper Lunatics* (qv).
— *Doubts Concerning the Expediency of immediately proceeding to provide a Lunatic Asylum for the County of Gloucester*. Printed at the office of the *Gloucester Journal*, 1813.

Pearson, Karl, *The Life, Letters and Labours of Francis Galton*, Cambridge UP, 1914, 4 vols.

Penrose, L. S., *The Biology of Mental Defect*, Sidgwick & Jackson, 1949.

Percy, Reuben and Percy, Sholto (pseud.), *The Percy Anecdotes*, 1870, 3 vols.

Pinel, Philippe, *L'Alienation Mentale*, translated as *A Treatise on Insanity*, by D. D. Davis, Sheffield, 1806.

Pinsent, Dame Ellen (Mrs Hume Pinsent), 'On the Permanent Care of the Feeble-Minded', *Lancet*, 21 February 1903.
— *The Oxford Mental Health Services*, Oxford UP, 1937.

Porritt, see *Medical Services Review Committee*.

Raffald, E., *Raffald's Manchester Directory*.

Rapaport, R., *Community as Doctor*, Tavistock, 1961.

Rehin, G. and Martin, F. M., *Patterns of Performance in Community Care*, Oxford UP, 1968.
— *Psychiatric Services in 1975*, PEP, vol. xxix, no. 468, 1963.

Reid, D. D., *Epidemiological Methods in the Study of Mental Disorders*. Public Health Papers no. 2, World Health Organisation, 1960.

Retreat, *The State of an Institution called the Retreat for Persons afflicted with Disorders of the Mind* (anon.), Whitby, 1803.

Rigby, E., *Further Facts relating to the Care of the Poor in the City of Norwich*, 1812.

Robb, Barbara (ed.), *Sans Everything—A Case to Answer*, Nelson, 1967.

Robinson, Kenneth, *Policy for Mental Health*, Fabian Research Series, 1958.

Rooff, M., *Voluntary Societies and Social Policy*, Routledge & Kegan Paul, 1957.

Rose, George, *Diaries and Correspondence of the Rt Hon. George Rose*, ed. Vernon Harcourt, Bentley, 1860, 2 vols.
— *Observations on the Poor Laws and the Management of the Poor*, 2nd ed., Hatchard, 1805.

Ross, J. Stirling, *The National Health Service in Great Britain*, Oxford UP, 1952.

Roth, (Sir) Martin, see Mayer-Gross.

Rothman, D. J., *The Discovery of the Asylum: social order and disorder in the New Republic*, Little, Brown, New York, 1971.

Royal College of Psychiatry, see Royal Medico-Psychological Association.

Royal Medico-Psychological Association, *Report of Medical Planning Committee: a Memorandum on the future organisation of the Psychiatric Services*, RMPA, 1945.

Runwell Hospital, *Brochure* prepared for the official opening, 1937.

Selborne, Roundell Palmer, 1st Earl, *Memoirs, Personal and Political, 1865–1895*, Macmillan, 1898.

Semelaigne, Rene, *Philippe Pinel et son Oeuvre*, Paris, 1888.

Shaftesbury, (ed. Rand), *The Life, Letters and Philosophical Regimen of the Third Earl of Shaftesbury*, New York, 1900.

Shaftesbury, Seventh Earl, see Hammond.

Shepherd, M., Goodman, N., and Watt, D. C., 'The Application of Hospital Statistics in the Evaluation of Pharmacotherapy in a Psychiatric Population', *Comprehensive Psychiatry*, II, 1 February 1961.

Siegler, M., Osmund, H. and Mann, H., 'Laing's Models of Madness', *Br. J. Psychiat.*, 115 (1969), 947–58.

Siegler, M. and Osmund, H., 'Goffman's Model of Mental Illness', *B.J. Psychiat.*, 119 (1971), 419–24.

Sketches in Bethlem, see Bethlem.

Society for the Improvement of Prison Discipline, *5th Report*, 1823; *7th Report*, 1827.

Somervell, D. C., *English Thought in the Nineteenth Century*, Methuen, 1964.

Sprigge, S. S., *Life and Times of Thomas Wakley*, Longmans, Green, 1897.

Stafford-Clark, D., see Clark.

Stanton, A. H. and Schwarz, M. S., *The Patient and the Mental Hospital*, Tavistock, 1954.

Stirling Ross, see Ross.

Summers, Montague, *The History of Witchcraft and Demonology*, Kegan Paul, 1926.

Surrey Asylum, *Rules*. Printed with *Reports of Visiting Justices of Surrey Asylum, 1844–6*, 1847.

Szasz, T. S., *The Myth of Mental Illness*, Secker & Warburg, 1962.

Taylor, Wallis, see Gore.

Thurnam, J., *Observations on the Statistics of Insanity*, Simpkin Marshall, 1845.

Timms, N., *Psychiatric Social Work in Great Britain*, Routledge & Kegan Paul, 1964.

Titmuss, R. M., 'Problems of Social Policy', *History of World War II*, UK Civil Series, HMSO and Longmans, 1950.

Tizard, J., *Community Services for the Mentally Handicapped*, Oxford UP, 1964.

Tizard, J. and Grad, J., *The Mentally Handicapped and their Families*, Oxford UP, 1961.

— see also O'Connor.

Tooth, G. C. and Brooke, E., 'Trends in the Mental Hospital Population and their effect on Future Planning', *Lancet*, 1 April 1961.

Townsend, P., *The Last Refuge: a survey of Residential Institutions and Homes for the Aged in England and Wales*, Routledge & Kegan Paul, 1962.

Tredgold, R. F., *Mental Deficiency*, 1st ed., Ballière, Tindall and Cox, 1908.

Tuke, D. H., *Chapters in the History of the Insane in the British Isles*, Kegan Paul, 1882.

Tuke, S., *A Description of the Retreat*, York, 1813.

Ullman, L. P., *Institution and Outcome*, Pergamon, 1967.

Verba, S., *Small Groups and Political Behaviour: a study of leadership*, Princeton UP, 1961.

Walk, A., 'Mental Hospitals', in *The Evolution of Hospitals in Britain*, Pitman Medical Publishing Co., 1958.

— 'The History of Mental Nursing', *J. Ment. Sci.* 107, 446, January 1966.

Walk, A., with D. L. Walker, 'Gloucester and the Beginnings of the RMPA', *J. Ment. Sci.*, 107, 449, July 1961.

Ward, Brian, see Gore.

Warneford Asylum, *Refutation of the Assertions made by the writer of an article in the Quarterly Review for October* 1844 . . . *as far as they relate to the Conduct and Practice of the Warneford Asylum*, Oxford, 1844.

Webb, Sidney and Webb, Beatrice, *Grants in Aid*, 1911.

— *English Poor Law History*, 3 vols., being vols. 7–9 for the series. *Government from the Revolution to the Municipal Corporation Act*, published 1900–29, 9 vols.

— *English Poor Law Policy*, 1910.

Wedgwood, Josiah, *Memoirs of a Fighting Life*, 1940.

Welfare, Marjorie U., 'Dame Evelyn Fox'. Reprint from *Social Service*, Spring 1955.

Wesley, John, *Primitive Physick, or An Easy and Natural Way of Curing Most Diseases*, 1st ed., 1780.

Willcocks, A. J., *The Creation of the National Health Service*, Routledge & Kegan Paul, 1967.

Willey, B., *The Eighteenth Century Background*, Chatto & Windus, 1940.

Wing, J. K., Bennett, D. H., and Denham, J., *The Industrial Rehabilitation of Long-stay Schizophrenic Patients*, Medical Research Council Memorandum no. 42, HMSO, 1964.

— see also Brown, G.

Workhouses, *An Account of Several Workhouses in Great Britain in the year 1732, shewing their original number and the particular management of them at the above period. With many useful remarks on the state of the poor* (anon.), 3rd ed., 1786.

Wormald, J. and Wormald, S., *A Guide to the Mental Deficiency Act, 1913*, King, 1913.

Younghusband, Dame Eileen, *The Employment and Training of Social Workers*, Carnegie UK Trust, 1947.

— *Social Work in Britain*, Carnegie UK Trust, 1951.

— see also Ministry of Health, Working Party, *Report*, 1959.

Zeitlyn, B. B., 'The Therapeutic Community—Fact or Fiction?' *Br. J. Psychiat.*, 113, (1967), 1083–6.

Zilboorg, G. and Henrey, G., *History of Medical Psychology*, Norton, New York, 1941.

Index

405

International Library of Sociology

Edited by

John Rex

University of Warwick

Founded by

Karl Mannheim

as The International Library of Sociology
and Social Reconstruction

*This Catalogue also contains other Social Science
series published by Routledge*

Routledge & Kegan Paul   London and Boston

68-74 Carter Lane London EC4V 5EL
9 Park Street Boston Mass 02108

Contents

● *Books so marked are available in paperback*
All books are in Metric Demy 8vo format (216 × 138mm approx.)

GENERAL SOCIOLOGY

Belshaw, Cyril. The Conditions of Social Performance. *An Exploratory Theory. 144 pp.*

Brown, Robert. Explanation in Social Science. *208 pp.*

Cain, Maureen E. Society and the Policeman's Role. *About 300 pp.*

Gibson, Quentin. The Logic of Social Enquiry. *240 pp.*

Homans, George C. Sentiments and Activities: *Essays in Social Science. 336 pp.*

Isajiw, Wsevold W. Causation and Functionalism in Sociology. *165 pp.*

Johnson, Harry M. Sociology: *a Systematic Introduction. Foreword by Robert K. Merton. 710 pp.*

Mannheim, Karl. Essays on Sociology and Social Psychology. *Edited by Paul Keckskemeti. With Editorial Note by Adolph Lowe. 344 pp.*

Systematic Sociology: *An Introduction to the Study of Society. Edited by J. S. Erös and Professor W. A. C. Stewart. 220 pp.*

Martindale, Don. The Nature and Types of Sociological Theory. *292 pp.*

● **Maus, Heinz.** A Short History of Sociology. *234 pp.*

Mey, Harald. Field-Theory. *A Study of its Application in the Social Sciences. 352 pp.*

Myrdal, Gunnar. Value in Social Theory: *A Collection of Essays on Methodology. Edited by Paul Streeten. 332 pp.*

Ogburn, William F., and **Nimkoff, Meyer F.** A Handbook of Sociology. *Preface by Karl Mannheim. 656 pp. 46 figures. 35 tables.*

Parsons, Talcott, and **Smelser, Neil J.** Economy and Society: *A Study in the Integration of Economic and Social Theory. 362 pp.*

● **Rex, John.** Key Problems of Sociological Theory. *220 pp.*

Stark, Werner. The Fundamental Forms of Social Thought. *280 pp.*

FOREIGN CLASSICS OF SOCIOLOGY

● **Durkheim, Emile.** Suicide. *A Study in Sociology. Edited and with an Introduction by George Simpson. 404 pp.*

Professional Ethics and Civic Morals. *Translated by Cornelia Brookfield. 288 pp.*

● **Gerth, H. H.,** and **Mills, C. Wright.** From Max Weber: *Essays in Sociology. 502 pp.*

Tönnies, Ferdinand. Community and Association. *(Gemeinschaft und Gesellschaft.) Translated and Supplemented by Charles P. Loomis. Foreword by Pitirim A. Sorokin. 334 pp.*

SOCIAL STRUCTURE

Andreski, Stanislav. Military Organization and Society. *Foreword by Professor A. R. Radcliffe-Brown. 226 pp. 1 folder.*

● **Cole, G. D. H.** Studies in Class Structure. *220 p.*

Coontz, Sydney H. Population Theories and the Economic Interpretation. *202 pp.*

Coser, Lewis. The Functions of Social Conflict. *204 pp.*

Dickie-Clark, H. F. Marginal Situation: *A Sociological Study of a Coloured Group. 240 pp. 11 tables.*

Glass, D. V. (Ed.). Social Mobility in Britain. *Contributions by J. Berent, T. Bottomore, R. C. Chambers, J. Floud, D. V. Glass, J. R. Hall, H. T. Himmelweit, R. K. Kelsall, F. M. Martin, C. A. Moser, R. Mukherjee, and W. Ziegel. 420 pp.*

Glaser, Barney, and **Strauss, Anselm L.** Status Passage. *A Formal Theory. 208 pp.*

Jones, Garth N. Planned Organizational Change: *An Exploratory Study Using an Empirical Approach. 268 pp.*

Kelsall, R. K. Higher Civil Servants in Britain: *From 1870 to the Present Day. 268 pp. 31 tables.*

König, René. The Community. *232 pp. Illustrated.*

● **Lawton, Denis.** Social Class, Language and Education. *192 pp.*

McLeish, John. The Theory of Social Change: *Four Views Considered. 128 pp.*

Marsh, David C. The Changing Social Structure in England and Wales, 1871-1961. *272 pp.*

Mouzelis, Nicos. Organization and Bureaucracy. *An Analysis of Modern Theories. 240 pp.*

Mulkay, M. J. Functionalism, Exchange and Theoretical Strategy. *272 pp.*

Ossowski, Stanislaw. Class Structure in the Social Consciousness. *210 pp.*

SOCIOLOGY AND POLITICS

Crick, Bernard. The American Science of Politics: *Its Origins and Conditions. 284 pp.*

Hertz, Frederick. Nationality in History and Politics: *A Psychology and Sociology of National Sentiment and Nationalism. 432 pp.*

Kornhauser, William. The Politics of Mass Society. *272 pp. 20 tables.*

Laidler, Harry W. History of Socialism. *Social-Economic Movements: An Historical and Comparative Survey of Socialism, Communism, Co-operation, Utopianism; and other Systems of Reform and Reconstruction. 992 pp.*

Mannheim, Karl. Freedom, Power and Democratic Planning. *Edited by Hans Gerth and Ernest K. Bramstedt. 424 pp.*

Mansur, Fatma. Process of Independence. *Foreword by A. H. Hanson. 208 pp.*

Martin, David A. Pacificism: *an Historical and Sociological Study. 262 pp.*

Myrdal, Gunnar. The Political Element in the Development of Economic Theory. *Translated from the German by Paul Streeten. 282 pp.*

Verney, Douglas V. The Analysis of Political Systems. *264 pp.*

Wootton, Graham. Workers, Unions and the State. *188 pp.*

FOREIGN AFFAIRS: THEIR SOCIAL, POLITICAL AND ECONOMIC FOUNDATIONS

Bonné, Alfred. State and Economics in the Middle East: *A Society in Transition. 482 pp.*
Studies in Economic Development: *with special reference to Conditions in the Under-developed Areas of Western Asia and India. 322 pp. 84 tables.*
Mayer, J. P. Political Thought in France from the Revolution to the Fifth Republic. *164 pp.*

CRIMINOLOGY

Ancel, Marc. Social Defence: *A Modern Approach to Criminal Problems. Foreword by Leon Radzinowicz. 240 pp.*
Cloward, Richard A., and **Ohlin, Lloyd E.** Delinquency and Opportunity: *A Theory of Delinquent Gangs. 248 pp.*
Downes, David M. The Delinquent Solution. *A Study in Subcultural Theory. 296 pp.*
Dunlop, A. B., and **McCabe, S.** Young Men in Detention Centres. *192 pp.*
Friedlander, Kate. The Psycho-Analytical Approach to Juvenile Delinquency: *Theory, Case Studies, Treatment. 320 pp.*
Glueck, Sheldon, and **Eleanor.** Family Environment and Delinquency. *With the statistical assistance of Rose W. Kneznek. 340 pp.*
Lopez-Rey, Manuel. Crime. *An Analytical Appraisal. 288 pp.*
Mannheim, Hermann. Comparative Criminology: *a Text Book. Two volumes. 442 pp. and 380 pp.*
Morris, Terence. The Criminal Area: *A Study in Social Ecology. Foreword by Hermann Mannheim. 232 pp. 25 tables. 4 maps.*
Trasler, Gordon. The Explanation of Criminality. *144 pp.*

SOCIAL PSYCHOLOGY

Bagley, Christopher. The Social Psychology of the Child with Epilepsy. *320 pp.*
Barbu, Zevedei. Problems of Historical Psychology. *248 pp.*
Blackburn, Julian. Psychology and the Social Pattern. *184 pp.*
● **Fleming, C. M.** Adolescence: *Its Social Psychology: With an Introduction to recent findings from the fields of Anthropology, Physiology, Medicine, Psychometrics and Sociometry. 288 pp.*
● The Social Psychology of Education: *An Introduction and Guide to Its Study. 136 pp.*
Homans, George C. The Human Group. *Foreword by Bernard DeVoto. Introduction by Robert K. Merton. 526 pp.*
Social Behaviour: *its Elementary Forms. 416 pp.*

5

Klein, Josephine. The Study of Groups. *226 pp. 31 figures. 5 tables.*

Linton, Ralph. The Cultural Background of Personality. *132 pp.*

Mayo, Elton. The Social Problems of an Industrial Civilization. *With an appendix on the Political Problem. 180 pp.*

Ottaway, A. K. C. Learning Through Group Experience. *176 pp.*

Ridder, J. C. de. The Personality of the Urban African in South Africa. *A Thematic Apperception Test Study. 196 pp. 12 plates.*

● **Rose, Arnold M.** (Ed.). Human Behaviour and Social Processes: *an Interactionist Approach. Contributions by Arnold M. Rose, Ralph H. Turner, Anselm Strauss, Everett C. Hughes, E. Franklin Frazier, Howard S. Becker, et al. 696 pp.*

Smelser, Neil J. Theory of Collective Behaviour. *448 pp.*

Stephenson, Geoffrey M. The Development of Conscience. *128 pp.*

Young, Kimball. Handbook of Social Psychology. *658 pp. 16 figures. 10 tables.*

SOCIOLOGY OF THE FAMILY

Banks, J. A. Prosperity and Parenthood: *A Study of Family Planning among The Victorian Middle Classes. 262 pp.*

Bell, Colin R. Middle Class Families: *Social and Geographical Mobility. 224 pp.*

Burton, Lindy. Vulnerable Children. *272 pp.*

Gavron, Hannah. The Captive Wife: *Conflicts of Household Mothers. 190 pp.*

George, Victor, and **Wilding, Paul.** Motherless Families. *220 pp.*

Klein, Josephine. Samples from English Cultures.
   1. Three Preliminary Studies and Aspects of Adult Life in England. *447 pp.*
   2. Child-Rearing Practices and Index. *247 pp.*

Klein, Viola. Britain's Married Women Workers. *180 pp.*
   The Feminine Character. *History of an Ideology. 244 pp.*

McWhinnie, Alexina M. Adopted Children. *How They Grow Up. 304 pp.*

Myrdal, Alva, and **Klein, Viola.** Women's Two Roles: *Home and Work. 238 pp. 27 tables.*

Parsons, Talcott, and **Bales, Robert F.** Family: *Socialization and Interaction Process. In collaboration with James Olds, Morris Zelditch and Philip E. Slater. 456 pp. 50 figures and tables.*

SOCIAL SERVICES

Bastide, Roger. The Sociology of Mental Disorder. *Translated from the French by Jean McNeil. 264 pp.*

Carlebach, Julius. Caring For Children in Trouble. *266 pp.*

Forder, R. A. (Ed.). Penelope Hall's Social Services of Modern England. *352 pp.*

George, Victor. Foster Care. *Theory and Practice. 234 pp.*
   Social Security: *Beveridge and After. 258 pp.*

● **Goetschius, George W.** Working with Community Groups. *256 pp.*

Goetschius, George W., and **Tash, Joan.** Working with Unattached Youth. *416 pp.*

Hall, M. P., and **Howes, I. V.** The Church in Social Work. *A Study of Moral Welfare Work undertaken by the Church of England. 320 pp.*

Heywood, Jean S. Children in Care: *the Development of the Service for the Deprived Child. 264 pp.*

Hoenig, J., and **Hamilton, Marian W.** The De-Segration of the Mentally Ill. *284 pp.*

Jones, Kathleen. Lunacy, Law and Conscience, *1744-1845: the Social History of the Care of the Insane. 268 pp.*

Mental Health and Social Policy, 1845-1959. *264 pp.*

King, Roy D., Raynes, Norma V., and **Tizard, Jack.** Patterns of Residential Care. *356 pp.*

Leigh, John. Young People and Leisure. *256 pp.*

Morris, Pauline. Put Away: *A Sociological Study of Institutions for the Mentally Retarded. 364 pp.*

Nokes, P. L. The Professional Task in Welfare Practice. *152 pp.*

Timms, Noel. Psychiatric Social Work in Great Britain (1939-1962). *280 pp.*

● Social Casework: *Principles and Practice. 256 pp.*

Trasler, Gordon. In Place of Parents: *A Study in Foster Care. 272 pp.*

Young, A. F., and **Ashton, E. T.** British Social Work in the Nineteenth Century. *288 pp.*

Young, A. F. Social Services in British Industry. *272 pp.*

SOCIOLOGY OF EDUCATION

Banks, Olive. Parity and Prestige in English Secondary Education: a Study in Educational Sociology. *272 pp.*

Bentwich, Joseph. Education in Israel. *224 pp. 8 pp. plates.*

● **Blyth, W. A. L.** English Primary Education. *A Sociological Description.*
  1. Schools. *232 pp.*
  2. Background. *168 pp.*

Collier, K. G. The Social Purposes of Education: *Personal and Social Values in Education. 268 pp.*

Dale, R. R., and **Griffith, S.** Down Stream: *Failure in the Grammar School. 108 pp.*

Dore, R. P. Education in Tokugawa Japan. *356 pp. 9 pp. plates*

Evans, K. M. Sociometry and Education. *158 pp.*

Foster, P. J. Education and Social Change in Ghana. *336 pp. 3 maps.*

Fraser, W. R. Education and Society in Modern France. *150 pp.*

Grace, Gerald R. Role Conflict and the Teacher. *About 200 pp.*

Hans, Nicholas. New Trends in Education in the Eighteenth Century. *278 pp. 19 tables.*

● Comparative Education: *A Study of Educational Factors and Traditions. 360 pp.*

Hargreaves, David. Interpersonal Relations and Education. *432 pp.*
● Social Relations in a Secondary School. *240 pp.*
Holmes, Brian. Problems in Education. *A Comparative Approach. 336 pp.*
King, Ronald. Values and Involvement in a Grammar School. *164 pp.*
● **Mannheim, Karl,** and **Stewart, W. A. C.** An Introduction to the Sociology of Education. *206 pp.*
Morris, Raymond N. The Sixth Form and College Entrance. *231 pp.*
● **Musgrove, F.** Youth and the Social Order. *176 pp.*
● **Ottaway, A. K. C.** Education and Society: *An Introduction to the Sociology of Education. With an Introduction by W. O. Lester Smith. 212 pp.*
Peers, Robert. Adult Education: *A Comparative Study. 398 pp.*
Pritchard, D. G. Education and the Handicapped: *1760 to 1960. 258 pp.*
Richardson, Helen. Adolescent Girls in Approved Schools. *308 pp.*
Simon, Brian, and **Joan** (Eds.). Educational Psychology in the U.S.S.R. *Introduction by Brian and Joan Simon. Translation by Joan Simon. Papers by D. N. Bogoiavlenski and N. A. Menchinskaia, D. B. Elkonin, E. A. Fleshner, Z. I. Kalmykova, G. S. Kostiuk, V. A. Krutetski, A. N. Leontiev, A. R. Luria, E. A. Milerian, R. G. Natadze, B. M. Teplov, L. S. Vygotski, L. V. Zankov. 296 pp.*
Stratta, Erica. The Education of Borstal Boys. *A Study of their Educational Experiences prior to, and during Borstal Training. 256 pp.*

SOCIOLOGY OF CULTURE

Eppel, E. M., and **M.** Adolescents and Morality: *A Study of some Moral Values and Dilemmas of Working Adolescents in the Context of a changing Climate of Opinion. Foreword by W. J. H. Sprott. 268 pp. 39 tables.*
● **Fromm, Erich.** The Fear of Freedom. *286 pp.*
The Sane Society. *400 pp.*
● **Mannheim, Karl.** Diagnosis of Our Time: *Wartime Essays of a Sociologist. 208 pp.*
Essays on the Sociology of Culture. *Edited by Ernst Mannheim in co-operation with Paul Kecskemeti. Editorial Note by Adolph Lowe. 280 pp.*
Weber, Alfred. Farewell to European History: *or The Conquest of Nihilism. Translated from the German by R. F. C. Hull. 224 pp.*

SOCIOLOGY OF RELIGION

Argyle, Michael. Religious Behaviour. *224 pp. 8 figures. 41 tables.*
Nelson, G. K. Spiritualism and Society. *313 pp.*

Stark, Werner. The Sociology of Religion. *A Study of Christendom.*
  Volume I. *Established Religion. 248 pp.*
  Volume II. *Sectarian Religion. 368 pp.*
  Volume III. *The Universal Church. 464 pp.*
  Volume IV. *Types of Religious Man. 352 pp.*
  Volume V. *Types of Religious Culture. 464 pp.*
Watt, W. Montgomery. Islam and the Integration of Society. *320 pp.*

SOCIOLOGY OF ART AND LITERATURE

Beljame, Alexandre. Men of Letters and the English Public in the Eighteenth
  Century: *1660-1744, Dryden, Addison, Pope. Edited with an Introduction
  and Notes by Bonamy Dobrée. Translated by E. O. Lorimer. 532 pp.*
Jarvie, Ian C. Towards a Sociology of the Cinema. *A Comparative Essay
  on the Structure and Functioning of a Major Entertainment Industry.
  405 pp.*
Rust, Frances S. Dance in Society. *An Analysis of the Relationships between
  the Social Dance and Society in England from the Middle Ages to the
  Present Day. 256 pp. 8 pp. of plates.*
Schücking, L. L. The Sociology of Literary Taste. *112 pp.*
Silbermann, Alphons. The Sociology of Music. *Translated from the German
  by Corbet Stewart. 222 pp.*

SOCIOLOGY OF KNOWLEDGE

Mannheim, Karl. Essays on the Sociology of Knowledge. *Edited by Paul
  Kecskemeti. Editorial note by Adolph Lowe. 353 pp.*
Stark, Werner. The Sociology of Knowledge: *An Essay in Aid of a Deeper
  Understanding of the History of Ideas. 384 pp.*

URBAN SOCIOLOGY

Ashworth, William. The Genesis of Modern British Town Planning: *A Study
  in Economic and Social History of the Nineteenth and Twentieth Centuries.
  288 pp.*
Cullingworth, J. B. Housing Needs and Planning Policy: *A Restatement of
  the Problems of Housing Need and 'Overspill' in England and Wales.
  232 pp. 44 tables. 8 maps.*
Dickinson, Robert E. City and Region: *A Geographical Interpretation.
  608 pp. 125 figures.*
  The West European City: *A Geographical Interpretation. 600 pp. 129 maps.
  29 plates.*
● The City Region in Western Europe. *320 pp. Maps.*

Humphreys, Alexander J. New Dubliners: *Urbanization and the Irish Family. Foreword by George C. Homans. 304 pp.*

Jackson, Brian. Working Class Community: *Some General Notions raised by a Series of Studies in Northern England. 192 pp.*

Jennings, Hilda. Societies in the Making: *a Study of Development and Re-development within a County Borough. Foreword by D. A. Clark. 286 pp.*

Kerr, Madeline. The People of Ship Street. *240 pp.*

● **Mann, P. H.** An Approach to Urban Sociology. *240 pp.*

Morris, R. N., and **Mogey, J.** The Sociology of Housing. *Studies at Berinsfield. 232 pp. 4 pp. plates.*

Rosser, C., and **Harris, C.** The Family and Social Change. *A Study of Family and Kinship in a South Wales Town. 352 pp. 8 maps.*

RURAL SOCIOLOGY

Chambers, R. J. H. Settlement Schemes in Africa: *A Selective Study. 268 pp.*

Haswell, M. R. The Economics of Development in Village India. *120 pp.*

Littlejohn, James. Westrigg: *the Sociology of a Cheviot Parish. 172 pp. 5 figures.*

Williams, W. M. The Country Craftsman: *A Study of Some Rural Crafts and the Rural Industries Organization in England. 248 pp. 9 figures. (Dartington Hall Studies in Rural Sociology.)*

The Sociology of an English Village: *Gosforth. 272 pp. 12 figures. 13 tables.*

SOCIOLOGY OF INDUSTRY AND DISTRIBUTION

Anderson, Nels. Work and Leisure. *280 pp.*

● **Blau, Peter M.,** and **Scott, W. Richard.** Formal Organizations: *a Comparative approach. Introduction and Additional Bibliography by J. H. Smith. 326 pp.*

Eldridge, J. E. T. Industrial Disputes. *Essays in the Sociology of Industrial Relations. 288 pp.*

Hetzler, Stanley. Technological Growth and Social Change. *Achieving Modernization. 269 pp.*

Hollowell, Peter G. The Lorry Driver. *272 pp.*

Jefferys, Margot, *with the assistance of Winifred Moss.* Mobility in the Labour Market: *Employment Changes in Battersea and Dagenham. Preface by Barbara Wootton. 186 pp. 51 tables.*

Millerson, Geoffrey. The Qualifying Associations: *a Study in Professionalization. 320 pp.*

Smelser, Neil J. Social Change in the Industrial Revolution: *An Application of Theory to the Lancashire Cotton Industry, 1770-1840. 468 pp. 12 figures. 14 tables.*

Williams, Gertrude. Recruitment to Skilled Trades. *240 pp.*

Young, A. F. Industrial Injuries Insurance: *an Examination of British Policy.* *192 pp.*

ANTHROPOLOGY

Ammar, Hamed. Growing up in an Egyptian Village: *Silwa, Province of Aswan. 336 pp.*

Brandel-Syrier, Mia. Reeftown Elite. *A Study of Social Mobility in a Modern African Community on the Reef. 376 pp.*

Crook, David, and **Isabel.** Revolution in a Chinese Village: *Ten Mile Inn. 230 pp. 8 plates. 1 map.*
The First Years of Yangyi Commune. *302 pp. 12 plates.*

Dickie-Clark, H. F. The Marginal Situation. *A Sociological Study of a Coloured Group. 236 pp.*

Dube, S. C. Indian Village. *Foreword by Morris Edward Opler. 276 pp. 4 plates.*
India's Changing Villages: *Human Factors in Community Development. 260 pp. 8 plates. 1 map.*

Firth, Raymond. Malay Fishermen. *Their Peasant Economy. 420 pp. 17 pp. plates.*

Gulliver, P. H. Social Control in an African Society: a Study of the Arusha, Agricultural Masai of Northern Tanganyika. *320 pp. 8 plates. 10 figures.*

Ishwaran, K. Shivapur. *A South Indian Village. 216 pp.*
Tradition and Economy in Village India: *An Interactionist Approach. Foreword by Conrad Arensburg. 176 pp.*

Jarvie, Ian C. The Revolution in Anthropology. *268 pp.*

Jarvie, Ian C., and **Agassi, Joseph.** Hong Kong. *A Society in Transition. 396 pp. Illustrated with plates and maps.*

Little, Kenneth L. Mende of Sierra Leone. *308 pp. and folder.*
Negroes in Britain. *With a New Introduction and Contemporary Study by Leonard Bloom. 320 pp.*

Lowie, Robert H. Social Organization. *494 pp.*

Mayer, Adrian C. Caste and Kinship in Central India: *A Village and its Region. 328 pp. 16 plates. 15 figures. 16 tables.*

Smith, Raymond T. The Negro Family in British Guiana: *Family Structure and Social Status in the Villages. With a Foreword by Meyer Fortes. 314 pp. 8 plates. 1 figure. 4 maps.*

DOCUMENTARY

Meek, Dorothea L. (Ed.). Soviet Youth: *Some Achievements and Problems. Excerpts from the Soviet Press, translated by the editor. 280 pp.*

Schlesinger, Rudolf (Ed.). Changing Attitudes in Soviet Russia.
2. *The Nationalities Problem and Soviet Administration. Selected Readings on the Development of Soviet Nationalities Policies. Introduced by the editor. Translated by W. W. Gottlieb. 324 pp.*

SOCIOLOGY AND PHILOSOPHY

Barnsley, John H. The Social Reality of Ethics. *A Comparative Analysis of Moral Codes. 448 pp.*

Douglas, Jack D. (Ed.). Understanding Everyday Life. *Toward the Reconstruction of Sociological Knowledge. Contributions by Alan F. Blum. Aaron W. Cicourel, Norman K. Denzin, Jack D. Douglas, John Heeren, Peter McHugh, Peter K. Manning, Melvin Power, Matthew Speier, Roy Turner, D. Lawrence Wieder, Thomas P. Wilson and Don H. Zimmerman. 358 pp.*

Jarvie, Ian C. Concepts and Society. *216 pp.*

Roche, Maurice. Phenomenology, Language and the Social Sciences. *About 400 pp.*

Sklair, Leslie. The Sociology of Progress. *320 pp.*

International Library of Social Policy

General Editor Kathleen Janes

Jones, Kathleen. Mental Health Services. *A history, 1744-1971. About 500 pp.*

Thomas, J. E. The English Prison Officer since 1850: *A Study in Conflict. 258 pp.*

Primary Socialization, Language and Education

General Editor Basil Bernstein

Bernstein, Basil. Class, Codes and Control. *2 volumes.*
1. *Theoretical Studies Towards a Sociology of Language. 254 pp.*
2. *Applied Studies Towards a Sociology of Language. About 400 pp.*

Brandis, Walter, and **Henderson, Dorothy.** Social Class, Language and Communication. *288 pp.*

Cook, Jenny. Socialization and Social Control. *About 300 pp.*

Gahagan, D. M., and **G. A.** Talk Reform. *Exploration in Language for Infant School Children. 160 pp.*

Robinson, W. P., and **Rackstraw, Susan, D. A.** A Question of Answers. *2 volumes. 192 pp. and 180 pp.*

Turner, Geoffrey, J., and **Mohan, Bernard, A.** A Linguistic Description and Computer Programme for Children's Speech. *208 pp.*

Reports of the Institute of Community Studies and the Institute of Social Studies in Medical Care

Cartwright, Ann. Human Relations and Hospital Care. *272 pp.*
Parents and Family Planning Services. *306 pp.*
Patients and their Doctors. *A Study of General Practice. 304 pp.*
Dunnell, Karen, and **Cartwright, Ann.** Medicine Takers, Prescribers and Hoarders. *About 140 pp.*
● **Jackson, Brian.** Streaming: *an Education System in Miniature. 168 pp.*
Jackson, Brian, and **Marsden, Dennis.** Education and the Working Class: *Some General Themes raised by a Study of 88 Working-class Children in a Northern Industrial City. 268 pp. 2 folders.*
Marris, Peter. Widows and their Families. *Foreword by Dr. John Bowlby. 184 pp. 18 tables. Statistical Summary.*
Family and Social Change in an African City. *A Study of Rehousing in Lagos. 196 pp. 1 map. 4 plates. 53 tables.*
The Experience of Higher Education. *232 pp. 27 tables.*
Marris, Peter, and **Rein, Martin.** Dilemmas of Social Reform. *Poverty and Community Action in the United States. 256 pp.*
Marris, Peter, and **Somerset, Anthony.** African Businessmen. *A Study of Entrepreneurship and Development in Kenya. 256 pp.*
Runciman, W. G. Relative Deprivation and Social Justice. *A Study of Attitudes to Social Inequality in Twentieth Century England. 352 pp.*
Townsend, Peter. The Family Life of Old People: *An Inquiry in East London. Foreword by J. H. Sheldon. 300 pp. 3 figures. 63 tables.*
Willmott, Peter. Adolescent Boys in East London. *230 pp.*
The Evolution of a Community: *a study of Dagenham after forty years. 168 pp. 2 maps.*
Willmott, Peter, and **Young, Michael.** Family and Class in a London Suburb. *202 pp. 47 tables.*
Young, Michael. Innovation and Research in Education. *192 pp.*
● **Young, Michael,** and **McGeeney, Patrick.** Learning Begins at Home. *A Study of a Junior School and its Parents. 128 pp.*
Young, Michael, and **Willmott, Peter.** Family and Kinship in East London. *Foreword by Richard M. Titmuss. 252 pp. 39 tables.*

Medicine, Illness and Society
General Editor W. M. Williams

Robinson, David. The Process of Becoming Ill.
Stacey, Margaret. *et al.* Hospitals, Children and Their Families. *The Report of a Pilot Study. 202 pp.*

Routledge Social Science Journals

The British Journal of Sociology. *Edited by Terence P. Morris. Vol. 1, No. 1, March 1950 and Quarterly. Roy. 8vo. Back numbers available. An international journal with articles on all aspects of sociology.*

Economy and Society. *Vol. 1, No. 1. February 1972 and Quarterly. Metric Roy. 8vo. A journal for all social scientists covering sociology, philosophy, anthropology, economics and history.*

Printed in Great Britain by Lewis Reprints Limited
Brown Knight & Truscott Group, London and Tonbridge   21972